STERLING
Test Prep

SAT Chemistry

Practice Questions

8th edition

www.Sterling-Prep.com

8   7   6   5   4   3   2   1

ISBN-13: 978-0-9892925-9-7

Sterling Test Prep products are available at special quantity discounts for sales, promotions, academic counseling offices and other educational purposes.

For more information contact our Sales Department at:

Sterling Test Prep
6 Liberty Square #11
Boston, MA 02109

info@sterling-prep.com

© 2017 Sterling Test Prep

Published by Sterling Test Prep

Congratulations on choosing this book as part of your SAT Chemistry preparation!

Scoring well on the SAT Chemistry is important for admission into college. To achieve a high score, you need to develop skills to properly apply the knowledge you have and quickly choose the correct answer. You must solve numerous practice questions that represent the style and content of the SAT questions. Understanding key science concepts is more valuable than memorizing terms.

This book provides 960 practice questions that test your knowledge of all SAT Chemistry topics. The explanations provide step-by-step solutions for quantitative questions and detailed explanations for conceptual questions. They also cover the foundations of important chemistry topics needed to answer related questions on the exam. By reading these explanations carefully and understanding how they apply to solving the question, you will learn important chemistry concepts and the relationships between them. This will prepare you for the test and you will significantly increase your score.

All the questions are prepared by our science editors who possess extensive credentials and are educated at top colleges and universities. Our editors are experts on teaching sciences, preparing students for standardized science tests and have coached thousands of undergraduate and graduate school applicants on admission strategies.

We wish you great success in your future academic achievements and look forward to being an important part of your successful test preparation!

Sterling Test Prep Team

170605gdx

Our Commitment to the Environment

Sterling Test Prep is committed to protecting our planet's resources by supporting environmental organizations with proven track records of conservation, environmental research and education and preservation of vital natural resources. A portion of our profits is donated to support these organizations so they can continue their important missions. These organizations include:

For over 40 years, Ocean Conservancy has been advocating for a healthy ocean by supporting sustainable solutions based on science and cleanup efforts. Among many environmental achievements, Ocean Conservancy laid the groundwork for an international moratorium on commercial whaling, played an instrumental role in protecting fur seals from overhunting and banning the international trade of sea turtles. The organization created national marine sanctuaries and served as the lead non-governmental organization in the designation of 10 of the 13 marine sanctuaries.

For 25 years, Rainforest Trust has been saving critical lands for conservation through land purchases and protected area designations. Rainforest Trust has played a central role in the creation of 73 new protected areas in 17 countries, including Falkland Islands, Costa Rica and Peru. Nearly 8 million acres have been saved thanks to Rainforest Trust's support of in-country partners across Latin America, with over 500,000 acres of critical lands purchased outright for reserves.

Since 1980, Pacific Whale Foundation has been saving whales from extinction and protecting our oceans through science and advocacy. As an international organization, with ongoing research projects in Hawaii, Australia and Ecuador, PWF is an active participant in global efforts to address threats to whales and other marine life. A pioneer in non-invasive whale research, PWF was an early leader in educating the public, from a scientific perspective, about whales and the need for ocean conservation.

Thank you for choosing our products to achieve your educational goals.

With your purchase you support environmental causes around the world.

Table of Contents

Table of Contents (*continued*)

We want to hear from you

Your feedback is important to us because we strive to provide the highest quality prep materials. If you have any questions, comments or suggestions, email us, so we can incorporate your feedback into future editions.

Customer Satisfaction Guarantee

If you have any concerns about this book, including printing issues, contact us and we will resolve any issues to your satisfaction.

info@sterling-prep.com

About SAT Chemistry Test

The SAT Chemistry test covers the material normally taught in a one-year college-prep level high school chemistry course to assess whether or not you have grasped the fundamental concepts of chemistry. It consists of 85 multiple-choice questions that must be answered in 60 minutes (an average of 42 seconds per question).

Calculators are not allowed, therefore it is important to know how to solve problems using ratios, direct and inverse proportions, scientific notation, and simple exponential functions. ETS will provide a periodic table that will have only the symbols of the elements along with their atomic numbers and masses.

There are eight different categories that ETS breaks the test down into and their respective percentages. These percentages are estimations and can vary from test to test. Please keep in mind that these categories are very broad. This simply serves as a way to know where to focus your studies if you are particularly weak in a certain section.

Topic	Approximate % on the test
Structure of matter • **Atomic Structure:** experimental evidence of atomic structure, quantum numbers and energy levels (orbitals), electron configurations, periodic trends • **Molecular Structure:** Lewis structures, three-dimensional molecular shapes, polarity • **Bonding:** ionic, covalent, metallic bonds, relationships of bonding to properties and structures; intermolecular forces such as hydrogen bonding, dipole-dipole, dispersion (London) forces	25%
States of Matter • **Gases:** the kinetic molecular theory, gas law relationships, molar volumes, density, and stoichiometry • **Liquids and Solids:** intermolecular forces in liquids and solids, types of solids, phase changes, and phase diagrams • **Solutions:** molarity and percent by mass concentrations, solution preparation and stoichiometry, factors affecting solubility of solids, liquids, and gases, qualitative aspects of colligative properties	16%

Reaction Types • **Acids and Bases:** Brønsted-Lowry theory, strong and weak acids and bases, pH, titrations, indicators • **Oxidation-Reduction:** recognition of oxidation-reduction reactions, combustion, oxidation numbers, activity series • **Precipitation:** basic solubility rules	14%
Stoichiometry • **Mole Concept:** molar mass, Avogadro's number, empirical and molecular formulas • **Chemical Equations:** balancing of equations, stoichiometric calculations, percent yield, and limiting reactants	14%
Equilibrium and Reaction Rates • **Equilibrium Systems**, including factors affecting position of equilibrium (LeChâtelier's principle) in gaseous and aqueous systems, equilibrium constants, and equilibrium expressions • **Rates of Reactions**, including factors affecting reaction rates, potential energy diagrams, activation energies	5%
Thermochemistry • Conservation of energy, calorimetry and specific heats, enthalpy (heat) changes associated with phase changes and chemical reactions, heating and cooling curves, entropy	6%
Descriptive Chemistry • Common elements, nomenclature of ions and compounds, periodic trends in chemical and physical properties of the elements, reactivity of elements and prediction of products of chemical reactions, examples of simple organic compounds and compounds of environmental concern	12%
Laboratory • Laboratory equipment, measurements, procedures, safety, observations, calculations, data analysis, interpretation of graphical data, conclusions from observations and data	8%

Format of the SAT Chemistry Test

The SAT Chemistry exam is broken down into three different types of questions. According to the College Board web site, the 85 multiple-choice type questions will fall into the following three types of skill.

Skill Being Tested	Approximate % on the test
Recall of knowledge: remembering fundamental concepts and specific information; demonstrating familiarity with terminology	20%
Application of knowledge: applying a single principle to unfamiliar and/or practical situations to obtain a qualitative result or solve a quantitative problem	45%
Synthesis of knowledge: inferring and deducing from qualitative and/or quantitative data; integrating two or more relationships to draw conclusions or solve problems	35%

The SAT Chemistry test tests you understanding of chemistry in three different ways. There are three different types of questions: *classification questions, relationship-analysis questions* and *five-choice completion questions.*

Classification Questions

In classification questions, the answers are given first and the questions follow. These are the reverse of an ordinary multiple-choice question. Any answer choice can be used more than once, only once, or not used at all; therefore you cannot eliminate an answer choiceif it matched on of the questions, which make things a bit more difficult. However, questions of classification can usually be answered more quickly than the five-choice completion because you only need to review one set of answer choices to answer a series of questions.

The difficulty level within the set of questions can vary. Therefore the beginning question won't always be easier than the last. With each set of classifications however, the difficulty level increases as you go through the test. This means that questions 1-4 will normally be easier than questions 11-13.

Relationship-Analysis Questions

These types of questions contain two specific statements: statement I and statement II. You should first determine whether statement I is true or false and then do the same for statement II. After determining the validity of both statements, you must decide if there is a relationship between them (for example, is statement II the reason that statement I is true?). These questions may seem a bit intimidating, but with the systematic approach you can feel just as comfortable with these types of questions as you would with any other. Relationship-analysis questions get a special section on the answer sheet.

Five-Choice Completion Questions

These are the common multiple-choice questions that you are used to. They ask a question, give you five possible answer choices, and you pick the appropriate one. This will be the third and final part of the exam.

Test Scoring

For every answer that is correct, you receive one point; for every incorrect answer you lose ¼ of a point. For every answer that you leave blank, you receive zero points. The SAT Chemistry test is scored the same way as all other SAT Subject Tests. These points are added up to calculate your raw score, which is than curved by ETS to generate your scaled score. This curve varies from test to test. On the next page, there is an approximate raw-to-scaled conversion chart.

Based on this chart, your score does not drop significantly with every question that you don't answer confidently. It is still possible to do very well on this test even if you do not know everything on it. You can even achieve the maximum 800 points providing wrong answers to a few questions and skipping some. To do well on the SAT Chemistry Test, it is important to have and follow a strategy that will allow you to read and answer all the questions you can, whether it be confidently or by taking an educated guess.

For example, you could score:*

- 800 if you answered 80 correct, 2 wrong and left 3 blank
- 750 if you answered 73 correct, 4 wrong, and left 8 blank
- 700 if you answered 66 correct, 6 wrong, and left 13 blank
- 650 if you answered 59 correct, 8 wrong, and left 18 blank
- 600 if you answered 53 correct, 12 wrong, and left 20 blank

* This is an approximation only. The actual score will depend on the conversion curve used by the ETS for your particular test administration.

Raw Score	Scaled Score	Raw Score	Scaled Score	Raw Score	Scaled Score
80	800	49	600	18	420
79	800	48	590	17	410
78	790	47	590	16	410
77	780	46	580	15	400
76	770	45	580	14	390
75	770	44	570	13	390
74	760	43	560	12	380
73	760	42	560	11	370
72	750	41	550	10	360
71	740	40	550	9	360
70	740	39	540	8	350
69	730	38	540	7	350
68	730	37	530	6	340
67	720	36	520	5	340
66	710	35	520	4	330
65	700	34	510	3	330
64	700	33	500	2	320
63	690	32	500	1	320
62	680	31	490	0	310
61	680	30	490	-1	310
60	670	29	480	-2	300
59	660	28	480	-3	300
58	660	27	470	-4	290
57	650	26	470	-5	280
56	640	25	460	-6	280
55	640	24	450	-7	270
54	630	23	450	-8	270
53	620	22	440	-9	260
52	620	21	440	-10	260
51	610	20	430		
50	600	19	420		

Set a Target Score

The task of pacing yourself will become easier if you are aware of the number of questions you need to answer to reach the score you want to get. Always strive for the highest score, but also be realistic about your level of preparation. It may be helpful if you research what counts as a good score for the colleges you are applying to. You can talk to admissions offices at colleges, research college guidebooks or specific college websites, or talk to your guidance counselor. Find the average score received by students that were admitted to the colleges of your choice and set your target score higher than the average. Take a look at the chart we provided earlier to see how many questions you would need to answer correctly to reach this target score. If the average score on SAT Chemistry for the school you're interested in is 700, set your target at about 750.

Test-Taking Strategies for SAT Chemistry

The best way to do well on SAT Chemistry is to be really good at chemistry. There is no way around that. Prepare for the test as much as you can, so you can answer with confidence as many questions as possible. With that being said, for multiple choice questions the only thing that matters is how many questions were answered correctly, not how much work you did to come up with those answers. A lucky guess will get you the same points as an answer you knew with confidence.

Below are some test-taking strategies to help you maximize your score. Many of these strategies you already know and they may seem like common sense. However, when a student is feeling the pressure of a timed test, these common sense strategies might be forgotten.

Mental Attitude

If you psych yourself out, chances are you will do poorly on the test. To do well on the test, particularly science, which calls for cool, systemic thinking, you must remain calm. If you start to panic, your mind won't be able to find correct solutions to the questions. Many steps can be taken before the test to increase your confidence level. Buying this book is a good start because you can begin to practice, learn the information you should know to master the topics and get used to answering chemistry questions. However, there are other things you should keep in mind:

Study in advance.
The information will be more manageable, and you will feel more confident if you've studied at regular intervals during the weeks leading up to the test. Cramming the night before is not a successful tactic.

Be well rested.
If you are up late the night before the test, chances are you will have a difficult time concentrating and focusing on the day of the test, as you will not feel fresh and alert.

Come up for air.
The best way to take this hour-long test is not to keep your head down, concentrating the full sixty minutes. Even though you only have 48 seconds per question and there is no time to waste, it is recommended to take a few seconds between the questions to take a deep breath and relax your muscles.

Time Management

Aside from good preparation, time management is the most important strategy that you should know how to use on any test. You have an average time of 48 seconds for each question. You will breeze through some in fifteen seconds and others you may be stuck on for two minutes.

Don't dwell on any one question for too long. You should aim to look at every question on the test. It would be unfortunate to not earn the points for a question you could have easily answered just because you did not get a chance to look at it. If you are still in the first half of the test and find yourself spending more than a minute on one question and don't see yourself getting closer to solving it, it is better to move on. It will be more productive if you come back to this question with a fresh mind at the end of the test. You do not want to lose points because you were stuck on one or few questions and did not get a chance to work with other questions that are easy for you.

Nail the easy questions quickly. On SAT subject tests, you get as many points for answering easy questions as you do for answering difficult questions. This means that you get a lot more points for five quickly answered questions than for one hard-earned victory. The questions do increase in difficulty as you progress throughout the test. However, each student has their strong and weak points, and you might be a master on a certain type of questions that are normally considered difficult. Skip the questions you are struggling with and nail the easy ones.

Skip the unfamiliar. If you come across a question that is totally unfamiliar to you, skip it. Do not try to figure out what is going on or what they are trying to ask. At the end of the test, you can go back to these questions if you have time. If you are encountering a question that you have no clue about, most likely you won't be able to answer it through analysis. The better strategy is to leave such questions to the end and use the guessing strategy on them at the end of the test.

Understanding the Question

It is important that you know what the question is asking before you select your answer choice. This seems obvious, but it is surprising how many students don't read a question carefully because they rush through the test and select a wrong answer choice.

A successful student will not just read the question, but will take a moment to understand the question before even looking at the answer choices. This student will be able to separate the important information from distracters and will not get confused on the questions that are asking to identify a false statement (which is the correct answer). Once you've identified what you're dealing with and what is being asked, you should be able to spend less time on picking the right answer. If the question is asking for a general concept, try to answer the question before looking at the answer choices, then look at the choices. If you see a choice that matches the answer you thought of, most likely it is the correct choice.

Correct Way to Guess

Random guessing won't help you on the test, but educated guessing is the strategy you should use in certain situations if you can eliminate at least one (or even two) of the five possible choices.

On SAT subject tests, you lose ¼ of a point for each wrong answer. This is done to prevent blind guessing, but not to punish you for making an educated guess. For example, if you just randomly entered responses for the first 20 questions, there is a 20% chance of guessing correctly on any given question. Therefore, the odds are you would guess right on 4 questions and wrong on 16 questions. Your raw score for those 20 questions would then be 0 because you get 4 points for 4 correct answers and lose 4 points for 16 wrong answers. This would be the same as leaving all 20 questions blank.

However, if for each of the 20 questions you can eliminate one answer choice because you know it to be wrong, you will have a 25% chance of being right. Therefore, your odds would move to 5 questions right and 15 questions wrong. This gives a raw score of 1.25 (gain 5 points and lose 3.75 points).

Guessing is not cheating and should not be viewed that way. Rather it is a form of "partial credit" because while you might not be sure of the correct answer, you do have relevant knowledge to identify one or two choices that are wrong.

SAT Chemistry Tips

Tip 1: Know the equations

Since many chemistry problems require that you know how to use the chemical equations, it is imperative that you memorize and understand when to use each one. It is not permitted to bring any papers with notes to the test. Therefore you must memorize all the equations you will need to solve the questions on the test, and there is no way around it.

As you work with this book, you will learn the application of all the important chemical equations and will use them in many different question types. If you are feeling nervous about having a lot of formulas and equations in your head and worry that it will affect your problem-solving skills, look over them right before you go into the testing space and write them down before you start the test. This way, you don't have to worry about remembering the formulas throughout the test. When you need to use them, you can refer back to where you wrote them down earlier.

Tip 2: Know how to manipulate the formulas

You must know how to apply the formulas in addition to just memorizing them. Questions will be worded in ways unfamiliar to you to test whether you can manipulate equations that you know to calculate the correct answer.

Tip 3: Estimating

This tip is only helpful for quantitative questions. For example, estimating can help you choose the correct answer if you have a general sense of the order of magnitude. This is especially applicable to questions where all answer choices have different orders of magnitude, and you can save time that you would have to spend on actual calculations.

Tip 4: Write the reaction

Don't hesitate to write, draw or graph your thought process once you have read and understood the question. This can help you determine what kind of information you are dealing with. Write out the reactions that need to be balanced or anything else that may be helpful. Even if a question does not require a graphic answer, drawing a graph can allow a solution to become obvious.

Tip 5: Eliminating wrong answers

This tip utilizes the strategy of educated guessing. You can usually eliminate one or two answer choices right away in most questions. In addition, there are certain types of questions for which you can use a particular elimination method. By using logical estimations for quantitative questions, you can eliminate the answer choices that are unreasonably high or unreasonably low.

In *classification questions*, the same five answer choices apply to several questions. It is helpful to keep in mind that it is not often that one answer choice is correct for more than one question (though it does happen sometimes). Some answer choices that you are confident to be correct for some questions are good elimination candidates for other questions where you're trying to use a guessing strategy. It is not a sure bet, but you should be aware of this option if you have to resort to guessing on some questions.

Roman numeral questions are multiple-choice questions that list a few possible answers with five different combinations of these answers. Supposing that you know that one of the Roman numeral choices is wrong, you can eliminate all answer choices that include it. These questions are usually difficult for most test takers because they tend to present more than one potentially correct statement which is often included in more than one answer choice. However, they have a certain upside if you can eliminate at least one wrong statement.

Last helpful tip: fill in your answers carefully

This seems like a simple thing, but it is extremely important. Many test takers make mistakes when filling in answers whether it is a paper test or computer-based test. Make sure you pay attention and check off the answer choice you actually chose as correct.

Common Chemistry Equations

Throughout the test the following symbols have the definitions specified unless otherwise noted.

L, mL	= liter(s), milliliter(s)	mm Hg	= millimeters of mercury
g	= gram(s)	J, kJ	= joule(s), kilojoule(s)
nm	= nanometer(s)	V	= volt(s)
atm	= atmosphere(s)	mol	= mole(s)

ATOMIC STRUCTURE

$$E = h\nu$$
$$c = \lambda\nu$$

E = energy
ν = frequency
λ = wavelength

Planck's constant, $h = 6.626 \times 10^{-34}$ J s

Speed of light, $c = 2.998 \times 10^{8}$ m s^{-1}

Avogadro's number $= 6.022 \times 10^{23}$ mol^{-1}

Electron charge, $e = -1.602 \times 10^{-19}$ coulomb

EQUILIBRIUM

$$K_c = \frac{[C]^c[D]^d}{[A]^a[B]^b}, \text{ where } a\,A + b\,B \rightleftarrows c\,C + d\,D$$

$$K_p = \frac{(P_C)^c(P_D)^d}{(P_A)^a(P_B)^b}$$

$$K_a = \frac{[H^+][A^-]}{[HA]}$$

$$K_b = \frac{[OH^-][HB^+]}{[B]}$$

$$K_w = [H^+][OH^-] = 1.0 \times 10^{-14} \text{ at } 25°C$$
$$= K_a \times K_b$$

$$pH = -\log[H^+], \quad pOH = -\log[OH^-]$$

$$14 = pH + pOH$$

$$pH = pK_a + \log\frac{[A^-]}{[HA]}$$

$$pK_a = -\log K_a, \quad pK_b = -\log K_b$$

Equilibrium Constants

K_c (molar concentrations)

K_p (gas pressures)

K_a (weak acid)

K_b (weak base)

K_w (water)

KINETICS

$$\ln[A]_t - \ln[A]_0 = -kt$$

$$\frac{1}{[A]_t} - \frac{1}{[A]_0} = kt$$

$$t_{1/2} = \frac{0.693}{k}$$

k = rate constant
t = time
$t_{1/2}$ = half-life

GASES, LIQUIDS, AND SOLUTIONS

$$PV = nRT$$

$$P_A = P_{total} \times X_A, \text{ where } X_A = \frac{\text{moles A}}{\text{total moles}}$$

$$P_{total} = P_A + P_B + P_C + \ldots$$

$$n = \frac{m}{M}$$

$$K = {}^\circ C + 273$$

$$D = \frac{m}{V}$$

$$KE \text{ per molecule} = \frac{1}{2}mv^2$$

Molarity, M = moles of solute per liter of solution

$$A = abc$$

P = pressure
V = volume
T = temperature
n = number of moles
m = mass
M = molar mass
D = density
KE = kinetic energy
v = velocity
A = absorbance
a = molar absorptivity
b = path length
c = concentration

Gas constant, R = 8.314 J mol^{-1} K^{-1}

$\qquad$ = 0.08206 L atm mol^{-1} K^{-1}

$\qquad$ = 62.36 L torr mol^{-1} K^{-1}

1 atm = 760 mm Hg

$\qquad$ = 760 torr

STP = 0.00 $^\circ$C and 1.000 atm

THERMOCHEMISTRY/ ELECTROCHEMISTRY

$$q = mc\Delta T$$

$$\Delta S^\circ = \sum S^\circ \text{ products} - \sum S^\circ \text{ reactants}$$

$$\Delta H^\circ = \sum \Delta H_f^\circ \text{ products} - \sum \Delta H_f^\circ \text{ reactants}$$

$$\Delta G^\circ = \sum \Delta G_f^\circ \text{ products} - \sum \Delta G_f^\circ \text{ reactants}$$

$$\Delta G^\circ = \Delta H^\circ - T\Delta S^\circ$$

$$= -RT \ln K$$

$$= -n F E^\circ$$

$$I = \frac{q}{t}$$

q = heat
m = mass
c = specific heat capacity
T = temperature
S° = standard entropy
H° = standard enthalpy
G° = standard free energy
n = number of moles
E° = standard reduction potential
I = current (amperes)
q = charge (coulombs)
t = time (seconds)

Faraday's constant, F = 96,485 coulombs per mole of electrons

$$1 \text{ volt} = \frac{1 \text{ joule}}{1 \text{ coulomb}}$$

Periodic Table of the Elements

How to Use This Book

To extract the maximum benefit from this book, we recommend that you start by doing the first diagnostic test and use the answer key to identify the topics you need to spend more time on. Spend some time going through the explanations to this diagnostic test. Review all the explanations, not only those that you got right. After this, practice with the topical questions for those topics you identified as your weak areas – take your time and master those questions.

Next, take the second diagnostic test. You should see a dramatic improvement in your performance on the topics that you practiced prior to this. Analyze your performance on the second diagnostic test and find new topics that you can improve on. Work with the corresponding topical practice questions.

Finally, take the third and fourth diagnostic tests. At this point, you should be very strong on all topics. If you still find weaknesses, spend extra time going through the solutions and do more practice. You may also find three additional diagnostic tests on our web site.

Ultimately, your goal should be to complete all three diagnostic tests, all topical practice questions and go through all the explanations.

Visit www.Sterling-Prep.com for SAT online practice tests

Our advanced online testing platform allows you to practice these and other SAT questions on the computer and generate Diagnostic Reports for each test.

By using our online SAT tests and Diagnostic Reports, you will be able to:

- Assess your knowledge of different topics tested on your SAT subject test

- Identify your areas of strength and weakness

- Learn important scientific topics and concepts

- Improve your test taking skills by solving numerous practice questions

> To access the online tests at a special pricing
> go to page 483 for web address

SAT Chemistry

Diagnostic Tests

Diagnostic Test #1

This Diagnostic Test is designed for you to assess your proficiency on each topic. Use your test results and identify areas of your strength and weakness to adjust your study plan and enhance your fundamental knowledge.

The length of the Diagnostic Tests is proven to be optimal for a single study session.

#	Answer:					Review	#	Answer:					Review
1:	A	B	C	D	E	___	31:	A	B	C	D	E	___
2:	A	B	C	D	E	___	32:	A	B	C	D	E	___
3:	A	B	C	D	E	___	33:	A	B	C	D	E	___
4:	A	B	C	D	E	___	34:	A	B	C	D	E	___
5:	A	B	C	D	E	___	35:	A	B	C	D	E	___
6:	A	B	C	D	E	___	36:	A	B	C	D	E	___
7:	A	B	C	D	E	___	37:	A	B	C	D	E	___
8:	A	B	C	D	E	___	38:	A	B	C	D	E	___
9:	A	B	C	D	E	___	39:	A	B	C	D	E	___
10:	A	B	C	D	E	___	40:	A	B	C	D	E	___
11:	A	B	C	D	E	___	41:	A	B	C	D	E	___
12:	A	B	C	D	E	___	42:	A	B	C	D	E	___
13:	A	B	C	D	E	___	43:	A	B	C	D	E	___
14:	A	B	C	D	E	___	44:	A	B	C	D	E	___
15:	A	B	C	D	E	___	45:	A	B	C	D	E	___
16:	A	B	C	D	E	___	46:	A	B	C	D	E	___
17:	A	B	C	D	E	___	47:	A	B	C	D	E	___
18:	A	B	C	D	E	___	48:	A	B	C	D	E	___
19:	A	B	C	D	E	___	49:	A	B	C	D	E	___
20:	A	B	C	D	E	___	50:	A	B	C	D	E	___
21:	A	B	C	D	E	___	51:	A	B	C	D	E	___
22:	A	B	C	D	E	___	52:	A	B	C	D	E	___
23:	A	B	C	D	E	___	53:	A	B	C	D	E	___
24:	A	B	C	D	E	___	54:	A	B	C	D	E	___
25:	A	B	C	D	E	___	55:	A	B	C	D	E	___
26:	A	B	C	D	E	___	56:	A	B	C	D	E	___
27:	A	B	C	D	E	___	57:	A	B	C	D	E	___
28:	A	B	C	D	E	___	58:	A	B	C	D	E	___
29:	A	B	C	D	E	___	59:	A	B	C	D	E	___
30:	A	B	C	D	E	___	60:	A	B	C	D	E	___

1. Which orbital is NOT correctly matched with its shape?

    I. *d*, spherically symmetrical
    II. *p*, dumbbell shaped
    III. *s*, spherically symmetrical

  A. I only
  B. II only
  C. III only
  D. I and II only
  E. I and III only

2. What is the molecular geometry of a NH_3 molecule?

  A. bent
  B. trigonal pyramidal
  C. tetrahedral
  D. trigonal planar
  E. linear

3. What is the new pressure if a sealed container with gas at 3.60 atm is heated from 30.0 K to 62.0 K?

  A. 0.500 atm
  B. 1.50 atm
  C. 4.50 atm
  D. 4.00 atm
  E. 7.44 atm

4. What are the formula masses of water (H_2O), propene (C_3H_6) and 2-propanol (C_3H_8O), respectively?

  A. water: 16 amu; propene: 44 amu; 2-propanol: 62 amu
  B. water: 18 amu; propene: 42 amu; 2-propanol: 60 amu
  C. water: 18 amu; propene: 44 amu; 2-propanol: 62 amu
  D. water: 16 amu; propene: 40 amu; 2-propanol: 58 amu
  E. water: 18 amu; propene: 42 amu; 2-propanol: 58 amu

5. Which of the following would have the same numerical magnitude?

  A. Heats of sublimation and deposition
  B. Heats of solidification and condensation
  C. Heats of fusion and deposition
  D. Heats of sublimation and condensation
  E. None of the above

6. If a catalyst is added, which statement is true?

  A. The forward and backward reaction rates are increased by the same proportion
  B. The equilibrium is shifted to the more energetically favorable product
  C. The forward reaction is favored
  D. The equilibrium concentrations shift
  E. The reverse reaction is favored

7. What are the products for this double-replacement reaction

$$AgNO_3\ (aq) + NaCl\ (aq) \rightarrow\ ?$$

A. $AgClO_3$ and $NaNO_2$ **C.** $AgCl$ and $NaNO_2$

B. $AgCl$ and $NaNO_3$ **D.** Ag_3N and $NaClO_3$ **E.** $AgClO_3$ and $NaNO_3$

8. If a salt to acid ratio is 1:10 for an acid with $K_a = 1 \times 10^{-4}$, what is the pH of the solution?

A. 2   **B.** 3   **C.** 4   **D.** 5   **E.** 6

9. What is the cell potential and is the following reaction spontaneous under standard conditions?

$$F_2\ (g) + 2\ Br^-\ (aq) \rightarrow Br_2\ (l) + 2\ F^-\ (aq)$$

Using the following half-reaction potentials:

$$Br_2\ (l) + 2\ e^- \rightarrow 2\ Br^-\ (aq) \qquad E° = 1.08\ V$$
$$F_2\ (g) + 2\ e^- \rightarrow 2\ F^-\ (aq) \qquad E° = 2.88\ V$$

A. $E° = 1.80$ V and nonspontaneous   **C.** $E° = 3.96$ V and spontaneous

B. $E° = 1.80$ V and spontaneous   **D.** $E° = -1.80$ V and nonspontaneous

                                              E. $E° = -1.80$ V and spontaneous

10. Which of the elements is an alkaline earth metal?

A. ^{85}At **B.** ^{34}Se **C.** ^{22}Ti **D.** ^{37}Rb **E.** ^{38}Sr

11. A water spider is able to walk on the surface of water because:

A. hydrophilic bonds hold H_2O molecules together

B. H_2O has strong covalent bonds within its molecules

C. surface tension from the adhesive properties of H_2O

D. surface tension from the cohesive properties of H_2O

E. a water spider is less dense than H_2O

12. Which transformation describes evaporation?

A. solid $\rightarrow$ liquid   **C.** liquid $\rightarrow$ solid

B. solid $\rightarrow$ gas   **D.** liquid $\rightarrow$ gas   **E.** gas $\rightarrow$ solid

13. What is the percent by mass of chlorine in the common aprotic solvent of carbon tetrachloride (CCl_4)?

A. 25%   **B.** 66%   **C.** 78%   **D.** 92%   **E.** 33%

14. Which statement is true for a chemical reaction, whereby ΔH is < 0 and ΔS is < 0?

   A. Reaction may or may not be spontaneous, but spontaneity is favored by low temperatures

   B. Reaction may or may not be spontaneous, but spontaneity is favored by high temperatures

   C. Reaction must be spontaneous, regardless of temperature and becomes more spontaneous as temperature increases

   D. Reaction must be spontaneous, regardless of temperature and becomes more spontaneous as temperature decreases

   E. No conclusion can be made from the information provided

15. What is the term for the difference in heat energy (ΔH) between the reactants and the products for a chemical reaction?

   A. Heat of reaction   **C.** Endothermic

   B. Exothermic   **D.** Activation energy   **E.** Entropy

16. What is the freezing point of an aqueous solution containing 30.0 g of a compound with a molecular weight of 100.0 g/mol dissolved in 50.0 g of water. (Note: the compound does not dissociate in solution and the molal freezing point constant of water = −1.86 °C/m)

   A. −4.5 °C   **C.** −11.2 °C

   B. −14.7 °C   **D.** −12.8 °C   **E.** −7.6 °C

17. Which of the following would be predominantly deprotonated in the stomach, if gastric juice has a pH of about 2?

   A. phosphoric acid (pK_a = 2.2)   **C.** acetic acid (pK_a = 4.8)

   B. lactic acid, (pK_a = 3.9)   **D.** phenol (pK_a = 9.8)

                                    E. hydrochloric acid (pK_a = −7.0)

18. The shell with a principal quantum number 3 can accommodate how many electrons?

   A. 2   **B.** 3   **C.** 10   **D.** 18   **E.** 8

19. What is the formula of a nitrate ion?

   A. NO_3^{1-} **C.** NO^{3-}

   B. NO_2 **D.** NO_3^{2-} **E.** NO_2^{1-}

20. Which of the following represent the standard temperature and pressure (STP) conditions (STP) for gases?

   A. temperature of 0.00 K; pressure of 1.000 atm
   B. temperature of 0.00 °C; pressure of 1.000 atm
   C. temperature of 273.15 K; pressure of 1.000 Pascal
   D. temperature of 298.15 K; pressure of 1.000 atm
   E. temperature of 298.15 K; pressure of 1.000 Pascal

21. Which of the following balanced equations is a *decomposition* reaction?

   A. $2 \, Cr \, (s) + 3 \, Cl_2 \, (g) \rightarrow 2 \, CrCl_3 \, (s)$ **C.** $C_7H_8O_2 \, (l) + 8 \, O_2 \, (g) \rightarrow 7 \, CO_2 \, (g) + 4 \, H_2O \, (l)$
   B. $6 \, Li \, (s) + N_2 \, (g) \rightarrow 2 \, Li_3N \, (s)$ **D.** $2 \, KClO_3 \, (s) \rightarrow 2 \, KCl \, (s) + 3 \, O_2 \, (g)$
   E. None of the above

22. Which statement(s) is/are true for an exothermic reaction?

   I. There is a net absorption of energy from a reaction
   II. The products have more energy than the reactants
   III. Heat is a product of the reaction

   A. I and II only   **C.** III only
   B. I and III only   **D.** II and III only   **E.** I, II and III

23. What happens when the concentration of H_2 is increased in the following reaction?

   $H_2 + F_2 \leftrightarrows 2 \, HF$

   I. equilibrium shifts to the left
   II. consumption of fluorine increases
   III. equilibrium shifts to the right

   A. I only   **B.** II only   **C.** III only   **D.** II and III only   **E.** I and III only

24. Which statement is true when a beam of light shines through a colloid suspension or a clear solution?

   A. The light beam is not visible in the colloid suspension, but visible in the solution
   B. The light beam is visible in the colloid suspension, but invisible in the solution
   C. The light beam is not visible in both the colloid suspension and the solution
   D. The light beam is visible in both the colloid suspension and the solution
   E. Depends on the temperature of the experiment

25. Which of the following compounds is NOT a strong base?

   A. $Mg(OH)_2$ **B.** $NaOH$ **C.** KOH **D.** $Al(OH)_3$ **E.** ^-OH

26. How many grams of Ag (s) plate at the cathode, if 6 amps of current pass for 3 minutes at the cathode in the following reaction? (Use the molecular mass of Ag = 108 g/mole)

$$Ag^+ + e^- \rightarrow Ag\ (s)$$

   A. 0.87 g   **B.** 1.20 g   **C.** 1.08 g   **D.** 1.14 g   **E.** 1.31 g

27. Isotopes have the same number of:

   A. neutrons, but a different number of electrons
   B. protons, but a different number of neutrons
   C. protons, but a different number of electrons
   D. neutrons and electrons
   E. protons and neutrons, but a different number of electrons

28. Which of the compounds is most likely ionic?

   A. N_2O_5 **B.** $SrBr_2$ **C.** CBr_4 **D.** GaAs   **E.** CH_2Cl_2

29. Which of the following statements is NOT correct for Boyle's Law?

   A. $P_1V_1 = P_2V_2$
   B. pressure × volume = constant
   C. pressure is proportional to 1/volume
   D. at constant temperature, a gas' pressure and volume are inversely proportional
   E. none of the above

30. Which of the following is the formula mass of $C_{12}H_{26}(COOH)_2$?

   A. 236.4 amu   **C.** 271.2 amu
   B. 252.5 amu   **D.** 260.4 amu   **E.** 291.5 amu

31. What does internal energy for an ideal gas depend upon?

   I. pressure   II. temperature   III. volume

   A. I only   **C.** I and III only
   B. II only   **D.** I, II and III   **E.** III only

32. Which of the following changes does NOT affect the equilibrium for the reversible reaction?

$$SO_3\ (g) + NO\ (g) + heat \leftrightarrow SO_2\ (g) + NO_2\ (g)$$

   A. Adding a catalyst   **C.** Increasing volume
   B. Adding helium gas   **D.** Decreasing volume   **E.** All of the above

---

33. Calculate the $[SO_4^{2-}]$ that must be exceeded before $PbSO_4$ precipitates, if the $[Pb^{2+}]$ of a solution is 1.10×10^{-3} M. (Use the solubility product (K_{sp}) of $PbSO_4$ at 25 °C = 1.70×10^{-8})

A. 1.25×10^{-5} M   **C.** 2.65×10^{-4} M

B. 8.20×10^{-4} M   **D.** 1.84×10^{-5} M   **E.** 1.55×10^{-5} M

34. Identify the acid and base for each substance in the following reaction.

$$HSO_4^- + H_2O \rightleftharpoons {}^-OH + H_2SO_4$$

A. HSO_4^- is a base, H_2O is a base, ⁻OH is a base, H_2SO_4 is an acid

B. HSO_4^- is an acid, H_2O is a base, ⁻OH is a base, H_2SO_4 is an acid

C. HSO_4^- is a base, H_2O is an acid, ⁻OH is an acid, H_2SO_4 is a base

D. HSO_4^- is an acid, H_2O is a base, ⁻OH is an acid, H_2SO_4 is a base

E. HSO_4^- is a base, H_2O is an acid, ⁻OH is a base, H_2SO_4 is an acid

35. Which choice below represents an element?

A. glucose   **C.** methanol

B. sodium chloride   **D.** hydrogen   **E.** brass

36. What is the name of the property that describes the energy required for an atom to lose an electron and form a positive ion?

A. electronegativity   **C.** hyperconjugation

B. ionization energy   **D.** electron affinity   **E.** induction

37. What is the volume percent of Ar in a 7.50 L flask that contains 0.30 mole of Ne, 0.40 mole He and 0.60 mole of Ar at STP?

A. 41.2%   **B.** 31.8%   **C.** 39.9%   **D.** 46.1%   **E.** 36.8%

38. For the following unbalanced reaction, how many moles of O_2 gas are required for combustion with two moles of $C_{12}H_{22}O_{11}$?

$$C_{12}H_{22}O_{11}\,(l) + O_2\,(g) \rightarrow CO_2\,(g) + H_2O\,(g)$$

A. 4   **B.** 8   **C.** 24   **D.** 12   **E.** 36

39. The internal energy of the system increases for which of the following situations?

I. A block of clay is dropped and sticks to the ground

II. Carbon and oxygen undergo an exothermic combustion reaction to form CO_2

III. A car travels at a constant speed while experiencing air resistance

A. II only   **B.** II and III only   **C.** I and III only   **D.** I, II and III   **E.** III only

40. Which component of the reaction mechanism results in the net production of free radicals?

I. initiation II. propagation III. termination

A. I only **C.** III only
B. II only **D.** II and III only **E.** I and III only

41. The *like dissolves like* rule for two liquids is illustrated by which of the following statements?

A. A nonpolar solute is immiscible with a nonpolar solvent
B. A nonpolar solute is miscible with a polar solvent
C. A polar solute is immiscible with a polar solvent
D. A polar solute is miscible with a nonpolar solvent
E. None of the above

42. Identify the correct acid-conjugate base pair for:

$$H_2PO_4^- + S^{2-} \rightarrow HS^- + HPO_4^{2-}$$

Acid	Conjugate Base
A. $H_2PO_4^-$	HPO_4^{2-}
B. HS^-	H_2PO4^-
C. S^{2-}	HS^-
D. $H_2PO_4^-$	S^{2-}
E. HPO_4^{2-}	$H_2PO_4^-$

43. Which of the following statements is true regarding the redox reaction occurring in a nonspontaneous electrochemical cell?

Electricity

$$Br_2 (l) + 2\, NaCl\, (aq) \quad \rightarrow \quad Cl_2 (g) + 2\, NaBr\, (aq)$$

A. Cl^- is produced at the anode **C.** Oxidation half-reaction: $Br_2 + 2\, e^- \rightarrow 2\, Br^-$
B. Br^- is produced at the anode **D.** Reduction half-reaction: $2\, Cl^- \rightarrow Cl_2 + 2\, e^-$
  E. Br^- is produced at the cathode

44. Which of the following statements about the periodic table is NOT true?

A. Elements are classified into groups by electronic structure
B. Noble gases represent the most stable period
C. Periods refer to the horizontal rows
D. Elements in the same groups have similar chemical properties
E. Vertical rows represent groups

45. Which of the following statement(s) about covalent bonds for aqueous solutions is accurate?

      I. Involve the sharing of electrons, so each atom acquires a noble gas configuration
      II. Can be either polar or nonpolar bonds
      III. Are stronger bonds than ionic bonds

    A. I only   **C.** III only
    B. II only   **D.** I and II only   **E.** I, II and III

46. Which of the following is true when comparing two compounds of similar molar mass, whereby compound A is comprised of nonpolar molecules, while compound B is composed of polar molecules?

    A. B boils at a higher temperature than A   **C.** A does not boil
    B. B boils at a lower temperature than A   **D.** B does not boil
    E. Both compounds have the same boiling point

47. What is the coefficient of $HClO_4$ when the following equation is balanced with smallest whole numbers?

$$Cl_2O_7 + H_2O \rightarrow HClO_4$$

    A. 1   **B.** 2   **C.** 3   **D.** 4   **E.** 7

48. Consider the enthalpy of the following balanced reaction.

$$2\ CO\ (g) + O_2\ (g) \rightarrow 2\ CO_2\ (g) + 134.8\ kcal$$

This reaction is [   ] because the sign of ΔH is [   ].

    A. endothermic; zero   **C.** endothermic; positive
    B. exothermic; negative   **D.** exothermic; positive   **E.** exothermic; zero

49. Given the expression: rate $= k[A]^2[B]^4$, what is the order of the reaction?

    A. 1   **B.** 2   **C.** 4   **D.** 6   **E.** 8

50. Which of the following solutions has the greatest osmolarity?

    A. 0.15 M KF   **C.** 0.7 M NaCl
    B. 0.25 M $CaBr_2$ **D.** 0.4 M $AlCl_3$ **E.** 0.10 M KNO_3

51. The [¯OH] and the pH of 0.04 M KOH at 25 °C are, respectively:

    A. 0.04 M and 12.6   **C.** 0.04 M and 1.40
    B. 4.0×10^{-13} M and 12.5   **D.** 0.4 M and 1.40   **E.** 4.0×10^{-13} and 1.40

52. Lavoisier, based on the Law of Mass Conservation, hypothesized that:

   A. an element is a combination of substances
   B. carbon dioxide is an element
   C. an element is made of a fundamental substance that cannot be broken down further
   D. elements can lose mass as temperature changes
   E. elements can gain mass as humidity changes

53. A covalent double bond is formed by how many electrons?

   A. 1   **B.** 2   **C.** 3   **D.** 4   **E.** 8

54. How many moles of carbon atoms are in a 22.4 liter sample of a gas at STP that contains, by volume, 30% C_2H_6, 50% CH_4 and 20% N_2?

   A. 0.60   **B.** 0.80   **C.** 1.10   **D.** 1.30   **E.** 1.60

55. What is the term given for the mass percent of each element in a compound?

   A. mass composition   **C.** compound composition
   B. percent composition   **D.** elemental composition
                                        E. molecular composition

56. As an extensive property, if the change in a value for the decomposition of 120 grams of a substance is –45 kJ, what is the change in this value when 360 grams decompose?

   A. –2.6 kJ   **C.** –135 kJ
   B. –45 kJ   **D.** –180 kJ   **E.** Cannot be determined

57. Identify the reaction described by the following equilibrium expression:

   $K_{eq} = [H_2]^2 \times [O_2] / [H_2O]^2$

   A. $2 H_2O (g) \leftrightarrow 2 H_2 (g) + O_2 (g)$ **C.** $H_2O (g) \leftrightarrow H_2 (g) + \frac{1}{2} O_2 (g)$
   B. $H_2O (g) \leftrightarrow 2 H (g) + O (g)$ **D.** $2 H_2 (g) + O_2 (g) \leftrightarrow 2 H_2O (g)$
                                                                  E. $2 H_2O (g) \leftrightarrow H_2 (g) + O_2 (g)$

58. Why does water boil at a lower temperature when at high altitudes?

   A. Vapor pressure of water is increased at high altitudes
   B. Ambient room temperature is higher than at low altitudes
   C. More energy is available to break liquid bonds at high altitudes
   D. Atmospheric pressure is lower at high altitudes
   E. Atmospheric pressure is lower at low altitudes

59. Which of the following is NOT an example of an acidic salt?

    A. sodium hydrogen sulfate   **C.** barium dihydrogen phosphate

    B. nickel (II) bichromate   **D.** aluminum bicarbonate

                                      E. potassium hydrogen chloride

60. How many Faradays are consumed to completely electrolyze 10 moles of H_2O_2 in the following reaction? (Use 1 mole of electrons = 1 faraday)

$$H_2O_2 + 2\,H^+ + 2\,e^- \rightleftarrows 2\,H_2O$$

    A. 0.2   **B.** 2.0   **C.** 5.0   **D.** 10.0   **E.** 20.0

Check your answers using the answer key. Then, go to the explanations section and review the explanations in detail, paying particular attention to questions you didn't answer correctly or marked for review. Note the topic that those questions belong to.

We recommend that you do this BEFORE taking the next Diagnostic Test.

Notes:

Diagnostic test #1 – Answer Key

1	A	Electronic Structure & Periodic Table	31	B	Thermochemistry
2	B	Bonding	32	E	Kinetics Equilibrium
3	E	Phases & Phase Equilibria	33	E	Solution Chemistry
4	B	Stoichiometry	34	E	Acids & Bases
5	A	Thermochemistry	35	D	Electronic Structure & Periodic Table
6	A	Kinetics Equilibrium	36	B	Bonding
7	B	Solution Chemistry	37	D	Phases & Phase Equilibria
8	B	Acids & Bases	38	C	Stoichiometry
9	B	Electrochemistry	39	C	Thermochemistry
10	E	Electronic Structure & Periodic Table	40	A	Kinetics Equilibrium
11	D	Bonding	41	E	Solution Chemistry
12	D	Phases & Phase Equilibria	42	A	Acids & Bases
13	D	Stoichiometry	43	E	Electrochemistry
14	A	Thermochemistry	44	B	Electronic Structure & Periodic Table
15	A	Kinetics Equilibrium	45	E	Bonding
16	C	Solution Chemistry	46	A	Phases & Phase Equilibria
17	E	Acids & Bases	47	B	Stoichiometry
18	D	Electronic Structure & Periodic Table	48	B	Thermochemistry
19	A	Bonding	49	D	Kinetics Equilibrium
20	B	Phases & Phase Equilibria	50	D	Solution Chemistry
21	D	Stoichiometry	51	A	Acids & Bases
22	C	Thermochemistry	52	C	Electronic Structure & Periodic Table
23	D	Kinetics Equilibrium	53	D	Bonding
24	B	Solution Chemistry	54	C	Phases & Phase Equilibria
25	D	Acids & Bases	55	B	Stoichiometry
26	C	Electrochemistry	56	C	Thermochemistry
27	B	Electronic Structure & Periodic Table	57	A	Kinetics Equilibrium
28	B	Bonding	58	D	Solution Chemistry
29	E	Phases & Phase Equilibria	59	E	Acids & Bases
30	D	Stoichiometry	60	E	Electrochemistry

Diagnostic Test #2

This Diagnostic Test is designed for you to assess your proficiency on each topic. Use your test results and identify areas of your strength and weakness to adjust your study plan and enhance your fundamental knowledge.

The length of the Diagnostic Tests is proven to be optimal for a single study session.

#	Answer:					Review	#	Answer:					Review
1:	A	B	C	D	E	___	31:	A	B	C	D	E	___
2:	A	B	C	D	E	___	32:	A	B	C	D	E	___
3:	A	B	C	D	E	___	33:	A	B	C	D	E	___
4:	A	B	C	D	E	___	34:	A	B	C	D	E	___
5:	A	B	C	D	E	___	35:	A	B	C	D	E	___
6:	A	B	C	D	E	___	36:	A	B	C	D	E	___
7:	A	B	C	D	E	___	37:	A	B	C	D	E	___
8:	A	B	C	D	E	___	38:	A	B	C	D	E	___
9:	A	B	C	D	E	___	39:	A	B	C	D	E	___
10:	A	B	C	D	E	___	40:	A	B	C	D	E	___
11:	A	B	C	D	E	___	41:	A	B	C	D	E	___
12:	A	B	C	D	E	___	42:	A	B	C	D	E	___
13:	A	B	C	D	E	___	43:	A	B	C	D	E	___
14:	A	B	C	D	E	___	44:	A	B	C	D	E	___
15:	A	B	C	D	E	___	45:	A	B	C	D	E	___
16:	A	B	C	D	E	___	46:	A	B	C	D	E	___
17:	A	B	C	D	E	___	47:	A	B	C	D	E	___
18:	A	B	C	D	E	___	48:	A	B	C	D	E	___
19:	A	B	C	D	E	___	49:	A	B	C	D	E	___
20:	A	B	C	D	E	___	50:	A	B	C	D	E	___
21:	A	B	C	D	E	___	51:	A	B	C	D	E	___
22:	A	B	C	D	E	___	52:	A	B	C	D	E	___
23:	A	B	C	D	E	___	53:	A	B	C	D	E	___
24:	A	B	C	D	E	___	54:	A	B	C	D	E	___
25:	A	B	C	D	E	___	55:	A	B	C	D	E	___
26:	A	B	C	D	E	___	56:	A	B	C	D	E	___
27:	A	B	C	D	E	___	57:	A	B	C	D	E	___
28:	A	B	C	D	E	___	58:	A	B	C	D	E	___
29:	A	B	C	D	E	___	59:	A	B	C	D	E	___
30:	A	B	C	D	E	___	60:	A	B	C	D	E	___

1. How many electrons are there in the outermost shell and subshell, respectively, in an atom with the electron configuration $1s^22s^22p^63s^23p^64s^23d^{10}4p^1$?

    A. 4, 1   **B.** 3, 1   **C.** 10, 1   **D.** 2, 2   **E.** 5,1

2. Based on the Lewis structure, how many non-bonding electrons are on N in the nitrate ion?

    A. 0   **B.** 2   **C.** 4   **D.** 6   **E.** 8

3. What volume is occupied by 7.4×10^{24} molecules of CO at STP? (Use Avogadro's number $= 6.02 \times 10^{23}$ molecules and the conversion of 1 mole occupies 22.4 L)

    A. 275.3 L   **B.** 4.24 L   **C.** 22.4 L   **D.** 0.54 L   **E.** 2.24 L

4. Which expression represents the balanced half reaction for *reduction* in the following unbalanced reaction?

$$\text{Fe } (s) + \text{CuSO}_4 \, (aq) \rightarrow \text{Fe}_2(\text{SO4})_3(aq) + \text{Cu } (s)$$

    A. $3\text{ Cu}^{2+} + 6\text{ e}^- \rightarrow 3\text{ Cu}$ **C.** $2\text{ Cu}^{3+} + 3\text{ e}^- \rightarrow 2\text{ Cu}$

    B. $2\text{ Fe} \rightarrow 2\text{ Fe}^{3+} + 6\text{e}^-$ **D.** $\text{Fe} + 3\text{ e}^- \rightarrow \text{Fe}^{3+}$ **E.** None of the above

5. A small bomb has exploded inside a sealed concrete bunker. What kind of system are the contents of the bunker, if no heat or vibrations are being detected by anyone leaning against its exterior wall?

    A. exergonic   **B.** entropic   **C.** open   **D.** closed   **E.** isolated

6. Which of the following statements is true?

    A. The equilibrium constant (K_{eq}) for a reaction can be determined in part from the activation energy

    B. The equilibrium concentrations of reactants can be determined in part from the activation energy

    C. The rate constant (k) of a reaction can be determined in part from the activation energy

    D. The order of a reaction can be determined in part from the activation energy

    E. None of the above is true

7. Which of the following illustrates the *like dissolves like* principle for two liquids?

    A. A nonpolar solute is miscible with a nonpolar solvent

    B. A nonpolar solvent is miscible with a polar solvent

    C. A polar solute is miscible with a nonpolar solvent

    D. A polar solute is immiscible with a polar solvent

    E. A polar solvent is immiscible with a polar solute

8. Which of the following describes why acetic acid is a weak acid in water?

   A. Only slightly dissociates into ions

   B. Unable to hold onto its hydrogen ion

   C. Only slightly soluble

   D. Dilute

   E. Completely dissociated into hydronium ions and acetate ions

9. Which of the following is the half-reaction that occurs at the cathode during electrolysis of aqueous $CuCl_2$ solution?

   A. $2\ H_2O + 2\ e^- \rightarrow H_2\,(g) + 2\ OH^-\,(aq)$ **C.** $Cl_2\,(g) + 2\ e^- \rightarrow 2\ Cl^-\,(aq)$

   B. $Cu^+\,(aq) + e^- \rightarrow Cu\,(s)$ **D.** $2\ Cl^-\,(aq) \rightarrow Cl_2\,(g) + 2\ e^-$

                                     E. $Cu^{2+}\,(aq) + 2\ e^- \rightarrow Cu\,(s)$

10. How many electrons are in the highest energy level of sulfur?

   A. 2   **B.** 4   **C.** 6   **D.** 8   **E.** 10

11. Which of the following molecules is polar?

   A. CF_4 **B.** C_2Cl_4 **C.** $BeCl_2$ **D.** CCl_4 **E.** NBr_3

12. Which characteristics best describe a gas?

   A. Volume and shape of container, no intermolecular attractions

   B. Defined volume; shape of container, weak intermolecular attractions

   C. Defined shape and volume, strong intermolecular attractions

   D. Defined volume; shape of container, moderate intermolecular attractions

   E. Volume and shape of container, strong intermolecular attractions

13. Which substance is functioning as the oxidizing agent in this reaction?

$$14\ H^+ + Cr_2O_7^{2-} + 3\ Ni \rightarrow 3\ Ni^{2+} + 2\ Cr^{3+} + 7\ H_2O$$

   A. H_2O **B.** $Cr_2O_7^{2-}$ **C.** $H+$ **D.** Ni **E.** Ni^{2+}

14. Use the following data to calculate the lattice energy ($\Delta H_{lattice}$) of sodium chloride:

      $Na\,(s) \rightarrow Na\,(g)$ $\Delta H_1 = +108\ kJ$

      $\frac{1}{2}\ Cl_2\,(g) \rightarrow Cl\,(g)$ $\Delta H_2 = +120\ kJ$

      $Na\,(g) \rightarrow Na^+\,(g) + e^-$ $\Delta H_3 = +496\ kJ$

      $Cl\,(g) + e^- \rightarrow Cl^-\,(g)$ $\Delta H_4 = -349\ kJ$

      $Na\,(s) + \frac{1}{2}\ Cl_2\,(g) \rightarrow NaCl\,(s)$ $\Delta H_f^\circ = -411\ kJ$

   A. −429 kJ/mol   **B.** −760 kJ/mol   **C.** −349 kJ/mol   **D.** 786 kJ/mol   **E.** −786 kJ/mol

15. Which method could be used to determine the rate law for a reaction?

      I. Measure the initial rate of the reaction at several reactant concentrations
      II. Graph the concentration of the reactants as a function of time
      III. Predict the reaction mechanism

   A. I only   **B.** III only   **C.** II only   **D.** II and III only   **E.** I, II and III

16. In a solution of 74 percent nitrogen and 26 percent oxygen, which substance is the solvent?

   A. nitrogen   **C.** both
   B. oxygen   **D.** neither   **E.** gases cannot form solutions

17. Why is sulfuric acid (H_2SO_4) a much stronger acid than carbonic acid (CO_3H_2)?

   A. The acid strength of two comparative molecules is directly proportional to the number of oxygens bonded to the central atom
   B. Since carbonic acid has resonance stabilization and sulfuric acid does not, sulfuric acid is less stable and more acidic
   C. The two double bonded oxygens in H_2SO_4 tend to destabilize the single bonded oxygen once the hydrogen ions form, thus making sulfuric acid more acidic
   D. In sulfuric acid, the negative charges move between 4 oxygen atoms, compared to 3 oxygen atoms in carbonic acid
   E. In carbonic acid, the positive charge moves between two additional oxygens, rather than only one for sulfuric acid

18. The magnetic quantum number does NOT:

   A. describe odd numbers of orbitals in a subshell
   B. have a range of $-l$ to $+l$
   C. describe the energy levels within a subshell
   D. identify the spin of the electron
   E. describe the orientation of the subshells

19. Which molecular geometry does NOT result in a nonpolar structure?

   A. diatomic covalent   **C.** tetrahedral
   B. square planar   **D.** trigonal planar   **E.** bent

20. Which of the following molecules can form hydrogen bonds?

      I. NH_3 II. H_2O III. HF

   A. I only   **C.** I and II only
   B. II only   **D.** II and III only   **E.** I, II and III

21. What is the approximate formula mass of sulfur dioxide (SO_2)?

    A. 28 amu   **B.** 36 amu   **C.** 62 amu   **D.** 64 amu   **E.** 68 amu

22. The mathematical equation that expresses the first law of thermodynamics is:

    A. $\Delta H = Q + W$ **C.** $\Delta H = \Delta E + P\Delta V$

    B. $\Delta H = Q + \Delta E$ **D.** $\Delta H = \Delta E - P\Delta V$ **E.** $\Delta E = Q + W$

23. Which statement is true regarding catalysts in chemical reactions?

    A. Shift the equilibrium towards products

    B. Are consumed in the reaction

    C. Lower the activation energy of the reaction

    D. Lower the energy of the products

    E. Increase the activation energy of the original reaction

24. Which of the following statements is/are true of a colloid?

        I. Dispersed particles are less than 1 nm in diameter

        II. Dispersed particles demonstrate the Tyndall effect

        III. Dispersed particles pass through biological membranes

    A. I only   **C.** I and II only

    B. II only   **D.** II and III only   **E.** I, II and III

25. Which is the balanced equation for the neutralization reaction between $Al(OH)_3$ and HCl (*aq*)?

    A. $Al(OH)_3 + 3\ HCl\ (aq) \rightarrow AlCl_3 + H^+ + {}^-OH$

    B. $Al^{3+} + {}^-OH + H^+ + Cl^- \rightarrow AlCl_3 + H_2O$

    C. $Al(OH)_3 + 3\ HCl\ (aq) \rightarrow AlCl_3 + 3\ H_2O$

    D. $Al(OH)_3 + HCl\ (aq) \rightarrow AlCl_3 + H_2O$

    E. $Al(OH)_3 + HCl\ (aq) \rightarrow AlCl_3 + 3\ H_2O$

26. For the following reaction for a battery, what is undergoing oxidation in the oxidation-reduction reaction?

        $Mn_2O_3 + ZnO \rightarrow 2\ MnO_2 + Zn$

    A. MnO_2 **C.** Zn

    B. ZnO   **D.** Mn_2O_3 **E.** Zn and MnO_2

27. Which element would most likely be a metalloid?

    A. B   **B.** Mg   **C.** Cl   **D.** H   **E.** C

28. What is the total number of electrons shown in a correctly written Lewis structure for OF_2?

   A. 20   **B.** 18   **C.** 10   **D.** 2   **E.** 12

29. A container contains only N_2, CO_2, O_2 and water vapor. What is the partial pressure of N_2 at STP, if the partial pressure of O_2 is 300 torr, CO_2 is 20 torr and water vapor is 8 torr? (Use STP = 760 torr)

   A. 165 torr   **B.** 432 torr   **C.** 760 torr   **D.** 330 torr   **E.** 864 torr

30. The number of moles of H_2O in a flask of water that contains 2.8×10^{21} molecules is:

   A. 3.4×10^{23} **B.** 2.1×10^{-23} **C.** 4.7×10^{-3} **D.** 2.4×10^{42} **E.** 2.4×10^{23}

31. Which of the following is true for a reaction where products have more stable bonds and more orderly arrangement than the reactants?

   A. ΔH is negative and ΔS is positive   **C.** ΔH is negative and ΔS is zero

   B. ΔH is positive and ΔS is negative   **D.** ΔH and ΔS are positive

                                                    E. ΔH and ΔS are negative

32. Which of the changes does NOT affect the equilibrium for the following reversible reaction?

   $SrCO_3\,(s) \leftrightarrow Sr^{2+}\,(aq) + CO_3^{2-}\,(aq)$

   A. Adding solid Na_2CO_3 **C.** Increasing $[CO_3^{2-}]$

   B. Adding solid $NaNO_3$ **D.** Increasing $[Sr^{2+}]$ **E.** Adding solid $Sr(NO_3)_2$

33. What is the volume of a solution that contains 3.40 moles of NaCl, if the concentration is 7.60 M NaCl?

   A. 0.936 L   **B.** 0.447 L   **C.** 2.34 L   **D.** 1.42 L   **E.** 0.234 L

34. By the Arrhenius definition of acids and bases, which statement is accurate for a base?

   A. produces ^-OH **C.** decreases pH

   B. decreases ^-OH **D.** decreases H_2O **E.** increases H_3O^+

35. All isotopes of an element possess the same:

   A. number of electrons, atomic number and mass, but have nothing else in common

   B. atomic number and mass, but have nothing else in common

   C. chemical properties and mass, but have nothing else in common

   D. number of electrons, atomic number and chemical properties

   E. mass only

36. Which of the following compounds is most likely to be ionic?

   A. CBr_4 **B.** H_2O **C.** CH_2Cl_2 **D.** CO_2 **E.** $SrBr_2$

37. What would be the new gas pressure, if a 440.0 mL gas sample at 360.0 mmHg is expanded to 820.0 mL with no change in temperature?

   A. 193.2 mmHg   **C.** 726.0 mmHg
   B. 364.2 mmHg   **D.** 766.0 mmHg   **E.** 810.0 mmHg

38. What is the oxidation number of C in BaC_2O_4?

   A. −3   **B.** −2   **C.** +2   **D.** +3   **E.** +4

39. What is the heat capacity of 68.0 g of H_2O? (Use the specific heat of H_2O = 4.184 J/g·°C)

   A. 16.3 J/°C   **B.** 413 J/°C   **C.** 92.3 J/°C   **D.** 155 J/°C   **E.** 285 J/°C

40. What conditions are required for a chemical reaction?

   A. Sufficient energy of collision and proper spatial orientation of the molecules
   B. Sufficient energy of collision only
   C. Proper spatial orientation of the molecules only
   D. Sufficient temperature and sufficient duration of molecular contact
   E. Sufficient energy of collision and sufficient duration of molecular content

41. If the concentration of a KCl solution is 18.0% (m/v), the mass of KCl in 28.0 mL of solution is:

   A. 5.04 g   **B.** 3.32 g   **C.** 0.643 g   **D.** 1.56 g   **E.** 8.0 g

42. The K_a of formic acid (HCOOH) is 1.7×10^{-4}. What is the pK_b of the formate ion?

   A. $14 - \log(1.7 \times 10^{-4})$ **C.** $-14 - \log(1.7 \times 10^{-4})$
   B. $14 + \log(1.7 \times 10^{-10})$ **D.** $-14 + \log(1.7 \times 10^{-4})$
                                                   E. $14 + \log(1.7 \times 10^{-4})$

43. Which of the following species undergoes reduction in the following reaction?

       $2\ CuBr \rightarrow 2\ Cu + Br_2$

   A. Br^- **B.** Cu^+ **C.** CuBr   **D.** Cu   **E.** Br_2

44. In which order must elements on the periodic table be listed for their properties to repeat at regular intervals?

    A. increasing atomic mass

    B. decreasing atomic mass

    C. increasing atomic number

    D. decreasing atomic number

    E. decreasing density

45. Which of the following is true of a hydrogen bond?

    A. The bond length is longer than a covalent bond

    B. The bond energy is less than a covalent bond

    C. The bond is between H and O, N or F

    D. The bond is between two polar molecules

    E. All of the above

46. The reason why ice floats in a glass of water is because, when frozen, H_2O is less dense due to:

    A. strengthening of cohesive forces

    B. high specific heat

    C. decreased number of hydrogen bonds

    D. weakening of cohesive forces

    E. increased number of hydrogen bonds

47. Which conversion factor is NOT consistent with the following unbalanced reaction?

    $NH_3 + O_2 \rightarrow NO + H_2O$

    A. 5 moles O_2 / 6 moles H_2O

    B. 4 moles NO / 4 moles NH_3

    C. 4 moles NH_3 / 5 moles H_2O

    D. 4 moles NO / 5 moles O_2

    E. All are correct

48. How much heat is needed to convert 15.0 g of ice at −8 °C to H_2O (*l*) at 15 °C? (Use the specific heat of ice = 2.09 J/g·°C; heat of fusion of ice = 334 J/g and specific heat of water = 4.18 J/g·°C)

    A. 3,410 J

    B. 6,201 J

    C. 5,763 J

    D. 2,474 J

    E. 8,266 J

49. Which of the following is true for the rate-determining step of a chemical reaction?

    A. It involves the fastest step

    B. It involves the slowest step

    C. It involves the molecules with the smallest molecular mass

    D. It involves the molecules with the greatest molecular mass

    E. It involves charged molecules transformed into neutral molecules

50. Which of the following compounds are soluble in water?

      I. LiF   II. FeS   III. CH_3COOH

A. I only   **C.** III only

B. II only   **D.** I and III only   **E.** I, II and III

51. Which compound is amphoteric?

A. NO_3 **C.** $CH_3CH_2COO^-$

B. HBr   **D.** BH_3 **E.** HSO_4^-

52. Which of the following atom has the largest atomic radius?

A. Li   **B.** Na   **C.** K   **D.** Rb   **E.** Cs

53. What is the approximate bond angle between atoms of a tetrahedral molecule?

A. 104.5°   **B.** 109.5°   **C.** 90°   **D.** 120°   **E.** 180°

54. The mathematical expression of Charles' law is:

A. $V_1T_1 = V_2T_2$ **C.** $V_1 + T_2 = V_2 + T_1$

B. $V_1 + T_1 = V_2 + T_2$ **D.** $V_1 / T_2 = T_1 / V_2$

                              E. $V_1 / T_1 = V_2 / T_2$

55. Which species is being oxidized and which is being reduced in the following reaction?

      $2Cr\ (s) + 3\ Cl_2\ (g) \rightarrow 2\ CrCl_3\ (s)$

A. Cr is oxidized; Cl_2 is reduced

B. Cl_2 is oxidized; Cr is reduced

C. Cr is oxidized; $CrCl_3$ is reduced

D. $CrCl_3$ is oxidized; Cr is reduced

E. Cr is reduced; $CrCl_3$ is reduced

56. Which of the following statements is true?

A. Reactions with $-\Delta H_f^o$ produce stable compounds

B. An endothermic reaction produces a relatively stable compound

C. Bond formation tends to increase the potential energy of the atoms

D. Compounds with $-\Delta H_f^o$ are unstable and spontaneously decompose into elements

E. Compounds with $+\Delta H_f^o$ are unstable and spontaneously decompose into elements

57. Which of the following is NOT an important condition for a chemical reaction?

    A. The molecules must make contact

    B. The molecules have enough energy to react once they collide

    C. The reacting molecules are in the correct orientation to one another

    D. The molecules are in the solid, liquid or gaseous state

    E. All are important

58. Molarity is defined as the number of:

    A. liters of solute per mole of solution

    B. moles of solute per liter of solvent

    C. grams of solute per liter of solution

    D. moles of solute per liter of solution

    E. grams of solute per mole of solution

59. Which of the following could NOT be a Brønsted-Lowry acid?

    A. CN^- **C.** HF

    B. HS^- **D.** $HC_2H_3O_2$ **E.** H_2SO_4

60. Which statement is correct about reduction if a galvanic cell that has two electrodes?

    A. Reduction occurs at the uncharged dynode

    B. Reduction occurs at the negatively charged cathode

    C. Reduction occurs at the positively charged anode

    D. Reduction occurs at the negatively charged anode

    E. Reduction occurs at the positively charged cathode

Check your answers using the answer key. Then, go to the explanations section and review the explanations in detail, paying particular attention to questions you didn't answer correctly or marked for review. Note the topic that those questions belong to.

We recommend that you do this BEFORE taking the next Diagnostic Test.

Diagnostic test #2 – Answer Key

1	B	Electronic Structure & Periodic Table	31	E	Thermochemistry
2	A	Bonding	32	B	Kinetics Equilibrium
3	A	Phases & Phase Equilibria	33	B	Solution Chemistry
4	A	Stoichiometry	34	A	Acids & Bases
5	E	Thermochemistry	35	D	Electronic Structure & Periodic Table
6	C	Kinetics Equilibrium	36	E	Bonding
7	A	Solution Chemistry	37	A	Phases & Phase Equilibria
8	A	Acids & Bases	38	D	Stoichiometry
9	E	Electrochemistry	39	E	Thermochemistry
10	C	Electronic Structure & Periodic Table	40	A	Kinetics Equilibrium
11	E	Bonding	41	A	Solution Chemistry
12	A	Phases & Phase Equilibria	42	E	Acids & Bases
13	B	Stoichiometry	43	B	Electrochemistry
14	E	Thermochemistry	44	C	Electronic Structure & Periodic Table
15	E	Kinetics Equilibrium	45	E	Bonding
16	A	Solution Chemistry	46	E	Phases & Phase Equilibria
17	D	Acids & Bases	47	C	Stoichiometry
18	D	Electronic Structure & Periodic Table	48	B	Thermochemistry
19	E	Bonding	49	B	Kinetics Equilibrium
20	E	Phases & Phase Equilibria	50	D	Solution Chemistry
21	D	Stoichiometry	51	E	Acids & Bases
22	E	Thermochemistry	52	E	Electronic Structure & Periodic Table
23	C	Kinetics Equilibrium	53	B	Bonding
24	B	Solution Chemistry	54	E	Phases & Phase Equilibria
25	C	Acids & Bases	55	A	Stoichiometry
26	D	Electrochemistry	56	A	Thermochemistry
27	A	Electronic Structure & Periodic Table	57	E	Kinetics Equilibrium
28	A	Bonding	58	D	Solution Chemistry
29	B	Phases & Phase Equilibria	59	A	Acids & Bases
30	C	Stoichiometry	60	E	Electrochemistry

Diagnostic Test #3

This Diagnostic Test is designed for you to assess your proficiency on each topic. Use your test results and identify areas of your strength and weakness to adjust your study plan and enhance your fundamental knowledge.

The length of the Diagnostic Tests is proven to be optimal for a single study session.

#	Answer:					Review	#	Answer:					Review
1:	A	B	C	D	E	___	31:	A	B	C	D	E	___
2:	A	B	C	D	E	___	32:	A	B	C	D	E	___
3:	A	B	C	D	E	___	33:	A	B	C	D	E	___
4:	A	B	C	D	E	___	34:	A	B	C	D	E	___
5:	A	B	C	D	E	___	35:	A	B	C	D	E	___
6:	A	B	C	D	E	___	36:	A	B	C	D	E	___
7:	A	B	C	D	E	___	37:	A	B	C	D	E	___
8:	A	B	C	D	E	___	38:	A	B	C	D	E	___
9:	A	B	C	D	E	___	39:	A	B	C	D	E	___
10:	A	B	C	D	E	___	40:	A	B	C	D	E	___
11:	A	B	C	D	E	___	41:	A	B	C	D	E	___
12:	A	B	C	D	E	___	42:	A	B	C	D	E	___
13:	A	B	C	D	E	___	43:	A	B	C	D	E	___
14:	A	B	C	D	E	___	44:	A	B	C	D	E	___
15:	A	B	C	D	E	___	45:	A	B	C	D	E	___
16:	A	B	C	D	E	___	46:	A	B	C	D	E	___
17:	A	B	C	D	E	___	47:	A	B	C	D	E	___
18:	A	B	C	D	E	___	48:	A	B	C	D	E	___
19:	A	B	C	D	E	___	49:	A	B	C	D	E	___
20:	A	B	C	D	E	___	50:	A	B	C	D	E	___
21:	A	B	C	D	E	___	51:	A	B	C	D	E	___
22:	A	B	C	D	E	___	52:	A	B	C	D	E	___
23:	A	B	C	D	E	___	53:	A	B	C	D	E	___
24:	A	B	C	D	E	___	54:	A	B	C	D	E	___
25:	A	B	C	D	E	___	55:	A	B	C	D	E	___
26:	A	B	C	D	E	___	56:	A	B	C	D	E	___
27:	A	B	C	D	E	___	57:	A	B	C	D	E	___
28:	A	B	C	D	E	___	58:	A	B	C	D	E	___
29:	A	B	C	D	E	___	59:	A	B	C	D	E	___
30:	A	B	C	D	E	___	60:	A	B	C	D	E	___

1. Sulfur has three common oxidation states of +2, 0 and –2. Which oxidation state has the largest atomic radius?

      I. neutral   II. anion   III. cation

  A. I only   **B.** II only   **C.** III only   **D.** I and II only   **E.** I, II and III

2. When drawing a Lewis dot structure of a compound, pairs of electrons that are not between atoms but are used to fill the octet are:

  A. excess electrons   **C.** lone pairs

  B. filled shells   **D.** bonding pairs   **E.** not shown on the structure

3. Which of these alkanes has the lowest boiling point?

  A. C_8H_{18} **B.** C_6H_{14} **C.** C_4H_{10} **D.** C_2H_6 **E.** $C_{10}H_{22}$

4. What is the oxidation number of Br in $NaBrO_4$?

  A. –6   **B.** –4   **C.** +7   **D.** +4   **E.** +5

5. From the given bond energies, how many kJ of energy are released or absorbed from the reaction of one mole of N_2 with three moles of H_2 to form two moles of NH_3?

      $N{\equiv}N + H{-}H + H{-}H + H{-}H \rightarrow NH_3 + NH_3$

      H–N: 389 kJ/mol   H–H: 436 kJ/mol $N{\equiv}N$: 946 kJ/mol

  A. –80 kJ/mol released   **C.** –946 kJ/mol released

  B. +89.5 kJ/mol absorbed   **D.** +895 kJ/mol absorbed   **E.** +946 kJ/mol absorbed

6. The data provides the rate of a reaction as affected by the concentration of the reactants. What is the order of the reaction rate?

Experiment	[X]	[Y]	[Z]	Rate (mol L^{-1} hr^{-1})
1	0.200 M	0.100 M	0.600 M	5.0
2	0.200 M	0.400 M	0.400 M	80.0
3	0.600 M	0.100 M	0.200 M	15.0
4	0.200 M	0.100 M	0.200 M	5.0
5	0.200 M	0.200 M	0.400 M	20.0

  A. Zero order with respect to X

  B. Order for X is minus one (rate proportional to 1 / [X])

  C. First order with respect to X

  D. Second order with respect to X

  E. Order for X cannot be determined from data

7. What are the products for the following unbalanced double-replacement reaction?

$$AgNO_3\,(aq) + Li_3PO_4\,(aq) \rightarrow$$

A. Ag_3PO_4 and $LiNO_2$ C. Ag_3PO_3 and $LiNO_2$

B. Ag_3PO_3 and $2\ LiNO_3$ D. Ag_3P and $3\ LiNO_3$ E. Ag_3PO_4 and $3\ LiNO_3$

8. In the following equation, which is the proton donor and which is the proton acceptor?

$$CO_3^{2-}\,(aq) + H_2O\,(l) \rightarrow HCO_3^-\,(aq) + {}^-OH\,(aq)$$

A. ^-OH is the donor and HCO_3^- is the acceptor
B. HCO_3^- is the donor and ^-OH is the acceptor
C. H_2O is the donor and CO_3^{2-} is the acceptor
D. CO_3^{2-} is the donor and H_2O is the acceptor
E. CO_3^{2-} is the donor and ^-OH is the acceptor

9. How many e^- are gained or lost in the following half-reaction: $Cl_2 \rightarrow 2\ Cl^-$?

A. $2\ e^-$ are gained   C. ½ e^- is gained

B. ½ e^- is lost   D. $2\ e^-$ are lost   E. $4\ e^-$ are gained

10. Which of the following elements is an alkaline earth metal?

A. Hydrogen   B. Calcium   C. Arsenic   D. Boron   E. Carbon

11. What is the molecular geometry of NCl_3?

A. tetrahedral   C. trigonal bipyramidal

B. trigonal planar   D. trigonal pyramidal   E. bent

12. Which of the following expression represents how the ideal gas equation CANNOT be written?

A. $PV = nRT$ C. $R = PV / nT$

B. $P = nRT / V$ D. $R = nT / PV$ E. None of the above

13. Balance the following equation: __$NO \rightarrow$ __$N_2O +$ __NO_2

A. 4, 4, 8   B. 1, 2, 4   C. 3, 1, 1   D. 3, 0, 0   E. 6, 2, 1

14. If a researcher is working with a sample of neon at 278 K, what phase change is observed when the pressure is reduced from 60 atm to 38 atm?

A. liquid $\rightarrow$ solid   C. solid $\rightarrow$ gas

B. solid $\rightarrow$ liquid   D. liquid $\rightarrow$ gas   E. gas $\rightarrow$ liquid

15. If the reaction is endothermic, which of the following is always true?

    A. The energy of the reactants is less than the products
    B. The energy of the reactants is greater than the products
    C. The reaction rate is slow
    D. The reaction rate is fast
    E. None of the above

16. Which of the following solid compounds are soluble in water?

    I. Li_2CO_3 II. $Cu(NO_3)_2$ III. $Ag(C_2H_3O_2)$

    A. I only   **C.** I and II only
    B. II and III only   **D.** I and III only   **E.** I, II and III

17. Calculate the hydrogen ion concentration in a solution with a pH = 6.35.

    A. 4.5×10^{-7} M   **C.** 7.35 M
    B. 7.55×10^{-8} M   **D.** 6.35 M   **E.** 6.35×10^{-8} M

18. Which of the following is true of an element in an excited state?

    A. It has emitted a photon and its energy has decreased
    B. It has emitted a photon and its energy has increased
    C. It has absorbed a photon and its energy has decreased
    D. It has absorbed a neutron and its energy has increased
    E. It has absorbed a photon and its energy has increased

19. Which of the following statements is NOT correct?

    A. Cations and anions combine in the simplest ratio which results in electrical neutrality
    B. In an ionic compound, the number of electrons lost by the cation equals the number of electrons gained by the anion
    C. Ionic compounds may contain one metal and one nonmetal
    D. Ionic compounds may contain one metal and one halogen
    E. Formulas of ionic compounds are written with the anion first, followed by the cation

20. Which of the following is assumed by the kinetic-molecular theory of ideal gases

    I. Gas molecules within the container have the same speed
    II. Gas molecules have negligible volume
    III. Gas molecules exert no attractive forces between each other

    A. I only   **C.** II and III only
    B. I and III only   **D.** III only   **E.** I, II and III

21. What is the percent by mass of nitrogen in NO_2?

    A. 12.0%   **B.** 25.5%   **C.** 30.4%   **D.** 33.3%   **E.** 50.0%

22. What term refers to a chemical reaction that absorbs heat energy?

    A. endothermic   **C.** exothermic
    B. isothermal   **D.** spontaneous   **E.** exergonic

23. If the temperature of a reaction increases, which of the following is true?

    I. Amount of product decreases
    II. Rate of reaction increases
    III. Heat of reaction increases

    A. I only   **B.** II only   **C.** III only   **D.** I and II only   **E.** I, II and III

24. What is the molarity of a hydrochloric acid solution prepared by diluting 500.0 mL of 1.00 M HCl to a total volume of 3.50 L?

    A. 2.30 M   **B.** 1.22 M   **C.** 2.56 M   **D.** 0.197 M   **E.** 0.143 M

25. Which volume of barium hydroxide is required to neutralize the acid when 25.0 mL of 0.100 M HCl is titrated with 0.150 M $Ba(OH)_2$?

$$2\ HCl\ (aq) + Ba(OH)_2\ (aq) \rightarrow BaCl_2\ (aq) + 2\ H_2O\ (l)$$

    A. 32.4 mL   **B.** 25.0 mL   **C.** 16.7 mL   **D.** 8.33 mL   **E.** 37.5 mL

26. What is E° for the electrochemical cell of $CuSO_4$ and LiCl?

$$Cu\ (s) + Li^+ \rightarrow Cu^{2+} + Li\ (s)$$

    $Cu^{2+} + 2\ e^- \rightarrow Cu\ (s)$ E° = 0.337
    $Li^+ + e^- \rightarrow Li\ (s)$ E° = −3.03

    A. 3.367 V   **B.** −3.367 V   **C.** 2.693 V   **D.** −2.693 V   **E.** −6.060 V

27. Except for helium, the valence shell of electrons in the noble gases has which of the following electron configurations?

    A. ns^2np^2 **B.** ns^2np^4 **C.** ns^8np^2 **D.** ns^2np^8 **E.** ns^2np^6

28. Which statement is true for a dipole?

    A. Nonpolar entity   **C.** Separation of charges
    B. Form of electronegativity   **D.** Molecule with parallel bonds
                               E. Forms by hyperconjugation

29. Which of the following molecules has only London dispersion forces as the primary attraction between molecules?

A. $CH_3CH_2NH_2$

B. $CH_3CH(OH)CH_3$

C. CH_3CH_3

D. H_2S

E. H_2O

30. Which of the following net ionic equations represents a disproportionation reaction?

A. $ClO^- + Cl^- + 2\,H^+ \rightarrow Cl_2 + H_2O$

B. $CH_4 + 2\,O_2 \rightarrow CO_2 + H_2O$

C. $Fe + 3\,Ag^+ \rightarrow Fe^{3+} + 3\,Ag$

D. $2\,HNO_3 + SO_2 \rightarrow H_2SO_4 + 2\,NO_2$

E. None of the above

31. What is heat a measure of?

A. temperature

B. internal thermal energy

C. average kinetic energy

D. potential energy

E. none of the above

32. Which condition(s) increase(s) the rate of a chemical reaction: $A\,(g) + B\,(g) \rightarrow C\,(s)$?

I. Decreasing the temperature of the chemical reaction

II. Significantly increasing the concentration of the reactants

III. Increasing the pressure on a gaseous reaction system

A. I only   B. II only   C. I and III only   D. II and III only   E. I, II and III

33. Which of the following is/are solution(s)?

I. Low concentration of NaCl in water

II. A mixture of 3% carbon dioxide and 97% water

III. Water vapor in N_2 gas

A. I only

B. II only

C. II and III only

D. I, II and III

E. I and II only

34. Which volume of 0.25 M H_2SO_4 is needed to neutralize 40 ml of 0.30 M NaOH?

A. 24 ml   B. 40 ml   C. 33 ml   D. 8 ml   E. 14 ml

35. Which of the following is/are characteristic of a nonmetallic element?

I. nonconductor of electricity

II. dull appearance

III. low melting point

A. I only

B. II only

C. II and III only

D. I and II only

E. I, II and III

36. What is the formula of the carbonate ion?

    A. $C_2O_4^{-2}$ **B.** $C_2O_4^{-1}$ **C.** CO_2^{-3} **D.** CO_3^{-2} **E.** $C_2H_3O_2^{-1}$

37. One liter of an ideal gas is placed in a piston at 27 °C. If the pressure is constant and the temperature is changed to 50 K, the final volume is:

    A. 108 ml   **B.** 131 ml   **C.** 136 ml   **D.** 167 ml   **E.** 184 ml

38. What is the percent by mass of chromium in K_2CrO_4?

    A. 26.8%   **B.** 31.6%   **C.** 41.3%   **D.** 43.7%   **E.** 52.6%

39. How much heat is required to raise the temperature of 5 grams of a material by 10 K, if it requires 35 calories to raise the temperature of 5 grams of this material by 10 °C?

    A. 0.10 cal   **B.** 35 cal   **C.** 10 cal   **D.** 50 cal   **E.** 3.5 cal

40. Which of the following is/are true regarding the K_{eq} expression?

    I. The value of K_{eq} is temperature dependent
    II. The K_{eq} expression contains only substances in the same physical state
    III. The K_{eq} expression was originally determined experimentally

    A. I only   **C.** I and III only
    B. I and II only   **D.** II and III only   **E.** I, II and III

41. Which of the following constitutes(s) a heterogeneous mixture that is opaque and has particles large enough to be filtered?

    I. colloid   II. suspension   III. solution

    A. I only   **B.** II only   **C.** I and II only   **D.** I and III only   **E.** I, II and III

42. Which characteristic of a molecule describes an acid?

    A. Donates hydrogen atoms   **C.** Donates hydrogen ions
    B. Dissolves metal   **D.** Accepts hydrogen atoms
                                      E. Donates hydronium ions

43. How many coulombs are required to electroplate 40.0 grams of chromium by passing an electrical current through a solution containing aqueous $CrCl_3$? (Use Faraday's constant = 96,500 C/mol and the molecular mass of Cr = 52.00 g/mol and Cl = 35.45 g/mol)

    A. 2.38×10^3 coulomb   **C.** 7.75×10^4 coulomb
    B. 5.64×10^4 coulomb   **D.** 2.23×10^5 coulomb   **E.** 1.13×10^6 coulomb

44. What is the term for the value that indicates the number of protons for an atom of a given element?

    A. atomic mass   **C.** atomic notation

    B. mass number   **D.** atomic number   **E.** isotope number

45. Water is a polar molecule because oxygen:

    A. is at one end with the hydrogens at the other end of the molecule

    B. has a partial negative charge, while the hydrogens have a partial positive charge

    C. has a partial positive charge, while the hydrogens have a partial negative charge

    D. is bonded between the two hydrogens

    E. attracts the hydrogen atoms

46. If the temperature of a liquid increases, what happens to its vapor pressure?

    A. unpredictable   **C.** decreases

    B. remains constant   **D.** increases   **E.** increases by $\sqrt{\text{temperature change}}$

47. What is the empirical formula of the compound that has a mass percent of 6% H and 94% O?

    A. HO   **B.** H_2O **C.** H_2O_2 **D.** H_3O_3 **E.** H_4O_2

48. For the Second law of thermodynamics, which statement(s) is/are true?

    I. Heat never flows from a cooler to a warmer object

    II. Heat cannot be converted completely to work in a cyclic process

    III. The entropy of the universe never decreases

    A. III only   **C.** II and III only

    B. I and II only   **D.** I, II and III   **E.** I and III only

49. A catalyst functions by:

    A. increasing the rate of a reaction by increasing the heat of reaction

    B. increasing the rate of a reaction by increasing the activation energy of the reverse reaction only

    C. decreasing the rate of a reaction by lowering the activation energy of the forward reaction only

    D. increasing the rate of a reaction by decreasing the heat of reaction

    E. increasing the rate of a reaction by providing an alternative pathway with a lower activation energy

50. Which is the correct order for nitrate, nitrite, sulfate and sulfite?

A. NO_2^-, NO_3^-, SO_4^{2-}, SO_3^{2-}

B. NO_3^-, NO_2^-, SO_4^{2-}, SO_3^{2-}

C. NO_3^-, NO_2^-, SO_3^{2-}, SO_4^{2-}

D. NO_2^-, NO_3^-, SO_3^{2-}, SO_4^{2-}

E. NO_2^-, SO_3^{2-}, NO_3^-, SO_4^{2-}

51. Identify the Brønsted-Lowry acid and base, respectively:

$$NH_3 + HCN \rightarrow NH_4^+ + CN^-$$

A. NH_3 and NH_4^+

B. NH_4^+ and CN^-

C. HCN and NH_3

D. NH_3 and HCN

E. NH_3 and NH_4^+

52. What is the term for the shorthand description of the arrangement of electrons by sublevels according to increasing energy?

A. continuous spectrum

B. electron configuration

C. atomic notation

D. atomic number

E. exited state

53. Which statement describes the relationship between bond length for a pair of atoms and the associated bond strength?

A. Doubling the bond length triples the bond energy

B. Bond length increases and bond energy increases

C. Bond length is not related to bond energy

D. Bond length increases and bond energy decreases

E. Doubling the bond length increases the bond energy by $\sqrt{2}$

54. Consider a 10.0 liters sample of helium and a 10.0 liters sample of neon, both at 23 °C, 2.0 atm. Which statement regarding these samples is NOT true?

A. The density of the neon sample is greater than the density of the helium sample

B. Each sample contains the same number of moles of gas

C. Each sample weighs the same amount

D. Each sample contains the same number of atoms of gas

E. All statements are true

55. Which substance is oxidized in the following redox reaction?

$$F_2 (g) + 2 Br^- (aq) \rightarrow 2 F^- (aq) + Br_2 (l)$$

A. Br_2

B. F^-

C. Br^-

D. F_2

E. None of the above

56. What is the term for the reaction, if $\Delta H° = -1{,}284$ kJ/mol?

$$P_4 (s) + 6 \; Cl_2 (g) \rightarrow 4 \; PCl_3 (l)$$

A. nonspontaneous   **C.** exothermic

B. spontaneous   **D.** endothermic   **E.** endergonic

57. $K_{eq} = 2$ with the initial concentrations of [A] = 4, [B] = 8 and [AB] = 16 at 23 °C.

$$AB + Heat \rightarrow A \; (g) + B \; (g)$$

After a stress has been absorbed by the reaction, the new equilibrium concentrations are: [A] = 2, [B] = 1, and [AB] = 64. Which of the following is the stress absorbed by the equilibrium system?

A. an increase in [AB]

B. a decrease in [B]

C. a decrease in [A]

D. a change in the reaction temperature resulting in the change to K_{eq}

E. a decrease in [A] and [B]

58. Which volume of 0.100 M hydrochloric acid reacts completely with 0.500 g of sodium carbonate, Na_2CO_3 (Use the molecular mass of $Na_2CO_3 = 105.99$ g/mol)?

$$Na_2CO_3 (s) + 2 \; HCl \; (aq) \rightarrow 2 \; NaCl \; (aq) + H_2O \; (l) + CO_2 (g)$$

A. 94.3 mL   **B.** 53.2 mL   **C.** 37.6 mL   **D.** 18.8 mL   **E.** 131 mL

59. Which are the products from the neutralization reaction?

$$HNO_3 \; (aq) + Ba(OH)_2 \; (aq) \rightarrow$$

A. $Ba(NO_2)_2$ and H_2O **C.** Ba_3N_2 and H_2O

B. $Ba(NO_3)_2$ and $2 \; H_2O$ **D.** $Ba(NO_2)_2$ and $2 \; H_2$ **E.** $Ba(NO_3)_2$ and H_2

60. In an electrolytic cell containing molten $MgCl_2 \; (l)$:

A. Mg^{2+} is oxidized at the cathode and Cl^- is reduced at the anode

B. Mg^{2+} is reduced at the anode and Cl^- is oxidized at the cathode

C. Mg^{2+} is oxidized at the anode and Cl^- is reduced at the cathode

D. Mg^{2+} is reduced at the cathode and Cl^- is oxidized at the anode

E. Mg^{2+} and Cl^- are reduced at the cathode

> Check your answers using the answer key. Then, go to the explanations section and review the explanations in detail, paying particular attention to questions you didn't answer correctly or marked for review. Note the topic that those questions belong to.

Diagnostic test #3 – Answer Key

1	B	Electronic Structure & Periodic Table	31	B	Thermochemistry
2	C	Bonding	32	D	Kinetics Equilibrium
3	D	Phases & Phase Equilibria	33	D	Solution Chemistry
4	C	Stoichiometry	34	A	Acids & Bases
5	A	Thermochemistry	35	E	Electronic Structure & Periodic Table
6	C	Kinetics Equilibrium	36	D	Bonding
7	E	Solution Chemistry	37	D	Phases & Phase Equilibria
8	C	Acids & Bases	38	A	Stoichiometry
9	A	Electrochemistry	39	B	Thermochemistry
10	B	Electronic Structure & Periodic Table	40	E	Kinetics Equilibrium
11	D	Bonding	41	B	Solution Chemistry
12	D	Phases & Phase Equilibria	42	C	Acids & Bases
13	C	Stoichiometry	43	D	Electrochemistry
14	D	Thermochemistry	44	D	Electronic Structure & Periodic Table
15	A	Kinetics Equilibrium	45	B	Bonding
16	E	Solution Chemistry	46	D	Phases & Phase Equilibria
17	A	Acids & Bases	47	A	Stoichiometry
18	E	Electronic Structure & Periodic Table	48	D	Thermochemistry
19	E	Bonding	49	E	Kinetics Equilibrium
20	C	Phases & Phase Equilibria	50	B	Solution Chemistry
21	C	Stoichiometry	51	C	Acids & Bases
22	A	Thermochemistry	52	B	Electronic Structure & Periodic Table
23	B	Kinetics Equilibrium	53	D	Bonding
24	E	Solution Chemistry	54	C	Phases & Phase Equilibria
25	D	Acids & Bases	55	C	Stoichiometry
26	B	Electrochemistry	56	C	Thermochemistry
27	E	Electronic Structure & Periodic Table	57	D	Kinetics Equilibrium
28	C	Bonding	58	A	Solution Chemistry
29	C	Phases & Phase Equilibria	59	B	Acids & Bases
30	A	Stoichiometry	60	D	Electrochemistry

Diagnostic Test #4

This Diagnostic Test is designed for you to assess your proficiency on each topic. Use your test results and identify areas of your strength and weakness to adjust your study plan and enhance your fundamental knowledge.

The length of the Diagnostic Tests is proven to be optimal for a single study session.

#	Answer:					Review	#	Answer:					Review
1:	A	B	C	D	E	___	31:	A	B	C	D	E	___
2:	A	B	C	D	E	___	32:	A	B	C	D	E	___
3:	A	B	C	D	E	___	33:	A	B	C	D	E	___
4:	A	B	C	D	E	___	34:	A	B	C	D	E	___
5:	A	B	C	D	E	___	35:	A	B	C	D	E	___
6:	A	B	C	D	E	___	36:	A	B	C	D	E	___
7:	A	B	C	D	E	___	37:	A	B	C	D	E	___
8:	A	B	C	D	E	___	38:	A	B	C	D	E	___
9:	A	B	C	D	E	___	39:	A	B	C	D	E	___
10:	A	B	C	D	E	___	40:	A	B	C	D	E	___
11:	A	B	C	D	E	___	41:	A	B	C	D	E	___
12:	A	B	C	D	E	___	42:	A	B	C	D	E	___
13:	A	B	C	D	E	___	43:	A	B	C	D	E	___
14:	A	B	C	D	E	___	44:	A	B	C	D	E	___
15:	A	B	C	D	E	___	45:	A	B	C	D	E	___
16:	A	B	C	D	E	___	46:	A	B	C	D	E	___
17:	A	B	C	D	E	___	47:	A	B	C	D	E	___
18:	A	B	C	D	E	___	48:	A	B	C	D	E	___
19:	A	B	C	D	E	___	49:	A	B	C	D	E	___
20:	A	B	C	D	E	___	50:	A	B	C	D	E	___
21:	A	B	C	D	E	___	51:	A	B	C	D	E	___
22:	A	B	C	D	E	___	52:	A	B	C	D	E	___
23:	A	B	C	D	E	___	53:	A	B	C	D	E	___
24:	A	B	C	D	E	___	54:	A	B	C	D	E	___
25:	A	B	C	D	E	___	55:	A	B	C	D	E	___
26:	A	B	C	D	E	___	56:	A	B	C	D	E	___
27:	A	B	C	D	E	___	57:	A	B	C	D	E	___
28:	A	B	C	D	E	___	58:	A	B	C	D	E	___
29:	A	B	C	D	E	___	59:	A	B	C	D	E	___
30:	A	B	C	D	E	___	60:	A	B	C	D	E	___

1. Which is a general characteristic of a metallic element?

   A. high melting point   **C.** ductile

   B. conducts electricity   **D.** appears shiny   **E.** all of the above

2. Based on the Lewis structure and formal charge considerations, how many equal energy resonance structures, if any, can be drawn for the PO_4^{3-} ion?

   A. original only   **B.** 2   **C.** 3   **D.** 4   **E.** 5

3. The conditions known as STP are:

   A. 1 mmHg and 273 K   **C.** 760 mmHg and 273 °C

   B. 1 atm and 273 °C   **D.** 760 atm and 273 K

                              E. 1 atm and 273 K

4. What is the oxidation number of the pure element zinc and zinc in the compound $ZnSO_4$, respectively?

   A. +1 and 0   **C.** 0 and 0

   B. 0 and +2   **D.** 0 and +1   **E.** +1 and +2

5. A chicken cutlet provides 6.90×10^2 food Calories (Cal). The heat energy provided by the chicken cutlet is sufficient to heat 57.4 kg of water by how many °C? (Use the specific heat of water = 4.18 J/g·°C and the conversion of 1 food Calorie = 4,180 J of heat energy)

   A. 5.32 °C   **C.** 5.91 °C

   B. 21.8 °C   **D.** 12.0 °C   **E.** 4.18 °C

6. Which of the following is always true about the reaction, if the E_{act} is lowered?

   A. It is endothermic   **C.** It proceeds slower

   B. It is exothermic   **D.** It proceeds faster   **E.** None of the above

7. Which of the following statements best explains the phrase "like dissolves like"?

   A. A solvent dissolves a solute that has a similar mass

   B. A solvent and a solute with different intermolecular forces form a solution

   C. A solvent and a solute with similar intermolecular forces form a solution

   D. Only true solutions are formed when hydrophobic solvents dissolve polar solutes

   E. Only homogeneous solutions are formed when water dissolves a nonpolar solute

8. Which compound is an example of a Brønsted-Lowry acid?

A. NH_3

B. NO_3^-

C. CH_3COOH

D. BH_3

E. CH_2Cl_2

9. Which of the following species is the reducing agent in the following reaction?

$$CuBr \rightarrow 2\,Cu + Br_2$$

A. Br^- B. Cu^+ C. $CuBr$ D. Cu E. Br_2

10. Elements have the same number of:

A. electrons

B. neutrons

C. protons + neutrons

D. protons

E. protons + electrons

11. How many valence electrons are in a chlorine atom and a chloride ion, respectively?

A. 17 and 18

B. 8 and 7

C. 7 and 8

D. 1 and 8

E. 6 and 7

12. A sample of a gas in a cylindrical chamber with a movable piston occupied a volume of 4.8 liters when the pressure was 0.96 atm and the temperature was 25.8 °C. By moving the piston, the pressure was adjusted to 1.4 atm. What is the volume occupied under the new conditions if the temperature remains constant?

A. 1.4 L   B. 3.3 L   C. 4.8 L   D. 5.7 L   E. 6.6 L

13. Which expression represents the net ionic reaction for the following balanced equation?

$$2\,AgNO_3\,(aq) + K_2SO_4\,(aq) \rightarrow 2\,KNO_3\,(aq) + Ag_2SO_4\,(s)$$

A. $2Ag^+ + SO_4^{2-} \rightarrow Ag_2SO_4$

B. $K^+ + NO_3^- \rightarrow KNO_3$

C. $2\,K^+ + SO_4^{2-} \rightarrow K_2SO_4$

D. $Ag^+ + NO_3^- \rightarrow AgNO_3$

E. $H^+ + OH^- \rightarrow H_2O$

14. What are the predicted products for this decomposition reaction?

$$Zn(HCO_3)_2\,(s) \rightarrow$$

A. $ZnCO_3$, $H_2 + CO_2$

B. $ZnCO_3 + H_2O$

C. Zn, $H_2 + CO_2$

D. Zn, $H_2O + CO_2$

E. $ZnCO_3$, $H_2O + CO_2$

15. If a reaction proceeds in several steps, the process with the highest activation energy is the:

    A. product formation step
    B. activated complex step
    C. transition step
    D. favorable step
    E. rate-determining step

16. Which of the following statements is an example of a colloid?

    A. A supersaturated solution of potassium chloride
    B. CO_2 molecules dissolving in a soft drink
    C. Hemoglobin molecules in cytosol
    D. Tiny sand particles dispersed in water settling as a precipitate
    E. Food coloring dispersed in water changing the color of the liquid

17. If [HF] (*aq*), [H^+] and [F^-] at equilibrium are 2.5×10^{-1} M, 5.0×10^{-2} M and 5.0×10^{-5} M respectively, what is the dissociation constant for HF(*aq*) for the reaction HF (*aq*) $\rightleftharpoons H^+ + F^-$?

    A. 1×10^{-5}
    B. 2.5×10^{-4}
    C. 3.0×10^{-3}
    D. 5.0×10^{-5}
    E. 3.0×10^{-2}

18. Which of the following elements is NOT a metal?

    A. rubidium
    B. sodium
    C. aluminum
    D. vanadium
    E. selenium

19. What is the molecular geometry of CH_2O?

    A. trigonal planar
    B. tetrahedral
    C. linear
    D. trigonal pyramidal
    E. bent

20. Which of the following compounds has the highest boiling point?

    A. $CH_3CH_2CH_3$
    B. $CH_3CH_2CH_2CH_2CH_3$
    C. CH_3CH_3
    D. CH_4
    E. $CH_3CH_2CH_2CH_3$

21. Which of the following reactions is NOT correctly classified?

    A. $AgNO_3 + KCl \rightarrow KNO_3 + AgCl$ (double-replacement)
    B. $CH_4 + 2 O_2 \rightarrow CO_2 + 2 H_2O$ (single-replacement)
    C. $Zn + H_2SO_4 \rightarrow ZnSO_4 + H_2$ (single-replacement)
    D. $2 KClO_3 \rightarrow 2 KCl + 3 O_2$ (decomposition)
    E. All are classified correctly

22. What is the product for the unbalanced combination reaction Li (s) + O$_2$ (g) → ?

A. LiO_2 **B.** Li_2O_3 **C.** LiO **D.** Li_3O_2 **E.** Li_2O

23. The rate of a chemical reaction in solution can be measured in the units:

A. $mol\ s\ L^{-1}$ **C.** $mol\ L^{-1}\ s^{-1}$

B. s^{-2} **D.** $L^2\ mol^{-1}\ s^{-1}$ **E.** $sec\ L^{-1}\ mol^{-1}$

24. When 1 ml of a 4 M solution of HCl is diluted to 20 ml, the new concentration of the HCl is:

A. 0.14 M   **B.** 0.24 M   **C.** 0.80 M   **D.** 0.06 M   **E.** 0.20 M

25. Which of the following is the correct definition of a Brønsted-Lowry acid?

A. acts as a H^+ acceptor in any system   **C.** increases $[H^+]$ when placed in H_2O

B. acts as a proton donor in any system   **D.** decreases $[H^+]$ when placed in H_2O

E. acts as lone pair acceptor in any system

26. What happens to an element when it is oxidized?

A. Loses electrons and its oxidation state decreases

B. Gains electrons and its oxidation remains the same

C. Gains electrons and its oxidation decreases

D. Gains electrons and its oxidation state increases

E. Loses electrons and its oxidation state increases

27. Which element is an alkali metal?

A. N   **B.** Sr   **C.** Cl   **D.** Ga   **E.** K

28. What bond holds hydrogens and oxygen of a water molecule together?

A. covalent   **C.** hydrophilic

B. dipole   **D.** hydrogen   **E.** van der Waals

29. A laser contains 0.40 mole Ar and 0.60 mole F$_2$, whereby the total pressure inside the laser cavity is 1.20 atm. What is the partial pressure of Ar inside the laser?

A. 0.80 atm   **B.** 0.05 atm   **C.** 0.60 atm   **D.** 1.0 atm   **E.** 0.48 atm

30. What is the coefficient (n) of H$_2$ gas for the balanced equation?

nN$_2$ (g) + nH$_2$ (g) → nNH$_3$ (g)

A. 1   **B.** 2   **C.** 3   **D.** 4   **E.** none of the above

31. Consider the following reaction: $N_2 + O_2 \rightarrow 2\,NO$. When 60.0 g of N_2 reacts, [ ] kcal will be [ ]. (Use the enthalpy, $\Delta H = 43$ kcal)

A. 36.7; produced
C. 73.4; produced
B. 92.0; consumed
D. 87.6; consumed
E. 43.8; produced

32. The rate constant for the conversion of methyl propanoate is $1 \times 10^{-4}\,s^{-1}$. A flask of methyl propanoate gas has a partial pressure of 100 torr. After 6.4 hours (approx. 23,000 seconds), what is the partial pressure of the methyl propanoate gas?

A. 1 torr
C. 5 torr
B. 10 torr
D. 30 torr
E. 12.5 torr

33. Which of the following can function as the solvent in a solution?

I. solid   II. liquid   III. gas

A. I only
C. III only
B. II only
D. I and II only
E. I, II and III

34. A base is a substance that:

A. contains a hydronium ion
C. accepts an ^-OH
B. accepts electrons
D. accepts an H^+
E. has a bitter taste

35. Which of the following elements is a metalloid?

A. Copper   B. Iron   C. Silicon   D. Bromine   E. Palladium

36. What is the geometry of a molecule with three pairs of bonded electrons and one pair of nonbonded electrons around a central atom?

A. octahedral
C. linear
B. trigonal planar
D. tetrahedral
E. trigonal pyramidal

37. A quantity of an ideal gas occupies 300 cm^3 at 28 °C. What is its volume at −170 °C at constant pressure?

A. 50 cm^3 B. 150 cm^3 C. 100 cm^3 D. 900 cm^3 E. 200 cm^3

38. Which of the following substance is functioning as the reducing agent?

$$14\,H^+ + Cr_2O_7^{2-} + 3\,Ni \rightarrow 3\,Ni^{2+} + 2\,Cr^{3+} + 7\,H_2O$$

A. $Cr_2O_7^{2-}$ B. H_2O C. Ni   D. H^+ E. Ni^{2+}

39. Which of the following describe(s) an intensive property?

        I. volume   II. density   III. specific heat

A. III only   **C.** II and III only

B. I and II only   **D.** I, II and III   **E.** II only

40. In the reaction described by the equation below, what is the rate of consumption of CH_4O (*g*), if the rate of consumption of O_2 (*g*) is 0.450 mol L^{-1} s^{-1}?

$$2\ CH_4O\ (g) + 3\ O_2\ (g) \rightarrow 2\ CO_2\ (g) + 4\ H_2O\ (g)$$

A. 0.15 mol L^{-1} s^{-1} **C.** 0.68 mol L^{-1} s^{-1}

B. 0.30 mol L^{-1} s^{1} **D.** 0.90 mol L^{-1} s^{-1} **E.** 0.45 mol L^{-1} s^{-1}

41. Which is the net ionic equation for the reaction that takes place when $HC_2H_3O_2$ (*aq*) is added to NH_3 (*aq*)?

A. $HC_2H_3O_2\ (aq) + OH^-\ (aq) \rightarrow C_2H_3O_2^-\ (aq) + H_2O\ (l)$

B. $H^+\ (aq) + NH_4OH\ (aq) \rightarrow NH_4^+\ (aq) + H_2O\ (l)$

C. $HC_2H_3O_2\ (aq) + NH_4OH\ (aq) \rightarrow H_2O\ (l) + NH_4ClO_4\ (aq)$

D. $H^+\ (aq) + OH^-\ (aq) \rightarrow H_2O\ (l)$

E. $HC_2H_3O_2\ (aq) + NH_3\ (aq) \rightarrow NH_4^+\ (aq) + C_2H_3O_2^-\ (aq)$

42. What is the best explanation for why a person might wash their hands with wood ashes?

A. The oils on the skin act as a base and react with the ashes to produce solutions of soap

B. After being burnt in the fire, the acids and bases of the log are neutralized, making it a gentle material to use on the hands

C. The ashes act as a base and react with skin oils to produce solutions of soap

D. The ashes act as an acid and react with the skin oils to produce solutions of soap

E. The amino acids on the skin act as a base and react with the ashes to produce solutions of soap

43. The net balanced reaction: $2\ Cu\ (s) + Li^+ \rightarrow Cu^{2+} + Li\ (s)$

        $Cu^{2+} + 2e^- \rightarrow Cu\ (s)$ $E° = 0.337$

        $Li^+ + e^- \rightarrow Li\ (s)$ $E° = -3.03$

The reaction for the data given for the electrochemical cell consisting of $CuSO_4$ and LiCl:

A. proceeds spontaneously as written   **C.** proceeds in the opposite direction

B. is at equilibrium   **D.** moves in both directions

                                        E. none of the above

44. Which of the following subshells is lowest in energy?

A. 5*f*   **B.** 4*s*   **C.** 3*d*   **D.** 6*s*   **E.** 5*p*

45. Which of the following pairs is NOT correctly matched?

Formula	Molecular polarity
A. PF_3	polar
B. BCl_3	nonpolar
C. H_2O	polar
D. BeF_2	polar
E. CCl_4	nonpolar

46. A sample of air at 9.50 atm is heated from 220 K to 440 K, while the volume remains constant. What is the final pressure?

A. 31.6 atm   **B.** 11.1 atm   **C.** 7.59 atm   **D.** 15.6 atm   **E.** 19.0 atm

47. Which of the following is the balanced equation for the reaction when a calcium nitrate solution is mixed with sodium phosphate solution?

A. $3 CaNO_3$ (*aq*) + Na_3PO_4 (*aq*) → Ca_3PO_4 (*aq*) + $3 NaNO_3$ (*s*)
B. $Ca(NO_3)_2$ (*aq*) + $2 NaPO_4$ (*aq*) → $Ca(PO_4)_2$ (*s*) + $2 NaNO_3$ (*aq*)
C. $3 Ca(NO_3)_2$ (*aq*) + $2 Na_3PO_4$ (*aq*) → $Ca_3(PO_4)_2$ (*aq*) + $6 NaNO_3$ (*aq*)
D. $2 Ca(NO_3)_2$ (*aq*) + $3 Na_3PO_4$ (*aq*) → $2 Ca_3(PO_4)_2$ (*s*) + $6 NaNO_3$ (*aq*)
E. $3 Ca(NO_3)_2$ (*aq*) + $2 Na_3PO_4$ (*aq*) → $Ca_3(PO_4)_2$ (*s*) + $6 NaNO_3$ (*aq*)

48. A nuclear power plant uses radioactive uranium to convert water to steam, which drives a turbine that turns a generator to produce electricity. The uranium and the steam represent which forms of energy, respectively?

A. Electrical and heat energy
B. Nuclear and heat energy
C. Chemical and mechanical energy
D. Chemical and heat energy
E. Nuclear and mechanical energy

49. Which of the following increases the collision frequency of molecules?

    I. Adding a catalyst
    II. Increasing the temperature
    III. Decreasing the concentration

A. I only   **B.** II only   **C.** III only   **D.** I and II only   **E.** I, II and III

50. Calculate the mass percent of a solution prepared by dissolving 16.5 g of NaCl in 172 g of water:

  A. 8.8%   **B.** 1.3%   **C.** 12.4%   **D.** 6.4%   **E.** 16.9%

51. Which of the following substances is produced during an acid/base reaction (i.e., neutralization)?

  A. NaOH   **B.** CO_2 **C.** H_2O **D.** H_2 **E.** NaCl

52. Which one of the following correctly represents the electron configuration of sulfur in an excited state?

  A. $1s^2 2s^2 2p^6 3s^2 3p^4 4s^1$ **C.** $1s^2 2s^2 2p^6 3s^2 3p^5$

  B. $1s^2 2s^2 2p^6 3s^2 3p^3 4s^1$ **D.** $1s^2 2s^2 2p^6 3s^2 3p^4$ **E.** $1s^2 2s^2 2p^6 3s^1 3p^5$

53. Which of the following is an example of a molecule that contains a coordinate covalent bond?

  A. CH_4 **B.** NH_3 **C.** NH_4^+ **D.** H_2O **E.** C_2H_4

54. A cylinder fitted with a movable piston and filled with a gas has a volume of 16.5 liters at 24.5 °C at an applied pressure of 770 torr. The temperature of the surrounding oil bath was increased to 186 °C, while the load on the piston was changed to adjust the volume to 16.8 liters. What is the final pressure in the system?

  A. 566 torr   **B.** 904.2 torr   **C.** 1,167 torr   **D.** 1,409 torr   **E.** 2,288 torr

55. What is the empirical formula of the compound with the following percent composition?

    C = 15.8%   S = 42.1%   N = 36.8%   H = 5.3%

  A. N_2H_4CS **B.** NH_2C_3S **C.** $N_2H_2C_3S$ **D.** N_3H_2CS **E.** $NH_2C_3S_4$

56. What is the standard enthalpy change for the following reaction? (Use the standard heats of formation shown below)

  $CaCO_3\,(s) \rightarrow CaO\,(s) + CO_2\,(g)$

Compound	ΔH_f°
$CaCO_3\,(s)$	–1206.5 Kj/mol
$CaO\,(s)$	–635.5 Kj/mol
$CO_2\,(g)$	–393.5 Kj/mol

  A. –571 kJ/mol   **C.** 177.5 kJ/mol

  B. –242 kJ/mol   **D.** 570 kJ/mol   **E.** –1,028.5 kJ/mol

57. How does a catalyst increase the rate of a reaction?

   A. It increases the energy difference between the reactants and products
   B. It has no effect on the rate of the reaction
   C. It is neither created nor consumed in a reaction
   D. It raises the activation energy of the reactants, which makes the reaction proceed faster
   E. It lowers the activation energy

58. Calculate the $[N_2]$ gas in water, if N_2 gas at a partial pressure above the water is 0.78 atm. (Use Henry's Law constant for N_2 in water $= 6.8 \times 10^{-4}$ mol/L·atm)

   A. 5.3×10^{-4} M   **C.** 3.2×10^3 M
   B. 7.2×10^{-3} M   **D.** 0.61 M   **E.** 7.2×10^{-5} M

59. Which atom bears the positive charge in the ammonium ion (NH_4^+)?

   A. Hydrogen atom   **C.** Neither atom bears a positive charge
   B. Nitrogen atom   **D.** Nitrogen and hydrogen equally share the positive charge
                          E. The spectator ion holds the positive charge

60. The following set of redox reactions takes place as shown:

       Vessel I   Vessel II

       $Fe \rightarrow Fe^{2+} + 2e^-$ $Cu^{2+} + 2e^- \rightarrow Cu$

If two vessels are filled with the ion solution described above, with a wire connecting a piece of iron (in vessel I) and a piece of copper (in vessel II) and a salt-bridge connecting the two vessels, in which direction do the electrons flow?

   A. From vessel I to vessel II
   B. From vessel II to vessel I
   C. There is no continuous flow of electrons between the two vessels
   D. The electrons only move within their original vessel
   E. The electrons flow back and forth between the two vessels

---

Check your answers using the answer key. Then, go to the explanations section and review the explanations in detail, paying particular attention to questions you didn't answer correctly or marked for review. Note the topic that those questions belong to.

Diagnostic test #4 – Answer Key

1	E	Electronic Structure & Periodic Table	31	B	Thermochemistry
2	D	Bonding	32	B	Kinetics Equilibrium
3	E	Phases & Phase Equilibria	33	E	Solution Chemistry
4	B	Stoichiometry	34	D	Acids & Bases
5	D	Thermochemistry	35	C	Electronic Structure & Periodic Table
6	D	Kinetics Equilibrium	36	E	Bonding
7	C	Solution Chemistry	37	C	Phases & Phase Equilibria
8	C	Acids & Bases	38	C	Stoichiometry
9	A	Electrochemistry	39	C	Thermochemistry
10	D	Electronic Structure & Periodic Table	40	B	Kinetics Equilibrium
11	C	Bonding	41	E	Solution Chemistry
12	B	Phases & Phase Equilibria	42	C	Acids & Bases
13	A	Stoichiometry	43	C	Electrochemistry
14	E	Thermochemistry	44	B	Electronic Structure & Periodic Table
15	E	Kinetics Equilibrium	45	D	Bonding
16	C	Solution Chemistry	46	E	Phases & Phase Equilibria
17	A	Acids & Bases	47	E	Stoichiometry
18	E	Electronic Structure & Periodic Table	48	B	Thermochemistry
19	A	Bonding	49	B	Kinetics Equilibrium
20	B	Phases & Phase Equilibria	50	A	Solution Chemistry
21	B	Stoichiometry	51	C	Acids & Bases
22	E	Thermochemistry	52	B	Electronic Structure & Periodic Table
23	C	Kinetics Equilibrium	53	C	Bonding
24	E	Solution Chemistry	54	C	Phases & Phase Equilibria
25	B	Acids & Bases	55	A	Stoichiometry
26	E	Electrochemistry	56	C	Thermochemistry
27	E	Electronic Structure & Periodic Table	57	E	Kinetics Equilibrium
28	A	Bonding	58	A	Solution Chemistry
29	E	Phases & Phase Equilibria	59	B	Acids & Bases
30	C	Stoichiometry	60	A	Electrochemistry

SAT Chemistry

Topical
Practice Questions

Atomic and Molecular Structure; Periodic Table

===

Practice Set 1: Questions 1–20

===

1. The property defined as the energy required to remove one electron from an atom in the gaseous state is:

    A. electronegativity   **C.** electron affinity

    B. ionization energy   **D.** hyperconjugation   **E.** none of the above

2. Which of the following elements most easily accepts an extra electron?

    A. He   **B.** Ca   **C.** Cl   **D.** Fr   **E.** Na

3. Which of the following pairs has one metalloid element and one nonmetal element?

    A. ^{82}Pb and ^{83}Bi   **C.** ^{51}Sb and ^{20}Ca

    B. ^{19}K and ^{9}F   **D.** ^{3}As and ^{14}Si   **E.** ^{32}Ge and ^{9}F

4. Periods on the periodic table represent elements:

    A. in the same group   **C.** known as isotopes

    B. with consecutive atomic numbers   **D.** with similar chemical properties

                                 E. known as ions

5. How many electrons can occupy the $n = 2$ shell?

    A. 2   **B.** 6   **C.** 8   **D.** 18   **E.** 32

6. Ignoring hydrogen, which area(s) of the periodic table contain(s) both metals and nonmetals?

        I. *s* area   II. *p* area   III. *d* areas

    A. I only   **C.** III only

    B. II only   **D.** I and II only   **E.** I, II and III

7. What is the number of known nonmetals relative to the number of metals?

    A. About two times greater   **C.** About five times less

    B. About fifty percent   **D.** About twenty-five percent greater

                                   E. About three times greater

8. Based on experimental evidence, Dalton postulated that:

    A. atoms of different elements have the same mass

    B. not all atoms of a given element are identical

    C. atoms can be created and destroyed in chemical reactions

    D. each element consists of indivisible minute particles called atoms

    E. none of the above

9. Which statement is true regarding the average mass of a naturally occurring isotope of iron that has an atomic mass equal to 55.43 amu?

    A. 55.43 / 1.0079 times greater than a ^1H atom

    B. 55.43 / 12.000 times greater than a ^{12}C atom

    C. 55.43 times greater than a ^{12}C atom

    D. 55.43 times greater than a ^1H atom

    E. none of the above

10. Which is the principal quantum number?

    A. n **B.** m **C.** l **D.** s **E.** $+\frac{1}{2}$

11. How many electrons can occupy the $4s$ subshell?

    A. 1   **B.** 2   **C.** 6   **D.** 8   **E.** 10

12. An excited hydrogen atom emits a light spectrum of specific, characteristic wavelengths. The light spectrum is a result of:

    A. energy released as H atoms form H_2 molecules

    B. the light wavelengths, which are not absorbed by valence electrons when white light passes through the sample

    C. particles being emitted as the hydrogen nuclei decay

    D. excited electrons being promoted to higher energy levels

    E. excited electrons dropping to lower energy levels

13. Which has the largest radius?

    A. Br^- **B.** K^+ **C.** Ar   **D.** Ca^{2+} **E.** Cl^-

14. In its ground state, how many unpaired electrons does a sulfur atom have?

    A. 0   **B.** 1   **C.** 2   **D.** 3   **E.** 4

15. Which of the elements would be in the same group as the element whose electronic configuration is $1s^2 2s^2 2p^6 3s^2 3p^6 4s^1$?

    A. Ar   **B.** Se   **C.** Mg   **D.** P   **E.** Li

16. When an atom is most stable, how many electrons does it contain in its valence shell?

    A. 4   **B.** 6   **C.** 8   **D.** 10   **E.** 12

17. Which characteristic(s) is/are responsible for the changes seen in ionization energy when moving down a column?

    I. Increased shielding of electrons
    II. Larger atomic radii
    III. Decreasing nuclear attraction for electrons

    A. I only   **C.** III only
    B. II only   **D.** I and II only
                                      E. I, II and III

18. What is the maximum number of electrons that can occupy the $4f$ subshell?

    A. 6   **B.** 8   **C.** 14   **D.** 16   **E.** 18

19. The property that describes the energy released by a gas phase atom from adding an electron is:

    A. ionization energy   **C.** electron affinity
    B. electronegativity   **D.** hyperconjugation   **E.** none of the above

20. The attraction of the nucleus on the outermost electron in an atom tends to:

    A. decrease from right to left and bottom to top on the periodic table
    B. decrease from left to right and bottom to top on the periodic table
    C. decrease from left to right and top to bottom of the periodic table
    D. increase from right to left and top to bottom on the periodic table
    E. decrease from right to left and top to bottom on the periodic table

Practice Set 2: Questions 21–40

21. How many protons and neutrons are in ^{35}Cl, respectively?

A. 35; 18   **C.** 17; 18

B. 18; 17   **D.** 17; 17   **E.** 35; 17

22. What must be the same if two atoms represent the same element?

A. number of neutrons   **C.** number of electron shells

B. atomic mass   **D.** atomic number

E. number of valence electrons

23. Referring to the periodic table, which of the following is NOT a solid metal under normal conditions?

A. Ce   **B.** Os   **C.** Ba   **D.** Cr   **E.** Hg

24. Which of the following describe electron affinity?

  I. Ability of an atom to attract electrons when it bonds with another atom

  II. Energy needed to remove an electron from a neutral atom of the element in the gas phase

  III. Energy liberated when an electron is added to a gaseous neutral atom converting it to an anion

A. I only   **C.** III only

B. II only   **D.** I and II only   **E.** I, II and III

25. Metalloids are elements:

A. larger than nonmetals

B. found in asteroids

C. smaller than metals

D. that have some properties like metals and some like nonmetals

E. that have properties different from either the metals or the nonmetals

26. Which of the following represent(s) halogens?

  I. Br   II. H   III. I

A. I only   **C.** III only

B. II only   **D.** I and III   **E.** I and II

27. According to John Dalton, atoms of an element:

A. are divisible   **C.** are identical

B. have the same shape   **D.** have different masses   **E.** none of the above

28. Which of the following represents a pair of isotopes?

A. $^{32}_{16}S$, $^{32}_{16}S^{2-}$ **C.** $^{14}_{6}C$, $^{14}_{7}N$

B. O_2, O_3 **D.** $^{1}_{1}H$, $^{2}_{1}H$ **E.** None of the above

29. Early investigators proposed that the ray of the cathode tube was actually a negatively charged particle because the ray was:

A. not seen from the positively charged anode

B. diverted by a magnetic field

C. observed in the presence or absence of a gas

D. able to change colors depending on which gas was within the tube

E. attracted to positively charged electric plates

30. What is the value of quantum numbers n and l in the highest occupied orbital for the element carbon that has an atomic number of 6?

A. $n = 1, l = 1$ **C.** $n = 1, l = 2$

B. $n = 2, l = 1$ **D.** $n = 2, l = 2$ **E.** $n = 3, l = 3$

31. Which type of subshell is filled by the distinguishing electron in an alkaline earth metal?

A. s **B.** p **C.** f **D.** d **E.** both s and p

32. If an element has an electron configuration ending in $3p^4$, which statements about the element's electron configuration is NOT correct?

A. There are six electrons in the 3rd shell

B. Five different subshells contain electrons

C. There are eight electrons in the 2nd shell

D. The 3rd shell needs two more electrons to be completely filled

E. All are correct statements

33. Halogens form cations and anions by:

A. gaining two electrons   **C.** gaining one neutron

B. gaining one electron   **D.** losing one electron

                                         E. losing two electrons

34. What is the term for a broad uninterrupted band of radiant energy?

    A. Ultraviolet spectrum   **C.** Continuous spectrum

    B. Visible spectrum   **D.** Radiant energy spectrum

                              E. None of the above

35. Which of the following is the correct order of increasing atomic radius?

    A. Te < Sb < In < Sr < Rb   **C.** Te < Sb < In < Rb < Sr

    B. In < Sb < Te < Sr < Rb   **D.** Rb < Sr < In < Sb < Te

                              E. In < Sb < Te < Rb < Sr

36. Which of the following electron configurations represents an excited state of an atom?

    A. $1s^2 2s^2 2p^6 3s^2 3d^3 3p^6 4s^2$ **C.** $1s^2 2s^2 2p^6 3s^2 3d^{10}$

    B. $1s^2 2s^2 2p^6 3s^2 3p^6 3d^{10} 4s^2 4p^6$ **D.** $1s^2 2s^2 2p^6 3s^2 3p^6 4s^1$

                              E. $1s^2 2s^2 2p^6 3s^2 3p^6 3d^{10} 4s^2 4p^3$

37. Which of the following elements has the greatest ionization energy?

    A. rubidium   **C.** potassium

    B. neon   **D.** calcium   **E.** magnesium

38. Which of the following elements is a nonmetal?

    A. Sodium   **C.** Aluminum

    B. Chlorine   **D.** Magnesium   **E.** Palladium

39. An atom that contains 47 protons, 47 electrons and 60 neutrons is an isotope of:

    A. Nd   **C.** Ag

    B. Bh   **D.** Al   **E.** cannot be determined

40. The shell level of an electron is defined by which quantum number?

    A. electron spin quantum number

    B. magnetic quantum number

    C. azimuthal quantum number

    D. principal quantum number

    E. principal quantum number and electron spin quantum number

==

Practice Set 3: Questions 41–60

==

41. How many neutrons are in a Beryllium atom with an atomic number of 4 and atomic mass of 9?

   A. 4   **B.** 5   **C.** 9   **D.** 13   **E.** 18

42. Which characteristics describe the mass, charge and location of an electron, respectively?

   A. approximate mass 5×10^{-4} amu; charge –1; outside nucleus
   B. approximate mass 5×10^{-4} amu; charge 0; inside nucleus
   C. approximate mass 1 amu; charge –1; inside nucleus
   D. approximate mass 1 amu; charge +1; outside nucleus
   E. approximate mass 1 amu; charge 0; outside nucleus

43. What is the name of the compound $CaCl_2$?

   A. dichloromethane   **C.** carbon chloride
   B. dichlorocalcium   **D.** calcium chloride   **E.** dicalcium chloride

44. What is the name for elements in the same column of the periodic table that have similar chemical properties?

   A. congeners   **C.** diastereomers
   B. stereoisomers   **D.** epimers   **E.** anomers

45. Which of the following sets of elements consist of members of the same group on the periodic table?

   A. ^{14}Si, ^{15}P and ^{16}S **C.** ^{9}F, ^{10}Ne and ^{11}Na
   B. ^{20}Ca, ^{26}Fe and ^{34}Se **D.** ^{31}Ga, ^{49}In and ^{81}Tl **E.** ^{11}Na, ^{20}Ca and ^{39}Y

46. Which element would most likely be a metal with a low melting point?

   A. K   **B.** B   **C.** N   **D.** C   **E.** Cl

47. Mg is an example of a(n):

   A. transition metal   **C.** alkali metal
   B. noble gas   **D.** halogen   **E.** alkaline earth metal

48. Metalloids:

      I. have some metallic and some nonmetallic properties

      II. may have low electrical conductivities

      III. contain elements in group IIIB

A. I and III only   **C.** II and III only

B. II only   **D.** I and II only

                     E. I, II and III

49. Which element is a halogen?

A. Os   **B.** I   **C.** O   **D.** Te   **E.** Se

50. Silicon exists as three isotopes: ^{28}Si, ^{29}Si, and ^{30}Si with atomic masses of 27.98 amu, 28.98 amu and 29.97 amu, respectively. Which isotope is the most abundant in nature?

A. ^{28}Si   **C.** ^{30}Si

B. ^{29}Si   **D.** ^{28}Si and ^{30}Si are equally abundant

                     E. All are equally abundant

51. Which statement supports the reason why early investigators proposed that the ray of the cathode ray tube was due to the cathode?

A. The ray was diverted by a magnetic field

B. The ray was not seen from the positively charged anode

C. The ray was attracted to the electric plates that were positively charged

D. The ray changed color depending on the gas used within the tube

E. The ray was observed in the presence or absence of a gas

52. Which of the following is implied by the spin quantum number?

      I. The two spinning electrons generate magnetic fields

      II. The values are $+\frac{1}{2}$ or $-\frac{1}{2}$

      III. Orbital electrons have opposite spins

A. II only   **C.** I and III only

B. I and II only   **D.** II and III only

                     E. I, II and III

53. How many quantum numbers are needed to describe a single electron in an atom?

A. 1   **B.** 2   **C.** 3   **D.** 4   **E.** 5

54. Which of the following has the correct order of increasing energy in a subshell?

A. 3*s*, 3*p*, 4*s*, 3*d*, 4*p*, 5*s*, 4*d*

B. 3*s*, 3*p*, 4*s*, 3*d*, 4*p*, 4*d*, 5*s*

C. 3*s*, 3*p*, 3*d*, 4*s*, 4*p*, 4*d*, 5*s*

D. 3*s*, 3*p*, 3*d*, 4*s*, 4*p*, 5*s*, 4*d*

E. 3*s*, 3*p*, 4*s*, 3*d*, 4*d*, 4*p*, 5*s*

55. Rank the elements below in order of decreasing atomic radius.

A. Al > P > Cl > Na > Mg

B. Cl > Al > P > Na > Mg

C. Mg > Na > P > Al > Cl

D. Na > Mg > Al > P > Cl

E. P > Al > Cl > Mg > Na

56. Which of the following is the electron configuration of a boron atom?

A. $1s^2 2s^1 2p^2$

B. $1s^2 2p^3$

C. $1s^2 2s^2 2p^2$

D. $1s^2 2s^2 2p^1$

E. $1s^2 2s^1 2p^1$

57. Which element has the electron configuration $1s^2 2s^2 2p^6 3s^2 3p^6 4s^2 3d^{10} 4p^6 5s^2 4d^{10} 5p^2$?

A. Sn   **B.** As   **C.** Pb   **D.** Sb   **E.** In

58. Which of the following elements has the greatest ionization energy?

A. Ar   **B.** Sr   **C.** Br   **D.** In   **E.** Sn

59. Which element has the lowest electronegativity?

A. Mg   **B.** Al   **C.** Cl   **D.** Br   **E.** I

60. Refer to the periodic table and predict which of the following is a solid nonmetal under normal conditions.

A. Cl   **B.** F   **C.** Se   **D.** As   **E.** Ar

==

Practice Set 4: Questions 61–80

==

61. Lines were observed in the spectrum of uranium ore identical to those of helium in the spectrum of the Sun. Which of the following produced the lines in the helium spectrum?

    A. Excited protons jumping to a higher energy level
    B. Excited protons dropping to a lower energy level
    C. Excited electrons jumping to a higher energy level
    D. Excited electrons dropping to a lower energy level
    E. None of the above

62. Which set of quantum numbers is possible?

    A. $n = 1$; $l = 2$; $m_l = 3$; $m_s = -\frac{1}{2}$
    C. $n = 2$; $l = 1$; $m_l = 2$; $m_s = -\frac{1}{2}$
    B. $n = 4$; $l = 2$; $m_l = 2$; $m_s = -\frac{1}{2}$
    D. $n = 3$; $l = 3$; $m_l = 2$; $m_s = -\frac{1}{2}$
    E. $n = 2$; $l = 3$; $m_l = 2$; $m_s = -\frac{1}{2}$

63. The number of neutrons in an atom is equal to:

    A. the mass number
    C. mass number minus atomic number
    B. the atomic number
    D. atomic number minus mass number
    E. mass number plus atomic number

64. Which of the following represent(s) a compound rather than an element?

    I. O_3 II. CCl_4 III. S_8

    A. I and III only
    C. I and II only
    B. II only
    D. III only
    E. I only

65. Which of the following elements is NOT correctly classified?

    A. Mo – transition element
    C. K – representative element
    B. Sr – alkaline earth metal
    D. Ar – noble gas
    E. Po – halogen

66. Which is the name of the elements that have properties of both metals and nonmetals?

    A. alkaline earth metals
    C. nonmetals
    B. metalloids
    D. metals   **E.** halogens

67. Which of the following is the correct sequence of atomic radii from smallest to largest?

A. $Al < S < Al^{3+} < S^{2-}$ **C.** $Al^{3+} < Al < S^{2-} < S$

B. $S < S^{2-} < Al < Al^{3+}$ **D.** $Al^{3+} < S < S^{2-} < Al$ **E.** $Al^{3+} < Al < S^{2-} < S$

68. Which of the following elements contains 6 valence electrons?

A. S   **B.** Cl   **C.** Si   **D.** P   **E.** Ca^{2+}

69. From the periodic table, which of the following elements is a semimetal?

A. Ar   **B.** As   **C.** Al   **D.** Ac   **E.** Am

70. Which statement does NOT describe the noble gases?

A. The more massive noble gases react with other elements
B. They belong to group VIIIA (or 18)
C. They contain at least one metalloid
D. He, Ne, Ar, Kr, Xe and Rn are included in the group
E. They were once known as the inert gases

71. Which is a good experimental method to distinguish between ordinary hydrogen and deuterium, the rare isotope of hydrogen?

      I. Measure the density of the gas at STP
      II. Measure the rate at which the gas effuses
      III. Infrared spectroscopy

A. I only   **C.** I and II only

B. II only   **D.** I, II and III   **E.** II and III only

72. Which statement is true regarding the relative abundances of the ^{6}lithium or ^{7}lithium isotopes?

A. The relative proportions change as neutrons move between the nuclei
B. The isotopes are in roughly equal proportions
C. The relative ratio depends on the temperature of the element
D. ^{6}Lithium is much more abundant
E. ^{7}Lithium is much more abundant

73. Which represents the charge on 1 mole of electrons?

A. 6.02×10^{23} e$^-$ **C.** 6.02×10^{23} grams

B. 6.02×10^{23} C   **D.** 1 C   **E.** 1 e

74. Which of the following statement(s) is/are true?

      I. The *f* subshell contains 7 orbitals
      II. The *d* subshell contains 5 orbitals
      III. The third energy shell ($n = 3$) has no *f* orbitals

    A. I only   **C.** I and II only
    B. II only   **D.** II and III only   **E.** I, II and III

75. Which element has the greatest ionization energy?

    A. Fr   **B.** Cl   **C.** Ga   **D.** I   **E.** Cs

76. Electrons fill up subshells in order of:

      I. decreasing distance from the nucleus
      II. increasing distance from the nucleus
      III. increasing energy

    A. I only   **C.** I and II only
    B. II only   **D.** II and III only   **E.** I, II and III

77. Which of the following produces the "atomic fingerprint" of an element?

    A. Excited protons dropping to a lower energy level
    B. Excited protons jumping to a higher energy level
    C. Excited electrons dropping to a lower energy level
    D. Excited electrons jumping to a higher energy level
    E. None of the above

78. Which of the following is the electron configuration for manganese (Mn)?

    A. $1s^2 2s^2 2p^6 3s^2 3p^6$ **C.** $1s^2 2s^2 2p^6 3s^2 3p^6 4s^2 3d^6$
    B. $1s^2 2s^2 2p^6 3s^2 3p^6 4s^2 3d^{10} 4p^1$ **D.** $1s^2 2s^2 2p^6 3s^2 3p^6 4s^2 3d^6$
                                          E. $1s^2 2s^2 2p^6 3s^2 3p^6 4s^2 3d^5$

79. Which element listed below has the greatest electronegativity?

    A. I   **B.** Fr   **C.** H   **D.** He   **E.** F

80. Which of the following is NOT an alkali metal?

    A. Fr   **B.** Cs   **C.** Ca   **D.** Na   **E.** Rb

This page is intentionally left blank

Atomic and Molecular Structure; Periodic Table – Answer Key

1: B	21: C	41: B	61: D
2: C	22: D	42: A	62: B
3: E	23: E	43: D	63: C
4: B	24: C	44: A	64: B
5: C	25: D	45: D	65: E
6: B	26: D	46: A	66: B
7: C	27: C	47: E	67: D
8: D	28: D	48: D	68: A
9: B	29: E	49: B	69: B
10: A	30: B	50: A	70: C
11: B	31: A	51: E	71: D
12: E	32: D	52: E	72: E
13: A	33: B	53: D	73: A
14: C	34: C	54: A	74: E
15: E	35: A	55: D	75: B
16: C	36: C	56: D	76: D
17: D	37: B	57: A	77: C
18: C	38: B	58: A	78: E
19: C	39: C	59: A	79: E
20: E	40: D	60: C	80: C

Chemical Bonding

Practice Set 1: Questions 1–20

1. What is the number of valence electrons in tin (Sn)?

   A. 14   **B.** 8   **C.** 2   **D.** 4   **E.** 5

2. Unhybridized *p* orbitals participate in π bonds as double and triple bonds. How many distinct and degenerate *p* orbitals exist in the second electron shell, where n = 2?

   A. 3   **B.** 2   **C.** 1   **D.** 0   **E.** 4

3. What is the total number of valence electrons in a sulfite ion, SO_3^{2-}?

   A. 22   **B.** 24   **C.** 26   **D.** 34   **E.** none of the above

4. Which type of attractive forces occurs in all molecules regardless of the atoms they possess?

   A. Dipole–ion interactions   **C.** Dipole–dipole attractions
   B. Ion–ion interactions   **D.** Hydrogen bonding
                                        E. London dispersion forces

5. Given the structure of glucose below, which statement explains the hydrogen bonding between glucose and water?

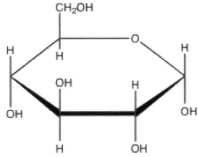

   A. Due to the cyclic structure of glucose, there is no H–bonding with water
   B. Each glucose molecule could H–bond with up to 17 water molecules
   C. H–bonds form, with water always being the H–bond donor
   D. H–bonds form, with glucose always being the H–bond donor
   E. Each glucose molecule could H–bond with up to 5 water molecules

6. How many valence electrons are in the Lewis dot structure of C_2H_6?

    A. 2   **B.** 14   **C.** 6   **D.** 8   **E.** 12

7. For two ions with charges q_1 and q_2 that are separated by distance r, the potential energy can be calculated from Coulomb's law. What is the amount of energy released when 1 mole NaCl is formed? (Use Coulomb's law of $E = q_1q_2 / k \cdot r$, rate constant $k = 1.11 \times 10^{-10}$ $C^2/J \cdot m$, charge on $Na^+ = +e$, charge on $Cl^- = -e$, charge of electron $e = 1.602 \times 10^{-19}$ C and radius $r = 282$ pm)

    A. –494 kJ/mol   **C.** +91.2 kJ/mol

    B. –288 kJ/mol   **D.** +421 kJ/mol   **E.** –464 kJ/mol

8. What is the name for the weak forces of attraction between nonpolar molecules due to temporary dipoles between adjacent nonpolar molecules?

    A. van der Waals forces   **C.** hydrogen bonding forces

    B. hydrophobic forces   **D.** nonpolar covalent forces

                                        E. hydrophilic forces

9. Nitrogen has five valence electrons; which of the following types of bonding is/are possible?

        I. one single and one double bond
        II. three single bonds
        III. one triple bond

    A. I only   **C.** I and III only

    B. II only   **D.** I, II and III   **E.** none of the above

10. What is the number of valence electrons in antimony (Sb)?

    A. 1   **B.** 2   **C.** 3   **D.** 4   **E.** 5

11. How many total resonance structures, if any, can be drawn for a nitrite ion?

    A. 1   **B.** 2   **C.** 3   **D.** 4   **E.** 5

12. What is the formula of the ammonium ion?

    A. NH_4^- **B.** N_4H^+ **C.** NH_4^{2-} **D.** NH_4^{2+} **E.** NH_4^+

13. What is the type of bond that forms between oppositely charged ions?

    A. dipole   **B.** covalent   **C.** London   **D.** induced dipole   **E.** ionic

14. Which of the following series of elements are arranged in the order of increasing electronegativity?

A. Fr, Mg, Si, O

C. F, B, O, Li

B. Br, Cl, S, P

D. Cl, S, Se, Te

E. Br, Mg, Si, N

15. The attraction due to London dispersion forces between molecules depends on what two factors?

A. Volatility and shape

C. Vapor pressure and size

B. Molar mass and volatility

D. Molar mass and shape

E. Molar mass and vapor pressure

16. Which of the substances below would have the largest dipole?

A. CO_2

C. H_2O

B. SO_2^-

D. CCl_4

E. CH_4

17. What is the name for the attraction between H_2O molecules?

A. adhesion

C. cohesion

B. polarity

D. van der Waals

E. hydrophilicity

18. Which compound contains only covalent bonds?

A. $HC_2H_3O_2$

C. NH_4OH

B. NaCl

D. $Ca_3(PO_4)_2$

E. LiF

19. The distance between two atomic nuclei in a chemical bond is determined by the:

A. size of the valence electrons

B. size of the nucleus

C. size of the protons

D. balance between the repulsion of the nuclei and the attraction of the nuclei for the bonding electrons

E. size of the neutrons

20. Carbonic acid has the chemical formula of H_2CO_3. The carbonate has the molecular formula of CO_3^{2-}. From the Lewis structure for the CO_3^{2-} ion, what is the number of reasonable resonance structures for the anion?

A. original structure only   **B.** 2   **C.** 3   **D.** 4   **E.** 5

==

Practice Set 2: Questions 21–40

==

21. Which of the following molecules would contain a dipole?

    A. F–F   **B.** H–H   **C.** Cl–Cl   **D.** H–F   **E.** *trans*-dichoroethene

22. Which is the correct formula for the ionic compound formed between Ca and I?

    A. Ca_3I_2 **B.** Ca_2I_3 **C.** CaI_2 **D.** Ca_2I **E.** Ca_3I_5

23. Which bonding is NOT possible for a carbon atom that has four valence electrons?

    A. 1 single and 1 triple bond   **C.** 4 single bonds
    B. 1 double and 1 triple bond   **D.** 2 single and 1 double bond
                                        E. 2 double bonds

24. During strenuous exercise, why does perspiration on a person's skin forms droplets?

    A. Ability of H_2O to dissipate heat   **C.** Adhesive properties of H_2O
    B. High specific heat of H_2O **D.** Cohesive properties of H_2O
                                          E. High NaCl content of perspiration

25. If an ionic bond is stronger than a dipole–dipole interaction, why does water dissolve an ionic compound?

    A. Ions do not overcome their interatomic attraction and therefore are not soluble
    B. Ion–dipole interaction causes the ions to heat up and vibrate free of the crystal
    C. Ionic bond is weakened by the ion–dipole interactions and ionic repulsion ejects the ions from the crystal
    D. Ion-dipole interactions of several water molecules aggregate with the ionic bond and dissociate it into the solution
    E. None of the above

26. Which one of these molecules can act as a hydrogen bond acceptor, but not a donor?

    A. CH_3NH_2 **C.** H_2O
    B. CH_3CO_2H **D.** C_2H_5OH **E.** $CH_3–O–CH_3$

27. When NaCl dissolves in water, what is the force of attraction between Na^+ and H_2O?

    A. ion–dipole   **C.** ion–ion
    B. hydrogen bonding   **D.** dipole–dipole   **E.** van der Waals

28. Based on the Lewis structure, how many polar and nonpolar bonds are present in H_2CO?

    A. 1 polar bond and 2 nonpolar bonds
    B. 2 polar bonds and 1 nonpolar bond
    C. 3 polar bonds and 0 nonpolar bonds
    D. 0 polar bonds and 3 nonpolar bonds
    E. 2 polar bonds and 2 nonpolar bonds

29. How many more electrons can fit within the valence shell of a hydrogen atom?

    A. 1   **B.** 2   **C.** 7   **D.** 0   **E.** 3

30. Which element likely forms a cation with a +2 charge?

    A. Na   **B.** S   **C.** Si   **D.** Mg   **E.** Br

31. Which of the statements is an accurate description of the structure of the ionic compound NaCl?

    A. Alternating rows of Na^+ and Cl^- ions are present
    B. Each ion present is surrounded by six ions of opposite charge
    C. Alternating layers of Na and Cl atoms are present
    D. Alternating layers of Na^+ and Cl^- ions are present
    E. Repeating layers of Na^+ and Cl^- ions are present

32. What is the name for the force holding two atoms together in a chemical bond?

    A. gravitational force   **C.** weak hydrophobic force
    B. strong nuclear force   **D.** weak nuclear force
                                      E. electrostatic force

33. Which of the following diatomic molecules contains the bond of greatest polarity?

    A. CH_4 **B.** BrI   **C.** Cl–F   **D.** P_4 **E.** Te–F

34. Why does H_2O have an unusually high boiling point compared to H_2S?

    A. Hydrogen bonding
    B. Van der Waals forces
    C. H_2O molecules pack more closely than H_2S
    D. Covalent bonds are stronger in H_2O
    E. This is a false statement, because H_2O has a similar boiling point to H_2S

35. What is the geometry of a molecule in which the central atom has 2 bonding electron pairs and 2 nonbonding electron pairs?

A. trigonal planar   **C.** linear

B. trigonal pyramidal   **D.** bent   **E.** tetrahedral

36. Which of the following represents the breaking of a noncovalent interaction?

A. Ionization of water   **C.** Hydrolysis of an ester

B. Decomposition of hydrogen peroxide   **D.** Dissolving of salt crystals

     E. None of the above

37. Which pair of elements is most likely to form an ionic compound when reacted together?

A. C and Cl   **C.** Ga and Si

B. K and I   **D.** Fe and Mg   **E.** H and O

38. Which of the following statements concerning coordinate covalent bonds is correct?

A. Once formed, they are indistinguishable from any other covalent bond

B. They are always single bonds

C. One of the atoms involved must be a metal and the other a nonmetal

D. Both atoms involved in the bond contribute an equal number of electrons to the bond

E. The bond is formed between two Lewis bases

39. The greatest dipole moment within a bond is when:

A. both bonding elements have low electronegativity

B. one bonding element has high electronegativity and the other has low electronegativity

C. both bonding elements have high electronegativity

D. one bonding element has high electronegativity and the other has moderate electronegativity

E. both bonding elements have moderate electronegativity

40. Which of the following must occur for an atom to obtain the noble gas configuration?

A. lose, gain or share an electron   **C.** lose an electron

B. lose or gain an electron   **D.** share an electron

     E. share or gain an electron

Practice Set 3: Questions 41–60

41. Based on the Lewis structure for hydrogen peroxide, H_2O_2, how many polar bonds and nonpolar bonds are present?

    A. 3 polar and 0 nonpolar bonds
    B. 2 polar and 2 nonpolar bonds
    C. 1 polar and 2 nonpolar bonds
    D. 0 polar and 3 nonpolar bonds
    E. 2 polar and 1 nonpolar bond

42. To form an octet, an atom of selenium must:

    A. gain 2 electrons
    B. lose 2 electrons
    C. gain 6 electrons
    D. lose 6 electrons
    E. gain 4 electrons

43. Which of the following is an example of a chemical reaction?

    A. two solids mix to form a heterogeneous mixture
    B. two liquids mix to form a homogeneous mixture
    C. one or more new compounds are formed by rearranging atoms
    D. a new element is formed by rearranging nucleons
    E. a liquid undergoes a phase change and produces a solid

44. Which compound is NOT correctly matched with the predominant intermolecular force associated with that compound in the liquid state?

Compound	Intermolecular force
A. CH_3OH	hydrogen bonding
B. HF	hydrogen bonding
C. Cl_2O	dipole–dipole interactions
D. HBr	van der Waals interactions
E. CH_4	van der Waals interactions

45. Which element forms an ion with the greatest positive charge?

    A. Mg   **B.** Ca   **C.** Al   **D.** Na   **E.** Rb

46. What is the difference between a dipole–dipole and an ion–dipole interaction?

    A. One interaction involves dipole attraction between neutral molecules, while the other involves dipole interactions with ions

    B. One interaction involves ionic molecules interacting with other ionic molecules, while the other deals with polar molecules

    C. One interaction involves salts and water, while the other does not involve water

    D. One interaction involves hydrogen bonding, while the other do not

    E. None of the above

47. Which is a true statement about H_2O as it begins to freeze?

    A. Hydrogen bonds break   **C.** Covalent bond strength increases

    B. Number of hydrogen bonds decreases   **D.** Molecules move closer together

                                     E. Number of hydrogen bonds increases

48. In the process of forming sodium nitride (Na_3N) from its elements, what happens to the electrons of each sodium atom and the electrons of each nitride atom, respectively?

    A. one lost; three gained   **C.** three lost; one gained

    B. three lost; three gained   **D.** one lost; two gained   **E.** two lost; three gained

49. Which species below has the least number of valence electrons in its Lewis symbol?

    A. S^{2-} **B.** Mg^{2+} **C.** Ar^+ **D.** Ga^+ **E.** F^-

50. Which of the following occur(s) naturally as nonpolar diatomic molecules?

    I. sulfur   II. chlorine   III. argon

    A. I only   **C.** I and III only

    B. II only   **D.** I and II only   **E.** I, II and III

51. In a chemical reaction, the bonds being formed are:

    A. more energetic than the ones broken   **C.** the same as the bonds broken

    B. less energetic than the ones broken   **D.** different from the ones broken

                                         E. none of the above

52. The charge on a sulfide ion is:

    A. +1   **B.** +2   **C.** 0   **D.** −2   **E.** −3

53. Which formula for an ionic compound is NOT correct?

    A. $Al_2(CO_3)_3$ **B.** Li_2SO_4 **C.** Na_2S **D.** $MgHCO_3$ **E.** K_2O

54. What term best describes the smallest whole number repeating ratio of ions in an ionic compound?

    A. lattice   **C.** formula unit

    B. unit cell   **D.** covalent unit   **E.** ionic unit

55. In the nitrogen monoxide molecule, the dipole moment is 0.16 D and the bond length is 115 pm. What is the sign and magnitude of the charge on the oxygen atom? (Use the conversion factor of 1 D = 3.34×10^{-30} C·m and the charge of 1 electron = 1.602×10^{-19} C)

    A. $-0.098\ e$ **B.** $-0.71\ e$ **C.** $-1.3\ e$ **D.** $-0.029\ e$ **E.** $+1.3\ e$

56. From the electronegativity below, which covalent single bond is the most polar?

Element:	H	C	N	O
Electronegativity	2.1	2.5	3.0	3.5

    A. O–C   **B.** O–N   **C.** N–C   **D.** C–H   **E.** C–C

57. Which of the following pairs is NOT correctly matched?

    Formula   Molecular Geometry

    A. CH_4 tetrahedral

    B. OF_2 bent

    C. PCl_3 trigonal planar

    D. Cl_2CO trigonal planar

    E. $^+CH_3$ trigonal planar

58. Why are adjacent water molecules attracted to each other?

    A. Ionic bonding between the hydrogens of H_2O

    B. Covalent bonding between adjacent oxygens

    C. Electrostatic attraction between the H of one H_2O and the O of another

    D. Covalent bonding between the H of one H_2O and the O of another

    E. Electrostatic attraction between the O of one H_2O and the O of another

59. What is the chemical formula for a compound that contains K^+ and CO_3^{2-} ions?

    A. $K(CO_3)_3$ **B.** $K_3(CO_3)_2$ **C.** $K_3(CO_3)_3$ **D.** KCO_3 **E.** K_2CO_3

60. Under what conditions is graphite converted to diamond?

    A. low temperature, high pressure   **C.** high temperature, high pressure

    B. high temperature, low pressure   **D.** low temperature, low pressure

                                            E. none of the above

===

Practice Set 4: Questions 61–80

===

61. Which of the following molecules is a Lewis acid?

A. NO_3^- **B.** NH_3 **C.** NH_4^+ **D.** CH_3COOH **E.** BH_3

62. Which molecule(s) is/are most likely to show a dipole-dipole interaction?

I. $H–C≡C–H$ II. CH_4 III. CH_3SH IV. CH_3CH_2OH

A. I only
B. II only
C. III only
D. III and IV only
E. I and IV only

63. $C=C$, $C=O$, $C=N$ and $N=N$ bonds are observed in many organic compounds. However, $C=S$, $C=P$, $C=Si$ and other similar bonds are not often found. What is the most probable explanation for this observation?

A. The comparative sizes of $3p$ atomic orbitals make effective overlap between them less likely than between two $2p$ orbitals
B. S, P and Si do not undergo hybridization of orbitals
C. S, P and Si do not form π bonds due to the lack of occupied p orbitals in their ground state electron configurations
D. Carbon does not combine with elements found below the second row of the periodic table
E. None of the above

64. Write the formula for the ionic compound formed from magnesium and sulfur:

A. Mg_2S **B.** Mg_3S_2 **C.** MgS_2 **D.** MgS_3 **E.** MgS

65. Explain why chlorine, Cl_2, is a gas at room temperature, while bromine, Br_2, is a liquid.

A. Bromine ions are held together by ionic bonds
B. Chlorine molecules are smaller and, therefore, pack tighter in their physical orientation
C. Bromine atoms are larger, which causes the formation of a stronger induced dipole–induced dipole attraction
D. Chlorine atoms are larger, which causes the formation of a stronger induced dipole–induced dipole attraction
E. Bromine molecules are smaller and therefore pack tighter in their physical orientation

66. What is the major intermolecular force in $(CH_3)_2NH$?

A. hydrogen bonding

B. dipole–dipole attractions

C. London dispersion forces

D. ion–dipole attractions

E. van der Waals forces

67. Which of the following correctly describes the molecule potassium oxide and its bond?

A. It is a weak electrolyte with an ionic bond

B. It is a strong electrolyte with an ionic bond

C. It is a non-electrolyte with a covalent bond

D. It is a strong electrolyte with a covalent bond

E. It is a non-electrolyte with a hydrogen bond

68. An ion with an atomic number of 34 and 36 electrons has what charge?

A. +2   B. −36   C. +34   D. −2   E. neutral

69. Based on the Lewis structure for $H_3C–NH_2$, the formal charge on N is:

A. −1   B. 0   C. +2   D. +1   E. −2

70. The name of S^{2-} is:

A. sulfite ion

B. sulfide ion

C. sulfur

D. sulfate ion

E. sulfurous acid

71. An ionic bond forms between two atoms when:

A. protons are transferred from the nucleus of the nonmetal to the nucleus of the metal

B. each atom acquires a negative charge

C. electron pairs are shared

D. four electrons are shared

E. electrons are transferred from metallic to nonmetallic atoms

72. Which of the following pairings of ions is NOT consistent with the formula?

A. Co_2S_3 (Co^{3+} and S^{2-})

B. K_2O (K^+ and O^-)

C. Na_3P (Na^+ and P^{3-})

D. BaF_2 (Ba^{2+} and F^-)

E. KCl (K^+ and Cl^-)

73. Which of the following solids is likely to have the smallest exothermic lattice energy?

A. Al_2O_3 B. KF   C. NaCl   D. LiF   E. NaOH

74. In chlorine monoxide, chlorine has a charge of +0.167 e. If the bond length is 154.6 pm, what is the dipole moment of the molecule? (Use 1 meter = 1×10^{-12} m/pm and 1 electron = 1.602×10^{-19} C)

    A. 2.30 D   **B.** 0.167 D   **C.** 1.24 D   **D.** 3.11 D   **E.** 1.65 D

75. All of the following are examples of polar molecules, EXCEPT:

    A. H_2O **B.** CCl_4 **C.** CH_2Cl_2 **D.** HF   **E.** CO

76. Which is the most likely noncovalent interaction between an alcohol and a carboxylic acid at pH = 10?

    A. formation of an anhydride bond   **C.** dipole–charge interaction

    B. dipole–dipole interaction   **D.** charge–charge interaction

                                   E. induced dipole–dipole interaction

77. Which of the following describes the orbital geometry of an sp^2 hybridized atom?

    A. linear   **C.** trigonal bipyramidal

    B. tetrahedral   **D.** bent   **E.** trigonal planar

78. Which of the following statements about noble gases is NOT correct?

    A. They have very stable electron arrangements

    B. They are the most reactive of all gases

    C. They exist in nature as individual atoms rather than in molecular form

    D. They have 8 valence electrons

    E. They have a complete octet

79. How are intermolecular forces and solubility related?

    A. Solubility is a measure of how weak the intermolecular forces in the solute are

    B. Solubility is a measure of how strong a solvent's intermolecular forces are

    C. Solubility depends on the solute's ability to overcome the intermolecular forces in the solvent

    D. Solubility depends on the solvent's ability to overcome the intermolecular forces in a solute

    E. None of the above

80. In a bond between any two of the following atoms, the bonding electrons would be most strongly attracted to:

    A. I   **B.** He   **C.** Cs   **D.** Cl   **E.** Fr

This page is intentionally left blank

Chemical Bonding – Answer Key

1: D	21: D	41: E	61: E
2: A	22: C	42: A	62: D
3: C	23: B	43: C	63: A
4: E	24: D	44: D	64: E
5: B	25: D	45: C	65: C
6: B	26: E	46: A	66: A
7: A	27: A	47: E	67: B
8: A	28: C	48: A	68: D
9: D	29: A	49: D	69: B
10: E	30: D	50: B	70: B
11: B	31: B	51: D	71: E
12: E	32: E	52: D	72: B
13: E	33: E	53: D	73: C
14: A	34: A	54: C	74: C
15: D	35: D	55: D	75: B
16: C	36: D	56: A	76: C
17: C	37: B	57: C	77: E
18: A	38: A	58: C	78: B
19: D	39: B	59: E	79: D
20: C	40: A	60: C	80: D

States of Matter: Gases, Liquids, Solids

==

Practice Set 1: Questions 1–20

==

1. Which statement is NOT true regarding vapor pressure?

>   I. Solids do not have a vapor pressure
>   II. Vapor pressure of a pure liquid does not depend on the amount of vapor present
>   III. Vapor pressure of a pure liquid does not depend on the amount of liquid present

A. I only   **B.** II only   **C.** III only   **D.** I and II only   **E.** I, II and III

2. How does the volume of a fixed sample of gas change if the temperature is doubled at a constant pressure?

A. Decreases by a factor of 2   **C.** Doubles
B. Increases by a factor of 4   **D.** Remains the same   **E.** Requires more information

3. When a solute is added to a pure solvent, the boiling point [   ] and freezing point [   ]?

A. decreases … decreases   **C.** increases … decreases
B. decreases … increases   **D.** increases … increases
                                 E. remains the same … remains the same

4. Consider the phase diagram for H_2O. The termination of the gas-liquid transition at which distinct or liquid phases do NOT exist is the:

A. critical point   **C.** triple point
B. end point   **D.** condensation point   **E.** inflection point

5. The van der Waals equation of state for a real gas is expressed as: $[P + n^2a / V^2]\cdot(V - nb) = nRT$. The van der Waals constant, *a*, represents a correction for:
  A. negative deviation in the measured value of P from that of an ideal gas due to the attractive forces between the molecules of a real gas
  B. positive deviation in the measured value of P from that of an ideal gas due to the attractive forces between the molecules of a real gas
  C. negative deviation in the measured value of P from that of an ideal gas due to the finite volume of space occupied by molecules of a real gas
  D. positive deviation in the measured value of P from that of an ideal gas due to the finite volume of space occupied by molecules of a real gas
  E. positive deviation in the measured value of P from that of an ideal gas due to the finite mass of the molecules of a real gas

6. What is the value of the ideal gas constant, expressed in units (torr × mL) / mole × K?

    A. 62.4   **B.** 62,400   **C.** 0.0821   **D.** 1 / 0.0821   **E.** 8.21

7. If both the pressure and the temperature of a gas are halved, the volume is:

    A. halved   **C.** doubled

    B. the same   **D.** quadrupled   **E.** decreased by a factor of 4

8. If container X is occupied by 2.0 moles of O_2 gas, while container Y is occupied by 10.0 grams of N_2 gas, and both containers are maintained at 5.0 °C and 760 torr, then:

    A. container X must have a volume of 22.4 L

    B. the average kinetic energy of the molecules in X is equal to the average kinetic energy of the molecules in Y

    C. container Y must be larger than container X

    D. the average speed of the molecules in container X is greater than that of the molecules in container Y

    E. the number of atoms in container Y is greater than the number of atoms in container X

9. Among the following choices, how tall should a properly designed Torricelli mercury barometer be?

    A. 100 in   **B.** 380 mm   **C.** 76 mm   **D.** 400 mm   **E.** 800 mm

10. When volatile solvents X and Y are mixed in equal proportions, heat is released to the surroundings. If pure X has a higher boiling point than pure Y, which of the following statements is NOT true?

    A. The vapor pressure of the mixture is lower than that of pure Y

    B. The vapor pressure of the mixture is lower than that of pure X

    C. The boiling point of the mixture is lower than that of pure X

    D. The boiling point of the mixture is lower than that of pure Y

    E. Not enough information is provided

11. For the balanced reaction $2 Na + Cl_2 \rightarrow 2 NaCl$, which of the following is a gas?

    I. Na   II. Cl_2 III. NaCl

    A. I only   **B.** II only   **C.** III only   **D.** I and II only   **E.** I, II and III

12. How does a real gas deviate from an ideal gas?

    I. Molecules occupy a significant amount of space

    II. Intermolecular forces may exist

    III. Pressure is created from molecular collisions with the walls of the container

    A. I only   **B.** II only   **C.** I and II only   **D.** II and III only   **E.** I, II and III

13. A 2.75 L sample of He gas has a pressure of 0.95 atm. What is the pressure of the gas if the volume is reduced to 0.45 L?

    A. 5.80 atm   **B.** 0.52 atm   **C.** 0.23 atm   **D.** 0.96 atm   **E.** 3.40 atm

14. Avogadro's law, in its alternate form, is very similar in form to:

    I. Boyle's law
    II. Charles' law
    III. Gay-Lussac's law

    A. I only   **C.** III only   **B.** II only   **D.** II and III only   **E.** I, II and III

15. What is the relationship between the pressure and volume of a fixed amount of gas at constant temperature?

    A. directly proportional   **C.** inversely proportional
    B. equal   **D.** decreased by a factor of 2   **E.** none of the above

16. What is the term for a change of state from a liquid to a gas?

    A. vaporization   **C.** deposition
    B. melting   **D.** condensing   **E.** sublimation

17. The combined gas law can NOT be written as:

    A. $V_2 = V_1 \times P_1 / P_2 \times T_2 / T_1$ **C.** $T_2 = T_1 \times P_1 / P_2 \times V_2 / V_1$
    B. $P_1 = P_2 \times V_2 / V_1 \times T_1 / T_2$ **D.** $V1 = V_2 \times P_2 / P_1 \times T_1 / T_2$
    E. none of the above

18. Which singular molecule is most likely to show a dipole-dipole interaction?

    A. CH_4 **B.** $H–C{\equiv}C–H$ **C.** SO_2 **D.** CO_2 **E.** CCl_4

19. What happens if the pressure of a gas above a liquid increases, such as by pressing a piston above a liquid?

    A. Pressure goes down and the gas moves out of the solvent
    B. Pressure goes down and the gas goes into the solvent
    C. The gas is forced into solution and the solubility increases
    D. The solution is compressed and the gas is forced out of the solvent
    E. The amount of gas in the solution remains constant

20. Which of the following two variables are present in mathematical statements of Avogadro's law?

    A. P and V   **B.** n and P   **C.** n and T   **D.** V and T   **E.** n and V

===

Practice Set 2: Questions 21–40

===

21. Which of the following acids has the lowest boiling point elevation?

Monoprotic Acids	Ka
Acid I	1.4×10^{-8}
Acid II	1.6×10^{-9}
Acid III	3.9×10^{-10}
Acid IV	2.1×10^{-8}

A. I   **C.** III

B. II   **D.** IV   **E.** Requires more information

22. An ideal gas differs from a real gas because the molecules of an ideal gas have:

A. no attraction to each other   **C.** molecular weight equal to zero

B. no kinetic energy   **D.** appreciable volumes

     E. none of the above

23. Which of the following is the definition of standard temperature and pressure?

A. 0 K and 1 atm   **C.** 298 K and 1 atm

B. 298 K and 760 mmHg   **D.** 273 °C and 760 torr

     E. 273 K and 760 mmHg

24. At constant volume, as the temperature of a sample of gas is decreased, the gas deviates from ideal behavior. Compared to the pressure predicted by the ideal gas law, actual pressure would be:

A. higher, because of the volume of the gas molecules

B. higher, because of intermolecular attractions between gas molecules

C. lower, because of the volume of the gas molecules

D. lower, because of intermolecular attractions among gas molecules

E. higher, because of intramolecular attractions between gas molecules

25. A flask contains a mixture of O_2, N_2 and CO_2. The pressure exerted by N_2 is 320 torr and by CO_2 is 240 torr. If the total pressure of the gas mixture is 740 torr, what is the percent pressure of O_2?

A. 14%   **B.** 18%   **C.** 21%   **D.** 24%   **E.** 29%

26. A balloon contains 40 grams of He with a pressure of 1,000 torr. When He is released from the balloon, the new pressure is 900 torr and the volume is half of the original. If the temperature is the same, how many grams of He remains in the balloon?

A. 18 grams
B. 22 grams
C. 10 grams
D. 40 grams
E. 28 grams

27. Which of the following is a true statement regarding evaporation?

A. Increasing the surface area of the liquid decreases the rate of evaporation
B. The temperature of the liquid changes during evaporation
C. Decreasing the surface area of the liquid increases the rate of evaporation
D. Molecules with greater kinetic energy escape from the liquid
E. Not enough information is provided to make any conclusions

28. Under which conditions does a real gas behave most nearly like an ideal gas?

A. High temperature and high pressure
B. High temperature and low pressure
C. Low temperature and low pressure
D. Low temperature and high pressure
E. If it remains in the gaseous state regardless of temperature or pressure

29. Which of the following compounds has the highest boiling point?

A. CH_3OH
B. $CH_3CH_2CH_2CH_2CH_2OH$
C. $CH_3OCH_2CH_2CH_2CH_3$
D. $CH_3CH_2OCH_2CH_2CH_3$
E. $CH_3CH_2CH_2C(OH)HOH$

30. According to the kinetic theory of gases, which of the following is the average kinetic energy of the gas particles directly proportional to?

A. temperature
B. molar mass
C. volume
D. pressure
E. number of moles of gas

31. Under ideal conitions, which of the following gases is least likely to behave as an ideal gas?

A. CF_4
B. CH_3OH
C. N_2
D. O_3
E. CO_2

32. Which statement is true regarding gases when compared to liquids?

    A. Gases have lower compressibility and higher density

    B. Gases have lower compressibility and lower density

    C. Gases have higher compressibility and higher density

    D. Gases have higher compressibility and lower density

    E. None of the above

33. When nonvolatile solute molecules are added to a solution, the vapor pressure of the solution:

    A. stays the same

    B. increases

    C. decreases

    D. is directly proportional to the second power of the amount added

    E. is directly proportional to the square root of the amount added

34. Which of the following laws states that the pressure exerted by a mixture of gases is equal to the sum of the individual gas pressures?

    A. Gay-Lussac's law   **C.** Charles's law

    B. Dalton's law   **D.** Boyle's law

                             E. Avogadro's law

35. Which characteristics best describe a solid?

    A. Definite volume; shape of container; no intermolecular attractions

    B. Volume and shape of container; no intermolecular attractions

    C. Definite shape and volume; strong intermolecular attractions

    D. Definite volume; shape of container; moderate intermolecular attractions

    E. Volume and shape of container; strong intermolecular attractions

36. Which of the following statements is true, if three 2.0 L flasks are filled with H_2, O_2 and He, respectively, at STP?

    A. There are twice as many He atoms as H_2 or O_2 molecules

    B. There are four times as many H_2 or O_2 molecules as He atoms

    C. Each flask contains the same number of atoms

    D. There are twice as many H_2 or O_2 molecules as He atoms

    E. The number of H_2 or O_2 molecules is the same as the number of He atoms

37. Which of the following atoms could interact through a hydrogen bond?

 A. The hydrogen of an amine and the oxygen of an alcohol
 B. The hydrogen on an aromatic ring and the oxygen of carbon dioxide
 C. The oxygen of a ketone and the hydrogen of an aldehyde
 D. The oxygen of methanol and a hydrogen on the methyl carbon of methanol
 E. None of the above

38. Which of the following laws states that for a gas at constant temperature, the pressure and volume are inversely proportional?

 A. Dalton's law   **C.** Boyle's law
 B. Gay-Lussac's law   **D.** Charles's law   **E.** Avogadro's law

39. As an automobile travels the highway, the temperature of the air inside the tires [   ] and the pressure [   ]?

 A. increases … decreases   **C.** decreases … decreases
 B. increases … increases   **D.** decreases … increases
                   E. none of the above

40. Using the following unbalanced chemical reaction, what volume of H_2 gas at 780 mmHg and 23 °C is required to produce 12.5 L of NH_3 gas at the same temperature and pressure?

$$N_2\,(g) + H_2\,(g) \rightarrow NH_3\,(g)$$

 A. 21.4 L   **B.** 15.0 L   **C.** 18.8 L   **D.** 13.0 L   **E.** 12.5 L

===

Practice Set 3 Questions 41–60

===

41. A mixture of gases containing 16 g of O_2, 14 g of N_2 and 88 g of CO_2 is collected above water at a temperature of 23 °C. The total pressure is 1 atm and the vapor pressure of water is 38 torr. What is the partial pressure exerted by CO_2?

    A. 283 torr   **B.** 367 torr   **C.** 481 torr   **D.** 549 torr   **E.** 583 torr

42. Which of the following demonstrate colligative properties?

       I. Freezing point   II. Boiling point   III. Vapor pressure

    A. I only   **B.** II only   **C.** III only   **D.** I and II only   **E.** I, II and III

43. What is the proportionality relationship between the pressure of a gas and its volume?

    A. directly   **C.** pressure is raised to the 2nd power

    B. inversely   **D.** pressure raised to the $\sqrt{2}$ power   **E.** none of the above

44. Which of the following statements about gases is correct?

    A. Formation of homogeneous mixtures, regardless of the nature of non-reacting gas components

    B. Relatively long distances between molecules

    C. High compressibility

    D. No attractive forces between gas molecules

    E. All of the above

45. Which of the following describes a substance in the solid physical state?

       I. It compresses negligibly

       II. It has a fixed volume

       III. It has a fixed shape

    A. I only   **B.** II only   **C.** I and III only   **D.** II and III only   **E.** I, II and III

46. Which of the following is NOT a unit used in measuring pressure?

    A. kilometers Hg   **C.** atmosphere

    B. millimeters Hg   **D.** inches Hg   **E.** torr

47. Which of the following compounds has the highest boiling point?

    A. CH_4 **B.** $CHCl_3$ **C.** CH_3COOH **D.** NH_3 **E.** CH_2Cl_2

48. Identify the decreasing ordering of attractions among particles in the three states of matter.

A. gas > liquid > solid

B. gas > solid > liquid

C. solid > liquid > gas

D. liquid > solid > gas

E. solid > gas > liquid

49. A sample of N_2 gas occupies a volume of 190 mL at STP. What volume will it occupy at 660 mmHg and 295 K?

A. 1.15 L   **B.** 0.760 L   **C.** 0.236 L   **D.** 1.84 L   **E.** 0.197 L

50. A nonvolatile liquid would have:

A. a highly explosive propensity

B. strong attractive forces between molecules

C. weak attractive forces between molecules

D. a high vapor pressure at room temperature

E. weak attractive forces within molecules

51. A closed-end manometer was constructed from a U-shaped glass tube. It was loaded with mercury, so that the closed side was filled to the top, which was 820 mm above the neck, while the open end was 160 mm above the neck. The manometer was taken into a chamber used for training astronauts. What is the highest pressure that can be read with assurance on this manometer?

A. 66.0 torr

B. 660 torr

C. 220 torr

D. 760 torr

E. 5.13 torr

52. Vessels X and Y each contain 1.00 L of a gas at STP, but vessel X contains oxygen, while vessel Y contains nitrogen. Assuming the gases behave as ideal, they have the same:

    I. number of molecules   II. density   III. kinetic energy

A. II only

B. III only

C. I and III only

D. I, II and III

E. I only

53. What condition must be satisfied for the noble gas Xe to exist in the liquid phase at 180 K, which is a temperature significantly greater than its normal boiling point?

A. external pressure > vapor pressure of xenon

B. external pressure < vapor pressure of xenon

C. external pressure = partial pressure of water

D. temperature is increased quickly

E. temperature is increased slowly

54. Matter is nearly incompressible in which of these states?

      I. solid   II. liquid   III. gas

    A. I only   **C.** III only

    B. II only   **D.** I and II only   **E.** I, II and III

55. Which of the following laws states that for a gas at constant pressure, volume and temperature are directly proportional?

    A. Gay-Lussac's law   **C.** Charles' law

    B. Dalton's law   **D.** Boyle's law   **E.** Avogadro's law

56. Which transformation describes sublimation?

    A. solid → liquid   **C.** liquid → solid

    B. solid → gas   **D.** liquid → gas   **E.** gas → liquid

57. What is the ratio of the diffusion rate of O_2 molecules to the diffusion rate of H_2 molecules, if six moles of O_2 gas and six moles of H_2 gas are placed in a large vessel, and the gases and vessel are at the same temperature?

    A. 4:1   **B.** 1:4   **C.** 12:1   **D.** 1:1   **E.** 2:1

58. How many molecules of neon gas are present in 6 liters at 10 °C and 320 mmHg? (Use the ideal gas constant R = 0.0821 L·atm K^{-1} mol^{-1})

    A. (320 mmHg / 760 atm)(0.821)·(6 L) / (6 × 10^{23})·(283 K)

    B. (320 mmHg / 760 atm)·(6 L)·(6 × 10^{23}) / (0.0821)·(283 K)

    C. (320 mmHg)·(6 L)·(283 K)·(6 × 10^{23})

    D. (320 mmHg / 760 atm)·(6 L)·(283 K)·(6 × 10^{23}) / (0.821)

    E. (320 mmHg / 283 K)·(6 L)·(6 × 10^{23}) / [(0.0821)·(760 atm)

59. Which gas has the greatest density at STP:

    A. CO_2 **B.** O_2 **C.** N_2 **D.** NO   **E.** more than one

60. A hydrogen bond is a special type of:

    A. dipole–dipole attraction involving hydrogen bonded to another hydrogen atom

    B. attraction involving any molecules that contain hydrogens

    C. dipole-dipole attraction involving hydrogen bonded to a highly electronegative atom

    D. dipole–dipole attraction involving hydrogen bonded to any other atom

    E. London dispersion force involving a hydrogen bonded to an electropositive atom

==

Practice Set 4: Questions 61–80

==

61. What is the mole fraction of H in a gaseous mixture that consists of 9.50 g of H_2 and 14.0 g of Ne in a 4.50 liter container maintained at 37.5 °C?

   A. 0.13   **B.** 0.43   **C.** 0.67   **D.** 0.87   **E.** 1.2

62. Which of the following is true about Liquid A, if the vapor pressure of Liquid A is greater than that of Liquid B?

   A. Liquid A has a higher heat of fusion   **C.** Liquid A forms stronger bonds

   B. Liquid A has a higher heat of vaporization   **D.** Liquid A boils at a higher temperature

                                             E. Liquid A boils at a lower temperature

63. When 25 g of non-ionizable compound X is dissolved in 1 kg of camphor, the freezing point of the camphor falls 2.0 K. What is the approximate molecular weight of compound X? (Use $K_{camphor} = 40$)

   A. 50 g/mol   **C.** 5,000 g/mol

   B. 500 g/mol   **D.** 5,500 g/mol   **E.** 5,750 g/mol

64. The boiling point of a liquid is the temperature:

   A. where sublimation occurs

   B. where the vapor pressure of the liquid is less than the atmospheric pressure over the liquid

   C. equal to or greater than 100 °C

   D. where the rate of sublimation equals evaporation

   E. where the vapor pressure of the liquid equals the atmospheric pressure over the liquid

65. The van der Waals equation $[(P + n^2a / v^2) \cdot (V - nb) = nRT]$ is used to describe nonideal gases. The terms n^2a / v^2 and nb stand for, respectively:

   A. volume of gas molecules and intermolecular forces

   B. nonrandom movement and intermolecular forces between gas molecules

   C. nonelastic collisions and volume of gas molecules

   D. intermolecular forces and volume of gas molecules

   E. nonrandom movement and volume of gas molecules

66. What are the units of the gas constant R?

   A. atm·K/l·mol   **C.** mol·l/atm·K

   B. atm·K/mol·l   **D.** mol·K/l·atm   **E.** l·atm/mol·K

---

67. A sample of a gas occupying a volume of 120.0 ml at STP was placed in a different vessel with a volume of 155.0 ml, in which the pressure was measured as 0.80 atm. What was its temperature?

    A. 9.1 °C   **B.** 43.1 °C   **C.** 4.1 °C   **D.** 93.6 °C   **E.** 108.3 °C

68. Why does a beaker of water begin to boil at 22 °C when it is placed in a closed chamber and a vacuum pump is used to evacuate the air from the chamber?

    A. The vapor pressure decreases   **C.** The atmospheric pressure decreases

    B. Air is released from the water   **D.** The vapor pressure increases

                                             E. The atmospheric pressure increases

69. According to the kinetic theory, what happens to the kinetic energy of gaseous molecules when the temperature of a gas decreases?

    A. Increase as does velocity   **C.** Increases and velocity decreases

    B. Remains constant as does velocity   **D.** Decreases and velocity increases

                                             E. Decreases as does velocity

70. A sample of SO_3 gas is decomposed to SO_2 and O_2.

      $2\,SO_3\,(g) \rightarrow 2\,SO_2\,(g) + O_2\,(g)$

If the total pressure of SO_2 and O_2 is 1,250 torr, what is the partial pressure of O_2 in torr?

    A. 417 torr   **C.** 1,250 torr

    B. 1,040 torr   **D.** 884 torr   **E.** 12.50 torr

71. For the balanced reaction $2\,Na + Cl_2 \rightarrow 2\,NaCl$, which of the following is a solid?

      I. Na   II. Cl   III. NaCl

    A. I only   **C.** III only

    B. II only   **D.** I and III only   **E.** I, II and III

72. According to Charles's law, what happens to a gas as temperature increases?

    A. volume decreases   **C.** pressure decreases

    B. volume increases   **D.** pressure increases   **E.** mole fraction increases

73. How does the pressure of a sample of gas change, if the moles of a gas remain constant while the volume is halved and temperature is quadrupled?

    A. decrease by a factor of 8   **C.** decrease by a factor of 4

    B. quadruple   **D.** decrease by a factor of 2   **E.** increase by a factor of 8

74. For a fixed quantity of gas, gas laws describe in mathematical terms the relationships between pressure and which two variables?

    A. chemical identity; mass   **C.** temperature; volume

    B. volume; chemical identity   **D.** temperature; size   **E.** volume; size

75. What is the term for a direct change of state from a solid to a gas?

    A. sublimation   **C.** condensation

    B. vaporization   **D.** deposition   **E.** melting

76. The average speed at which a methane molecule effuses at 28.5 °C is 631 m/s. The average speed at which a krypton molecule effuses at the same temperature is:

    A. 123 m/s   **B.** 276 m/s   **C.** 312 m/s   **D.** 421 m/s   **E.** 633 m/s

77. A chemical reaction A (*s*) → B (*s*) + C (*g*) occurs when substance A is vigorously heated. The molecular mass of the gaseous product was determined from the following experimental data:

    Mass of A before reaction: 5.2 g

    Mass of A after reaction: 0 g

    Mass of residue B after cooling and weighing when no more gas evolved: 3.8 g

    When all of the gas C evolved, it was collected and stored in a 668.5 mL glass vessel at 32.0 °C, and the gas exerted a pressure of 745.5 torr.

    Use the ideal gas constant R equals 0.0821 L·atm K⁻¹ mol⁻¹

From this data, determine the apparent molecular mass of *C*, assuming it behaves as an ideal gas:

    A. 6.46 g/mol   **B.** 46.3 g/mol   **C.** 53.9 g/mol   **D.** 72.2 g/mol   **E.** 142.7 g/mol

78. Which of the following describes a substance in the liquid physical state?

    I. It has a variable shape

    II. It compresses negligibly

    III. It has a fixed volume

    A. I only   **B.** II only   **C.** I and III only   **D.** II and III only   **E.** I, II and III

79. Which is the strongest form of intermolecular attraction between water molecules?

    A. ion-dipole   **C.** induced dipole-induced dipole

    B. covalent bonding   **D.** hydrogen bonding

                         E. polar-induced dipolar

80. When a helium balloon is placed in a freezer, the temperature in the balloon [   ] and the volume [   ]?

A. increases … increases

B. increases … decreases

C. decreases … increases

D. decreases … decreases

E. none of the above

States of Matter: Gases, Liquids, Solids – Answer Key

1: A	21: E	41: C	61: D
2: C	22: A	42: E	62: E
3: C	23: E	43: B	63: B
4: A	24: D	44: E	64: E
5: A	25: D	45: E	65: D
6: B	26: A	46: A	66: E
7: B	27: D	47: C	67: A
8: B	28: B	48: C	68: C
9: E	29: E	49: C	69: E
10: D	30: A	50: B	70: A
11: B	31: B	51: B	71: D
12: C	32: D	52: C	72: B
13: A	33: C	53: A	73: E
14: D	34: B	54: D	74: C
15: C	35: C	55: C	75: A
16: A	36: E	56: B	76: B
17: C	37: A	57: B	77: C
18: C	38: C	58: B	78: E
19: C	39: B	59: A	79: D
20: E	40: C	60: C	80: D

Stoichiometry

Practice Set 1: Questions 1–20

1. What is the volume of three moles of O_2 at STP?

    A. 11.2 L   **B.** 22.4 L   **C.** 67.2 L   **D.** 32.0 L   **E.** 5.51 L

2. In the following reaction, which of the following describes H_2SO_4?

    $$H_2SO_4 + HI \rightarrow I_2 + SO_2 + H_2O$$

    A. reducing agent and is reduced   **C.** oxidizing agent and is reduced
    B. reducing agent and is oxidized   **D.** oxidizing agent and is oxidized
                                              E. neither oxidizing nor reducing agent

3. Select the balanced chemical equation for the reaction: $C_6H_{14} + O_2 \rightarrow CO_2 + H_2O$

    A. $3\ C_6H_{14} + O_2 \rightarrow 18\ CO_2 + 22\ H_2O$
    B. $2\ C_6H_{14} + 12\ O_2 \rightarrow 12\ CO_2 + 14\ H_2O$
    C. $2\ C_6H_{14} + 19\ O_2 \rightarrow 12\ CO_2 + 14\ H_2O$
    D. $2\ C_6H_{14} + 9\ O_2 \rightarrow 12\ CO_2 + 7\ H_2O$
    E. $C_6H_{14} + O_2 \rightarrow CO_2 + H_2O$

4. An oxidation number is the [   ] that an atom [   ] when the electrons in each bond are assigned to the [   ] electronegative of the two atoms involved in the bond."

    A. charge… definitely has… more
    B. charge… definitely has… less
    C. number of electrons… definitely has… more
    D. number of electrons… appears to have… less
    E. charge… appears to have… more

5. What is the empirical formula of acetic acid, CH_3COOH?

    A. CH_3COOH **B.** $C_2H_4O_2$ **C.** CH_2O **D.** CO_2H_2 **E.** CHO

6. In which of the following compounds does Cl have an oxidation number of +7?

    A. $NaClO_2$ **B.** $Al(ClO_4)_3$ **C.** $Ca(ClO_3)_2$ **D.** $LiClO_3$ **E.** none of the above

7. What is the formula mass of a molecule of CO_2?

   A. 44 amu

   B. 52 amu

   C. 56.5 amu

   D. 112 amu

   E. None of the above

8. What is the product of heating cadmium metal and powdered sulfur?

   A. CdS_2

   B. Cd_2S_3

   C. CdS

   D. Cd_2S

   E. Cd_3S_2

9. After balancing the following redox reaction, what is the coefficient of NaCl?

   $$Cl_2\ (g) + NaI\ (aq) \rightarrow I_2\ (s) + NaCl\ (aq)$$

   A. 1   **B.** 2   **C.** 3   **D.** 5   **E.** none of the above

10. Which substance listed below is the strongest reducing agent, given the following *spontaneous* redox reaction?

    $$FeCl_3\ (aq) + NaI\ (aq) \rightarrow I_2\ (s) + FeCl_2\ (aq) + NaCl\ (aq)$$

    A. $FeCl_2$ **B.** I_2 **C.** NaI   **D.** $FeCl_3$ **E.** NaCl

11. 14.5 moles of N_2 gas are mixed with 34 moles of H_2 gas in the following reaction:

    $$N_2\ (g) + 3\ H_2\ (g) \rightarrow 2\ NH_3\ (g)$$

    How many moles of N_2 gas remain, if the reaction produces 18 moles of NH_3 gas when performed at 600 K?

    A. 0.6 moles

    B. 1.4 moles

    C. 5.5 moles

    D. 7.4 moles

    E. 9.6 moles

12. Which equation is NOT correctly classified by the type of chemical reaction?

    A. $AgNO_3 + NaCl \rightarrow AgCl + NaNO_3$ (double-replacement/non-redox)

    B. $Cl_2 + F_2 \rightarrow 2\ ClF$ (synthesis/redox)

    C. $H_2O + SO_2 \rightarrow H_2SO_3$ (synthesis/non-redox)

    D. $CaCO_3 \rightarrow CaO + CO_2$ (decomposition/redox)

    E. All are correctly classified

13. How many grams of H_2O can be formed from a reaction between 10 grams of oxygen and 1 gram of hydrogen?

    A. 11 grams of H_2O are formed since mass must be conserved

    B. 10 grams of H_2O are formed since the mass of water produced cannot be greater than the amount of oxygen reacting

    C. 9 grams of H_2O are formed because oxygen and hydrogen react in an 8:1 mass ratio

    D. No H_2O is formed because there is insufficient hydrogen to react with the oxygen

    E. Not enough information is provided

14. How many grams of Ba^{2+} ions are in an aqueous solution of $BaCl_2$ that contains 6.8×10^{22} Cl ions?

    A. 3.2×10^{48} g   **B.** 12 g   **C.** 14.5 g   **D.** 7.8 g   **E.** 9.8 g

15. What is the oxidation number of Br in $NaBrO_3$?

    A. −1   **B.** +1   **C.** +3   **D.** +5   **E.** none of the above

16. When aluminum metal reacts with ferric oxide (Fe_2O_3), a displacement reaction yields two products with one being metallic iron. What is the sum of the coefficients of the products of the balanced reaction?

    A. 4   **B.** 6   **C.** 2   **D.** 5   **E.** 3

17. Which of the following reactions is NOT correctly classified?

    A. $AgNO_3$ (*aq*) + KOH (*aq*) → KNO_3 (*aq*) + AgOH (*s*) : non-redox / double-replacement

    B. 2 H_2O_2 (*s*) → 2 H_2O (*l*) + O_2 (*g*) : non-redox / decomposition

    C. $Pb(NO_3)_2$ (*aq*) + 2 Na (*s*) → Pb (*s*) + 2 $NaNO_3$ (*aq*) : redox / single-replacement

    D. HNO_3 (*aq*) + LiOH (*aq*) → $LiNO_3$ (*aq*) + H_2O (*l*) : non-redox / double-replacement

    E. All are correctly classified

18. Calculate the number of O_2 molecules, if a 15.0 L cylinder was filled with O_2 gas at STP. (Use the conversion factor of 1 mole of $O_2 = 6.02 \times 10^{23}$ O_2 molecules)

    A. 443 molecules

    B. 6.59×10^{24} molecules

    C. 4.03×10^{23} molecules

    D. 2.77×10^{22} molecules

    E. 4,430 molecules

19. Which of the following is a guideline for balancing redox equations by the oxidation number method?

    A. Verify that the total number of atoms and the total ionic charge are the same for reactants and products

    B. In front of the substance reduced, place a coefficient that corresponds to the number of electrons lost by the substance oxidized

    C. In front of the substance oxidized, place a coefficient that corresponds to the number of electrons gained by the substance reduced

    D. Determine the electrons lost by the substance oxidized and gained by the substance reduced

    E. All of the above

20. Which of the following represents the oxidation of Co^{2+}?

    A. $Co \rightarrow Co^{2+} + 2\ e^-$ **C.** $Co^{2+} + 2\ e^- \rightarrow Co$

    B. $Co^{3+} + e^- \rightarrow Co^{2+}$ **D.** $Co^{2+} \rightarrow Co^{3+} + e^-$

                                      E. $Co^{3+} + 2\ e^- \rightarrow Co^+$

==

Practice Set 2: Questions 21–40

==

21. How many moles of phosphorous trichloride are required to produce 365 grams of HCl when the reaction yields 75%?

$$PCl_3 (g) + 3 NH_3 (g) \rightarrow P(NH_2)_3 + 3 HCl (g)$$

  A. 1 mol   **B.** 2.5 mol   **C.** 3.5 mol   **D.** 4.5 mol   **E.** 5 mol

22. What is the oxidation number of liquid bromine in the elemental state?

  A. 0   **B.** –1   **C.** –2   **D.** –3   **E.** None of the above

23. Propane burners are used by campers for cooking. What volume of H_2O is produced by the complete combustion, as shown in the unbalanced equation, of 2.6 L of propane (C_3H_8) gas when measured at the same temperature and pressure?

$$C_3H_8 (g) + O_2 (g) \rightarrow CO_2 (g) + H_2O (g)$$

  A. 0.65 L   **B.** 10.4 L   **C.** 5.2 L   **D.** 2.6 L   **E.** 26.0 L

24. Which substance is reduced in the following redox reaction?

$$HgCl_2 (aq) + Sn^{2+} (aq) \rightarrow Sn^{4+} (aq) + Hg_2Cl_2 (s) + Cl^- (aq)$$

  A. Sn^{4+} **B.** Hg_2Cl_2 **C.** $HgCl_2$ **D.** Sn^{2+} **E.** None of the above

25. What is the coefficient (n) of P for the balanced equation: $nP (s) + nO_2 (g) \rightarrow nP_2O_5 (s)$?

  A. 1   **B.** 2   **C.** 4   **D.** 5   **E.** none of the above

26. In basic solution, which of the following are guidelines for balancing a redox equation by the half–reaction method?

   I.   Add the two half–reactions together and cancel identical species on each side of the equation
   II. Multiply each half–reaction by a whole number so that the number of electrons lost by the substance oxidized is equal to the electrons gained by the substance reduced
   III. Write a balanced half-reaction for the substance oxidized and the substance reduced

  A. II only   **B.** III only   **C.** I and III only   **D.** II and III only   **E.** I, II and III

121

27. What is the molecular formula of galactose, if the empirical formula is CH_2O, and the approximate molar mass is 180 g/mol?

A. $C_6H_{12}O_6$

B. CH_2O_6

C. CH_2O

D. CHO

E. $C_{12}H_{22}O_{11}$

28. How many formula units of lithium iodide (LiI) have a mass equal to 6.45 g? (Use the molecular mass of LiI = 133.85 g)

A. 3.45×10^{23} formula units

B. 6.43×10^{23} formula units

C. 1.65×10^{24} formula units

D. 7.74×10^{25} formula units

E. 2.90×10^{22} formula units

29. What is/are the product(s) of the reaction of N_2 and O_2 gases in a combustion engine?

I. NO   II. NO_2 III. N_2O

A. I only

B. II only

C. III only

D. I and II only

E. I, II and III

30. What is the coefficient (n) of O_2 gas for the balanced equation?

$$nP\ (s) + nO_2\ (g) \rightarrow nP_2O_3\ (s)$$

A. 1   **B.** 2   **C.** 3   **D.** 5   **E.** None of the above

31. Which substance is the weakest reducing agent given the spontaneous redox reaction?

$$Mg\ (s) + Sn^{2+}\ (aq) \rightarrow Mg^{2+}\ (aq) + Sn\ (s)$$

A. Sn   **B.** Mg^{2+} **C.** Sn^{2+} **D.** Mg   **E.** None of the above

32. After balancing the following redox reaction in acidic solution, what is the coefficient of H^+?

$$Mg\ (s) + NO_3^-\ (aq) \rightarrow Mg^{2+}\ (aq) + NO_2\ (aq)$$

A. 1   **B.** 2   **C.** 4   **D.** 6   **E.** None of the above

33. Which substance contains the greatest number of moles in a 10 g sample?

A. SiO_2 **B.** SO_2 **C.** CBr_4 **D.** CO_2 **E.** CH_4

34. Which chemistry law is illustrated when ethyl alcohol always contains 52% carbon, 13% hydrogen, and 35% oxygen by mass?

A. law of constant composition   C. law of multiple proportions

B. law of constant percentages   D. law of conservation of mass

                                          E. none of the above

35. Which could NOT be true for the following reaction: $N_2(g) + 3 H_2(g) \rightarrow 2 NH_3(g)$?

A. 25 grams of N_2 gas reacts with 75 grams of H_2 gas to form 50 grams of NH_3 gas

B. 28 grams of N_2 gas reacts with 6 grams of H_2 gas to form 34 grams of NH_3 gas

C. 15 moles of N_2 gas reacts with 45 moles of H_2 gas to form 30 moles of NH_3 gas

D. 5 molecules of N_2 gas reacts with 15 molecules of H_2 gas to form 10 molecules of NH_3 gas

E. None of the above

36. From the following reaction, if 0.2 mole of Al is allowed to react with 0.4 mole of Fe_2O_3, how many grams of aluminum oxide are produced?

$$2 Al + Fe_2O_3 \rightarrow 2 Fe + Al_2O_3$$

A. 2.8 g   B. 5.1 g   C. 10.2 g   D. 14.2 g   E. 18.6 g

37. In all of the following compounds, the oxidation number of hydrogen is +1, EXCEPT:

A. NH_3 B. $HClO_2$ C. H_2SO_4 D. NaH   E. none of the above

38. Which equation is NOT correctly classified by the type of chemical reaction?

A. $PbO + C \rightarrow Pb + CO$: single-replacement/non-redox

B. $2 Na + 2HCl \rightarrow 2 NaCl + H_2$: single-replacement/redox

C. $NaHCO_3 + HCl \rightarrow NaCl + H_2O + CO_2$: double-replacement/non-redox

D. $2 Na + H_2 \rightarrow 2 NaH$: synthesis/redox

E. All are correctly classified

39. What are the oxidation states of sulfur in H_2SO_4 and H_2SO_3, respectively?

A. +4 and +4   C. +2 and +4

B. +6 and +4   D. +4 and +2   E. +4 and +6

40. A latex balloon has a volume of 500 mL when filled with gas at a pressure of 780 torr and a temperature of 320 K. How many moles of gas does the balloon contain? (Use the ideal gas constant R = 0.08206 L·atm K^{-1} mol^{-1})

A. 0.0195   B. 0.822   C. 3.156   D. 18.87   E. 1.282

===

Practice Set 3: Questions 41–60

===

41. What is the term for a substance that causes the reduction of another substance in a redox reaction?

    A. oxidizing agent   **C.** anode

    B. reducing agent   **D.** cathode   **E.** none of the above

42. Which of the following is a method for balancing a redox equation in acidic solution by the half-reaction method?

    A. Multiply each half-reaction by a whole number, so that the number of electrons lost by the substance oxidized is equal to the electrons gained by the substance reduced

    B. Add the two half-reactions together and cancel identical species from each side of the equation

    C. Write a half-reaction for the substance oxidized and the substance reduced

    D. Balance the atoms in each half-reaction; balance oxygen with water and hydrogen with H^+

    E. All of the above

43. What is the formula mass of a molecule of $C_6H_{12}O_6$?

    A. 148 amu   **B.** 27 amu   **C.** 91 amu   **D.** 180 amu   **E.** None of the above

44. Is it possible to have a macroscopic sample of oxygen that has a mass of 12 atomic mass units?

    A. No, because oxygen is a gas at room temperature

    B. Yes, because it would have the same density as nitrogen

    C. No, because this is less than a macroscopic quantity

    D. Yes, but it would need to be made of isotopes of oxygen atoms

    E. No, because this is less than the mass of a single oxygen atom

45. What is the coefficient for O_2 when balanced with the lowest whole number coefficients?

    $C_2H_6 + O_2 \rightarrow CO_2 + H_2O$

    A. 3   **B.** 4   **C.** 6   **D.** 7   **E.** 9

46. Which element is reduced in the following redox reaction?

    $BaSO_4 + 4\,C \rightarrow BaS + 4\,CO$

    A. O in CO   **B.** Ba in BaS   **C.** S in BaS   **D.** C in CO   **E.** S in $BaSO_4$

47. Ethanol (C_2H_5OH) is blended with gasoline as a fuel additive. If combustion of ethanol produces carbon dioxide and water, what is the coefficient of oxygen in the balanced equation?

Spark

__C_2H_5OH (g) + __O_2 (g) → __CO_2 (g) + __H_2O (g)

A. 1   **B.** 2   **C.** 3   **D.** 6   **E.** None of the above

48. How many moles of C are in a 4.50 g sample, if the atomic mass of C is 12.011 amu?

A. 5.40 moles   **C.** 1.00 moles
B. 2.67 moles   **D.** 0.54 moles   **E.** 0.375 moles

49. Upon combustion analysis, a 6.84 g sample of a hydrocarbon yielded 8.98 grams of carbon dioxide. The percent, by mass, of carbon in the hydrocarbon is:

A. 18.6%   **B.** 23.7%   **C.** 35.8%   **D.** 11.4%   **E.** 52.8%

50. Select the balanced chemical equation:

A. $2 C_2H_5OH + 2 Na_2Cr_2O_7 + 8 H_2SO_4 \rightarrow 2 HC_2H_3O_2 + 2 Cr_2(SO_4)_3 + 4 Na_2SO_4 + 11 H_2O$
B. $2 C_2H_5OH + Na_2Cr_2O_7 + 8 H_2SO_4 \rightarrow 3 HC_2H_3O_2 + 2 Cr_2(SO_4)_3 + 2 Na_2SO_4 + 11 H_2O$
C. $C_2H_5OH + 2 Na_2Cr_2O_7 + 8 H_2SO_4 \rightarrow HC_2H_3O_2 + 2 Cr_2(SO_4)_3 + 2 Na_2SO_4 + 11 H_2O$
D. $C_2H_5OH + Na_2Cr_2O_7 + 2 H_2SO_4 \rightarrow HC_2H_3O_2 + Cr_2(SO_4)_3 + 2 Na_2SO_4 + 11 H_2O$
E. $3 C_2H_5OH + 2 Na_2Cr_2O_7 + 8 H_2SO_4 \rightarrow 3 HC_2H_3O_2 + 2 Cr_2(SO_4)_3 + 2 Na_2SO_4 + 11 H_2O$

51. Under acidic conditions, what is the sum of the coefficients in the balanced reaction below?

$Fe^{2+} + Cr_2O_7^{2-} \rightarrow Fe^{3+} + Cr^{3+}$

A. 8   **B.** 14   **C.** 17   **D.** 36   **E.** none of the above

52. Assuming STP, if 49 g of H_2SO_4 are produced in the following reaction, what volume of O_2 must be used in the reaction?

RuS (s) + O_2 + H_2O → Ru_2O_3 (s) + H_2SO_4

A. 20.6 liters   **C.** 28.3 liters
B. 31.2 liters   **D.** 29.1 liters   **E.** 25.2 liters

53. From the following reaction, if 0.20 mole of Al is allowed to react with 0.40 mole of Fe_2O_3, how many moles of iron are produced?

$2 Al + Fe_2O_3 \rightarrow 2 Fe + Al_2O_3$

A. 0.05 mole   **B.** 0.075 mole   **C.** 0.20 mole   **D.** 0.10 mole   **E.** 0.25 mole

54. What is the oxidation number of sulfur in the $S_2O_8^{2-}$ ion?

    A. −1   **B.** +7   **C.** +2   **D.** +6   **E.** +1

55. What are the oxidation numbers for the elements in Na_2CrO_4?

    A. +2 for Na, +5 for Cr and −6 for O   **C.** +1 for Na, +4 for Cr and −6 for O

    B. +2 for Na, +3 for Cr and −2 for O   **D.** +1 for Na, +6 for Cr and −2 for O

                                                  E. +1 for Na, +5 for Cr and −2 for O

56. What is the oxidation state of sulfur in sulfuric acid?

    A. +8   **B.** +6   **C.** −2   **D.** −6   **E.** +4

57. Which substance is oxidized in the following redox reaction?

$$HgCl_2\,(aq) + Sn^{2+}\,(aq) \rightarrow Sn^{4+}\,(aq) + Hg_2Cl_2\,(s) + Cl^-\,(aq)$$

    A. Hg_2Cl_2 **C.** Sn^{2+}

    B. Sn^{4+} **D.** $HgCl_2$ **E.** None of the above

58. Which of the following statements that is NOT true with respect to the balanced equation?

$$Na_2SO_4\,(aq) + BaCl_2\,(aq) \rightarrow 2\,NaCl\,(aq) + BaSO_4\,(s)$$

    A. Barium sulfate and sodium chloride are products

    B. Barium chloride is dissolved in water

    C. Barium sulfate is a solid

    D. $2\,NaCl\,(aq)$ could also be written as $Na_2Cl_2\,(aq)$

    E. Sodium sulfate has a coefficient of one

59. Which of the following represents 1 mol of phosphine gas (PH_3)?

    I. 22.4 L phosphine gas at STP

    II. 34.00 g phosphine gas

    III. 6.02×10^{23} phosphine molecules

    A. I only   **C.** III only

    B. II only   **D.** I and II only   **E.** I, II and III

60. Which of the following represents the oxidation of Co^{2+}?

    A. $Co \rightarrow Co^{2+} + 2\,e^-$ **C.** $Co^{2+} + 2\,e^- \rightarrow Co$

    B. $Co^{3+} + e^- \rightarrow Co^{2+}$ **D.** $Co^{2+} \rightarrow Co^{3+} + e^-$

                                           E. $Co^{3+} + 2\,e^- \rightarrow Co^+$

Practice Set 4: Questions 61–80

61. What is the term for a substance that causes oxidation in a redox reaction?

    A. oxidized   **C.** anode

    B. reducing agent   **D.** cathode   **E.** oxidizing agent

62. Carbon tetrachloride (CCl_4) is a potent hepatotoxin (toxic to the liver) commonly used in the past in fire extinguishers and as a refrigerant. What is the percent by mass of Cl in carbon tetrachloride?

    A. 25%   **B.** 66%   **C.** 78%   **D.** 92%   **E.** 33%

63. In order for a redox reaction to be balanced, which of the following is true?

    I. Total ionic charge of reactants must equal total ionic charge of products

    II. Atoms of each reactant must equal atoms of product

    III. Electron gain must equal electron loss

    A. I only   **C.** I and II only

    B. II only   **D.** I and III only   **E.** I, II and III

64. The mass percent of a compound is as follows: 71% Cl, 24% C and 4% H. If the molecular weight of the compound is 99 g/mol, what is the molecular formula of the compound?

    A. $Cl_2C_3H_6$ **C.** $ClCH_3$

    B. $Cl_2C_2H_4$ **D.** ClC_2H_2 **E.** CCl_4

65. In the early 1980s, benzene that had been used as a solvent for waxes and oils was listed as a carcinogen by the EPA. What is the molecular formula of benzene, if the empirical formula is C_1H_1 and the approximate molar mass is 78 g/mol?

    A. CH_{12} **B.** $C_{12}H_{12}$ **C.** CH   **D.** CH_6 **E.** C_6H_6

66. How many O atoms are in the formula unit $GaO(NO_3)_2$?

    A. 3   **B.** 4   **C.** 5   **D.** 7   **E.** 8

67. Which reaction represents the balanced reaction for the combustion of ethanol?

    A. $4 C_2H_5OH + 13 O_2 \rightarrow 8 CO_2 + 10 H_2$
    B. $C_2H_5OH + 3 O_2 \rightarrow 2 CO_2 + 3 H_2O$
    C. $C_2H_5OH + 2 O_2 \rightarrow 2CO_2 + 2 H_2O$
    D. $C_2H_5OH + O_2 \rightarrow CO_2 + H_2O$
    E. $C_2H_5OH + \frac{1}{2} O_2 \rightarrow 2 CO_2 + 3 H_2O$

68. What is the coefficient for O_2 when the following equation is balanced with the lowest whole number coefficients?

$$\_\_C_3H_7OH + \_\_O_2 \rightarrow \_\_CO_2 + \_\_H_2O$$

    A. 3   **B.** 6   **C.** 9   **D.** 13/2   **E.** 12

69. After balancing the following redox reaction, what is the coefficient of CO_2?

$$\_\_Co_2O_3 \ (s) + \_\_CO \ (g) \rightarrow \_\_Co \ (s) + \_\_CO_2 \ (g)$$

    A. 1   **B.** 2   **C.** 3   **D.** 4   **E.** 5

70. What is the term for the volume occupied by 1 mol of any gas at STP?

    A. STP volume   **C.** standard volume
    B. molar volume   **D.** Avogadro's volume   **E.** none of the above

71. Which substance listed below is the weakest oxidizing agent given the following spontaneous redox reaction?

$$Mg \ (s) + Sn^{2+} \ (aq) \rightarrow Mg^{2+} \ (aq) + Sn \ (s)$$

    A. Mg^{2+} **B.** Sn   **C.** Mg   **D.** Sn^{2+} **E.** none of the above

72. In the following reaction performed at 500 K, 18.0 moles of N_2 gas are mixed with 24.0 moles of H_2 gas. What is the percent yield of NH_3, if the reaction produces 13.5 moles of NH_3?

$$N_2 \ (g) + 3 H_2 \ (g) \rightarrow 2 NH_3 \ (g)$$

    A. 16%   **B.** 66%   **C.** 72%   **D.** 84%   **E.** 100%

73. How many grams of H_2O can be produced from the reaction of 25.0 grams of H_2 and 225 grams of O_2?

    A. 266 grams   **C.** 184 grams
    B. 223 grams   **D.** 27 grams   **E.** 2.5 grams

74. What is the oxidation number of Cl in $LiClO_2$?

   A. −1   **B.** +1   **C.** +3   **D.** +5   **E.** None of the above

75. In acidic conditions, what is the sum of the coefficients in the products of the balanced reaction?

$$MnO_4^- + C_3H_7OH \rightarrow Mn^{2+} + C_2H_5COOH$$

   A. 12   **B.** 16   **C.** 18   **D.** 20   **E.** 24

76. Which reaction is NOT correctly classified?

   A. PbO (*s*) + C (*s*) → Pb (*s*) + CO (*g*) : (double-replacement)
   B. CaO (*s*) + H_2O (*l*) → $Ca(OH)_2$ (*aq*) : (synthesis)
   C. $Pb(NO_3)_2$ (*aq*) + $2LiCl$ (*aq*) → 2 $LiNO_3$ (*aq*) + $PbCl_2$ (*s*) : (double-replacement)
   D. Mg (*s*) + 2 HCl (*aq*) → $MgCl_2$ (*aq*) + H_2 (*g*) : (single-replacement)
   E. All are classified correctly

77. The reactants for this chemical reaction are:

$$C_6H_{12}O_6 + 6\ H_2O + 6\ O_2 \rightarrow 6\ CO_2 + 12\ H_2O$$

   A. $C_6H_{12}O_6$, H_2O, O_2 and CO_2 **C.** $C_6H_{12}O_6$
   B. $C_6H_{12}O_6$ and H_2O **D.** $C_6H_{12}O_6$ and CO_2
                                                E. $C_6H_{12}O_6$, H_2O and O_2

78. What is the total charge of all the electrons in 4 grams of He? (Use Faraday constant F = 96,500 C/mol)

   A. 48,250 C   **C.** 193,000 C
   B. 96,500 C   **D.** 386,000 C   **E.** Cannot be determined

79. What is the oxidation number of iron in the compound $FeBr_3$?

   A. −2   **B.** +1   **C.** +2   **D.** +3   **E.** −1

80. What is the term for the amount of substance that contains 6.02×10^{23} particles?

   A. molar mass   **C.** Avogadro's number
   B. mole   **D.** formula mass
                                           E. none of the above

Stoichiometry – Answer Key

1: C	21: D	41: B	61: E
2: C	22: A	42: E	62: D
3: C	23: B	43: D	63: E
4: E	24: C	44: E	64: B
5: C	25: C	45: D	65: E
6: B	26: E	46: E	66: D
7: A	27: A	47: C	67: B
8: C	28: E	48: E	68: C
9: B	29: E	49: C	69: C
10: C	30: C	50: E	70: B
11: C	31: A	51: D	71: A
12: D	32: C	52: E	72: D
13: C	33: E	53: C	73: B
14: D	34: A	54: B	74: C
15: D	35: A	55: D	75: D
16: E	36: C	56: B	76: A
17: B	37: D	57: C	77: E
18: C	38: A	58: D	78: C
19: E	39: B	59: E	79: D
20: D	40: A	60: D	80: B

Thermochemistry

==

Practice Set 1: Questions 1–20

==

1. Which of the following statement regarding the symbol ΔG is NOT true?

    A. Specifies the enthalpy of the reaction
    B. Refers to the free energy of the reaction
    C. Predicts the spontaneity of a reaction
    D. Describes the effect of both enthalpy and entropy on a reaction
    E. None of the above

2. What happens to the kinetic energy of a gas molecule when the gas is heated?

    A. Depends on the gas
    B. Kinetic energy increases
    C. Kinetic energy decreases
    D. Kinetic energy remains constant
    E. None of the above

3. How much heat energy (in Joules) is required to heat 21.0 g of copper from 21.0 °C to 68.5 °C? (Use specific heat c of Cu = 0.382 J/g·°C)

    A. 462 J   B. 188 J   C. 522 J   D. 662 J   E. 381 J

4. For n moles of gas, which term expresses the kinetic energy?

    A. nPA, where n = number of moles of gas, P = total pressure and A = surface area of the container walls
    B. ½nPA, where n = number of moles of gas, P = total pressure and A = surface area of the container walls
    C. ½MV^2, where M = molar mass of the gas and V = volume of the container
    D. MV^2, where M = molar mass of the gas and V = volume of the container
    E. 3/2 nRT, where n = number of moles of gas, R = ideal gas constant and T = absolute temperature

5. Which of the following is NOT an endothermic process?

    A. Condensation of water vapor
    B. Boiling liquid
    C. Water evaporating
    D. Ice melting
    E. All are endothermic

---

6. What is true of an endothermic reaction if it causes a decrease in ΔS of the system?

   A. Only occurs at low temperatures when ΔS is insignificant
   B. Occurs if coupled to an endergonic reaction
   C. Never occurs because it decreases ΔS of the system
   D. Never occurs because ΔG is positive
   E. None of the above

7. Which of the following terms describe(s) energy contained in an object or transferred to an object?

   I. chemical   II. electrical   III. heat

   A. I only   **B.** II only   **C.** I and II only   **D.** I and III only   **E.** I, II and III

8. The greatest entropy is observed for which 10 g sample of CO_2?

   A. $CO_2\,(g)$ **B.** $CO_2\,(aq)$ **C.** $CO_2\,(s)$ **D.** $CO_2\,(l)$ **E.** All are equivalent

9. What is the term for a reaction that proceeds by absorbing heat energy?

   A. Isothermal reaction   **C.** Endothermic reaction
   B. Exothermic reaction   **D.** Spontaneous   **E.** None of the above

10. If a chemical reaction has $\Delta H = X$, $\Delta S = Y$, $\Delta G = X - RY$ and occurs at R °K, the reaction is:

   A. spontaneous   **C.** nonspontaneous
   B. at equilibrium   **D.** irreversible   **E.** cannot be determined

11. The thermodynamic systems that have high stability tend to demonstrate:

   A. maximum ΔH and maximum ΔS **C.** minimum ΔH and maximum ΔS
   B. maximum ΔH and minimum ΔS **D.** minimum ΔH and minimum ΔS
                                                           E. none of the above

12. Whether a reaction is endothermic or exothermic is determined by:

   A. an energy balance between bond breaking and bond forming, resulting in a net loss or gain of energy
   B. the presence of a catalyst
   C. the activation energy
   D. the physical state of the reaction system
   E. none of the above

13. What role does entropy play in chemical reactions?

   A. The entropy change determines whether the reaction occurs spontaneously
   B. The entropy change determines whether the chemical reaction is favorable
   C. The entropy determines how much product is actually produced
   D. The entropy change determines whether the reaction is exothermic or endothermic
   E. The entropy determines how much reactant remains

14. Calculate the value of $\Delta H°$ of reaction using provided bond energies.

   $H_2C=CH_2\,(g) + H_2\,(g) \rightarrow H_3C–CH_3\,(g)$

   C–C: 348 KJ   C≡C: 960 kJ

   C=C: 612 kJ   C–H: 412 kJ   H–H: 436 kJ

   A. –348 kJ   **B.** +134 kJ   **C.** –546 kJ   **D.** –124 kJ   **E.** –238 kJ

15. The bond dissociation energy is:

   I. useful in estimating the enthalpy change in a reaction
   II. the energy required to break a bond between two gaseous atoms
   III. the energy released when a bond between two gaseous atoms is broken

   A. I only   **C.** I and II only
   B. II only   **D.** I and III only   **E.** I, II and III

16. Based on the following reaction, which statement is true?

   $N_2 + O_2 \rightarrow 2\,NO$ (Use the value for enthalpy, $\Delta H = 43.3$ kcal)

   A. 43.3 kcal are consumed when 2.0 mole of O_2 reacts
   B. 43.3 kcal are consumed when 2.0 moles of NO are produced
   C. 43.3 kcal are produced when 1.0 g of N_2 reacts
   D. 43.3 kcal are consumed when 2.0 g of O_2 reacts
   E. 43.3 kcal are produced when 2.0 g of NO are produced

17. Which of the following properties of a gas is/are a state functions?

   I. temperature   II. heat   III. work

   A. I only   **C.** II and III only
   B. I and II only   **D.** I, II and III   **E.** II only

18. All of the following statements concerning temperature change as a substance is heated are correct, EXCEPT:

    A. As a liquid is heated, its temperature rises until its boiling point is reached

    B. During the time a liquid is changing to the gaseous state, the temperature gradually increases until all the liquid is changed

    C. As a solid is heated, its temperature rises until its melting point is reached

    D. During the time for a solid to melt to a liquid, the temperature remains constant

    E. The temperature remains the same during the phase change

19. Calculate the value of $\Delta H°$ of reaction for:

$$O=C=O \ (g) + 3 \ H_2 \ (g) \rightarrow CH_3–O–H \ (g) + H–O–H \ (g)$$

Use the following bond energies, $\Delta H°$:

C–C: 348 kJ	C=C: 612 kJ	C≡C: 960 kJ	C–H: 412 kJ
C–O: 360 kJ	C=O: 743 kJ	H–H: 436 kJ	H–O: 463 kJ

    A. –348 kJ   **C.** –191 kJ

    B. +612 kJ   **D.** –769 kJ   **E.** +5,779 kJ

20. Which statement(s) is/are true for ΔS?

    I. ΔS of the universe is conserved

    II. ΔS of a system is conserved

    III. ΔS of the universe increases with each reaction

    A. I only   **C.** III only

    B. II only   **D.** I and II only   **E.** I and III only

==

Practice Set 2: Questions 21–40

==

21. Which of the following reaction energies is the most endothermic?

A. 360 kJ/mole   **C.** 88 kJ/mole

B. –360 kJ/mole   **D.** –88 kJ/mole   **E.** 0 kJ/mole

22. A fuel cell contains hydrogen and oxygen gas that react explosively and the energy converts water to steam which drives a turbine to turn a generator that produces electricity. The fuel cell and the steam represent which forms of energy, respectively?

A. Electrical and heat energy   **C.** Chemical and heat energy

B. Electrical and chemical energy   **D.** Chemical and mechanical energy

     E. Nuclear and mechanical energy

23. Which of the following is true for the ΔG of formation for N_2 (g) at 25 °C?

A. 0 kJ/mol   **C.** negative

B. positive   **D.** 1 kJ/mol   **E.** more information is needed

24. Which of the statements best describes the following reaction?

$HC_2H_3O_2$ (*aq*) + NaOH (*aq*) → $NaC_2H_3O_2$ (*aq*) + H_2O (*l*)

A. Acetic acid and NaOH solutions produce sodium acetate and H_2O

B. Aqueous solutions of acetic acid and NaOH produce aqueous sodium acetate and H_2O

C. Acetic acid and NaOH solutions produce sodium acetate solution and H_2O

D. Acetic acid and NaOH produce sodium acetate and H_2O

E. An acid plus a base produce H_2O and a salt

25. If a chemical reaction is spontaneous, which value must be negative?

A. C_p **B.** ΔS **C.** ΔG **D.** ΔH **E.** K_{eq}

26. What is the purpose of the hollow walls in a closed hollow-walled container that is effective at maintaining the temperature inside?

A. To trap air trying to escape from the container, which minimizes convection

B. To act as an effective insulator, which minimizes convection

C. To act as an effective insulator, which minimizes conduction

D. To provide an additional source of heat for the container

E. Reactions occur within the walls that maintain the temperature within the container

27. If the heat of reaction is exothermic, which of the following is always true?

    A. Energy of the reactants is greater than the products

    B. Energy of the reactants is less than the products

    C. Reaction rate is fast

    D. Reaction rate is slow

    E. Energy of the reactants is equal to that of the products

28. How much heat must be absorbed to evaporate 16 g of NH_3 to its condensation point at $-33\ °C$? (Use heat of condensation for $NH_3 = 1,380$ J/g)

    A. 86.5 J   **C.** 118 J

    B. 2,846 J   **D.** 22,080 J

                               E. 1,380 J

29. Which of the reactions is the most exothermic, assuming that the following energy profiles have the same scale? (Use the notation of R = reactants and P = products)

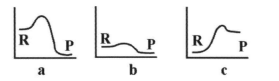

    A. a   **B.** b   **C.** c   **D.** d   **E.** Cannot be determined

30. What is the heat of formation of $NH_3\ (g)$ of the following reaction:

$$2\ NH_3\ (g) \rightarrow N_2\ (g) + 3\ H_2\ (g)$$

(Use $\Delta H° = 92.4$ kJ/mol)

    A. -92.4 kJ/mol   **C.** 46.2 kJ/mol

    B. -184.4 kJ/mol   **D.** 92.4 kJ/mol

                               E. -46.2 kJ/mol

31. If a chemical reaction has a positive ΔH and a negative ΔS, the reaction tends to be:

    A. at equilibrium   **C.** spontaneous

    B. nonspontaneous   **D.** irreversible

                               E. unable to be determined

32. What happens to the entropy of a system as the components of the system are introduced to a larger number of possible arrangements, such as when liquid water transforms into water vapor?

    A. Entropy of a system is solely dependent upon the amount of material undergoing reaction

    B. Entropy of a system is independent of introducing the components of the system to a larger number of possible arrangements

    C. Entropy increases because there are more ways for the energy to disperse

    D. Entropy decreases because there are less ways in which the energy can disperse

    E. Entropy increases because there are less ways for the energy to disperse

33. Which of the following quantities is needed to calculate the amount of heat energy released as water turns to ice at 0 °C?

    A. Heat of condensation for water and the mass

    B. Heat of vaporization for water and the mass

    C. Heat of fusion for water and the mass

    D. Heat of solidification for water and the mass

    E. Heat of fusion for water only

34. A nuclear power plant uses ^{235}U to convert water to steam that drives a turbine which turns a generator to produce electricity. What are the initial and final forms of energy, respectively?

    A. Heat energy and electrical energy

    B. Nuclear energy and electrical energy

    C. Chemical energy and mechanical energy

    D. Chemical energy and heat energy

    E. Nuclear energy and mechanical energy

35. Which statement(s) is/are correct for the entropy?

    I. Higher for a sample of gas than for the same sample of liquid

    II. A measure of the disorder in a system

    III. Available energy for conversion into mechanical work

    A. I only   **C.** III only

    B. II only   **D.** I and II only   **E.** I, II and III

36. Given the following data, what is the heat of formation for ethanol?

$$C_2H_5OH + 3\ O_2 \rightarrow 2\ CO_2 + 3\ H_2O : \Delta H = 327.0\ kcal/mole$$

$$H_2O \rightarrow H_2 + \frac{1}{2}\ O_2 : \Delta H = +68.3\ kcal/mole$$

$$C + O_2 \rightarrow CO_2 : \Delta H = -94.1\ kcal/mole$$

A. –720.1 kcal   **C.** +62.6 kcal

B. –327.0 kcal   **D.** +720.1 kcal   **E.** +327.0 kcal

37. Based on the reaction shown, which statement is true?

$$S + O_2 \rightarrow SO_2 + 69.8\ kcal$$

A. 69.8 kcal are consumed when 32.1 g of sulfur reacts

B. 69.8 kcal are produced when 32.1 g of sulfur reacts

C. 69.8 kcal are consumed when 1 g of sulfur reacts

D. 69.8 kcal are produced when 1 g of sulfur reacts

E. 69.8 kcal are produced when 1 g of sulfur dioxide is produced

38. In the reaction, $2\ H_2\ (g) + O_2\ (g) \rightarrow 2\ H_2O\ (g)$, entropy is:

A. increasing   **C.** inversely proportional

B. the same   **D.** decreasing

                    E. unable to be determined

39. For an isolated system, which of the following can NOT be exchanged between the system and its surroundings?

        I. Temperature   II. Matter   III. Energy

A. I only   **C.** III only

B. II only   **D.** II and III only   **E.** I, II and III

40. Which is a state function?

        I. ΔG II. ΔH III. ΔS

A. I only   **C.** III only

B. II only   **D.** I and II only   **E.** I, II and III

===

Practice Set 3: Questions 41–60

===

41. To simplify comparisons, the energy value of fuels is expressed in units of:

A. kcal/g   **C.** J/kcal

B. kcal/L   **D.** kcal/mol   **E.** kcal

42. Which process is slowed down when an office worker places a lid on a hot cup of coffee?

       I. Radiation   II. Conduction   III. Convection

A. I only   **C.** III only

B. II only   **D.** I and III only   **E.** I, II and III

43. Which statement below is always true for a spontaneous chemical reaction?

A. $\Delta S_{sys} - \Delta S_{surr} = 0$ **C.** $\Delta S_{sys} + \Delta S_{surr} < 0$

B. $\Delta S_{sys} + \Delta S_{surr} > 0$ **D.** $\Delta S_{sys} + \Delta S_{surr} = 0$

                                           E. $\Delta S_{sys} - \Delta S_{surr} < 0$

44. A fuel cell contains hydrogen and oxygen gas that react explosively and the energy converts water to steam, which drives a turbine to turn a generator that produces electricity. What energy changes are employed in the process?

       I. Mechanical → electrical energy

       II. Heat → mechanical energy

       III. Chemical → heat energy

A. I only   **C.** I and II only

B. II only   **D.** I and III only   **E.** I, II and III

45. Determine the value of $\Delta E°_{rxn}$ for this reaction, whereby the standard enthalpy of reaction ($\Delta H°_{rxn}$) is –311.5 kJ mol^{-1}:

       $C_2H_2\,(g) + 2\,H_2\,(g) \rightarrow C_2H_6\,(g)$

A. –306.5 kJ mol^{-1} **C.** +346.0 kJ mol^{-1}

B. –318.0 kJ mol^{-1} **D.** +306.5 kJ mol^{-1} **E.** +466 kJ mol^{-1}

46. Which is true for the thermodynamic functions G, H and S in $\Delta G = \Delta H - T\Delta S$?

    A. G refers to the universe, H to the surroundings and S to the system

    B. G, H and S refer to the system

    C. G and H refers to the surroundings and S to the system

    D. G and H refer to the system and S to the surroundings

    E. G and S refers to the system and H to the surroundings

47. Which reaction is accompanied by an *increase* in entropy?

    A. $Na_2CO_3 (s) + CO_2 (g) + H_2O (g) \rightarrow 2\ NaHCO_3 (s)$

    B. $BaO (s) + CO_2 (g) \rightarrow BaCO_3 (s)$

    C. $CH_4 (g) + H_2O (g) \rightarrow CO (g) + 3\ H_2 (g)$

    D. $ZnS (s) + 3/2\ O_2 (g) \rightarrow ZnO (s) + SO_2 (g)$

    E. $N_2 (g) + 3\ H_2 (g) \rightarrow 2\ NH_3 (g)$

48. Under standard conditions, which reaction has the largest difference between the energy of reaction and enthalpy?

    A. C (*graphite*) $\rightarrow$ C (*diamond*)

    B. C (*graphite*) $+ O_2 (g) \rightarrow$ C (*diamond*)

    C. 2 C (*graphite*) $+ O_2 (g) \rightarrow 2\ CO (g)$

    D. C (*graphite*) $+ O_2 (g) \rightarrow CO_2 (g)$

    E. $CO (g) + NO_2 (g) \rightarrow CO_2 (g) + NO (g)$

49. Which type of reaction tends to be the most stable?

    I. Isothermic   II. Exergonic   III. Endergonic

    A. I only   **C.** III only

    B. II only   **D.** I and II only   **E.** I and III only

50. Which is true for the thermodynamic functions G, H and S in $\Delta G = \Delta H - T\Delta S$?

    A. G refers to the universe, H to the surroundings and S to the system

    B. G, H and S refer to the system

    C. G and H refers to the surroundings and S to the system

    D. G and H refer to the system and S to the surroundings

    E. G and S refers to the system and H to the surroundings

51. Which of the following statements is true for the following reaction? (Use the change in enthalpy, $\Delta H° = -113.4$ kJ/mol and the change in entropy, $\Delta S° = -145.7$ J/K mol)

$$2 \text{ NO } (g) + \text{O}_2 (g) \rightarrow 2 \text{ NO}_2 (g)$$

   A. Reaction is at equilibrium at 25 °C under standard conditions

   B. Reaction is spontaneous at only high temperatures

   C. Reaction is spontaneous only at low temperatures

   D. Reaction is spontaneous at all temperatures

   E. $\Delta G°$ becomes more favorable as temperature increases

52. Which of the following expressions defines enthalpy? (Use the conventions: q = heat, U = internal energy, P = pressure and V = volume)

   A. $q - \Delta U$ **B.** $U + q$ **C.** q **D.** ΔU **E.** $U + PV$

53. Which statement is true regarding entropy?

   I. It is a state function

   II. It is an extensive property

   III. It has an absolute zero value

   A. I only   **C.** I and II only

   B. III only   **D.** I and III only   **E.** I, II and III

54. Where does the energy released during an exothermic reaction originate from?

   A. Kinetic energy of the surrounding

   B. Kinetic energy of the reacting molecules

   C. Potential energy of the reacting molecules

   D. Thermal energy of the reactants

   E. Potential energy of the surrounding

55. The species in the reaction $\text{KClO}_3 (s) \rightarrow \text{KCl } (s) + 3/2\text{O}_2 (g)$ have the values for standard enthalpies of formation at 25 °C. At constant physical states, assume that the values of $\Delta H°$ and $\Delta S°$ are constant throughout a broad temperature range. Which of the following conditions may apply for the reaction? (Use $\text{KClO}_3 (s)$ with $\Delta H_f° = -391.2$ kJ mol^{-1} and $\text{KCl } (s)$ with $\Delta H_f° = -436.8$ kJ mol^{-1})

   A. Nonspontaneous at low temperatures, but spontaneous at high temperatures

   B. Spontaneous at low temperatures, but nonspontaneous at high temperatures

   C. Nonspontaneous at all temperatures over a broad temperature range

   D. Spontaneous at all temperatures over a broad temperature range

   E. No conclusion can be drawn about spontaneity based on the information

56. What is the standard enthalpy change for the reaction?

$$P_4\ (s) + 6\ Cl_2\ (g) \rightarrow 4\ PCl_3\ (l) \quad \Delta H^\circ = -1,289\ kJ$$

$$3\ P_4\ (s) + 18\ Cl_2\ (g) \rightarrow 12\ PCl_3\ (l)$$

A. 426 kJ   **C.** −366 kJ

B. −1,345 kJ   **D.** 1,289 kJ   **E.** −3,837 kJ

57. Which of the following reactions is endothermic?

A. $PCl_3 + Cl_2 \rightarrow PCl_5 + heat$ **C.** $CH_4 + NH_3 + heat \rightarrow HCN + 3\ H_2$

B. $2\ NO_2 \rightarrow N_2 + 2\ O_2 + heat$ **D.** $NH_3 + HBr \rightarrow NH_4Br$

               E. $PCl_3 + Cl_2 \rightarrow PCl_5 + heat$

58. When the system undergoes a spontaneous reaction, is it possible for entropy of a system to decrease?

A. No, because this violates the second law of thermodynamics

B. No, because this violates the first law of thermodynamics

C. Yes, but only if the reaction is endothermic

D. Yes, but only if the entropy gain of the environment is greater than the entropy loss in the system

E. Yes, but only if the entropy gain of the environment is smaller than the entropy loss in the system

59. A 500 ml beaker of distilled water is placed under a bell jar, which is then covered by a layer of opaque insulation. After several days, some of the water evaporated. The contents of the bell jar are what kind of system?

A. endothermic   **C.** closed

B. exergonic   **D.** open   **E.** isolated

60. Which law explains the observation that the amount of heat transfer accompanying a change in one direction is equal in magnitude but opposite in sign to the amount of heat transfer in the opposite direction?

A. Law of Conservation of Mass

B. Law of Definite Proportions

C. Avogadro's Law

D. Boyle's Law

E. Law of Conservation of Energy

===

Practice Set 4: Questions 61–80

===

61. What is the term for a reaction that proceeds by releasing heat energy?

A. Endothermic reaction
B. Isothermal reaction

C. Exothermic reaction
D. Nonspontaneous
E. None of the above

62. If a stationary gas has a kinetic energy of 500 J at 25 °C, what is its kinetic energy at 50 °C?

A. 125 J   **B.** 450 J   C. 540 J   D. 1,120 J   E. 270 J

63. Which is NOT true for entropy in a closed system according to the equation $\Delta S = Q / T$?

A. Entropy is a measure of energy dispersal of the system
B. Equation is only valid for a reversible process
C. Changes due to heat transfer are greater at low temperatures
D. Disorder of the system decreases as heat is transferred out of the system
E. Increases as temperature decreases

64. In which of the following pairs of physical changes both processes are exothermic?

A. Melting and condensation
B. Freezing and condensation

C. Sublimation and evaporation
D. Freezing and sublimation
E. None of the above

65. A fuel cell contains hydrogen and oxygen gas that react explosively and the energy converts water to steam which drives a turbine to turn a generator that produces electricity. What are the initial and final forms of energy, respectively?

A. Chemical and electrical energy
B. Nuclear and electrical energy

C. Chemical and mechanical energy
D. Chemical and heat energy
E. Nuclear and mechanical energy

66. Which must be true concerning a solution at equilibrium where chemicals are mixed in a redox reaction and allowed to come to equilibrium?

A. $\Delta G° = \Delta G$
B. $E = 0$

C. $\Delta G° < 1$
D. $K = 1$ E. $K < 1$

---

67. A solid sample at room temperature spontaneously sublimes forming a gas. This change in state is accompanied by which of the changes in the sample?

A. Entropy decreases and energy increases

B. Entropy increases and energy decreases

C. Entropy and energy decrease

D. Entropy and energy increase

E. Entropy and energy are equal

68. At constant temperature and pressure, a negative ΔG indicates that the:

A. reaction is nonspontaneous

B. reaction is fast

C. reaction is spontaneous

D. reaction is endothermic

E. $\Delta S > 0$

69. The process of H_2O (*g*) → H_2O (*l*) is nonspontaneous under pressure of 760 torr and temperatures of 378 K because:

A. $\Delta H = T\Delta S$ B. $\Delta G < 0$ C. $\Delta H > 0$ D. $\Delta H < T\Delta S$ E. $\Delta H > T\Delta S$

70. Consider the contribution of entropy to the spontaneity of the reaction:

$$2\ Al_2O_3\ (s) \rightarrow 4\ Al\ (s) + 3\ O_2\ (g),\ \Delta G = +138\ kcal.$$

As written, the reaction is [   ] and the entropy of the system [   ].

A. non-spontaneous… decreases

B. non-spontaneous… increases

C. spontaneous… decreases

D. spontaneous… increases

E. non-spontaneous… does not change

71. The ΔG of a reaction is the maximum energy that the reaction releases to do:

A. P–V work only

B. work and release heat

C. any type of work

D. non P–V work only

E. work and generate heat

72. Which of the following represent forms of internal energy?

    I. bond energy   II. thermal energy   III. gravitational energy

A. I only   B. II only   C. I and II only   D. I and III only   E. I, II and III

73. If it takes energy to break bonds and energy is gained in the formation of bonds, how can some reactions be exothermic, while others are endothermic?

A. Some products have more energy than others and always require energy to be formed

B. Some reactants have more energetic bonds than others and always release energy

C. It is the total number of bonds that is determinative. Since all bonds have same amount of energy, the net gain or net loss of energy depends on the number of bonds

D. It is the total amount of energy that is determinative. Some bonds are stronger than others, so there is a net gain or net loss of energy when formed

E. None of the above

74. Which constant is represented by A in the following calculation to determine how much heat is required to convert 60 g of ice at −25 °C to steam at 320 °C?

$$\text{Total heat} = [(A)\cdot(60\text{ g})\cdot(25\text{ °C})] + [(\text{heat of fusion})\cdot(60\text{ g})] +$$
$$+ [(4.18\text{ J/g}\cdot\text{°C})\cdot(60\text{ g})\cdot(100\text{ °C})] + [(B)\cdot(60\text{ g})] + [(C)\cdot(60\text{ g})\cdot(220\text{ °C})]$$

A. Specific heat of water   **C.** Heat of condensation

B. Heat of vaporization of water   **D.** Heat capacity of steam   **E.** Specific heat of ice

75. The heat of formation of water vapor is:

A. positive, but greater than the heat of formation for H_2O (*l*)

B. positive and smaller than the heat of formation for H_2O (*l*)

C. negative, but greater than the heat of formation for H_2O (*l*)

D. negative and smaller than the heat of formation for H_2O (*l*)

E. positive and equal to the heat of formation for H_2O (*l*)

76. Entropy can be defined as the amount of:

A. equilibrium in a system

B. chemical bonds that are changed during a reaction

C. energy required to initiate a reaction

D. energy required to rearrange chemical bonds

E. disorder in a system

77. Which is true of an atomic fission bomb according to the conservation of mass and energy law?

A. The mass of the bomb and the fission products are identical

B. A small amount of mass is converted into energy

C. The energy of the bomb and the fission products are identical

D. The mass of the fission bomb is greater than the mass of the products

E. None of the above

78. Once an object enters a black hole, astronomers consider it to have left the universe which means the universe is:

A. entropic   **B.** isolated   **C.** closed   **D.** open   **E.** exergonic

79. Which ranking from lowest to highest entropy per gram of NaCl is correct?

A. NaCl (*s*) < NaCl (*l*) < NaCl (*aq*) < NaCl (*g*)

B. NaCl (*s*) < NaCl (*l*) < NaCl (*g*) < NaCl (*aq*)

C. NaCl (*g*) < NaCl (*aq*) < NaCl (*l*) < NaCl (*s*)

D. NaCl (*s*), NaCl (*aq*), NaCl (*l*), NaCl (*g*)

E. NaCl (*l*) < NaCl (*aq*) < NaCl (*g*) < NaCl (*s*)

80. For a closed system, what can be exchanged between the system and its surroundings?

    I. Heat   II. Matter   III. Energy

  A. I only   **B.** II only   **C.** III only   **D.** I and III only   **E.** I, II and III

Thermochemistry – Answer Key

1: A	21: A	41: A	61: C
2: B	22: C	42: C	62: C
3: E	23: A	43: B	63: C
4: E	24: B	44: E	64: B
5: A	25: C	45: A	65: A
6: D	26: C	46: B	66: B
7: E	27: A	47: C	67: D
8: A	28: D	48: C	68: C
9: C	29: A	49: B	69: E
10: E	30: E	50: B	70: B
11: C	31: B	51: C	71: D
12: A	32: C	52: E	72: C
13: B	33: D	53: C	73: D
14: D	34: B	54: C	74: E
15: C	35: D	55: D	75: C
16: B	36: A	56: E	76: E
17: A	37: B	57: C	77: B
18: B	38: D	58: D	78: D
19: C	39: D	59: E	79: A
20: C	40: E	60: E	80: D

Equilibrium and Reaction Rates

===

Practice Set 1: Questions 1–20

===

1. What is the general equilibrium constant (K_{eq}) expression for the following reversible reaction?

$$2\,A + 3\,B \leftrightarrow C$$

A. $K_{eq} = [C] / [A]^2 \cdot [B]^3$

C. $K_{eq} = [A] \cdot [B] / [C]$

B. $K_{eq} = [C] / [A] \cdot [B]$

D. $K_{eq} = [A]^2 \cdot [B]^3 / [C]$　　　**E.** none of the above

2. What are gases A and B likely to be, if a mixture of gas A and B has the average velocity of gas A twice that of B?

A. Ar and Kr　　　**B.** N and Fe　　　**C.** Ne and Ar　　　**D.** Mg and K　　　**E.** B and Ne

3. For a hypothetical reaction, $A + B \rightarrow C$, predict which reaction occurs at the slowest rate from the following reaction conditions.

Reaction	Activation energy	Temperature
1	103 kJ/mol	15 °C
2	46 kJ/mol	22 °C
3	103 kJ/mol	24 °C
4	46 kJ/mol	30 °C

A. 1　　　**B.** 2　　　**C.** 3　　　**D.** 4　　　**E.** requires more information

4. From the data below, what is the order of the reaction with respect to reactant A?

Determining Rate Law from Experimental Data

$$A + B \rightarrow \text{Products}$$

Exp.	Initial [A]	Initial [B]	Initial Rate M/s
1	0.015	0.022	0.125
2	0.030	0.044	0.500
3	0.060	0.044	0.500
4	0.060	0.066	1.125
5	0.085	0.088	?

A. Zero　　　**B.** First　　　**C.** Second　　　**D.** Third　　　**E.** Fourth

5. For the combustion of ethanol (C_2H_6O) to form carbon dioxide and water, what is the rate at which carbon dioxide is produced, if the ethanol is consumed at a rate of 4.0 M s^{-1}?

A. 1.5 M s^{-1}

C. 8.0 M s^{-1}

B. 12.0 M s^{-1}

D. 9.0 M s^{-1}

E. 10.0 M s^{-1}

6. Which is the correct equilibrium constant (K_{eq}) expression for the following reaction?

$$2\ Ag\ (s) + Cl_2\ (g) \leftrightarrow 2\ AgCl\ (s)$$

A. $K_{eq} = [AgCl] / [Ag]^2 \times [Cl_2]$

C. $K_{eq} = [AgCl]^2 / [Ag]^2 \times [Cl_2]$

B. $K_{eq} = [2AgCl] / [2Ag] \times [Cl_2]$

D. $K_{eq} = 1 / [Cl_2]$

E. $K_{eq} = [2AgCl]^2 / [2Ag]^2 \times [Cl_2]$

7. The position of the equilibrium for a system where $K_{eq} = 6.3 \times 10^{-14}$ can be described as being favored for [   ] and the concentration of products is relatively [   ].

A. the left; large

C. the right; large

B. the left; small

D. the right; small

E. neither direction; large

8. What can be deduced about the activation energy of a reaction that takes billions of years to go to completion and a reaction that takes only a fraction of a millisecond?

A. The slow reaction has a high activation energy, while the fast reaction has a low activation energy

B. The slow reaction must have a low activation energy, while the fast reaction must have a high activation energy

C. The activation energy of both reactions is very low

D. The activation energy of both reactions is very high

E. The activation energy of both reactions is equal

9. Which influences the rate of a chemical reaction?

I. catalyst

II. temperature

III. concentration

A. I only

C. I and III only

B. I and II only

D. II and III only

E. I, II and III

Questions **10** through **14** are based on the following:

Energy profiles for four reactions (with the same scale).

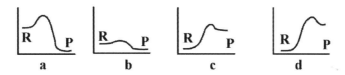

R = reactants   P = products

10. Which reaction requires the most energy?

  A. a   **B.** b   **C.** c   **D.** d   **E.** None of the above

11. Which reaction has the highest activation energy?

  A. a   **B.** b   **C.** c   **D.** d   **E.** c and d

12. Which reaction has the lowest activation energy?

  A. a   **B.** b   **C.** c   **D.** d   **E.** a and b

13. Which reaction proceeds the slowest?

  A. a   **B.** b   **C.** c   **D.** d   **E.** c and d

14. If the graphs are for the same reaction, which most likely has a catalyst?

  A. a   **B.** b   **C.** c   **D.** d   **E.** All have a catalyst

15. What is an explanation for the observation that the reaction stops before all reactants are converted to products in the following reaction?

$$NH_3\,(aq) + HC_2H_3O_2\,(aq) \rightarrow NH_4^+\,(aq) + C_2H_3O_2^-\,(aq)$$

  A. The catalyst is depleted
  B. The reverse rate increases, while the forward rate decreases until they are equal
  C. As [products] increases, the acetic acid begins to dissociate, stopping the reaction
  D. As [reactants] decreases, NH_3 and $HC_2H_3O_2$ molecules stop colliding
  E. As [products] increases, NH_3 and $HC_2H_3O_2$ molecules stop colliding

16. What is the term for the principle that the rate of reaction is regulated by the frequency, energy and orientation of molecules striking each other?

A. orientation theory

B. frequency theory

C. energy theory

D. collision theory

E. rate theory

17. What is the effect on the energy of the activated complex and on the rate of the reaction when a catalyst is added to a chemical reaction?

A. Energy of the activated complex increases and the reaction rate decreases

B. Energy of the activated complex decreases and the reaction rate increases

C. Energy of the activated complex and the reaction rate increase

D. Energy of the activated complex and the reaction rate decrease

E. Energy of the activated complex remains the same, while the reaction rate decreases

18. Which change shifts the equilibrium to the right for the reversible reaction in an aqueous solution?

$$HNO_2 \, (aq) \leftrightarrow H^+ \, (aq) + NO_2^- \, (aq)$$

I. Add solid NaOH

II. Decrease $[NO_2^-]$

III. Decrease $[H^+]$

IV. Increase $[HNO_2]$

A. I and II only

B. I and III only

C. III and IV only

D. I, II and IV only

E. I, II, III and IV

19. Which conditions would favor driving the reaction to completion?

$$2 \, N_2 \, (g) + 6 \, H_2O \, (g) + heat \leftrightarrow 4 \, NH_3 \, (g) + 3 \, O_2 \, (g)$$

A. Increasing the reaction temperature

B. Continual addition of NH_3 gas to the reaction mixture

C. Decreasing the pressure on the reaction vessel

D. Continual removal of N_2 gas

E. Decreases reaction temperature

20. The system, $H_2 \, (g) + X_2 \, (g) \leftrightarrow 2 \, HX \, (g)$ has a value of 24.4 for K_c. A catalyst was introduced into a reaction within a 4.0-liters reactor containing 0.20 moles of H_2, 0.20 moles of X_2 and 0.800 moles of HX. The reaction proceeds in which direction?

A. to the right, $Q > K_c$

B. to the left, $Q > K_c$

C. to the right, $Q < K_c$

D. to the left, $Q < K_c$

E. requires more information

Practice Set 2: Questions 21–40

21. Which is the K_c equilibrium expression for the following reaction?

$$4 \, CuO \, (s) + CH_4 \, (g) \leftrightarrow CO_2 \, (g) + 4 \, Cu \, (s) + 2 \, H_2O \, (g)$$

   A. $[Cu]^4 / [CuO]^4$ **C.** $[CH_4] / [CO_2][H_2O]^2$

   B. $[CH_4]^2 / [CO_2]\cdot[H_2O]$ **D.** $[CuO]^4 / [Cu]^4$ **E.** $[CO_2][H_2O]^2 / [CH_4]$

22. Which of the following concentrations of CH_2Cl_2 should be used in the rate law for Step 2, if CH_2Cl_2 is a product of the fast (first) step and a reactant of the slow (second) step?

   A. $[CH_2Cl_2]$ at equilibrium

   B. $[CH_2Cl_2]$ in Step 2 cannot be predicted because Step 1 is the fast step

   C. Zero moles per liter

   D. $[CH_2Cl_2]$ after Step 1 is completed

   E. None of the above

23. What is the term for a substance that allows a reaction to proceed faster by lowering the energy of activation?

   A. rate barrier   **C.** collision energy

   B. energy barrier   **D.** activation energy   **E.** catalyst

24. Which statement is true for the grams of products present after a chemical reaction reaches equilibrium?

   A. Must equal the grams of the initial reactants

   B. May be less than, equal to, or greater than the grams of reactants present, depending upon the chemical reaction

   C. Must be greater than the grams of the initial reactants

   D. Must be less than the grams of the initial reactants

   E. None of the above

25. What is the rate law when rates were measured at different concentrations for the dissociation of hydrogen gas: $H_2 \, (g) \rightarrow 2 \, H \, (g)$?

$[H_2]$	Rate M/s s^{-1}
1.0	1.3×10^5
1.5	2.6×10^5
2.0	5.2×10^5

   A. rate $= k^2[H] / [H_2]$ **C.** rate $= k[H_2]^2$

   B. rate $= k[H]^2 / [H_2]$ **D.** rate $= k[H_2] / [H]^2$ **E.** requires more information

26. What is the equilibrium constant (K_{eq}) expression for the following reaction at 26 °C? (Use the value of $\Delta G°_{rxn}$ = –68.4 kJ/mol and the universal gas constant R = 8.314 J/mol·K)

$$2 \text{ NO } (g) + \text{O}_2 (g) \leftrightarrow 2 \text{ NO}_2 (g)$$

A. 8.77×10^{11} **C.** 4.72×10^{8}

B. 7.37×10^{-4} **D.** 3.64×10^{6} **E.** 6.16×10^{9}

27. Which statement is NOT correct for $a\text{A} + b\text{B} \rightarrow d\text{D} + e\text{E}$ whereby rate = $k[\text{A}]^q[\text{B}]^r$?

  A. The overall order of the reaction is $q + r$
  B. The exponents q and r are equal to the coefficients a and b, respectively
  C. The exponents q and r must be determined experimentally
  D. The exponents q and r are often integers
  E. The symbol k represents the rate constant

28. Which is the correct equilibrium constant (K_{eq}) expression for the following reaction?

$$\text{CO } (g) + 2 \text{ H}_2 (g) \leftrightarrow \text{CH}_3\text{OH } (l)$$

  A. $K_{eq} = 1 / [\text{CO}]\cdot[\text{H}_2]^2$ **C.** $K_{eq} = [\text{CH}_3\text{OH}] / [\text{CO}]\cdot[\text{H}_2]^2$
  B. $K_{eq} = [\text{CO}]\cdot[\text{H}_2]^2$ **D.** $K_{eq} = [\text{CH}_3\text{OH}] / [\text{CO}]\cdot[\text{H}_2]$
              E. None of the above

Questions **29-32** are based on the following graph and net reaction:

The reaction proceeds in two consecutive steps.

$$\text{XY} + \text{Z} \leftrightarrow \text{XYZ} \leftrightarrow \text{X} + \text{YZ}$$

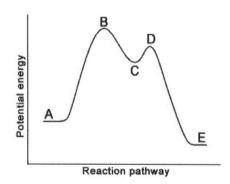

29. Where is the activated complex for this reaction?

  A. A   **C.** C

  B. A and C   **D.** E   **E.** B and D

30. The activation energy of the slow step for the forward reaction is given by:

    A. A → B   **C.** B → C

    B. A → C   **D.** C → E   **E.** A → E

31. The activation energy of the slow step for the reverse reaction is given by:

    A. C → A   **C.** C → B

    B. E → C   **D.** E → D   **E.** E → A

32. The change in energy (ΔE) of the overall reaction is given by the difference between:

    A. A and B   **C.** A and C

    B. A and E   **D.** B and D   **E.** B and C

33. Which of the following increases the collision energy of gaseous molecules?

    I. Increasing the temperature

    II. Adding a catalyst

    III. Increasing the concentration

    A. I only   **C.** III only

    B. II only   **D.** I and II only   **E.** I and III only

34. Which of the following conditions favors the formation of NO (*g*) in a closed container?

    N_2 (*g*) + O_2 (*g*) ↔ 2 NO (*g*)

    (Use ΔH = +181 kJ/mol)

    A. Increasing the temperature

    B. Decreasing the temperature

    C. Increasing the pressure

    D. Decreasing the pressure

    E. Decreasing the temperature and decreasing the pressure

35. A chemical system is considered to have reached dynamic equilibrium when the:

    A. activation energy of the forward reaction equals the activation energy of the reverse reaction

    B. rate of production of each of the products equals the rate of their consumption by the reverse reaction

    C. frequency of collisions between the reactant molecules equals the frequency of collisions between the product molecules

    D. sum of the concentrations of each of the reactant species equals the sum of the concentrations of each of the product species

    E. none of the above

36. Chemical equilibrium is reached in a system when:

   A. complete conversion of reactants to products has occurred
   B. product molecules begin reacting with each other
   C. reactant concentrations steadily decrease
   D. reactant concentrations steadily increase
   E. product and reactant concentrations remain constant

37. At a given temperature, $K = 46.0$ for the reaction:

$$4 \text{ HCl } (g) + O_2 (g) \leftrightarrow 2 \text{ H}_2\text{O } (g) + 2 \text{ Cl}_2 (g)$$

At equilibrium, [HCl] = 0.150, [O_2] = 0.395 and [H_2O] = 0.625. What is the concentration of Cl_2 at equilibrium?

   A. 0.153 M   **B.** 0.444 M   **C.** 1.14 M   **D.** 0.00547 M   **E.** 2.64 M

38. If, at equilibrium, reactant concentrations are slightly smaller than product concentrations, the equilibrium constant would be:

   A. slightly greater than 1   **C.** much lower than 1
   B. slightly lower than 1   **D.** much greater than 1
                                          E. equal to zero

39. Hydrogen gas reacts with iron (III) oxide to form iron metal (which produces steel), as shown in the reaction below. Which statement is NOT correct concerning the equilibrium system?

$$\text{Fe}_2\text{O}_3 (s) + 3 \text{ H}_2 (g) + heat \leftrightarrow 2 \text{ Fe } (s) + 3 \text{ H}_2\text{O } (g)$$

   A. Continually removing water from the reaction chamber increases the yield of iron
   B. Decreasing the volume of hydrogen gas reduces the yield of iron
   C. Lowering the reaction temperature increases the concentration of hydrogen gas
   D. Increasing the pressure on the reaction chamber increases the formation of products
   E. Decreasing the pressure on the reaction chamber favors the formation of products

40. Which of the changes shifts the equilibrium to the right for the following reversible reaction?

$$\text{CO } (g) + \text{H}_2\text{O } (g) \leftrightarrow \text{CO}_2 (g) + \text{H}_2 (g) + heat$$

   A. increasing volume   **C.** increasing [CO_2]
   B. increasing temperature   **D.** adding a catalyst
                                          E. increasing [CO]

===

Practice Set 3: Questions 41–60

===

41. Which is the correct equilibrium constant (K_{eq}) expression for the following reaction?

$$4 \, NH_3 \, (g) + 5 \, O_2 \, (g) \leftrightarrow 4 \, NO \, (g) + 6 \, H_2O \, (g)$$

A. $K_{eq} = [NO]^4 \times [H_2O]^6 / [NH_3]^4 \times [O_2]^5$

B. $K_{eq} = [NH_3]^4 \times [O_2]^5 / [NO]^4 \times [H_2O]^6$

C. $K_{eq} = [NO] \times [H_2O] / [NH_3] \times [O_2]$

D. $K_{eq} = [NH_3] \times [O_2] / [NO] \times [H_2O]$

E. $K_{eq} = [NH_3]^2 \times [O_2]^5 / [NO]^2 \times [H_2O]^3$

42. Carbonic acid equilibrium in blood:

$$CO_2 \, (g) + H_2O \, (l) \leftrightarrow H_2CO_3 \, (aq) \leftrightarrow H^+ \, (aq) + HCO_3^- \, (aq)$$

If a person hyperventilates, the rapid breathing expels carbon dioxide gas. Which of the following decreases when a person hyperventilates?

    I. $[HCO_3^-]$ II. $[H^+]$ III. $[H_2CO_3]$

A. I only   **B.** II only   **C.** III only   **D.** I and II only   **E.** I, II and III

43. What is the overall order of the reaction if the units of the rate constant for a particular reaction are min^{-1}?

A. Zero   **B.** First   **C.** Second   **D.** Third   **E.** Fourth

44. Heat is often added to chemical reactions performed in the laboratory to:

A. compensate for the natural tendency of energy to disperse

B. increase the rate at which reactants collide

C. allow a greater number of reactants to overcome the barrier of the activation energy

D. increase the energy of the reactant molecules

E. all of the above

45. Predict which reaction occurs at a faster rate for a hypothetical reaction $X + Y \rightarrow W + Z$.

Reaction	Activation energy	Temperature
1	low	low
2	low	high
3	high	high
4	high	low

A. 1   **B.** 2   **C.** 3   **D.** 4   **E.** 1 and 4

46. For the reaction, $2\,XO + O_2 \rightarrow 2\,XO_2$, data obtained from measurement of the initial rate of reaction at varying concentrations are:

Experiment	[XO]	[O₂]	Rate (mmol L⁻¹ s⁻¹)
1	0.010	0.010	2.5
2	0.010	0.020	5.0
3	0.030	0.020	45.0

What is the expression for the rate law?

A. rate $= k[XO]\cdot[O_2]$ **C.** rate $= k[XO]^2\cdot[O_2]$

B. rate $= k[XO]^2\cdot[O_2]^2$ **D.** rate $= k[XO]\cdot[O_2]^2$ **E.** rate $= k[XO]^2 / [O_2]^2$

47. What is the equilibrium (K_{eq}) expression for the following reaction?

$$CaO\,(s) + CO_2\,(g) \leftrightarrow CaCO_3\,(s)$$

A. $K_{eq} = [CaCO_3] / [CaO]$

B. $K_{eq} = 1 / [CO_2]$

C. $K_{eq} = [CaCO_3] / [CaO]\cdot[CO_2]$

D. $K_{eq} = [CO_2]$

E. $K_{eq} = [CaO]\cdot[CO_2] / [CaCO_3]$

48. If a reaction does not occur extensively and gives a low concentration of products at equilibrium, which of the following is true?

A. The rate of the forward reaction is greater than the reverse reaction

B. The rate of the reverse reaction is greater than the forward reaction

C. The equilibrium constant is greater than one; that is, K_{eq} is larger than 1

D. The equilibrium constant is less than one; that is, K_{eq} is smaller than 1

E. The equilibrium constant equals 1

49. Which of the following changes most likely decreases the rate of a reaction?

A. Increasing the reaction temperature

B. Increasing the concentration of a reactant

C. Increasing the activation energy for the reaction

D. Decreasing the activation energy for the reaction

E. Increasing the reaction pressure

50. Which factors would increase the rate of a reversible chemical reaction?

I. Increasing the temperature of the reaction

II. Removing products as they form

III. Adding a catalyst to the reaction vessel

A. I only   **B.** II only   **C.** I and II only   **D.** I and III only   **E.** I, II and III

51. What is the ionization equilibrium constant (K_i) expression for the following weak acid?

$$H_2S \ (aq) \leftrightarrow H^+ \ (aq) + HS^- \ (aq)$$

A. $K_i = [H^+]^2 \cdot [S^{2-}] \, / \, [H_2S]$

B. $K_i = [H_2S] \, / \, [H^+] \cdot [HS^-]$

C. $K_i = [H^+] \cdot [HS^-] \, / \, [H_2S]$

D. $K_i = [H^+]^2 \cdot [HS^-] \, / \, [H_2S]$

E. $K_i = [H_2S] \, / \, [H^+]^2 \cdot [HS^-]$

52. Increasing the temperature of a chemical reaction:

A. increases the reaction rate by lowering the activation energy

B. increases the reaction rate by increasing reactant collisions per unit time

C. increases the activation energy, thus increasing the reaction rate

D. raises the activation energy, thus decreasing the reaction rate

E. causes fewer reactant collisions to take place

53. Reaction rates are determined by all of the following factors, EXCEPT:

A. orientation of collisions between molecules

B. spontaneity of the reaction

C. force of collisions between molecules

D. number of collisions between molecules

E. the activation energy of the reaction

54. Coal burning plants release sulfur dioxide, into the atmosphere, while nitrogen monoxide is released into the atmosphere via industrial processes and from combustion engines. Sulfur dioxide can also be produced in the atmosphere by the following equilibrium reaction:

$$SO_3 \ (g) + NO \ (g) + heat \leftrightarrow SO_2 \ (g) + NO_2 \ (g)$$

Which of the following does NOT shift the equilibrium to the right?

A. $[NO_2]$ decrease

B. $[NO]$ increase

C. Decrease the reaction chamber volume

D. Temperature increase

E. All of the above shift the equilibrium to the right

55. Which of the following statements can be assumed to be true about how reactions occur?

A. Reactant particles must collide with each other

B. Energy must be released as the reaction proceeds

C. Catalysts must be present in the reaction

D. Energy must be absorbed as the reaction proceeds

E. The energy of activation must have a negative value

56. At equilibrium, increasing the temperature of an exothermic reaction likely:

    A. increases the heat of reaction

    B. decreases the heat of reaction

    C. increases the forward reaction

    D. decreases the forward reaction

    E. increases the heat of reaction and increases the forward reaction

57. Which shifts the equilibrium to the left for the reversible reaction in an aqueous solution?

$$HC_2H_3O_2 \,(aq) \leftrightarrow H^+ \,(aq) + C_2H_3O_2^- \,(aq)$$

    A. add solid KOH   **C.** increase pH

    B. add solid KNO_3 **D.** increase $[HC_2H_3O_2]$ **E.** add solid $KC_2H_3O_2$

58. Which of the following statements is true concerning the equilibrium system, whereby S combines with H_2 to form hydrogen sulfide, a toxic gas from the decay of organic material? (Use the equilibrium constant, $K_{eq} = 2.8 \times 10^{-21}$)

$$S \,(g) + H_2 \,(g) \leftrightarrow H_2S \,(g)$$

    A. Almost all the starting molecules are converted to product

    B. Decreasing $[H_2S]$ shifts the equilibrium to the left

    C. Decreasing $[H_2]$ shifts the equilibrium to the right

    D. Increasing the volume of the sealed reaction container shifts the equilibrium to the right

    E. Very little hydrogen sulfide gas is present in the equilibrium

59. Which of the following conditions characterizes a system in a state of chemical equilibrium?

    A. Product concentrations are greater than reactant concentrations

    B. Reactant molecules no longer react with each other

    C. Concentrations of reactants and products are equal

    D. Rate of forward reaction has dropped to zero

    E. Reactants are being consumed at the same rate they are being produced

60. Which statement is NOT true regarding an equilibrium constant for a particular reaction?

    A. It does not change as product is removed

    B. It does not change as additional quantity of a reactant is added

    C. It changes when a catalyst is added

    D. It changes as the temperature increases

    E. All are true statements

Practice Set 4: Questions 61–80

> Questions **61** through **63** refer to the rate data
> for the conversion of reactants W, X, and Y to product Z.

Trial Number	Concentration (moles/L)			Rate of Formation of Z (moles/l·s)
	W	X	Y	
1	0.01	0.05	0.04	0.04
2	0.015	0.07	0.06	0.08
3	0.01	0.15	0.04	0.36
4	0.03	0.07	0.06	0.08
5	0.01	0.05	0.16	0.08

61. From the above data, what is the overall order of the reaction?

　A. 3½　　　　**B.** 4　　　　**C.** 3　　　　**D.** 2　　　　**E.** 2½

62. From the above data, the order with respect to W suggests that the rate of formation of Z is:

　A. dependent on [W]　　　　　　**C.** semidependent on [W]
　B. independent of [W]　　　　　　**D.** unable to be determined
　　　　　　　　　　　　　　　　　　E. inversely proportional to [W]

63. From the above data, the magnitude of k for trial 1 is:

　A. 20　　　　**B.** 40　　　　**C.** 60　　　　**D.** 80　　　　**E.** 90

64. Which of the following changes shifts the equilibrium to the left for the given reversible reaction?

$SO_3 (g) + NO (g) + heat \leftrightarrow SO_2 (g) + NO_2 (g)$

　A. Decrease temperature　　　　　**C.** Increase [NO]
　B. Decrease volume　　　　　　　**D.** Decrease [SO_2]
　　　　　　　　　　　　　　　　　　E. Add a catalyst

65. What is the ionization equilibrium constant (K_i) expression for the following weak acid?

$$H_3PO_4 \, (aq) \leftrightarrow H^+ \, (aq) + H_2PO_4^- \, (aq)$$

A. $K_i = [H_3PO_4] / [H^+] \cdot [H_2PO_4^-]$

B. $K_i = [H^+]^3 \cdot [PO_4^{3-}] / [H_3PO_4]$

C. $K_i = [H^+]^3 \cdot [H_2PO_4^-] / [H_3PO_4]$

D. $K_i = [H^+] \cdot [H_2PO_4^-] / [H_3PO_4]$

E. $K_i = [H_3PO_4] / [H^+]^3 \cdot [PO_4^{3-}]$

66. What effect does a catalyst have on an equilibrium?

A. It increases the rate of the forward reaction

B. It shifts the reaction to the right

C. It increases the rate at which equilibrium is reached without changing ΔG

D. It increases the rate at which equilibrium is reached and lowers ΔG

E. It slows the reverse reaction

67. What is the correct ionization equilibrium constant (K_i) expression for the following weak acid?

$$H_2SO_3 \, (aq) \leftrightarrow H^+ \, (aq) + HSO_3^- \, (aq)$$

A. $K_i = [H_2SO_3] / [H^+] \cdot [HSO_3^-]$

B. $K_i = [H^+]^2 \cdot [SO_3^{2-}] / [H_2SO_3]$

C. $K_i = [H^+]^2 \cdot [HSO_3^-] / [H_2SO_3]$

D. $K_i = [H^+] \cdot [HSO_3^-] / [H_2SO_3]$

E. $K_i = [H_2SO_3] / [H^+]^2 \cdot [SO_3^{2-}]$

68. Which of the following is true if a reaction occurs extensively and yields a high concentration of products at equilibrium?

A. The rate of the reverse reaction is greater than the forward reaction

B. The rate of the forward reaction is greater than the reverse reaction

C. The equilibrium constant is less than one; K_{eq} is much smaller than 1

D. The equilibrium constant is greater than one; K_{eq} is much larger than 1

E. The equilibrium constant equals 1

69. The minimum combined kinetic energy reactants must possess for collisions to result in a reaction is:

A. orientation energy   **C.** collision energy

B. activation energy   **D.** dissociation energy   **E.** bond energy

70. Which factors decrease the rate of a reaction?

    I. Lowering the temperature

    II. Increasing the concentration of reactants

    III. Adding a catalyst to the reaction vessel

A. I only   **B.** II only   **C.** III only   **D.** I and II only   **E.** I, II and III

71. For a collision between molecules to result in a reaction, the molecules must possess both a favorable orientation relative to each other and:

A. be in the gaseous state

B. have a certain minimum energy

C. adhere for at least 2 nanoseconds

D. exchange electrons

E. be in the liquid state

72. Most reactions are carried out in liquid solution or in the gaseous phase, because in such situations:

A. kinetic energies of reactants are lower

B. reactant collisions occur more frequently

C. activation energies are higher

D. reactant activation energies are lower

E. reactant collisions occur less frequently

73. Find the reaction rate for A + B → C:

Trial	$[A]_{t=0}$	$[B]_{t=0}$	Initial rate (M/s)
1	0.05 M	1.0 M	1.0×10^{-3}
2	0.05 M	4.0 M	16.0×10^{-3}
3	0.15 M	1.0 M	3.0×10^{-3}

A. rate = $k[A]^2 \cdot [B]^2$

B. rate = $k[A] \cdot [B]^2$

C. rate = $k[A]^2 \cdot [B]$

D. rate = $k[A] \cdot [B]$

E. rate = $k[A]^2 \cdot [B]^3$

74. Why does a glowing splint of wood burn only slowly in air, but rapidly in a burst of flames when placed in pure oxygen?

A. A glowing wood splint is actually extinguished within pure oxygen because oxygen inhibits the smoke

B. Pure oxygen is able to absorb carbon dioxide at a faster rate

C. Oxygen is a flammable gas

D. There is an increased number of collisions between the wood and oxygen molecules

E. There is a decreased number of collisions between the wood and oxygen

75. Which of the changes shift the equilibrium to the right for the following system at equilibrium?

N_2 (g) + 3 H_2 (g) ↔ 2 NH_3 (g) + 92.94 kJ

I. Removing NH_3

II. Adding NH_3

III. Removing N_2

IV. Adding N_2

A. I and III

B. II and III

C. II and IV

D. I and IV

E. None of the above

76. Which of the changes has no effect on the equilibrium for the reversible reaction in an aqueous solution?

$$HC_2H_3O_2 \,(aq) \leftrightarrow H^+ \,(aq) + C_2H_3O_2^- \,(aq)$$

A. Adding solid $NaC_2H_3O_2$ **C.** Increasing $[HC_2H_3O_2]$

B. Adding solid $NaNO_3$ **D.** Increasing $[H^+]$

                                               E. Adding solid NaOH

77. Consider the following reaction: $H_2 \,(g) + I_2 \,(g) \rightarrow 2\,HI \,(g)$

At 160 K, this reaction has an equilibrium constant of 35. If, at 160 K, the concentration of hydrogen gas is 0.4 M, iodine gas is 0.6 M, and hydrogen iodide gas is 3 M:

A. system is at equilibrium   **C.** [hydrogen iodide] increases

B. [iodine] decreases   **D.** [hydrogen iodide] decreases

                                               E. [hydrogen] decreases

78. If the concentration of reactants decreases, which of the following is true?

    I. The amount of products increases

    II. The heat of reaction decreases

    III. The rate of reaction decreases

A. I only   **B.** II only   **C.** III only   **D.** II and III only   **E.** I, II and III

79. What does a chemical equilibrium expression of a reaction depend on?

    I. mechanism

    II. stoichiometry

    III. rate

A. I only   **B.** II only   **C.** III only   **D.** I and II only   **E.** I, II and III

80. For the following reaction where $\Delta H < 0$, which factor decreases the magnitude of the equilibrium constant K?

$$CO \,(g) + 2\,H_2O \,(g) \leftrightarrow CH_3OH \,(g)$$

A. Decreasing the temperature of this system

B. Decreasing volume

C. Decreasing the pressure of this system

D. All of the above

E. None of the above

This page is intentionally left blank

Equilibrium and Reaction Rates – Answer Key

1: A	21: E	41: A	61: E
2: B	22: A	42: E	62: B
3: A	23: E	43: B	63: D
4: A	24: B	44: E	64: A
5: C	25: C	45: B	65: D
6: D	26: A	46: C	66: C
7: B	27: B	47: B	67: D
8: A	28: A	48: D	68: D
9: E	29: E	49: C	69: B
10: D	30: A	50: E	70: A
11: D	31: C	51: C	71: B
12: B	32: B	52: B	72: B
13: D	33: A	53: B	73: B
14: B	34: A	54: C	74: D
15: B	35: B	55: A	75: D
16: D	36: E	56: D	76: B
17: B	37: A	57: E	77: D
18: E	38: A	58: E	78: C
19: A	39: D	59: E	79: B
20: C	40: E	60: C	80: E

Solution Chemistry

==

Practice Set 1: Questions 1–20

==

1. If the solubility of nitrogen in blood is 1.90 cc/100 cc at 1.00 atm, what is the solubility of nitrogen in a scuba diver's blood at a depth of 125 feet where the pressure is 4.5 atm?

   A. 1.90 cc/100 cc   **C.** 4.5 cc/100 cc

   B. 2.36 cc/100 cc   **D.** 0.236 cc/100 cc   **E.** 8.55 cc/100 cc

2. All of the statements about molarity are correct, EXCEPT:

   A. volume = moles/molarity

   B. moles = molarity × volume

   C. molarity of a diluted solution is less than the molarity of the original solution

   D. abbreviation is M

   E. molarity equals moles of solute per mole of solvent

3. Which of the following molecules is expected to be most soluble in water?

   A. $NaCl$ **C.** $CH_3CH_2CH_2OH$

   B. $CH_3CH_2CH_2COOH$ **D.** $Al(OH)_3$ **E.** CH_4

4. The equation for the reaction shown below can be written as an ionic equation.

$$BaCl_2\,(aq) + K_2CrO_4\,(aq) \rightarrow BaCrO_4\,(s) + 2\,KCl\,(aq)$$

In the ionic equation, the spectator ions are:

   A. K^+ and Cl^- **C.** Ba^{2+} and K^+

   B. Ba^{2+} and CrO_4^{2-} **D.** K^+ and CrO_4^{2-} **E.** Cl^- and CrO_4^{2-}

5. In commercially prepared soft drinks, carbon dioxide gas is injected into soda. Under what conditions is carbon dioxide gas most soluble?

   A. High temperature, high pressure   **C.** Low temperature, low pressure

   B. High temperature, low pressure   **D.** Low temperature, high pressure

                                      E. Solubility is the same for all conditions

6. A solute is a:

   A. substance that dissolves into a solvent

   B. substance containing a solid, liquid or gas

   C. solid substance that does not dissolve into water

   D. solid substance that does not dissolve at a given temperature

   E. liquid that does not dissolve into another liquid

7. How many ions are produced in solution by dissociation of one formula unit of $Co(NO_3)_2 \cdot 6H_2O$?

   A. 2   **B.** 3   **C.** 4   **D.** 6   **E.** 9

8. 15 grams of an unknown substance are dissolved in 60 grams of water. When the solution is transferred to another container, it weighs 78 grams. Which of the following is a possible explanation?

   A. The solution reacted with the second container, forming a precipitate

   B. Some of the solution remained in the first container

   C. The reaction was endothermic, which increased the average molecular speed

   D. The solution reacted with the first container, causing some byproducts to be transferred with the solution

   E. The reaction was exothermic, which increased the average molecular speed

9. Which of the following is NOT soluble in H_2O?

   A. Iron (III) hydroxide   **C.** Potassium sulfate

   B. Iron (III) nitrate   **D.** Ammonium sulfate   **E.** Sodium chloride

10. What is the v/v% concentration of a solution made by adding 25 mL of acetone to 75 mL of water?

   A. 33% v/v   **C.** 25% v/v

   B. 0.33% v/v   **D.** 2.5% v/v   **E.** 3.3% v/v

11. Why is octane less soluble in H_2O than in benzene?

   A. Bonds between benzene and octane are much stronger than the bonds between H_2O and octane

   B. Octane cannot dissociate in the presence of H_2O

   C. Bonds between H_2O and octane are weaker than the bonds between H_2O molecules

   D. Octane and benzene have similar molecular weights

   E. H_2O dissociates in the presence of octane

12. What is the K_{sp} for slightly soluble copper (II) phosphate in an aqueous solution?

$$Cu_3(PO_4)_2\,(s) \leftrightarrow 3\,Cu^{2+}\,(aq) + 2\,PO_4^{3-}\,(aq)$$

   A. $K_{sp} = [Cu^{2+}]^3 \cdot [PO_4^{3-}]^2$ **C.** $K_{sp} = [Cu^{2+}]^3 \cdot [PO_4^{3-}]$

   B. $K_{sp} = [Cu^{2+}] \cdot [PO_4^{3-}]^2$ **D.** $K_{sp} = [Cu^{2+}] \cdot [PO_4^{3-}]$

                                         E. $K_{sp} = [Cu^{2+}]^2 \cdot [PO_4^{3-}]^3$

13. Apply the *like dissolves like* rule to predict which of the following liquids is miscible with water:

       I.   carbon tetrachloride, CCl_4
      II. toluene, C_7H_8
    III. ethanol, C_2H_5OH

  A. I only   **B.** II only   **C.** III only   **D.** I and II only   **E.** I, II and III

14. In which of the following pairs of substances would both species in the pair be written in molecular form in a net ionic equation?

      I. CO_2 and H_2SO_4 II. LiOH and H_2 III. HF and CO_2

  A. I only   **B.** II only   **C.** III only   **D.** I, II and III   **E.** None of the above

15. Which statement best describes a supersaturated solution?

  A. It contains dissolved solute in equilibrium with undissolved solid
  B. It rapidly precipitates if a seed crystal is added
  C. It contains as much solvent as it can accommodate
  D. It contains no double bonds
  E. It contains only electrolytes

16. What is the mass of a 7.50% urine sample that contains 122 g of dissolved solute?

  A. 1,250 g   **B.** 935 g   **C.** 49.35 g   **D.** 155.4 g   **E.** 1,627 g

17. Calculate the molarity of a solution prepared by dissolving 15.0 g of NH_3 in 250 g of water with a final density of 0.974 g/mL.

  A. 36.2 M   **B.** 3.42 M   **C.** 0.0462 M   **D.** 0.664 M   **E.** 6.80 M

18. Which of the following compounds has the highest boiling point?

  A. 0.2 M $Al(NO_3)_3$ **C.** 0.2 M glucose ($C_6H_{12}O_6$)
  B. 0.2 M $MgCl_2$ **D.** 0.2 M Na_2SO_4 **E.** Pure H_2O

19. Which compound produces four ions per formula unit by dissociation when dissolved in water?

  A. Li_3PO_4 **B.** $Ca(NO_3)_2$ **C.** $MgSO_4$ **D.** $(NH_4)_2SO_4$ **E.** $(NH_4)_4Fe(CN)_6$

20. Which of the following would be a weak electrolyte in a solution?

  A. HBr (*aq*)   **B.** KCl   **C.** KOH   **D.** $HC_2H_3O_2$ **E.** HI

Practice Set 2: Questions 21–40

21. The ions Ca^{2+}, Mg^{2+}, Fe^{2+}, Fe^{3+}, which are present in all ground water, can be removed by pretreating the water with:

A. $PbSO_4$
B. $Na_2CO_3 \cdot 10H_2O$

C. KNO_3
D. $CaCl_2$

E. 0.05 M HCl

22. Choose the spectator ions: $Pb(NO_3)_2$ (*aq*) + H_2SO_4 (*aq*) → ?

A. NO_3^- and H^+
B. H^+ and SO_4^{2-}

C. Pb^{2+} and H^+
D. Pb^{2+} and NO_3^-

E. Pb^{2+} and SO_4^{2-}

23. From the *like dissolves like* rule, predict which of the following vitamins is soluble in water:

A. α-tocopherol ($C_{29}H_{50}O_2$)
B. calciferol ($C_{27}H_{44}O$)

C. ascorbic acid ($C_6H_8O_6$)
D. retinol ($C_{20}H_{30}O$)
E. none of the above

24. How much water must be added when 125 mL of a 2.00 M solution of HCl is diluted to a final concentration of 0.400 M?

A. 150 mL
B. 850 mL

C. 625 mL
D. 750 mL

E. 500 mL

25. Which of the following is the sulfate ion?

A. SO_4^{2-}
B. S^{2-}
C. CO_3^{2-}
D. PO_4^{3-}
E. S^-

26. Which of the following explains why bubbles form on the inside of a pot of water when the pot of water is heated?

A. As temperature increases, the vapor pressure increases
B. As temperature increases, the atmospheric pressure decreases
C. As temperature increases, the solubility of air decreases
D. As temperature increases, the kinetic energy decreases
E. None of the above

27. A solution in which the rate of crystallization is equal to the rate of dissolution is:

A. saturated
B. supersaturated

C. dilute
D. unsaturated

E. impossible to determine

28. What is the term that refers to liquids that do not dissolve in one another and separate into two layers?

A. Soluble   **B.** Miscible   **C.** Insoluble   **D.** Immiscible   **E.** None of the above

29. Which is a correctly balanced hydration equation for the hydration of Na_2SO_4?

A. $Na_2SO_4 \, (s) \xrightarrow{H_2O} Na^+ \, (aq) + 2SO_4^{2-} \, (aq)$

B. $Na_2SO_4 \, (s) \xrightarrow{H_2O} 2 \, Na^{2+} \, (aq) + S^{2-} \, (aq) + O_4^{2-} \, (aq)$

C. $Na_2SO_4 \, (s) \xrightarrow{H_2O} Na_2^{2+} \, (aq) + SO_4^{2-} \, (aq)$

D. $Na_2SO_4 \, (s) \xrightarrow{H_2O} 2 \, Na^+ \, (aq) + SO_4^{2-} \, (aq)$

E. $Na_2SO_4 \, (s) \xrightarrow{H_2O} 2 \, Na^{2+} \, (aq) + S^{2-} \, (aq) + SO_4^{2-} \, (aq) + O_4^{2-} \, (aq)$

30. Soft drinks are carbonated by injection with carbon dioxide gas. Under what conditions is carbon dioxide gas least soluble?

A. High temperature, low pressure

B. High temperature, high pressure

C. Low temperature, high pressure

D. Low temperature, low pressure

E. None of the above

31. Which type of compound is likely to dissolve in H_2O?

    I.   One with hydrogen bonds

    II. Highly polar compound

    III. Salt

A. I only   **B.** II only   **C.** III only   **D.** I and III only   **E.** I, II and III

32. Which of the following might have the best solubility in water?

A. CH_3CH_3 **B.** CH_3OH **C.** CCl_4 **D.** O_2 **E.** None of the above

33. What is the K_{sp} for slightly soluble gold (III) chloride in an aqueous solution for the reaction shown?

$$AuCl_3 \, (s) \leftrightarrow Au^{3+} \, (aq) + 3 \, Cl^- \, (aq)$$

A. $K_{sp} = [Au^{3+}]^3 \, [Cl^-] \, / \, [AuCl_3]$

B. $K_{sp} = [Au^{3+}] \cdot [Cl^-]^3$

C. $K_{sp} = [Au^{3+}]^3 \, [Cl^-]$

D. $K_{sp} = [Au^{3+}] \cdot [Cl^-]$

E. $K_{sp} = [Au^{3+}] \cdot [Cl^-]^3 \, / \, [AuCl_3]$

34. What is the net ionic equation for the reaction shown?

$$CaCO_3 + 2\ HNO_3 \rightarrow Ca(NO_3)_2 + CO_2 + H_2O$$

A. $CO_3^{2-} + H^+ \rightarrow CO_2$
B. $CaCO_3 + 2\ H^+ \rightarrow Ca^{2+} + CO_2 + H_2O$
C. $Ca^{2+} + 2\ NO_3^- \rightarrow Ca(NO_3)_2$
D. $CaCO_3 + 2\ NO_3^- \rightarrow Ca(NO_3)_2 + CO_3^{2-}$
E. None of the above

35. What is the volume of a 0.550 M $Fe(NO_3)_3$ solution needed to supply 0.950 moles of nitrate ions?

A. 265 mL   **B.** 0.828 mL   **C.** 22.2 mL   **D.** 576 mL   **E.** 384 mL

36. What is the molarity of a solution that contains 48 mEq Ca^{2+} per liter?

A. 0.024 M   **B.** 0.048 M   **C.** 1.8 M   **D.** 2.4 M   **E.** 0.96 M

37. If 36.0 g of LiOH is dissolved in water to make 975 mL of solution, what is the molarity of the LiOH solution? (Use molecular mass of LiOH = 24.0 g/mol)

A. 1.54 M   **B.** 2.48 M   **C.** 0. 844 M   **D.** 0.268 M   **E.** 0.229 M

38. Which has the highest boiling point?

A. 0.2 M $Al(NO_3)_3$ **C.** 0.2 M glucose ($C_6H_{12}O_6$)
B. 0.2 M $MgCl_2$ **D.** 0.2 M Na_2SO_4 **E.** Pure H_2O

39. In an AgCl solution, if the K_{sp} for AgCl is A and the concentration Cl^- in a container is B molar, what is the concentration of Ag (in moles/liter)?

I. A moles/liter   II. B moles/liter   III. A/B moles/liter

A. I only   **C.** III only
B. II only   **D.** II and III only   **E.** I and III only

40. Which statement below is generally true?

A. All bases are strong electrolytes and ionize completely when dissolved in water
B. All salts are strong electrolytes and dissociate completely when dissolved in water
C. All acids are strong electrolytes and ionize completely when dissolved in water
D. All bases are weak electrolytes and ionize completely when dissolved in water
E. All salts are weak electrolytes and ionize partially when dissolved in water

==

Practice Set 3: Questions 41–60

==

41. Which of the following intermolecular attractions is/are important for the formation of a solution?

       I. solute-solute   II. solvent-solute   III. solvent-solvent

  A. I only   **C.** I and II only
  B. III only   **D.** II and III only   **E.** I, II and III

42. What is the concentration of I^- ions in a 0.40 M solution of magnesium iodide?

  A. 0.05 M   **C.** 0.60 M
  B. 0.80 M   **D.** 0.20 M   **E.** 0.40 M

43. Which is most likely soluble in NH_3?

  A. CO_2 **C.** CCl_4
  B. SO_2 **D.** N_2 **E.** H_2

44. Which of the following represents the symbol for the chlorite ion?

  A. ClO_2^- **B.** ClO^- **C.** ClO_4^- **D.** ClO_3^- **E.** ClO_2

45. Which of the following statements best describes what is happening in a water softening unit?

  A. Sodium is removed from the water, making the water interact less with the soap molecules
  B. Ions in the water softener are softened by chemically bonding with sodium
  C. Hard ions are all trapped in the softener, which filters out all the ions
  D. Hard ions in water are exchanged for ions that do not interact as strongly with soaps
  E. None of the above

46. Which of the following compounds are soluble in water?

       I. $Mn(OH)_2$ II. $Cr(NO_3)_3$ III. $Ni_3(PO_4)_2$

  A. I only   **C.** III only
  B. II only   **D.** I and III only   **E.** I, II and III

47. The hydration number of an ion is the number of:

   A. water molecules bonded to an ion in an aqueous solution
   B. water molecules required to dissolve one mole of ions
   C. ions bonded to one mole of water molecules
   D. ions dissolved in one liter of an aqueous solution
   E. water molecules required to dissolve the compound

48. When a solid dissolves, each molecule is removed from the crystal by interaction with the solvent. This process of surrounding each ion with solvent molecules is called:

   A. hemolysis   **C.** crenation
   B. electrolysis   **D.** dilution   **E.** solvation

49. The term *miscible* describes which type of solution?

   A. Solid/solid   **C.** Liquid/solid
   B. Liquid/gas   **D.** Liquid/liquid   **E.** Solid/gas

50. Apply the *like dissolves like* rule to predict which of the following vitamins is insoluble in water:

   A. niacinamide ($C_6H_6N_2O$)   **C.** retinol ($C_{20}H_{30}O$)
   B. pyridoxine ($C_8H_{11}NO_3$)   **D.** thiamine ($C_{12}H_{17}N_4OS$)
                                              E. cyanocobalamin ($C_{63}H_{88}CoN_{14}O_{14}P$)

51. Which species is NOT written as its constituent ions when the equation is expanded into the ionic equation?

$$Mg(OH)_2 \ (s) + 2 \ HCl \ (aq) \rightarrow MgCl_2 \ (aq) + 2 \ H_2O \ (l)$$

   A. $Mg(OH)_2$ only   **C.** HCl
   B. H_2O and $Mg(OH)_2$ **D.** $MgCl_2$ **E.** HCl and $MgCl_2$

52. If x moles of $PbCl_2$ fully dissociate in 1 liter of H_2O, the K_{sp} is equivalent to:

   A. x^2 **B.** $2x^4$ **C.** $3x^2$ **D.** $2x^3$ **E.** $4x^3$

53. Which of the following are strong electrolytes?

   I. salts   II. strong bases   III. weak acids

   A. I only   **C.** III only
   B. I and II only   **D.** I, II and III   **E.** I and III only

54. What are the spectator ions in the reaction between KOH and HNO_3?

A. K^+ and NO_3^-
C. K^+ and H^+
B. H^+ and NO_3^-
D. H^+ and ^-OH
E. K^+ and ^-OH

55. What volume of 14 M acid must be diluted with distilled water to prepare 6.0 L of 0.20 M acid?

A. 86 mL **B.** 62 mL **C.** 0.94 mL **D.** 6.8 mL **E.** 120 mL

56. What is the molarity of the solution obtained by diluting 160 mL of 4.50 M NaOH to 595 mL?

A. 0.242 M **C.** 2.42 M
B. 1.21 M **D.** 1.72 M **E.** 0.115 M

57. Which compound is most likely to be more soluble in the nonpolar solvent of benzene than in water?

A. SO_2 **C.** Silver chloride
B. CO_2 **D.** H_2S **E.** CH_2Cl_2

58. Which of the following concentrations is dependent on temperature?

A. Mole fraction **C.** Mass percent
B. Molarity **D.** Molality **E.** More than one of the above

59. Which of the following solutions is the most concentrated?

A. One liter of water with 1 gram of sugar
B. One liter of water with 2 grams of sugar
C. One liter of water with 5 grams of sugar
D. One liter of water with 10 grams of sugar
E. All are the same

60. What mass of NaOH is contained in 75.0 mL of a 5.0% (w/v) NaOH solution?

A. 6.50 g **B.** 15.0 g **C.** 7.50 g **D.** 0.65 g **E.** 3.75 g

==

Practice Set 4: Questions 61–80

==

Questions **61** through **63** are based on the following data:

	K_{sp}
$PbCl_2$	1.0×10^{-5}
$AgCl$	1.0×10^{-10}
$PbCO_3$	1.0×10^{-15}

61. Consider a saturated solution of $PbCl_2$. The addition of NaCl would:

    I.   decrease $[Pb^{2+}]$

    II. increase the precipitation of $PbCl_2$

    III. have no effect on the precipitation of $PbCl_2$

  A. I only   **B.** II only   **C.** III only   **D.** I and II only   **E.** I and III only

62. What occurs when $AgNO_3$ is added to a saturated solution of $PbCl_2$?

    I.   AgCl precipitates

    II. $Pb(NO_3)_2$ forms a white precipitate

    III. More $PbCl_2$ forms

  A. I only   **B.** II only   **C.** III only   **D.** I, II and III   **E.** I and II only

63. Comparing equal volumes of saturated solutions for $PbCl_2$ and AgCl, which solution contains a greater concentration of Cl^-?

    I. $PbCl_2$

    II. AgCl

    III. Both have the same concentration of Cl^-

  A. I only   **B.** II only   **C.** III only   **D.** I and II only   **E.** Cannot be determined

64. Which of the following is the reason why hexane is significantly soluble in octane?

  A. Entropy increases for the two substances as the dominant factor in the ΔG when mixed

  B. Hexane hydrogen bonds with octane

  C. Intermolecular bonds between hexane-octane are much stronger than either hexane-hexane or octane-octane molecular bonds

  D. ΔH for hexane-octane is greater than hexane-H_2O

  E. Hexane and octane have similar molecular weights

65. Which of the following are characteristics of an ideally dilute solution?

    I.   Solute molecules do not interact with each other
    II. Solvent molecules do not interact with each other
    III. The mole fraction of the solvent approaches 1

A. I only   **B.** II only   **C.** I and III only   **D.** I, II and III   **E.** I and II only

66. Which principle states that the solubility of a gas in a liquid is proportional to the partial pressure of the gas above the liquid?

A. Solubility principle   **C.** Colloid principle
B. Tyndall effect   **D.** Henry's law   **E.** None of the above

67. Water and methanol are two liquids that dissolve in each other. When the two are mixed they form one layer, because the liquids are:

A. unsaturated   **C.** miscible
B. saturated   **D.** immiscible   **E.** supersaturated

68. What is the molarity of a glucose solution that contains 10.0 g of $C_6H_{12}O_6$ dissolved in 100.0 mL of solution? (Use the molecular mass of $C_6H_{12}O_6 = 180.0$ g/mol)

A. 1.80 M   **C.** 0.0555 M
B. 0.555 M   **D.** 0.00555 M   **E.** 18.0 M

69. Which of the following solid compounds is insoluble in water?

    I. $BaSO_4$ II. Hg_2Cl_2 III. $PbCl_2$

A. I only   **C.** III only
B. II only   **D.** I and III only   **E.** I, II and III

70. The net ionic equation for the reaction between zinc and hydrochloric acid solution is:

A. $Zn^{2+}(aq) + H_2(g) \rightarrow ZnS(s) + 2H^+(aq)$
B. $ZnCl_2(aq) + H_2(g) \rightarrow ZnS(s) + 2HCl(aq)$
C. $Zn(s) + 2H^+(aq) \rightarrow Zn^{2+}(aq) + H_2(g)$
D. $Zn(s) + 2HCl(aq) \rightarrow ZnCl_2(aq) + H_2(g)$
E. None of the above

71. Apply the *like dissolves like* rule to predict which of the following liquids is/are miscible with water:

        I. methyl ethyl ketone, C_4H_8O
        II. glycerin, $C_3H_5(OH)_3$
        III. formic acid, $HCHO_2$

    A. I only
    B. II only
             C. III only
             D. I and II only
        E. I, II and III

72. What is the K_{sp} for calcium fluoride (CaF_2) if the calcium ion concentration in a saturated solution is 0.00021 *M*?

    A. $K_{sp} = 3.7 \times 10^{-11}$
    B. $K_{sp} = 2.6 \times 10^{-10}$
             C. $K_{sp} = 3.6 \times 10^{-9}$
             D. $K_{sp} = 8.1 \times 10^{-10}$
        E. $K_{sp} = 7.3 \times 10^{-11}$

73. A 4 M solution of H_3A is completely dissociated in water. How many equivalents of H^+ are found in 1/3 liter?

    A. ¼
    B. 1
    C. 1.5
    D. 3
    E. 4

74. Which of the following aqueous solutions is a poor conductor of electricity?

        I. sucrose, $C_{12}H_{22}O_{11}$
        II. barium nitrate, $Ba(NO_3)_2$
        III. calcium bromide, $CaBr_2$

    A. I only
    B. II only
              C. III only
             D. I and II only
        E. I, II and III

75. Which of the following solid compounds is insoluble in water?

    A. $BaSO_4$
    B. Na_2S
             C. $(NH_4)_2CO_3$
             D. K_2CrO_4
        E. $Sr(OH)_2$

76. Which is true if the ion concentration product of a solution of AgCl is less than the K_{sp}?

        I. Precipitation occurs
        II. The ions are insoluble in water
        III. Precipitation does not occur

    A. I only
    B. II only
              C. III only
             D. I and II only
        E. II and III only

77. Under which conditions is the expected solubility of oxygen gas in water the highest?

    A. High temperature and high O_2 pressure above the solution

    B. Low temperature and low O_2 pressure above the solution

    C. Low temperature and high O_2 pressure above the solution

    D. High temperature and low O_2 pressure above the solution

    E. The O_2 solubility is independent of temperature and pressure

78. What is the molarity of an 8.60 molal solution of methanol (CH_3OH) with a density of 0.94 g/mL?

    A. 0.155 M   **C.** 6.34 M

    B. 23.5 M   **D.** 9.68 M   **E.** 2.35 M

79. Which of the following is NOT a unit factor related to a 15.0% aqueous solution of potassium iodide (KI)?

    A. 100 g solution / 85.0 g water   **C.** 85.0 g water / 100 g solution

    B. 85.0 g water / 15.0 g KI   **D.** 15.0 g KI / 85.0 g water

                                                E. 15.0 g KI / 100 g water

80. What is the molar concentration of a solution containing 0.75 mol of solute in 75 cm^3 of solution?

    A. 0.1 M   **B.** 1.5 M   **C.** 3 M   **D.** 10 M   **E.** 1 M

Solution Chemistry – Answer Key

1: E	21: B	41: E	61: D
2: E	22: A	42: B	62: A
3: A	23: C	43: B	63: A
4: A	24: E	44: A	64: A
5: D	25: A	45: D	65: C
6: A	26: C	46: B	66: D
7: B	27: A	47: A	67: C
8: D	28: D	48: E	68: B
9: A	29: D	49: D	69: E
10: C	30: A	50: C	70: C
11: C	31: E	51: B	71: E
12: A	32: B	52: E	72: A
13: C	33: B	53: B	73: E
14: C	34: B	54: A	74: A
15: B	35: D	55: A	75: A
16: E	36: A	56: B	76: C
17: B	37: A	57: B	77: C
18: A	38: A	58: B	78: C
19: A	39: D	59: D	79: E
20: D	40: B	60: E	80: D

Acids and Bases

Practice Set 1: Questions 1–20

1. Which is the conjugate acid–base pair in the reaction?

$$CH_3NH_2 + HCl \leftrightarrow CH_3NH_3^+ + Cl^-$$

A. HCl and Cl^-

B. $CH_3NH_3^+$ and Cl^-

C. CH_3NH_2 and Cl^-

D. CH_3NH_2 and HCl

E. HCl and H_3O^+

2. What is the pH of an aqueous solution if the $[H^+] = 0.10$ M?

A. 0.0   **B.** 1.0   **C.** 2.0   **D.** 10.0   **E.** 13.0

3. In which of the following pairs of substances are both species salts?

A. NH_4F and KCl

B. $CaCl_2$ and HCN

C. LiOH and K_2CO_3

D. NaOH and $CaCl_2$

E. HCN and K_2CO_3

4. Which reactant is a Brønsted-Lowry acid?

$$HCl\ (aq) + KHS\ (aq) \rightarrow KCl\ (aq) + H_2S\ (aq)$$

A. KCl   **B.** H_2S **C.** HCl   **D.** KHS   **E.** None of the above

5. If a light bulb in a conductivity apparatus glows brightly when testing a solution, which of the following must be true about the solution?

A. It is highly reactive

B. It is slightly reactive

C. It is highly ionized

D. It is slightly ionized

E. It is not an electrolyte

6. What is the term for a substance capable of either donating or accepting a proton in an acid–base reaction?

          I. Nonprotic   II. Aprotic   III. Amphoteric

A. I only   **B.** II only   **C.** III only   **D.** I and III only   **E.** II and III only

7. Which of the following compounds is a strong acid?

          I. $HClO_4\ (aq)$ II. $H_2SO_4\ (aq)$ III. $HNO_3\ (aq)$

A. I only   **B.** II only   **C.** II and III only   **D.** I and II only   **E.** I, II and III

8. What is the approximate pH of a solution of a strong acid where $[H_3O^+] = 8.30 \times 10^{-9}$?

    A. 9   **B.** 11   **C.** 7   **D.** 6   **E.** 8

9. Which of the following reactions represents the ionization of H_2O?

    A. $H_2O + H_2O \rightarrow 2\,H_2 + O_2$ **C.** $H_2O + H_3O^+ \rightarrow H_3O^+ + H_2O$

    B. $H_2O + H_2O \rightarrow H_3O^+ + {}^-OH$ **D.** $H_3O^+ + \rightarrow H_2O + H_2O$

                                                   E. None of the above

10. Which set below contains only weak electrolytes?

    A. $NH_4Cl\ (aq)$, $HClO_2\ (aq)$, $HCN\ (aq)$

    B. $NH_3\ (aq)$, $HC_2H_3O_2\ (aq)$, $HCN\ (aq)$

    C. $KOH\ (aq)$, $H_3PO_4\ (aq)$, $NaClO_4\ (aq)$

    D. $HNO_3\ (aq)$, $H_2SO_4\ (aq)$, $HCN\ (aq)$

    E. $NaOH\ (aq)$, $H_2SO_4\ (aq)$, $HC_2H_3O_2\ (aq)$

11. Which of the following statements describes a neutral solution?

    A. $[H_3O^+] / [{}^-OH] = 1 \times 10^{-14}$ **C.** $[H_3O^+] < [{}^-OH]$

    B. $[H_3O^+] / [{}^-OH] = 1$ **D.** $[H_3O^+] > [{}^-OH]$

                                           E. $[H_3O^+] \times [{}^-OH] \neq 1 \times 10^{-14}$

12. Which of the following is an example of an Arrhenius acid?

    A. $H_2O\ (l)$ **C.** $Ba(OH)_2\ (aq)$

    B. $RbOH\ (aq)$ **D.** $Al(OH)_3\ (s)$ **E.** None of the above

13. In the following reaction, which reactant is a Brønsted-Lowry base?

$$H_2CO_3\ (aq) + Na_2HPO_4\ (aq) \rightarrow NaHCO_3\ (aq) + NaH_2PO_4\ (aq)$$

    A. $NaHCO_3$ **C.** Na_2HPO_4

    B. NaH_2PO_4 **D.** H_2CO_3 **E.** None of the above

14. Which of the following is the conjugate base of ^-OH?

    A. O_2 **B.** O^{2-} **C.** H_2O **D.** O^- **E.** H_3O^+

15. Which of the following describes the solution for a vinegar sample at pH of 5?

    A. Weakly basic   **C.** Weakly acidic

    B. Neutral   **D.** Strongly acidic   **E.** Strongly basic

16. What is the pI for glutamic acid that contains two carboxylic acid groups and an amino group? (Use the carboxyl $pK_{a1} = 2.2$, carboxyl $pK_{a2} = 4.2$ and amino $pK_a = 9.7$)

    A. 3.2   **B.** 1.0   **C.** 6.4   **D.** 5.4   **E.** 5.95

17. Which of the following compounds cannot act as an acid?

    A. NH_3 **B.** H_2SO_4 **C.** HSO_4^{1-} **D.** SO_4^{2-} **E.** CH_3CO_2H

18. A weak acid is titrated with a strong base. When the concentration of the conjugate base is equal to the concentration of the acid, the titration is at the:

    A. end point   **B.** equivalence point
    C. buffering region   **D.** diprotic point
                                E. indicator zone

19. If $[H_3O^+]$ in an aqueous solution is 7.5×10^{-9} M, what is the $[^-OH]$?

    A. 6.4×10^{-5} M   **C.** 7.5×10^{-23} M
    B. $3.8 \times 10^{+8}$ M   **D.** 1.3×10^{-6} M   **E.** 9.0×10^{-9} M

20. Which species has a K_a of 5.7×10^{-10} if NH_3 has a K_b of 1.8×10^{-5}?

    A. H^+ **B.** NH_2^- **C.** NH_4^+ **D.** H_2O **E.** NH_3

Practice Set 2: Questions 21–40

21. Which of the following are the conjugate bases of HSO_4^-, CH_3OH and H_3O^+, respectively:

A. SO_4^{2-}, CH_2OH^- and ^-OH

B. CH_3O^-, SO_4^{2-} and H_2O

C. SO_4^-, CH_3O^- and ^-OH

D. SO_4^-, CH_2OH^- and H_2O

E. SO_4^{2-}, CH_3O^- and H_2O

22. If 30.0 mL of 0.10 M $Ca(OH)_2$ is titrated with 0.20 M HNO_3, what volume of nitric acid is required to neutralize the base according to the following expression?

$$2\ HNO_3\ (aq) + Ca(OH)_2\ (aq) \rightarrow 2\ Ca(NO_3)_2\ (aq) + 2\ H_2O\ (l)$$

A. 30.0 mL

B. 15.0 mL

C. 10.0 mL

D. 20.0 mL

E. 45.0 mL

23. Which of the following expressions describes an acidic solution?

A. $[H_3O^+] / [^-OH] = 1 \times 10^{-14}$

B. $[H_3O^+] \times [^-OH] \neq 1 \times 10^{-14}$

C. $[H_3O^+] < [^-OH]$

D. $[H_3O^+] > [^-OH]$

E. $[H_3O^+] / [^-OH] = 1$

24. Which is incorrectly classified as an acid, a base, or an amphoteric species?

A. LiOH / base

B. H_2O / amphoteric

C. H_2S / acid

D. NH_4^+ / base

E. None of the above

25. Which of the following is the strongest weak acid?

A. CH_3COOH; $K_a = 1.8 \times 10^{-5}$

B. HF; $K_a = 6.5 \times 10^{-4}$

C. HCN; $K_a = 6.3 \times 10^{-10}$

D. HClO; $K_a = 3.0 \times 10^{-8}$

E. HNO_2; $K_a = 4.5 \times 10^{-4}$

26. What are the products from the complete neutralization of phosphoric acid with aqueous lithium hydroxide?

A. $LiHPO_4$ (aq) and H_2O (l)

B. Li_3PO_4 (aq) and H_2O (l)

C. Li_2HPO4 (aq) and H_2O (l)

D. LiH_2PO_4 (aq) and H_2O (l)

E. Li_2PO_4 (aq) and H_2O (l)

27. Which of the following compounds is NOT a strong base?

A. $Ca(OH)_2$

B. $Fe(OH)_3$

C. KOH

D. NaOH

E. $^-NH_2$

28. What is the $[H^+]$ in stomach acid that registers a pH of 2.0 on a strip of pH paper?

A. 0.2 M   **B.** 0.1 M   **C.** 0.02 M   **D.** 0.01 M   **E.** 2 M

29. Which statement is true about distinguishing between dissociation and ionization?

A. Some acids are weak electrolytes and ionize completely when dissolved in H_2O

B. Some acids are strong electrolytes and dissociate completely when dissolved in H_2O

C. Some acids are strong electrolytes and ionize completely when dissolved in H_2O

D. All acids are strong electrolytes and dissociate completely when dissolved in H_2O

E. All acids are weak electrolytes and dissociate completely when dissolved in H_2O

30. Which of the following is a general property of a basic solution?

    I. Turns litmus paper red

    II. Tastes sour

    III. Causes the skin of the fingers to feel slippery

A. I only   **B.** II only   **C.** III only   **D.** I and II only   **E.** I, II and III

31. Which of the following compound-classification pairs is incorrectly matched?

A. HF – weak acid   **C.** NH_3 – weak base

B. $LiC_2H_3O_2$ – salt   **D.** HI – strong acid   **E.** $Ca(OH)_2$ – weak base

32. What is the term for a substance that releases H^+ in H_2O?

A. Brønsted-Lowry acid   **C.** Arrhenius acid

B. Brønsted-Lowry base   **D.** Arrhenius base   **E.** Lewis acid

33. Which molecule is acting as a base in the following reaction?

$$^-OH + NH_4^+ \rightarrow H_2O + NH_3$$

A. ^-OH **B.** NH_4^+ **C.** H_2O **D.** NH_3 **E.** H_3O^+

34. Citric acid is a triprotic acid with three carboxylic acid groups having pK_a values of 3.2, 4.8 and 6.4. At a pH of 5.7, what is the predominant protonation state of citric acid?

A. All three carboxylic acid groups are deprotonated

B. All three carboxylic acid groups are protonated

C. One carboxylic acid group is deprotonated, while two are protonated

D. Two carboxylic acid groups are deprotonated, while one is protonated

E. The protonation state cannot be determined

35. When fully neutralized by treatment with barium hydroxide, a phosphoric acid yields $Ba_2P_2O_7$ as one of its products. The parent acid for the anion in this compound is:

   A. monoprotic acid   **C.** triprotic acid

   B. diprotic acid   **D.** hexaprotic acid   **E.** tetraprotic acid

36. Does a solution become more or less acidic when a weak acid solution is added to a concentrated solution of HCl?

   A. Less acidic, because the concentration of OH^- increases

   B. No change in acidity, because [HCl] is too high to be changed by the weak solution

   C. Less acidic, because the solution becomes more dilute with a less concentrated solution of H_3O^+ being added

   D. More acidic, because more H_3O^+ is being added to the solution

   E. More acidic, because the solution becomes more dilute with a less concentrated solution of H_3O^+ being added

37. Which of the following is a triprotic acid?

   A. HNO_3 **B.** H_3PO_4 **C.** H_2SO_3 **D.** $HC_2H_3O_2$ **E.** CH_2COOH

38. For which of the following pairs of substances do the two members of the pair NOT react?

   A. Na_3PO_4 and HCl   **C.** HF and LiOH

   B. KCl and NaI   **D.** $PbCl_2$ and H_2SO_4

                           E. All react to form products

39. What happens to the pH when sodium acetate is added to a solution of acetic acid?

   A. Decreases due to the common ion effect

   B. Increases due to the common ion effect

   C. Remains constant, because sodium acetate is a buffer

   D. Remains constant, because sodium acetate is neither acidic nor basic

   E. Remains constant due to the common ion effect

40. Which of the following is the acidic anhydride of phosphoric acid (H_3PO_4)?

   A. P_2O **B.** P_2O_3 **C.** PO_3 **D.** PO_2 **E.** P_4O_{10}

Practice Set 3: Questions 41–60

41. Which of the following does NOT act as a Brønsted-Lowry acid?

A. CO_3^{2-} **B.** HS^- **C.** HSO_4^- **D.** H_2O **E.** H_2SO_4

42. Which of the following is the strongest weak acid?

A. HF; $pK_a = 3.17$
B. HCO_3^-; $pK_a = 10.32$
C. $H_2PO_4^-$; $pK_a = 7.18$
D. NH_4^+; $pK_a = 9.20$ **E.** $HC_2H_3O_2$; $pK_a = 4.76$

43. Why does boiler scale form on the walls of hot water pipes from ground water?

A. Transformation of $H_2PO_4^-$ ions to PO_4^{3-} ions, which precipitate with the "hardness ions," Ca^{2+}, Mg^{2+}, Fe^{2+}/Fe^{3+}
B. Transformation of HSO_4^- ions to SO_4^{2-} ions, which precipitate with the "hardness ions," Ca^{2+}, Mg^{2+}, Fe^{2+}/Fe^{3+}
C. Transformation of HSO_3^- ions to SO_3^{2-} ions, which precipitate with the "hardness ions," Ca^{2+}, Mg^{2+}, Fe^{2+}/Fe^{3+}
D. Transformation of HCO_3^- ions to CO_3^{2-} ions, which precipitate with the "hardness ions," Ca^{2+}, Mg^{2+}, Fe^{2+}/Fe^{3+}
E. The reaction of the CO_3^{2-} ions present in all ground water with the "hardness ions," Ca^{2+}, Mg^{2+}, Fe^{2+}/Fe^{3+}

44. Which of the following substances, when added to a solution of sulfuric acid (H_2SO_2), could be used to prepare a buffer solution?

A. H_2O
B. $HC_2H_3O_2$
C. KCl
D. HCl
E. $NaHSO_2$

45. Which of the following statements is NOT correct?

A. Acidic salts are formed by partial neutralization of a diprotic acid by a diprotic base
B. Acidic salts are formed by partial neutralization of a triprotic acid by a diprotic base
C. Acidic salts are formed by partial neutralization of a monoprotic acid by a monoprotic base
D. Acidic salts are formed by partial neutralization of a diprotic acid by a monoprotic base
E. Acidic salts are formed by partial neutralization of a polyprotic acid by a monoprotic base

46. Which of the following is the acid anhydride for $HClO_4$?

A. ClO   **B.** ClO_2 **C.** ClO_3 **D.** ClO_4 **E.** Cl_2O_7

47. Identify the acid/base behavior of each substance for the reaction:

$$H_3O^+ + Cl^- \rightleftharpoons H_2O + HCl$$

A. H_3O^+ acts as an acid, Cl^- acts as a base, H_2O acts as a base and HCl acts as an acid

B. H_3O^+ acts as a base, Cl^- acts as an acid, H_2O acts as a base and HCl acts as an acid

C. H_3O^+ acts as an acid, Cl^- acts as a base, H_2O acts as an acid and HCl acts as a base

D. H_3O^+ acts as a base, Cl^- acts as an acid, H_2O acts as an acid and HCl acts as a base

E. H_3O^+ acts as an acid, Cl^- acts as a base, H_2O acts as a base and HCl acts as a base

48. Given the pK_a values for phosphoric acid of 2.15, 6.87 and 12.35, what is the ratio of HPO_4^{2-} / $H_2PO_4^-$ in a typical muscle cell when the pH is 7.35?

A. 6.32×10^{-6} **B.** 1.18×10^5 **C.** 0.46   **D.** 3.02   **E.** 3.31×10^3

49. If a light bulb in a conductivity apparatus glows dimly when testing a solution, which of the following must be true about the solution?

    I. It is slightly reactive

    II. It is slightly ionized

    III. It is highly ionized

A. I only   **B.** II only   **C.** III only   **D.** I and II only   **E.** II and III only

50. Which of the following properties is NOT characteristic of an acid?

A. It is neutralized by a base   **C.** It produces H^+ in water

B. It has a slippery feel   **D.** It tastes sour   **E.** Its pH reading is less than 7

51. What is the term for a substance that releases hydroxide ions in water?

A. Brønsted-Lowry base   **C.** Arrhenius base

B. Brønsted-Lowry acid   **D.** Arrhenius acid   **E.** Lewis base

52. For the reaction below, which of the following is the conjugate acid of C_5H_5N?

$$C_5H_5N + H_2CO_3 \leftrightarrow C_5H_6N^+ + HCO_3^-$$

A. $C_5H_6N^+$ **B.** HCO_3^- **C.** C_5H_5N **D.** H_2CO_3 **E.** H_3O^+

53. Which of the following terms applies to Cl^- in the reaction below?

$$HCl\ (aq) \rightarrow H^+ + Cl^-$$

A. Weak conjugate base   **C.** Weak conjugate acid

B. Strong conjugate base   **D.** Strong conjugate acid

                                     E. Strong conjugate base and weak conjugate acid

54. Which of the following compounds is a diprotic acid?

   A. HCl   **B.** H_3PO_4 **C.** HNO_3 **D.** H_2SO_3 **E.** H_2O

55. Lysine contains two amine groups ($pK_a = 9.0$ and 10.0) and a carboxylic acid group ($pK_a = 2.2$). In a solution of pH 9.5, which describes the protonation and charge state of lysine?

   A. Carboxylic acid is deprotonated and negative; amine (pK_a 9.0) is deprotonated and neutral, whereby the amine ($pK_a = 10.0$) is protonated and positive

   B. Carboxylic acid is deprotonated and negative; amine ($pK_a = 9.0$) is protonated and positive, whereby the amine ($pK_a = 10.0$) is deprotonated and neutral

   C. Carboxylic acid is deprotonated and neutral; both amines are protonated and positive

   D. Carboxylic acid is deprotonated and negative; both amines are deprotonated and neutral

   E. Carboxylic acid is deprotonated and neutral; amine ($pK_a = 9.0$) is deprotonated and neutral, whereby the amine ($pK_a = 10.0$) is protonated and positive

56. Which of the following is the chemical species present in all acidic solutions?

   A. H_2O^+ *(aq)*   **C.** H_2O *(aq)*

   B. H_3O^+ *(l)*   **D.** ^-OH *(aq)*   **E.** H_3O^+ *(aq)*

57. Which compound has a value of K_a that is approximately equal to 10^{-5}?

   A. $CH_3CH_2CH_2CO_2H$ **C.** NaBr

   B. KOH   **D.** HNO_3 **E.** NH_3

58. Relative to a pH of 7, a solution with a pH of 4 has:

   A. 30 times less $[H^+]$ **C.** 1,000 times greater $[H^+]$

   B. 300 times less $[H^+]$ **D.** 300 times greater $[H^+]$ **E.** 30 times greater $[H^+]$

59. What is the pH of this buffer system if the concentration of an undissociated weak acid is equal to the concentration of the conjugate base? (Use the K_a of the buffer = 4.6×10^{-4})

   A. 1 and 2   **C.** 5 and 6

   B. 3 and 4   **D.** 7 and 8   **E.** 9 and 10

60. Which of the following is the ionization constant expression for water?

   A. $K_w = [H_2O] / [H^+]\cdot[^-OH]$ **C.** $K_w = [H^+]\cdot[^-OH]$

   B. $K_w = [H+]\cdot[^-OH] / [H_2O]$ **D.** $K_w = [H_2O]\cdot[H_2O]$

                                                      E. None of the above

==

Practice Set 4: Questions 61–80

==

61. Which of the following statements about strong or weak acids is true?

   A. A weak acid reacts with a strong base
   B. A strong acid does not react with a strong base
   C. A weak acid readily forms ions when dissolved in water
   D. A weak acid and a strong acid at the same concentration are equally corrosive
   E. None of the above

62. What is the value of K_w at 25 °C?

   A. 1.0
   B. 1.0×10^{-7}
   C. 1.0×10^{-14}
   D. 1.0×10^{7}
   E. 1.0×10^{14}

63. Which of the statements below best describes the following reaction?

   $$HNO_3 \ (aq) + LiOH \ (aq) \rightarrow LiNO_3 \ (aq) + H_2O \ (l)$$

   A. Nitric acid and lithium hydroxide solutions produce lithium nitrate solution and H_2O
   B. Nitric acid and lithium hydroxide solutions produce lithium nitrate and H_2O
   C. Nitric acid and lithium hydroxide produce lithium nitrate and H_2O
   D. Aqueous solutions of nitric acid and lithium hydroxide produce aqueous lithium nitrate and H_2O
   E. An acid plus a base produces H_2O and a salt

64. The Brønsted-Lowry acid and base in the following reaction are, respectively:

   $$NH_4^+ + CN^- \rightarrow NH_3 + HCN$$

   A. NH_4^+ and ^-CN
   B. ^-CN and HCN
   C. NH_4^+ and HCN
   D. NH_3 and ^-CN
   E. NH_3 and NH_4^+

65. Which would NOT be used to make a buffer solution?

   A. H_2SO_4
   B. H_2CO_3
   C. NH_4OH
   D. CH_3COOH
   E. Tricene

66. Which of the following is a general property of an acidic solution?

   A. Turns litmus paper blue
   B. Neutralizes acids
   C. Tastes bitter
   D. Feels slippery
   E. None of the above

67. What is the term for a solution that is a good conductor of electricity?

A. Strong electrolyte   **C.** Non-electrolyte

B. Weak electrolyte   **D.** Aqueous electrolyte   **E.** None of the above

68. Which of the following compounds is an acid?

A. HBr   **B.** C_2H_6 **C.** KOH   **D.** NaF   **E.** $NaNH_2$

69. A metal and a salt solution react only if the metal introduced into the solution is:

A. below the replaced metal in the activity series

B. above the replaced metal in the activity series

C. below hydrogen in the activity series

D. above hydrogen in the activity series

E. equal to the replaced metal in the activity series

70. Which of the following is an example of an Arrhenius base?

    I. NaOH (*aq*)   II. $Al(OH)_3$ (*s*)   III. $Ca(OH)_2$ (*aq*)

A. I only   **B.** II only   **C.** III only   **D.** I and II only   **E.** I, II and III

71. Which of the following is NOT a conjugate acid/base pair?

A. S^{2-} / H_2S **C.** H_2O / ^-OH

B. HSO_4^- / SO_4^{2-} **D.** PH_4^+ / PH_3 **E.** All are conjugate acid/base pairs

72. If a buffer is made with the pH below the pK_a of the weak acid, the [base] / [acid] ratio is:

A. equal to 0   **C.** greater than 1

B. equal to 1   **D.** less than 1   **E.** undetermined

73. Which of the following acids listed below has the strongest conjugate base?

Monoprotic Acids	K_a
Acid I	1.3×10^{-8}
Acid II	2.9×10^{-9}
Acid III	4.2×10^{-10}
Acid IV	3.8×10^{-8}

A. I   **B.** II   **C.** III   **D.** IV   **E.** Not enough data to determine

74. Complete neutralization of phosphoric acid with barium hydroxide, when separated and dried, yields $Ba_3(PO_4)_2$ as one of the products. Therefore, which term describes phosphoric acid?

A. Monoprotic acid   **C.** Hexaprotic acid

B. Diprotic acid   **D.** Tetraprotic acid   **E.** Triprotic acid

75. Which is the correct net ionic equation for the hydrolysis reaction of Na_2S?

A. $Na^+ (aq) + H_2O (l) \rightarrow NaOH (aq) + H_2 (g)$

B. $Na^+ (aq) + 2 H_2O (l) \rightarrow NaOH (aq) + H_2O^+ (aq)$

C. $S^{2-} (aq) + H_2O (l) \rightarrow 2 HS^- (aq) + {}^-OH (aq)$

D. $S^{2-} (aq) + 2 H_2O (l) \rightarrow HS^- (aq) + H_3O^+ (aq)$

E. $S^{2-} (aq) + H_2O (l) \rightarrow HS^- (aq) + {}^-OH (aq)$

76. Calculate the pH of 0.0765 M HNO_3.

A. 1.1   **B.** 3.9   **C.** 11.7   **D.** 7. 9   **E.** 5.6

77. Which of the following compounds is NOT a strong acid?

A. HBr (aq) **B.** HNO_3 **C.** H_2CO_3 **D.** H_2SO_4 **E.** HCl (aq)

78. Which reaction produces $NiCr_2O_7$ as a product?

A. Nickel (II) hydroxide and dichromic acid

B. Nickel (II) hydroxide and chromic acid

C. Nickelic acid and chromium (II) hydroxide

D. Nickel (II) hydroxide and chromate acid

E. Nickel (II) hydroxide and trichromic acid

79. Which of the following statements describes a Brønsted-Lowry base?

A. Donates protons to other substances

B. Accepts protons from other substances

C. Produces hydrogen ions in aqueous solution

D. Produces hydroxide ions in aqueous solution

E. Accepts hydronium ions from other substances

80. When dissolved in water, the Arrhenius acid/bases KOH, H_2SO_4 and HNO_3 are, respectively:

A. base, acid and base   **C.** base, acid and acid

B. base, base and acid   **D.** acid, base and base   **E.** acid, acid and base

This page is intentionally left blank

Acids and Bases – Answer Key

1: A	21: E	41: A	61: A
2: B	22: A	42: A	62: C
3: A	23: D	43: D	63: D
4: C	24: D	44: E	64: A
5: C	25: B	45: C	65: A
6: C	26: B	46: E	66: E
7: E	27: B	47: A	67: A
8: E	28: D	48: D	68: A
9: B	29: C	49: B	69: B
10: B	30: C	50: B	70: E
11: B	31: E	51: C	71: A
12: E	32: C	52: A	72: D
13: C	33: A	53: A	73: C
14: B	34: D	54: D	74: E
15: C	35: E	55: A	75: E
16: A	36: C	56: E	76: A
17: D	37: B	57: A	77: C
18: C	38: B	58: C	78: A
19: D	39: B	59: B	79: B
20: C	40: E	60: C	80: C

Electrochemistry and Oxidation-Reduction Reactions

===

Practice Set 1: Questions 1–20

===

1. Which is NOT true regarding the redox reaction occurring in a spontaneous electrochemical cell?

$$Cl_2\,(g) + 2\,Br^-\,(aq) \rightarrow Br_2\,(l) + 2\,Cl^-\,(aq)$$

  A. Cations in the salt bridge flow from the Br_2 half-cell to the Cl_2 half-cell

  B. Electrons flow from the anode to the cathode

  C. Cl_2 is reduced at the cathode

  D. Br^- is oxidized at the cathode

  E. Br^- is oxidized at the anode

2. What is the relationship between an element's ionization energy and its ability to function as an oxidizing agent? As ionization energy increases:

  A. the ability of an element to function as an oxidizing agent remains the same

  B. the ability of an element to function as an oxidizing agent decreases

  C. the ability of an element to function as an oxidizing agent increases

  D. the ability of an element to function as a reducing agent remains the same

  E. the ability of an element to function as a reducing agent increases

3. How many electrons are needed to balance the following half reaction $H_2S \rightarrow S_8$ in acidic solution?

  A. 14 electrons to the left side   **C.** 12 electrons to the left side

  B. 6 electrons to the right side   **D.** 8 electrons to the right side

                                        E. 16 electrons to the right side

4. Which is NOT true regarding the following redox reaction occurring in an electrolytic cell?

$$\overset{\text{Electricity}}{3\,C + 2\,Co_2O_3 \quad \rightarrow \quad 4\,Co + 3\,CO_2}$$

  A. $CO_2\,(g)$ is produced at the anode

  B. Co metal is produced at the anode

  C. Oxidation half-reaction: $C + 2\,O^{2-} \rightarrow CO_2 + 4\,e^-$

  D. Reduction half-reaction: $Co^{3+} + 3\,e^- \rightarrow Co$

  E. Co metal is produced at the cathode

---

5. The anode in a galvanic cell attracts:

A. cations

B. neutral particles

C. anions

D. both anions and neutral particles

E. both cations and neutral particles

6. The electrode with the standard reduction potential of 0 V is assigned as the standard reference electrode and uses the half-reaction:

A. $2\,NH_4^+\,(aq) + 2\,e^- \leftrightarrow H_2\,(g) + 2\,NH_3\,(g)$

B. $Ag^+\,(aq) + e^- \leftrightarrow Ag\,(s)$

C. $Cu^{2+}\,(aq) + 2\,e^- \leftrightarrow Cu\,(s)$

D. $Zn^{2+}\,(aq) + 2\,e^- \leftrightarrow Zn\,(s)$

E. $2\,H^+\,(aq) + 2\,e^- \leftrightarrow H_2\,(g)$

7. In the reaction for a discharging nickel–cadmium (NiCad) battery, which substance is being oxidized?

$$Cd\,(s) + NiO_2\,(s) + 2\,H_2O\,(l) \rightarrow Cd(OH)_2\,(s) + Ni(OH)_2\,(s)$$

A. H_2O **B.** $Cd(OH)_2$ **C.** Cd **D.** NiO_2 **E.** $Ni(OH)_2$

8. What happens at the anode if rust forms when Fe is in contact with H_2O?

$$4\,Fe + 3\,O_2 \rightarrow 2\,Fe_2O_3$$

A. Fe is reduced

B. Oxygen is reduced

C. Oxygen is oxidized

D. Fe is oxidized

E. None of the above

9. Which is true regarding the redox reaction occurring in the spontaneous electrochemical cell for $Cl_2\,(g) + 2\,Br^-\,(aq) \rightarrow Br_2\,(l) + 2\,Cl^-\,(aq)$?

A. Electrons flow from the cathode to the anode

B. Cl_2 is oxidized at the cathode

C. Br^- is reduced at the anode

D. Cations in the salt bridge flow from the Br_2 half-cell to the Cl_2 half-cell

E. Br^- is reduced at the anode, and Cl_2 is oxidized at the cathode

10. What is the term for a chemical reaction that involves electron transfer between two reacting substances?

A. Reduction reaction

B. Electrochemical reaction

C. Oxidation reaction

D. Half-reaction

E. Redox reaction

11. Using the following metal ion/metal reaction potentials,

$$Cu^{2+}(aq)|Cu(s) \quad Ag^+(aq)|Ag(s) \quad Co^{2+}(aq)|Co(s) \quad Zn^{2+}(aq)|Zn(s)$$

$$+0.34\ V \qquad\quad +0.80\ V \qquad\quad -0.28\ V \qquad\quad -0.76\ V$$

calculate the standard cell potential for the cell whose reaction is:

$$Co(s) + Cu^{2+}(aq) \rightarrow Co^{2+}(aq) + Cu(s)$$

A. +0.62 V

B. –0.62 V

C. +0.48 V

D. –0.48 V

E. +0.68 V

12. How are photovoltaic cells different from many other forms of solar energy?

A. Light is reflected and the coolness of the shade is used to provide a temperature differential

B. Light is passively converted into heat

C. Light is converted into heat and then into steam

D. Light is converted into heat and then into electricity

E. Light is converted directly to electricity

13. What is the term for an electrochemical cell that has a single electrode where oxidation or reduction can occur?

A. Half-cell

B. Voltaic cell

C. Dry cell

D. Electrolytic cell

E. None of the above

14. By which method could electrolysis be used to raise the hull of a sunken ship?

A. Electrolysis could only be used to raise the hull if the ship is made of iron. If so, the electrolysis of the iron metal might produce sufficient gas to lift the ship

B. The gaseous products of the electrolysis of H_2O are collected with bags attached to the hull of the ship, and the inflated bags raise the ship

C. The electrolysis of the H_2O beneath the hull of the ship boils H_2O and creates upward pressure to raise the ship

D. An electric current passed through the hull of the ship produces electrolysis, and the gases trapped in compartments of the vessel would push it upwards

E. Electrolysis of the ship's hull decreases its mass and the reduced weight causes the ship to rise

15. What are the products for the single-replacement reaction $Zn(s) + CuSO_4(aq) \rightarrow$?

A. CuO and $ZnSO_4$

B. CuO and $ZnSO_3$

C. Cu and $ZnSO_4$

D. Cu and $ZnSO_3$

E. No reaction

16. Which of the following is a true statement about the electrochemical reaction for an electrochemical cell that has a cell potential of +0.36 V?

    A. The reaction favors the formation of reactants and would be considered a galvanic cell

    B. The reaction favors the formation of reactants and would be considered an electrolytic cell

    C. The reaction is at equilibrium and is a galvanic cell

    D. The reaction favors the formation of products and would be considered an electrolytic cell

    E. The reaction favors the formation of products and would be considered a galvanic cell

17. Which of the following is a unit of electrical energy?

    A. Coulomb   **B.** Joule   **C.** Watt   **D.** Ampere   **E.** Volt

18. Which observation describes the solution near the cathode when an aqueous solution of sodium chloride is electrolyzed and hydrogen gas is evolved at the cathode?

    A. Colored   **B.** Acidic   **C.** Basic   **D.** Frothy   **E.** Viscous

19. How many grams of Ag are deposited in the cathode of an electrolytic cell if a current of 3.50 A is applied to a solution of $AgNO_3$ for 12 minutes? (Use the molecular mass of Ag = 107.86 g/mol and the conversion of 1 mol $e^- = 9.65 \times 10^4$ C)

    A. 0.32 g   **B.** 0.86 g   **C.** 2.82 g   **D.** 3.86 g   **E.** 4.38 g

20. In an electrochemical cell, which of the following statements is FALSE?

    A. The anode is the electrode where oxidation occurs

    B. A salt bridge provides electrical contact between the half-cells

    C. The cathode is the electrode where reduction occurs

    D. A spontaneous electrochemical cell is called a galvanic cell

    E. All of the above are true

Practice Set 2: Questions 21–40

21. What is the relationship between an element's ionization energy and its ability to function as an oxidizing and reducing agent? Elements with high ionization energy are:

    A. strong oxidizing and weak reducing agents

    B. weak oxidizing and weak reducing agents

    C. strong oxidizing and strong reducing agents

    D. weak oxidizing and strong reducing agents

    E. weak oxidizing and neutral reducing agents

22. In a basic solution, how many electrons are needed to balance the following half-reaction?

$$C_8H_{10} \rightarrow C_8H_4O_4^{2-}$$

    A. 8 electrons on the left side

    B. 12 electrons on the left side

    C. 4 electrons on the left side

    D. 12 electrons on the right side

    E. 8 electrons on the right side

23. Which statement is true regarding the following redox reaction occurring in an electrolytic cell?

$$\overset{\text{Electricity}}{3\ C\ (s) + 2\ Co_2O_3\ (l)\ \rightarrow\ 4\ Co\ (l) + 3\ CO_2\ (g)}$$

    A. CO_2 gas is produced at the anode

    B. Co^{3+} is produced at the cathode

    C. Oxidation half-reaction: $Co^{3+} + 3\ e^- \rightarrow Co$

    D. Reduction half-reaction: $C + 2\ O^{2-} \rightarrow CO_2 + e^-$

    E. None of the above

24. Which is true regarding the following redox reaction occurring in a spontaneous electrochemical cell?

$$Sn\ (s) + Cu^{2+}\ (aq) \rightarrow Cu\ (s) + Sn^{2+}\ (aq)$$

    A. Anions in the salt bridge flow from the Cu half-cell to the Sn half-cell

    B. Electrons flow from the Cu electrode to the Sn electrode

    C. Cu^{2+} is oxidized at the cathode

    D. Sn is reduced at the anode

    E. None of the above

25. In galvanic cells, reduction occurs at the:

    I. salt bridge   II. cathode   III. anode

  A. I only   **B.** II only   **C.** III only   **D.** I and II only   **E.** I, II and III

26. For a battery, what is undergoing reduction in the following oxidation-reduction reaction?

    $Mn_2O_3 + ZnO \rightarrow 2\ MnO_2 + Zn$

  A. Mn_2O_3 **B.** MnO_2 **C.** ZnO **D.** Zn **E.** Mn_2O_3 and Zn

27. Given that the following redox reactions go essentially to completion, which of the metals listed below has the greatest tendency to undergo oxidation?

    $Ni\ (s) + Ag^+\ (aq) \rightarrow Ag\ (s) + Ni^{2+}\ (aq)$

    $Al\ (s) + Cd^{2+}\ (aq) \rightarrow Cd\ (s) + Al^{3+}\ (aq)$

    $Cd\ (s) + Ni^{2+}\ (aq) \rightarrow Ni\ (s) + Cd^{2+}\ (aq)$

    $Ag\ (s) + H^+\ (aq) \rightarrow$ no reaction

  A. (H)   **B.** Cd   **C.** Ni   **D.** Ag   **E.** Al

28. What is the purpose of the salt bridge in a voltaic cell?

  A. Allows for a balance of charge between the two chambers
  B. Allows the Fe^{2+} and the Cu^{2+} to flow freely between the two chambers
  C. Allows for the buildup of positively charged ions in one container and negatively charged ions in the other container
  D. Prevents any further migration of electrons through the wire
  E. None of the above

29. If $\Delta G°$ for a cell is positive, the E° is:

  A. neutral   **C.** positive
  B. negative   **D.** unable to be determined   **E.** greater than 1

30. In an electrochemical cell, which of the following statements is FALSE?

  A. Oxidation occurs at the anode
  B. Reduction occurs at the cathode
  C. Electrons flow through the salt bridge to complete the cell
  D. A spontaneous electrochemical cell is called a voltaic cell
  E. All of the above are true

31. Which of the following statements about electrochemistry is NOT true?

A. The study of how protons are transferred from one chemical compound to another

B. The use of electrical current to produce an oxidation-reduction reaction

C. The use of a set of oxidation-reduction reactions to produce electrical current

D. The study of how electrical energy and chemical reactions are related

E. The study of how electrons are transferred from one chemical compound to another

32. In an operating photovoltaic cell, electrons move through the external circuit to the negatively charged p-type silicon wafer. How can the electrons move to the negatively charged silicon wafer if electrons are negatively charged?

A. The p-type silicon wafer is positively charged

B. The energy of the sunlight moves electrons in a nonspontaneous direction

C. Advancements in photovoltaic technology have solved this technological impediment

D. An electric current occurs because the energy from the sun reverses the charge of the electrons

E. The p-type silicon wafer is negatively charged

33. What is the term for the value assigned to an atom in a substance that indicates whether the atom is electron-poor or electron-rich compared to a free atom?

A. Reduction number
B. Oxidation number

C. Cathode number
D. Anode number
E. None of the above

34. What is the term for the relative ability of a substance to undergo reduction?

A. Oxidation potential
B. Reduction potential

C. Anode potential
D. Cathode potential
E. None of the above

35. What is the primary difference between a fuel cell and a battery?

A. Fuel cells oxidize to supply electricity, while batteries reduce to supply electricity

B. Batteries supply electricity, while fuel cells supply heat

C. Batteries can be recharged, while fuel cells cannot

D. Fuel cells do not run down because they can be refueled, while batteries run down and need to be recharged

E. Fuel cells do not use metals as oxidants and reductants, while batteries have a static reservoir of oxidants and reductants

36. In balancing the equation for a disproportionation reaction, using the oxidation number method, the substance undergoing disproportionation is:

    A. initially written twice on the reactant side of the equation

    B. initially written twice on the product side of the equation

    C. initially written on both the reactant and product sides of the equation

    D. always assigned an oxidation number of zero

    E. always assigned an oxidation number of $+1$

37. What is the term for an electrochemical cell in which electrical energy is generated from a spontaneous redox reaction?

    A. Voltaic cell   **C.** Dry cell

    B. Photoelectric cell   **D.** Electrolytic cell   **E.** Wet cell

38. Which observation describes the solution near the anode when an aqueous solution of sodium sulfate is electrolyzed and a gas is evolved at the anode?

    A. Colored   **B.** Acidic   **C.** Basic   **D.** Frothy   **E.** Viscous

39. Which of the statements listed below is true regarding the following redox reaction occurring in a nonspontaneous electrochemical cell?

$$Cd\ (s) + Zn(NO_3)_2\ (aq) + electricity \rightarrow Zn\ (s) + Cd(NO_3)_2\ (aq)$$

    A. Oxidation half-reaction: $Zn^{2+} + 2\ e^- \rightarrow Zn$

    B. Reduction half-reaction: $Cd \rightarrow Cd^{2+} + 2\ e^-$

    C. Cd metal is produced at the anode

    D. Zn metal is produced at the cathode

    E. None of the above

40. Which statement is true for electrolysis?

    A. A spontaneous redox reaction produces electricity

    B. A nonspontaneous redox reaction is forced to occur by applying an electric current

    C. Only pure, drinkable water is produced

    D. There is a cell which reverses the flow of ions

    E. None of the above

Practice Set 3: Questions 41–60

41. Which relationship explains an element's electronegativity and its ability to act as an oxidizing and reducing agent?

    A. Atoms with large electronegativity tend to act as strong oxidizing and strong reducing agents

    B. Atoms with large electronegativity tend to act as weak oxidizing and strong reducing agents

    C. Atoms with large electronegativity tend to act as strong oxidizing and weak reducing agents

    D. Atoms with large electronegativity tend to act as weak oxidizing and weak reducing agents

    E. None of the above

42. Which substance is undergoing reduction for a battery if the following two oxidation-reduction reactions take place?

        Reaction I: $Zn + 2\ OH^- \rightarrow ZnO + H_2O + 2\ e^-$

        Reaction II: $2\ MnO_2 + H_2O + 2\ e^- \rightarrow Mn_2O_3 + 2\ OH^-$

  A. OH^- **B.** H_2O **C.** Zn **D.** ZnO **E.** MnO_2

43. What is the term for an electrochemical cell in which a nonspontaneous redox reaction occurs by forcing electricity through the cell?

    I. voltaic cell   II. dry cell   III. electrolytic cell

  A. I only   **C.** III only

  B. II only   **D.** I and II only   **E.** I and III only

44. Which of the statements is true regarding the following redox reaction occurring in a galvanic cell?

        $Cl_2\,(g) + 2\ Br^-\,(aq) \rightarrow Br_2\,(l) + 2\ Cl^-\,(aq)?$

    A. Cations in the salt bridge flow from the Cl_2 half-cell to the Br_2 half-cell

    B. Electrons flow from the anode to the cathode

    C. Cl_2 is reduced at the anode

    D. Br^- is oxidized at the cathode

    E. None of the above

45. Which of the statements listed below is true regarding the following redox reaction occurring in a nonspontaneous electrolytic cell?

$$3 \text{ C } (s) + 4 \text{ AlCl}_3 \, (l) \xrightarrow{\text{Electricity}} 4 \text{ Al } (l) + 3 \text{ CCl}_4 \, (g)$$

A. Cl^- is produced at the anode

B. Al metal is produced at the cathode

C. Oxidation half-reaction is $Al^{3+} + 3 \text{ e}^- \rightarrow Al$

D. Reduction half-reaction is $C + 4 \text{ Cl}^- \rightarrow CCl_4 + 4 \text{ e}^-$

E. None of the above

46. Which of the following materials is most likely to undergo oxidation?

   I. Cl^- II. Na   III. Na^+

A. I only   B. II only   C. III only   D. I and II only   E. I, II and III

47. Which of the statements is NOT true regarding the redox reaction occurring in a spontaneous electrochemical cell?

$$\text{Zn } (s) + Cd^{2+} \, (aq) \rightarrow Cd \, (s) + Zn^{2+} \, (aq)$$

A. Anions in the salt bridge flow from the Zn half-cell to the Cd half-cell

B. Electrons flow from the Zn electrode to the Cd electrode

C. Cd^{2+} is reduced at the cathode

D. Zn is oxidized at the anode

E. Anions in the salt bridge flow from the Cd half-cell to the Zn half-cell

48. Which is capable of oxidizing Cu (s) to Cu^{2+} (aq) when added to Cu (s) in solution?

A. Al^{3+} (aq) B. Ag^+ (aq) C. Ni (s) D. I^- (aq) E. Au^{3+} (aq)

49. Why is the anode of a battery indicated with a negative (−) sign?

A. Electrons move to the anode to react with NH_4Cl in the battery

B. It indicates the electrode where the chemicals are reduced

C. Electrons are attracted to the negative electrode

D. The cathode is the source of negatively charged electrons

E. The electrode is the source of negatively charged electrons

50. What is the term for the conversion of chemical energy to electrical energy from redox reactions?

A. Redox chemistry   C. Cell chemistry

B. Electrochemistry   D. Battery chemistry   E. None of the above

51. In electrolysis, E° tends to be:

    A. zero   **B.** neutral   **C.** positive   **D.** greater than 1   **E.** negative

52. A major source of chlorine gas is the electrolysis of concentrated salt water, NaCl (*aq*). What is the sign of the electrode where the chlorine gas is formed?

    A. Neither, since chlorine gas is a neutral molecule and there is no electrode attraction
    B. Negative, since the chlorine gas needs to deposit electrons to form chloride ions
    C. Positive, since the chloride ions lose electrons to form chlorine molecules
    D. Both, since the chloride ions from NaCl (*aq*) are attracted to the positive electrode to form chlorine molecules, while the produced chlorine gas molecules move to deposit electrons at the negative electrode
    E. Positive, since the chloride ions gain electrons to form chlorine molecules

53. Which statement is correct for an electrolytic cell that has two electrodes?

    A. Oxidation occurs at the anode, which is negatively charged
    B. Oxidation occurs at the anode, which is positively charged
    C. Oxidation occurs at the cathode, which is positively charged
    D. Oxidation occurs at the cathode, which is negatively charged
    E. Oxidation occurs at the dynode, which is uncharged

54. Which of the statements listed below is true regarding the following redox reaction occurring in a nonspontaneous electrochemical cell?

$$Cd\ (s) + Zn(NO_3)_2\ (aq) + electricity \rightarrow Zn\ (s) + Cd(NO_3)_2\ (aq)$$

    A. Oxidation half-reaction: $Zn^{2+} + 2\ e^- \rightarrow Zn$ **C.** Cd metal dissolves at the anode
    B. Reduction half-reaction: $Cd \rightarrow Cd^{2+} + 2\ e^-$ **D.** Zn metal dissolves at the cathode
        E. None of the above

55. Which battery system is based on half reactions involving zinc metal and manganese dioxide?

    A. Alkaline batteries   **C.** Lead-acid storage batteries
    B. Fuel cells   **D.** Dry-cell batteries
        E. None of the above

56. Which of the following equations is a disproportionation reaction?

    A. $2\ H_2O \rightarrow 2\ H_2 + O_2$ **C.** $HNO_2 \rightarrow NO + NO_3^-$
    B. $H_2SO_3 \rightarrow H_2O + SO_2$ **D.** $Mg + H_2SO_4 \rightarrow MgSO_4 + H_2$
        E. None of the above

57. How is electrolysis different from the chemical process inside a battery?

    A. Pure compounds cannot be generated *via* electrolysis

    B. Electrolysis only uses electrons from a cathode

    C. Electrolysis does not use electrons

    D. They are the same process in reverse

    E. Chemical changes do not occur in electrolysis

58. Which fact about fuel cells is FALSE?

    A. Fuel cell automobiles are powered by water and only emit hydrogen

    B. Fuel cells are based on the tendency of some elements to gain electrons from other elements

    C. Fuel cell automobiles are quiet

    D. Fuel cell automobiles are environmentally friendly

    E. All of the above

59. Which process occurs when copper is refined using the electrolysis technique?

    A. Impure copper goes into solution at the anode, and pure copper plates out on the cathode

    B. Impure copper goes into solution at the cathode, and pure copper plates out on the anode

    C. Pure copper goes into solution from the anode and forms a precipitate at the bottom of the tank

    D. Pure copper goes into solution from the cathode and forms a precipitate at the bottom of the tank

    E. Pure copper on the bottom of the tank goes into solution and plates out on the cathode

60. Which of the following statements describes electrolysis?

    A. A chemical reaction which results when electrical energy is passed through a metallic liquid

    B. A chemical reaction which results when electrical energy is passed through a liquid electrolyte

    C. The splitting of atomic nuclei by electrical energy

    D. The splitting of atoms by electrical energy

    E. The passage of electrical energy through a split-field armature

Practice Set 4: Questions 61–80

61. In a battery, which of the following species in the two oxidation-reduction reactions is undergoing oxidation?

Reaction I: $Zn + 2 OH^- \rightarrow ZnO + H_2O + 2 e^-$

Reaction II: $2 MnO_2 + H_2O + 2 e^- \rightarrow Mn_2O_3 + 2 OH^-$

A. H_2O **B.** MnO_2 **C.** ZnO **D.** Zn **E.** OH^-

62. What is the term for an electrochemical cell in which the anode and cathode reactions do not take place in aqueous solutions?

A. Voltaic cell   **C.** Dry cell

B. Electrolytic cell   **D.** Galvanic cell   **E.** None of the above

63. How many electrons are needed to balance the charge for the following half-reaction in an acidic solution?

$C_2H_6O \rightarrow HC_2H_3O_2$

A. 6 electrons to the right side   **C.** 3 electrons to the left side

B. 4 electrons to the right side   **D.** 2 electrons to the left side

                                                    E. 8 electrons to the right side

64. Which of the statements is true regarding the following redox reaction occurring in an electrolytic cell?

$$3 C (s) + 4 AlCl_3 (l) \xrightarrow{\text{Electricity}} 4 Al (l) + 3 CCl_4 (g)$$

A. Al^{3+} is produced at the cathode

B. CCl_4 gas is produced at the anode

C. Reduction half-reaction: $C + 4 Cl^- \rightarrow CCl_4 + 4 e^-$

D. Oxidation half-reaction: $Al^{3+} + 3 e^- \rightarrow Al$

E. None of the above

65. What is the term for any electrochemical cell that spontaneously produces electrical energy?

     I. half-cell   II. electrolytic cell   III. dry cell

A. I and II only   **C.** III only

B. II only   **D.** II and III only   **E.** None of the above

66. The anode of a battery is indicated with a negative (–) sign, because the anode is:

A. where electrons are adsorbed

B. positive

C. negative

D. where electrons are generated

E. determined by convention

67. Which is the strongest reducing agent for the following half-reaction potentials?

$$Sn^{4+} (aq) + 2\ e^- \rightarrow Sn^{2+} (aq) \qquad E° = -0.13\ V$$

$$Ag^+ (aq) + e^- \rightarrow Ag\ (s) \qquad E° = +0.81\ V$$

$$Cr^{3+} (aq) + 3\ e^- \rightarrow Cr\ (s) \qquad E° = -0.75\ V$$

$$Fe^{2+} (aq) + 2\ e^- \rightarrow Fe\ (s) \qquad E° = -0.43\ V$$

A. $Cr\ (s)$

B. $Fe^{2+} (aq)$

C. $Sn^{2+} (aq)$

D. $Ag\ (s)$

E. $Sn^{2+} (aq)$ and $Ag\ (s)$

68. Which is true for the redox reaction occurring in a spontaneous electrochemical cell?

$$Zn\ (s) + Cd^{2+} (aq) \rightarrow Cd\ (s) + Zn^{2+} (aq)$$

A. Electrons flow from the Cd electrode to the Zn electrode

B. Anions in the salt bridge flow from the Cd half-cell to the Zn half-cell

C. Zn is reduced at the anode

D. Cd^{2+} is oxidized at the cathode

E. None of the above

69. Based upon the reduction potential: $Zn^{2+} + 2\ e^- \rightarrow Zn\ (s)$; $E° = -0.76\ V$, does a reaction take place when Zinc (*s*) is added to aqueous HCl, under standard conditions?

A. Yes, because the reduction potential for H^+ is negative

B. Yes, because the reduction potential for H^+ is zero

C. No, because the oxidation potential for Cl^- is positive

D. No, because the reduction potential for Cl^- is negative

E. Yes, because the reduction potential for H^+ is positive

70. If 1 amp of current passes a cathode for 10 minutes, how much Zn (*s*) forms in the following reaction? (Use the molecular mass of Zn = 65 g/mole)

$$Zn^{2+} + 2\ e^- \rightarrow Zn\ (s)$$

A. 0.10 g

B. 10.0 g

C. 0.65 g

D. 2.20 g

E. 0.20 g

71. In the oxidation–reduction reaction Mg (s) + Cu^{2+} (aq) → Mg^{2+} (aq) + Cu (s), which atom/ion is reduced and which atom/ion is oxidized?

   A. The Cu^{2+} ion is reduced (gains electrons) to form Cu metal, while Mg metal is oxidized (loses electrons) to form Mg^{2+}

   B. Since Mg is transformed from a solid to an aqueous solution and Cu is transformed from an aqueous solution to a solid, no oxidation–reduction reaction occurs

   C. The Cu^{2+} ion is oxidized (i.e., gains electrons) from Cu metal, while Mg metal is reduced (i.e., loses electrons) to form Mg^{2+}

   D. The Mg^{2+} ion is reduced (i.e., gains electrons) from Cu metal, while Cu^{2+} is oxidized (i.e., loses electrons) to the Mg^{2+}

   E. None of the above

72. Electrolysis is an example of a(n):

   A. acid-base reaction   **C.** physical change

   B. exothermic reaction   **D.** chemical change   **E.** state function

73. What is the term for a process characterized by the loss of electrons?

   A. Redox   **C.** Electrochemistry

   B. Reduction   **D.** Oxidation   **E.** None of the above

74. Which of the following statements is true about a galvanic cell?

   A. The standard reduction potential for the anode reaction is always positive

   B. The standard reduction potential for the anode reaction is always negative

   C. The standard reduction potential for the cathode reaction is always positive

   D. E° for the cell is always positive

   E. E° for the cell is always negative

75. Which of the following statements is true?

   A. Galvanic cells were invented by Thomas Edison

   B. Galvanic cells generate electrical energy rather than consume it

   C. Electrolysis cells generate alternating current when their terminals are reversed

   D. Electrolysis was discovered by Lewis Latimer

   E. The laws of electrolysis were discovered by Granville Woods

76. Which statement is correct for an electrolysis cell that has two electrodes?

   A. Reduction occurs at the anode, which is positively charged

   B. Reduction occurs at the anode, which is negatively charged

   C. Reduction occurs at the cathode, which is positively charged

   D. Reduction occurs at the cathode, which is negatively charged

   E. Reduction occurs at the dynode, which is uncharged

77. How long would it take to deposit 4.00 grams of Cu from a $CuSO_4$ solution if a current of 2.5 A is applied? (Use the molecular mass of Cu = 63.55 g/mol and the conversion of 1 mol $e^- = 9.65 \times 10^4$ C and 1 C = A·s)

   A. 1.02 hours   **C.** 4.46 hours

   B. 1.36 hours   **D.** 6.38 hours   **E.** 7.72 hours

78. Which battery system is completely rechargeable?

   A. Alkaline batteries   **C.** Lead-acid storage batteries

   B. Fuel cells   **D.** Dry-cell batteries   **E.** None of the above

79. In which type of cell does the following reaction occur when electrons are forced into a system by applying an external voltage?

$$Fe^{2+} + 2e^- \rightarrow Fe\ (s) \qquad E° = -0.44\ V$$

   A. Concentration cell   **C.** Electrochemical cell

   B. Battery   **D.** Galvanic cell   **E.** Electrolytic cell

80. What is the term for a reaction that represents separate oxidation or reduction processes?

   A. Reduction reaction   **C.** Oxidation reaction

   B. Redox reaction   **D.** Half-reaction   **E.** None of the above

This page is intentionally left blank

Electrochemistry and Oxidation-Reduction Reactions – Answer Key

1: D	21: A	41: C	61: D
2: C	22: D	42: E	62: C
3: E	23: A	43: C	63: B
4: B	24: A	44: B	64: B
5: C	25: B	45: B	65: C
6: E	26: C	46: B	66: D
7: C	27: E	47: A	67: A
8: D	28: A	48: B	68: B
9: D	29: B	49: E	69: B
10: E	30: C	50: B	70: E
11: A	31: A	51: E	71: A
12: E	32: B	52: C	72: D
13: A	33: B	53: B	73: D
14: B	34: B	54: C	74: D
15: C	35: D	55: D	75: B
16: E	36: A	56: C	76: D
17: B	37: A	57: D	77: B
18: C	38: B	58: A	78: C
19: C	39: D	59: A	79: E
20: E	40: B	60: B	80: D

We want to hear from you

Your feedback is important to us because we strive to provide the highest quality prep materials. If you have any questions, comments or suggestions, email us, so we can incorporate your feedback into future editions.

Customer Satisfaction Guarantee

If you have any concerns about this book, including printing issues, contact us and we will resolve any issues to your satisfaction.

info@sterling-prep.com

Explanations:
Diagnostic Tests

Explanations: Diagnostic Test #1

1. A is correct.

Electrons cannot be precisely located in space at any point in time, and orbitals describe probability regions for finding the electrons.

The *s* subshells are spherically symmetrical, *p* orbitals have a dumbbell shape, and *d* orbitals have four lobes.

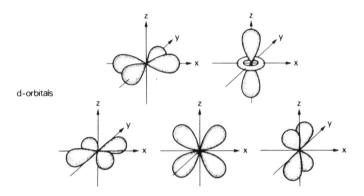

Representation of the three *p* orbitals

Representation of the five *d* orbitals

2. B is correct.

Nitrogen has 5 valence electrons.

Three substituents on a central atom that has a nonbonded pair of electrons indicate a trigonal pyramidal geometry.

3. E is correct.

Gay-Lussac's Law:

$$(P_1 / T_1) = (P_2 / T_2)$$

or

$$(P_1 T_2) = (P_2 T_1)$$

Solve for the final pressure:

$$P_2 = (P_1 T_2) / T_1$$

$$P_2 = [(3.60 \text{ atm}) \times (62.0 \text{ K})] / (30.0 \text{ K})$$

$$P_2 = 7.44 \text{ atm}$$

4. B is correct.

Use the periodic table to determine the atomic mass and formula masses:

H = 1 amu, O = 16 amu, C = 12 amu

Then, calculate the sum of mass for each molecule:

H_2O: (2 × 1 amu) + 16 amu = 18 amu

C_3H_6: (3 × 12 amu) + (6 × 1 amu) = 42 amu

C_3H_8O: (3 × 12 amu) + (8 × 1 amu) + (16 amu) = 60 amu

5. A is correct.

To have the same numerical magnitude, both phase changes must be the reverse of each other (between the same phases).

Here, both phase changes of heat of sublimation and deposition are between gas and solid phases.

Therefore, both heats of sublimation and deposition are equal in magnitude.

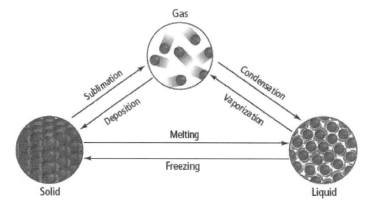

6. A is correct. Catalysts increase the rates of reactions by lowering the energy of activation (i.e., pathway of the reaction). Catalysts increase both the forward and backward reaction rates equally.

A catalyst does not shift the equilibrium, change equilibrium concentrations or the relative difference in energy between the reactants and products (ΔG).

7. B is correct.

Balance the reaction:

$$AgNO_3\ (aq) + NaCl\ (aq) \rightarrow AgCl + NaNO_3$$

For double-replacement reactions, one of the prerequisites is having at least one product molecule precipitating (e.g., $AgCl$). Know about the solubility of various salts.

8. B is correct.

Use the following relationship between pH and pK_a:

$$pH = pK_a + \log(\text{salt} / \text{acid})$$

Convert the given K_a into pK_a:

$$K_a = 1 \times 10^{-4}$$

$$pK_a = -\log(10^{-4})$$

$$pK_a = 4$$

Solve for pH:

$$pH = 4 + \log(1\ /10)$$

$$pH = 4 + \log(10^{-1})$$

$$pH = 4 + (-1)$$

$$pH = 3$$

9. B is correct.

Calculate E°:

$$2\ Br^-\ (aq) \rightarrow Br_2\ (l) + 2\ e^- \qquad E° = -1.08\ V$$

$$F_2\ (g) + 2\ e^- \rightarrow 2\ F^-\ (aq) \qquad E° = +2.88$$

$$F_2\ (g) + 2\ Br^-\ (aq) \rightarrow Br_2\ (l) + 2\ F^-\ (aq)$$

$$E° = +1.80\ V \text{ and spontaneous}$$

10. E is correct.

From the periodic table: alkaline earth metals are located in group 12/IIA.

11. D is correct.

The water spider remains on the surface of water because the water molecules are held very close together and participate in hydrogen bonding with adjacent water molecules. This cohesive property of water gives it surface tension and requires disruption of the hydrogen bonding for the water spider to penetrate the water's surface.

12. D is correct.

Evaporation is the phase change from a liquid to a gas. This occurs in the Earth's water cycle, when solar energy heats water and causes it to evaporate and become water vapor.

Evaporation is an endothermic process (i.e., heat is absorbed).

Sublimation is when a solid becomes a gas without becoming a liquid during the phase change.

13. D is correct.

Atomic mass of CCl_4:

$$[12 \text{ g/mol} + (4 \times 35.5 \text{ g/mol})] = 154 \text{ g/mol}$$

Atomic mass of Cl in CCl_4:

$$Cl = (4 \times 35.5 \text{ g/mol}) = 142 \text{ g/mol}$$

The % of Cl by mass:

$$(142 \text{ g/mole}) / (154 \text{ g/mol}) \times 100 = 92\%$$

14. A is correct.

Spontaneity is determined by the value of ΔG:

$$\Delta G = \Delta H - T\Delta S$$

A reaction is spontaneous if $\Delta G < 0$

Because $\Delta H < 0$ and $\Delta S < 0$, a lower temperature would likely yield a negative ΔG.

15. A is correct.

The difference between heat energies of reactants and products is heat of reaction.

Exothermic and endothermic are classifications of the heat of a reaction.

Activation energy is the minimum energy required to start a reaction and is not related to heat of reaction.

16. C is correct.

The concentration of the solute:

$$(0.30 \text{ mol}) / (0.05 \text{ kg}) = 6 \text{ m}$$

Given that the molecule does not dissociate (i.e., i = 1), the freezing point depression is:

$$\Delta T_f = k_f m$$

$$\Delta T_f = (-1.86 \text{ °C/m}) \cdot (6 \text{ m}) = -11.2 \text{ °C}$$

Thus, $T_f = (0 \text{ °C}) - (11.2 \text{ °C}) = -11.2 \text{ °C}$

17. E is correct.

In solution, an acid is deprotonated (i.e., ionized) if its pK_a is lower or close to the pH.

Henderson Hasselbalch expression:

$$pH = pK_a + \log[(\text{conjugate base}) / (\text{acid})]$$

Hydrochloric acid has the lowest pK_a of –7.0

Phosphoric acid ($pK_a = 2.2$) is closer to the pH of solution, but its pK_a is higher than the pH so it is less likely to be deprotonated.

18. D is correct.

For n = 3, *s*, *p*, and *d* orbitals are possible.

Two electrons can occupy the *s* orbitals, six electrons can occupy the *p* orbitals, and ten electrons can occupy the *d* orbitals.

Note, the n = 4 shell starts filling before the n = 3 shell is complete (however, not applicable).

19. A is correct.

Nitrate is a polyatomic ion with the molecular formula NO_3^- and is the conjugate base of nitric acid (HNO_3).

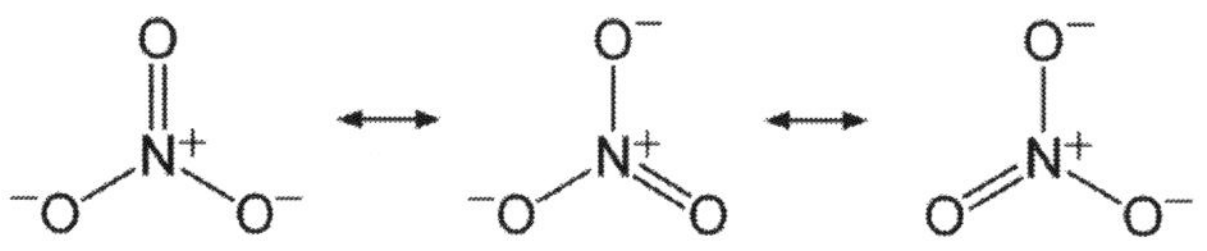

Three resonance forms of the nitrate ion

Nitrates also describe the organic functional group $RONO_2$

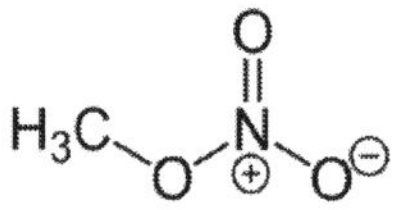

Methyl nitrate

20. B is correct.

$0\,°C$ and 1 atm are STP (standard temperature and pressure).

Other units for STP:

Temperature: $273.15\,K = 0\,°C$

Pressure: $101,325\,Pa = 1\,atm$

If choices do not have both $0\,°C$ and 1 atm, convert to an equivalent value for each unit.

21. D is correct.

$2\,KClO_3\,(s) \rightarrow 2\,KCl\,(s) + 3\,O_2\,(g)$ is a decomposition reaction, which occurs when one chemical compound is split into two or more compounds.

The compound $KClO_3$ is split into KCl and O_2.

$2\,Cr\,(s) + 3\,Cl_2\,(g) \rightarrow 2\,CrCl_3\,(s)$ is a synthesis reaction (composition reactions), because it forms a more complex chemical compound from individual elements.

$6\,Li\,(s) + N_2\,(g) \rightarrow 2\,Li_3N\,(s)$ is a synthesis reaction (composition reactions), because it forms a more complex chemical compound from individual elements.

$C_7H_8O_2\,(l) + 8\,O_2\,(g) \rightarrow 7\,CO_2\,(g) + 4\,H_2O\,(l)$ is a combustion reaction, because the hydrocarbon is reacting with oxygen. It is not a decomposition reaction because it involves two reactants rather than a single substance.

22. C is correct.

Heat is a product of a spontaneous (exothermic) reaction whereby the products are more stable than the reactants.

Endothermic reactions have a net absorption of energy from a reaction and the products have more energy than the reactants. Heat is required as a reactant for non-spontaneous (endothermic) reactions.

23. D is correct.

By Le Châtelier's principle, if the concentration of H_2 increases, then the equilibrium shifts to the right, which leads to a greater production of HF and increased consumption of F_2.

24. B is correct.

A colloidal suspension contains microscopically dispersed insoluble particles (i.e., colloid) suspended throughout the liquid.

The colloid particles are larger than those of the solution, but not large enough to precipitate due to gravity.

The Tyndall effect (i.e., light scattering by particles in a colloid) results when a beam of light that shines through a colloid suspension is dispersed, so that the beam becomes visible as the light rays are deflected by the particles.

In a non-colloidal solution, the beam shines through the solution and is not visible within the solution.

25. D is correct.

Strong bases are unstable anions.

All alkali and alkali metal (Groups IA and IIA) are strong bases.

Hydroxide ($^-$OH) is classified as a strong base.

26. C is correct. Calculating mass of metal deposited in cathode:

Step 1: Calculate total charge using current and time

Q = current × time

Q = 6 A × (3 minutes × 60 s/minute)

Q = 1,080 A·s = 1,080 C

Step 2: Calculate moles of electron that has the same amount of charge

moles e⁻ = Q / 96,500 C/mol

moles e⁻ = 1,080 C / 96,500 C/mol

moles e⁻ = 0.01 mol

Step 3: Calculate moles of metal deposited

Half-reaction of silver ion reduction:

$Ag^+ (aq) + e^- \rightarrow Ag (s)$

All coefficients in the reaction are 1:

moles e⁻ = moles Ag = 0.01 mol

Step 4: Calculate mass of metal deposited

mass Ag = moles Ag × molecular mass of Ag

mass Ag = 0.01 mol × 108 g/mol

mass Ag = 1.08 g

27. B is correct.

Isotopes are variants of the same element that have a different number of neutrons. Since they are the same element, they must have the same number of protons.

Ions are elements that have the same number of protons but a different number of electrons.

28. B is correct.

Ionic bonds are formed between elements with an electronegativity difference greater than 1.7 Pauling units (e.g., a metal atom and a non-metal atom).

Sr is in group IIA/2 (alkali earth metal), therefore the compound containing Sr is most likely to be ionic.

Ga is located in group IIIA/13 in the periodic table, which means that it is a metalloid: it has both metal and non-metal properties.

The other choices are incorrect because they do not have metal atoms; they have covalent bonds (between non-metals).

29. E is correct.

Boyle's Law:

$$P_1V_1 = P_2V_2$$

Pressure and volume are inversely related when temperature is constant.

The statement "pressure is proportional to 1/volume" is the shortened formula for Boyle's law.

Since temperature is constant, "pressure × volume = a constant" is true.

The two sets of conditions (pressure and volume) have the same ratio.

30. D is correct.

Formula mass is a synonym of molecular mass or molecular weight (MW).

$$MW = (14 \times \text{atomic mass of C}) + (28 \times \text{atomic mass of H}) + (4 \times \text{atomic mass of O})$$

$$MW = (14 \times 12.01 \text{ g/mole}) + (28 \times 1.01 \text{ g/mole}) + (4 \times 16.00 \text{ g/mole})$$

$$MW = (168.14 \text{ g/mole}) + (28.28 \text{ g/mole}) + (64 \text{ g/mole})$$

$$MW = 260.4 \text{ g/mole}$$

Note: 1 amu = 1 g/mole

31. B is correct.

For an ideal gas, internal energy is a function of temperature only.

An ideal gas has no attractive forces between molecules, so changing the distance between the molecules by changing pressure or volume (at a constant temperature) does not affect the internal energy.

The kinetic energy of the molecules is a function of temperature:

$$KE = 3/2 \, RT$$

32. E is correct. In equilibrium, only gaseous and aqueous species affect equilibrium.

Solids and liquids have no effect.

33. E is correct. The concentrations of the dissolved ions must exceed the value of the K_{sp} for precipitation. Given the dissolution of $PbSO_4$:

$$PbSO_4 \leftrightarrow Pb^{2+} (aq) + SO_4^{2-} (aq)$$

$$K_{sp} = [Pb^{2+}] \cdot [SO_4^{2-}]$$

The minimum concentration of SO_4^{2-} for precipitation is:

$$[SO_4^{2-}] = K_{sp} / [Pb^{2+}]$$

$$[SO_4^{2-}] = (1.70 \times 10^{-8}) / (1.10 \times 10^{-3})$$

$$[SO_4^{2-}] = 1.55 \times 10^{-5} \text{ M}$$

34. E is correct.

Bronsted-Lowry definition: acid is the H^+ (proton) donating substance to become the conjugate base. A base is the proton acceptor (which needs a lone pair of electrons) to become the conjugate acid.

Since this is a dynamic equilibrium reaction, there is a pair of acids and bases.

Forward reaction: HSO_4^- gains H^+ to form H_2SO_4; HSO_4^- is a base

H_2O loses H^+ to form ^-OH; H_2O is an acid

Reverse reaction: H_2SO_4 loses H^+ to form HSO_4^-; H_2SO_4 is an acid

^-OH gains H^+ to form H_2O; ^-OH is a base

35. D is correct.

An element is a pure chemical substance that consists of one type of atom. Every element has an atomic number based on the number of protons.

Hydrogen has the atomic number 1, and it is the first element on the periodic table of elements. Hydrogen gas (H_2) is a compound.

The other choices contain more than one type of atom bonded together and are referred to as chemical compounds.

Glucose and methanol contain carbon, oxygen and hydrogen atoms bonded together.

Sodium chloride, as its name suggests, contains sodium and chlorine bonded together.

Brass contains copper and zinc bonded together.

36. B is correct.

Ionization energy is the minimum amount of energy required to remove an electron from an atom or molecule in its gaseous state. When this electron (usually the outermost or highest-energy electron) is removed, the atom constitutes a positive ion (cation) because, it has more protons than electrons.

37. D is correct.

To obtain volume percent of Ar, set the total and partial volume/mole conditions of Ar equal:

$(V_T / n_T) = (V_{Ar} / n_{Ar})$

Solve for the volume of Ar:

$V_{Ar} = (0.600$ moles Ar$) \times [(7.50$ L total$) / (1.30$ moles total$)]$

$V_{Ar} = 3.46$ L Ar

Divide partial volume of Ar by total volume of flask, and multiply by 100%:

$V_{Ar}\% = [(3.46$ L Ar$) / (7.50$ L total$)] \times 100\% = 46.1\%$

38. C is correct.

Balance the reaction: $C_{12}H_{22}O_{11}$ (*l*) + 12 O_2 (*g*) → 12 CO_2 (*g*) + 11 H_2O (*g*)

12 moles of O_2 per $C_{12}H_{22}O_{11}$

12 moles × 2 = 24 moles

39. C is correct. To analyze each statement, it is important to define "the system."

Case I: thermal energy goes up for both the clay and the ground, so regardless of what the system is considered to be (just clay, just ground, or both), internal energy increases.

Case II: if only carbon and oxygen atoms constitute the system, then the internal energy decreases because some energy is given off as heat; if the system is carbon, oxygen and the environment (i.e., surroundings), then the internal energy remains constant, since the energy lost from the atoms goes into the environment. In either case, the internal energy is not increasing.

Case III: just like in case I, thermal energy increases, therefore internal energy is going up.

40. A is correct. Initiation reactions produce free radicals.

Propagation reactions involve no net loss of free radicals.

Termination reactions involve free radical reactants producing a nonradical product.

As an example, a free radial reaction for Cl_2 is shown:

Initiation: $Cl_2 \xrightarrow{\text{UV light}} 2Cl\cdot$

Propagation: $Cl\cdot + CH_4 \rightarrow CH_3\cdot + HCl$

Termination: $CH_3\cdot + Cl\cdot \rightarrow CH_3Cl$

41. E is correct.

The *like dissolves like* rule applies when a solvent is miscible with a solute that has similar properties.

A polar solute is miscible with a polar solvent and the rule applies for nonpolar solute/solvent.

42. A is correct.

An acid is the species that donates a proton (H^+).

Only $H_2PO_4^-$ acts as a proton-donating species.

Conjugate base is specific to each acid; it is the molecule after losing one H^+:

$$H_2PO_4^- \text{ (acid)} \rightarrow HPO_4^{2-} \text{ (conjugate base)} + H^+$$

For $H_2PO_4^-$, the acid listed is correct, but S^{2-} is not the conjugate base for this acid.

43. E is correct.

In an electrochemical cell:

oxidation (i.e., loss of electrons) occurs at the anode ($Cl^- \rightarrow Cl_2$)

reduction (i.e., gain of electrons) occurs at the cathode ($Br_2 \rightarrow Br^-$)

44. B is correct.

The noble gases are the most stable *group* (vertical column and not the horizontal period).

They are stable because of a complete octet of valence electrons.

45. E is correct.

With little or no difference in electronegativity (Pauling units < 0.4) between the atoms, it is a nonpolar covalent bond, whereby the electrons are shared between the two bonding atoms.

Polar covalent bonded atoms are covalently bonded compounds that involve unequal sharing of electrons due to large electronegativity differences (Pauling units of 0.4 to 1.7) between the atoms.

When the difference in electronegativity is greater than 1.7 Pauling units, the compounds form ionic bonds. Ionic bonds involve the transfer of an electron from the electropositive element (along the left-hand column/group) to the electronegative element (along the right-hand column/groups) on the periodic table.

In both covalent and polar covalent bonds, the electrons are shared so that each atom acquires a noble gas configuration.

In dry conditions, ionic bonds are stronger than covalent bonds.

In aqueous conditions, ionic bonds are weak and the compound spontaneously dissociates into ions (e.g., table salt in a glass of water).

46. A is correct.

Polar molecules have stronger dipole-dipole force between molecules because the partial positive end of one molecule bonds with the partial negative end of another molecule.

Nonpolar molecules have induced dipole-induced dipole intermolecular force, which is weak compared to dipole-dipole force.

47. B is correct.

Balance the number of hydrogen by adding 2 to $HClO_4$:

$$Cl_2O_7 + H_2O \rightarrow 2\ HClO_4$$

The reaction is balanced – confirm by counting number of Cl and O on both sides (e.g., 2 and 8 respectively).

48. B is correct.

This reaction releases some energy, which means that this reaction is exothermic.

By convention, exothermic reactions always have negative ΔH.

The total enthalpy (i.e., internal energy) of a system cannot be measured directly; the *enthalpy change* of a system is measured instead.

Enthalpy change is defined by the following equation: $\Delta H = H_f - H_i$

If the standard enthalpy of the products is less than the standard enthalpy of the reactants, the standard enthalpy of reaction is negative and the reaction is exothermic.

If the standard enthalpy of the products is more than the standard enthalpy of the reactants, the standard enthalpy of reaction is positive and the reaction is endothermic.

49. D is correct.

Add the exponents to determine the order of reaction: $2 + 4 = 6$

50. D is correct.

Osmolarity is the number of molecules contributing to osmotic pressure in solutions.

Every ion in ionic compounds contributes to osmotic pressure.

For example, in a solution, 1 mol of NaCl dissociates into 1 mol of Na^+ and 1 mol of Cl^-, osmolarity is (1 mol + 1 mol) = 2 moles.

Calculate the osmolarity by multiplying the molarity by the total number of ions.

KF: osmolarity = 0.15 M × 2 = 0.30 M

$CaBr_2$: osmolarity = 0.25 M × 3 = 0.75 M

NaCl: osmolarity = 0.7 M × 2 = 1.4 M

$AlCl_3$: osmolarity = 0.4 M × 4 = 1.6 M

KNO_3: osmolarity = 0.10 M × 2 = 0.2 M

$AlCl_3$ has the highest osmolarity value at 1.6 M.

51. A is correct.

KOH is a strong base: all KOH ions dissociates into K^+ and ^-OH.

[KOH] = [^-OH] = 0.04 M

To determine pH of bases, calculate pOH:

pOH = –log [^-OH]

pOH = –log 0.04

pOH = 1.40

Using pOH, determine the pH:

pH + pOH = 14

pH = 14 – pOH

pH = 14 – 1.40

pH = 12.6

52. C is correct.

French chemist Antoine Lavoisier performed a series of experiments that established the Law of Mass Conservation, which states that *whenever matter undergoes a change, the total mass of the products of the change is the same as the total mass of the reactants.*

From this idea, he further proposed that an element is any material made of a fundamental substance that cannot be broken down into another element.

53. D is correct.

Two electrons form each covalent bond. A double bond involves 2 electrons in the sigma (single) bond and another 2 electrons in the pi (double) bond.

54. C is correct.

22.4 liters of gas at STP = 1 mole.

Assume 1 mole:

C_2H_6 = 0.3 mole, CH_4 = 0.5 mole, N_2 = 0.2 mole

Total moles of carbon from C_2H_6 = (0.3 × 2 carbons) = 0.6 mole

(CH_4 = 0.5 mole) + (C_2H_6 = 0.6 mole) = 1.1 mole of carbon

55. B is correct.

Percent composition is a breakdown of each component's percentage in a compound.

56. C is correct. An extensive property is a property that varies with amount of matter.

An intensive property is a property that does not vary with amount of matter.

Because the problem indicates that change of heat is an extensive property, it is proportional to the amount of matter involved in the reaction.

Therefore, three times more mass results in three times the change in the property.

(360 grams / 120 grams) × (–45 kJ)

= 3 × (–45 kJ) = –135 kJ

57. A is correct.

General formula for the equilibrium constant K_{eq} of a reaction:

aA + bB ↔ cC + dD

K_{eq} = ([C]^c × [D]^d) / ([A]^a × [B]^b)

Analyze the given K_{eq} expression to determine the reaction:

K_{eq} = [H$_2$]^2 [O$_2$] / [H$_2$O]

Reaction = 2 H$_2$O ↔ 2 H$_2$ + O$_2$

58. D is correct.

Neither bond energy nor vapor pressure changes with a change in atmospheric pressure.

Boiling occurs when the vapor pressure of a liquid equals the atmospheric pressure. At high altitudes, water boils at a lower temperature because the atmospheric pressure decreases as altitude increases.

59. E is correct.

To determine acidity of a salt, evaluate the cations and anions of the salt.

If it is a conjugate of a strong acid (e.g., HCl, HBr or H_2SO_4), it is acidic, but only if it's paired with a cation that is a conjugate of a weak base (such as nickel).

A salt is basic if it is a conjugate of strong base (e.g., KOH, NaOH or $Ba(OH)_2$) and paired with a weak conjugate acid.

If both cation and anion are from strong acids and bases, the salt is neutral.

60. E is correct. To electrolyze 10 moles of H_2O_2, 20 moles of electrons are required.

20 moles of electrons = 20 faradays.

Explanations: Diagnostic Test #2

1. B is correct.

Outermost shell is the shell with the largest quantum number: n = 4.

The sum of electrons within the fourth shell: 2 for $4s^2$ + 1 for $4p^1$ = 3

Outermost subshell: the subshell within the shell that has the outermost electron/last added electron.

Usually it's the very last orbital in the electron configuration. It is $4p$, which only has 1 electron.

2. A is correct.

The nitrogen has 4 bonds and therefore has 0 nonbonding valence electrons.

The nitrate ion is NO_3^- and has the following resonance forms:

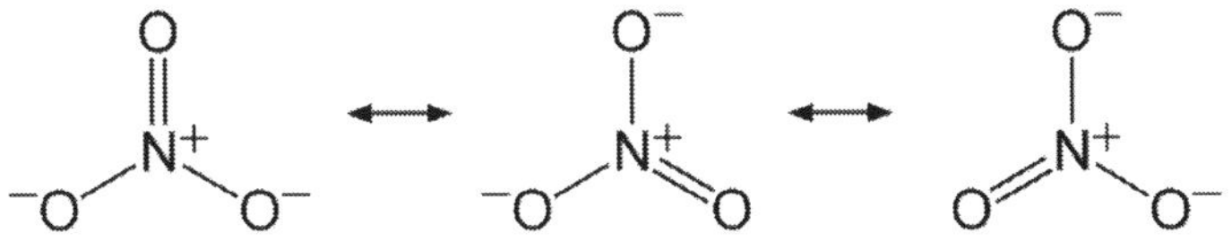

Nitrate, as a resonance hybrid, exists as a superposition of these three resonance forms.

3. A is correct.

1 mole of CO has 6.02×10^{23} CO molecules (Avogadro's number).

Calculate the moles of CO:

moles of CO = (7.4×10^{24} molecules) / (6.02×10^{23} molecules/mole)

moles of CO = 12.29 moles

In STP conditions, 1 mole of gas has a volume of 22.4 L.

Calculate volume of CO:

volume of CO = 12.29 moles × 22.4 L/mole

volume of CO = 275.3 L

4. A is correct.

Start by balancing the overall reaction:

$$2 \text{ Fe } (s) + 3 \text{ CuSO}_4 \ (aq) \rightarrow \text{Fe}_2(\text{SO}_4)_3 (aq) + 3 \text{ Cu } (s)$$

Identify the component that undergoes reduction (decreasing oxidation number).

It is Cu because it went from +2 in $CuSO_4$ to 0 in elemental Cu.

Write them in a half-reaction with their coefficients:

$$3 \text{ Cu}^{2+} \rightarrow 3 \text{ Cu}$$

Add electrons to balance the charges:

$$3 \text{ Cu}^{2+} + 6 \text{ e}^- \rightarrow 3 \text{ Cu}$$

5. E is correct.

In thermodynamics, an isolated system is a system enclosed by rigid immovable walls through which neither matter nor energy pass. Therefore, no matter or energy escapes from the system.

6. C is correct.

The rate constant (k) is related to the activation energy by the Arrhenius equation:

$$k = Ae^{-Ea/RT}$$

where, k = rate constant, Ea = activation energy, A = constant and R = 1.99 cal/mol·K

7. A is correct.

The *like dissolves like* rule applies when a solvent is miscible with a solute that has similar properties.

Therefore, a polar solute is miscible with a polar solvent and the rule applies for nonpolar solute / solvent.

8. A is correct.

Acetic acid is a weak acid (pKa = 4.75) and therefore only dissociates partially when placed in an aqueous solution.

Weak acids do not dissociate completely based on the relative instability of the resulting anion.

9. E is correct.

At the cathode, one cation is reduced and it is based on the electrochemical series.

Cu has a higher reduction potential than positive ion in water (H^+), so Cu is reduced.

10. C is correct.

Sulfur is in the third period (horizontal row) of the periodic table with a principal quantum number n = 3.

S is in group VI of the periodic table and has 6 valence electrons with an electronic configuration: ($3s^23p^4$).

11. E is correct.

Polar molecules have a net dipole due to difference in electronegativity between atoms.

Electronegativity is a chemical property to describe an atom's tendency to attract electrons to itself.

Consider geometry, as symmetrical molecules do not have a net dipole.

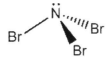

Nitrogen tribromide has a shape similar to ammonia (i.e., pyramidal) due to the three substituents and the remaining lone pair of electrons on the nitrogen. Therefore, the molecule has a net dipole toward the resulting vector from the electronegative bromines.

12. A is correct.

Gases do *not* have definite volumes and shapes; rather they take up the volume and shape of the container that they are in. This is different from liquids (which have a definite volume, but take up the shape of the container that they are in) and solids (which have both a definite volume and a definite shape).

Ideal gases are modeled as having perfectly elastic collisions, meaning that they have no intermolecular interactions. Essentially, the molecules in a gas (ideal or low pressure) are separate from one another.

13. B is correct.

The oxidizing agent is the substance that causes the other reactant(s) to be oxidized.

The oxidizing agent also undergoes reduction.

14. E is correct.

Criteria for calculating enthalpy:

When a reaction is reversed, the magnitude of ΔH stays the same, but the sign changes.

When the balanced equation for a reaction is multiplied by an integer, the corresponding value of ΔH must be multiplied by that integer as well.

The change in enthalpy for a reaction can be calculated from the enthalpies of formation of the reactants and the products.

Elements in their standard states make no contribution to the enthalpy calculations since the enthalpy of an element in its standard state is zero. Allotropes of an element (i.e., same chemical formula with different bonding arrangement) other than the standard state generally have non-zero standard enthalpies of formation.

Lattice energy is the energy released when one mole of a solid compound is created from its gaseous ions.

For NaCl, the lattice energy is represented by the reaction: $Na^+ (g) + Cl^- (g) \rightarrow NaCl (s)$

Arrange the reactions so when they are summed, all other terms cancel and the remaining reaction is the lattice reaction described above.

When reversing a reaction, change the positive/negative sign of ΔH.

$$Na (s) + \tfrac{1}{2}\, Cl_2 (g) \rightarrow NaCl (s) \quad \Delta H = -411 \text{ kJ}$$

$$Na (g) \rightarrow Na (s) \qquad\qquad\qquad \Delta H = -108 \text{ kJ}$$

$$Cl (g) \rightarrow \tfrac{1}{2}\, Cl_2 (g) \qquad\qquad \Delta H = -120 \text{ kJ}$$

$$Cl^- (g) \rightarrow Cl (g) + e^- \qquad\quad \Delta H = +349 \text{ kJ}$$

$$\underline{Na^+ (g) + e^- \rightarrow Na (g) \qquad\quad \Delta H = -496 \text{ kJ}}$$

$$Na^+ (g) + Cl^- (g) \rightarrow NaCl (s) \quad \Delta H = -786 \text{ kJ}$$

The lattice energy of a crystalline solid is usually defined as the energy of formation of the crystal from infinitely-separated ions (i.e., an exothermic process and hence the negative sign).

Some older textbooks define lattice energy with the opposite sign. The older notation was referring to the energy required to convert the crystal into infinitely separated gaseous ions in vacuum (i.e., an endothermic process and hence the positive sign).

15. E is correct. Methods I and II describe the experimental methods to determine reaction rates.

Method III tries to determine the rate law by predicting the mechanism, which affects the rate law.

16. A is correct.

The solvent is the molecule in the highest percentage.

17. D is correct.

When carbon dioxide dissolves in water, it exists in chemical equilibrium producing carbonic acid:

$$CO_2 + H_2O \leftrightarrow H_2CO_3$$

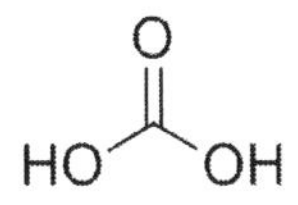

carbonic acid

The hydration reaction of sulfuric acid is highly exothermic (i.e., forward reaction is favored). Therefore, the dilution should always be performed by adding the acid to the water (not adding the water to the acid), so the *acid* is the limiting reagent.

This reaction is best thought of as the formation of hydronium ions:

$$H_2SO_4 + H_2O \rightarrow H_3O^+ + HSO_4^- \quad K_1 = 2.4 \times 10^6 \quad \text{(strong acid)}$$

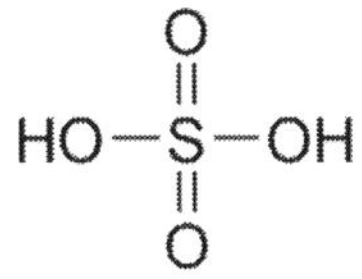

sulfuric acid

When all the hydrogens are removed, carbonic acid becomes carbonate ion (CO_3^{2-}), resonance forms shown below:

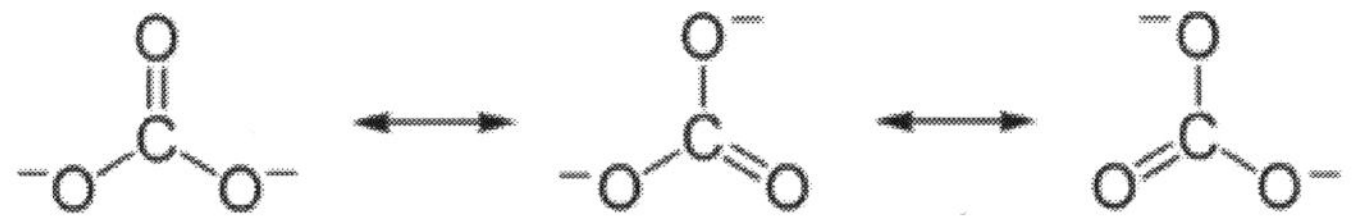

3 resonance structures for the carbonate ion

When all the hydrogens are removed, sulfuric acid becomes sulphate ion (SO_4^{2-}), resonance forms shown below.

6 resonance structures for the sulphate ion

Both ions have 2 extra electrons that reside with oxygen atoms. All oxygen atoms are equally capable of accommodating the extra electrons and the electrons are constantly moving (via resonance structures) between oxygens.

18. D is correct.

The magnetic quantum number m_l describes the particular orbitals in a subshell, their energy levels and the orientation of these subshells.

The value of m_l depends on the orbital angular momentum quantum number l; it can range from $-l$ to $+l$, and therefore can be a negative integer, zero, or a positive integer.

Restrictions on the possible values for m_l and the other quantum numbers give rise to the pattern of each subshell divided into orbitals that increase by odd numbers.

However, the magnetic quantum number does not describe the spin of the electrons; instead, this is the spin quantum number s.

19. E is correct.

Complete symmetry around the central atom is necessary for the molecule to be nonpolar.

For example, H_2O is a bent molecule (i.e., bond angle of 104.5° between the hydrogens) that lacks symmetry because both pairs of oxygen's lone pair electrons are on the same side of the central atom.

20. E is correct. Hydrogens, bonded directly to F, O or N, participate in hydrogen bonds. The hydrogen is partial positive (i.e., ∂+) due to the bond to these electronegative atoms.

The lone pair of electrons on the F, O or N interacts with the partial positive (∂+) hydrogen to form a hydrogen bond.

$$\delta^+ H \overset{\overset{\displaystyle \delta^-}{\displaystyle O}}{\diagdown} H \; \delta^+$$

Dipole in water molecule

21. D is correct. Formula mass is a synonym of molecular mass/molecular weight (MW).

Calculate MW of SO_2:

(atomic mass of S) + (2 × atomic mass of O)

(32.07 g/mole) + (2 × 16.00 g/mole)

MW of SO_2 = 64.02 g/mole

Note: 1 amu = 1 g/mole.

22. E is correct. The first law of thermodynamics describes the conservation of energy.

This equation describes that the change of energy (ΔE) equals heat (Q) released plus the magnitude of the work (W) generated.

23. C is correct. Catalysts lower activation energy by creating a new path towards the transition state.

Catalysts have no effect on the relative energy of the reactants, products or on the Gibbs free energy (ΔG) of the reaction.

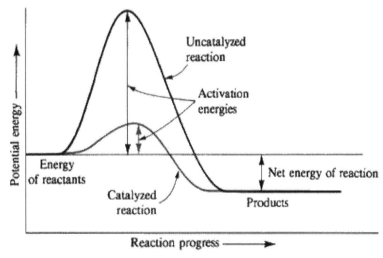

24. B is correct.

A colloidal suspension contains microscopically dispersed insoluble particles (i.e., colloid) suspended throughout the liquid. The colloid particles are larger than those of the solution, but not large enough to precipitate due to gravity.

The Tyndall effect is light scattering by particles in a colloid. Longer wavelength light is more transmitted while shorter wavelength light is reflected more. For example, the blue light emitted by an exhaust of a motorcycle, where burnt engine oil generates particles.

25. C is correct. With a neutralization reaction, the cations and anions on both reactants switch pairs, resulting in salt and water.

26. D is correct.

Determine the oxidation numbers of each atom on both sides of the reaction.

Mn has an oxidation number of +3 on the left and +4 on the right, so Mn was oxidized.

27. A is correct.

Metalloids are semimetallic elements (i.e., between metals and nonmetals). The metalloids are boron (B), silicon (Si), germanium (Ge), arsenic (As), antimony (Sb) and tellurium (Te). Some literature reports polonium (Po) and astatine (At) as metalloids.

They have properties between metals and nonmetals. They typically have a metallic appearance but are only fair conductors of electricity (as opposed to metals, which are excellent conductors), which makes them useable in the semi-conductor industry.

Metalloids tend to be brittle, and chemically they behave more like nonmetals.

28. A is correct.

OF_2 has 6 valence electrons for oxygen and 7 valence electrons for each of the fluorine atoms ($2 \times 7 = 14$).

Total number of valence electrons: $6 + 14 = 20$ electrons.

29. B is correct.

Dalton's Law of Partial Pressures:

$$P_T = P_1 + P_2 + P_3 + \ldots$$

Set the total pressure equal to partial pressures of each component of the container:

$$P_T = P_{H2O} + P_{N2} + P_{CO2} + P_{O2}$$

Solve for the partial pressure of nitrogen:

$$P_{N2} = P_T - [P_{O2} + P_{CO2} + P_{H2O}]$$

$$P_{N2} = (760 \text{ torr total}) - [300 \text{ torr } O_2 + 20 \text{ torr } CO_2 + 8 \text{ torr } H_2O)$$

$$P_{N2} = 432 \text{ torr } N_2$$

30. C is correct.

To determine the number of moles, divide the number of molecules by Avogadro's constant:

$$\text{number of moles} = 2.8 \times 10^{21} \text{ molecules} / (6.02 \times 10^{23} \text{ molecules/mol})$$

$$\text{number of moles} = 4.7 \times 10^{-3} \text{ mol}$$

31. E is correct.

More stable product means that the molecules lost energy: $-\Delta H$

A more orderly arrangement for products than the reactants means entropy decreased: $-\Delta S$

32. B is correct.

In equilibrium, only gaseous and aqueous species affect equilibrium.

Solids and liquids have no effect on equilibrium.

33. B is correct.

$$\text{Molarity} = \text{moles} / \text{volume}$$

Rearrange the equation to solve for volume:

$$\text{Volume} = \text{moles} / \text{molarity}$$

$$\text{Volume} = 3.40 \text{ mole} / 7.60 \text{ M}$$

$$\text{Volume} = 0.447 \text{ L}$$

34. A is correct.

By the Arrhenius definition, a base donates ⁻OH (hydroxide) ions in water.

In the Arrhenius theory, acids are defined as substances that dissociate in aqueous solution to give H^+ (hydrogen ions).

In the Arrhenius theory, bases are defined as substances that dissociate in aqueous solution to give OH^- (hydroxide ions).

35. D is correct.

Isotopes are variants of a particular element which differ in the number of neutrons. All isotopes of the element have the same number of protons and occupy the same position on the periodic table.

The number of protons within the atom's nucleus is the atomic number (Z) and is equal to the number of electrons in the neutral (non-ionized) atom. Each atomic number identifies a specific element, but not the isotope; an atom of a given element may have a wide range in its number of neutrons.

The number of both protons and neutrons (i.e., nucleons) in the nucleus is the atom's mass number (A), and each isotope of an element has a different mass number.

36. E is correct.

Whether a compound forms an ionic, polar covalent or covalent character, depends on the differences in electronegativity between the elements.

The value of electronegativity for an atom can be determined from the Pauling units assigned to each atom (e.g., F = 3.98, C = 2.55 and Fr = 0.7).

Covalent bonds have electrons equally shared between the atoms.

Ionic bonds form when one atom donates an electron completely to another atom. As a result, the donor atom acquires a (+) charge and the other atom acquires a (–) charge. The resulting (+) charge is strongly attracted to the (–) charge.

Metals, which lie on the left 2/3 of the periodic table, have low electronegativity.

Nonmetals, which lie in the right 1/3 of the periodic table, have high electronegativity.

For example, CsF, SrBr2, and PdCl2 are strongly ionic because the differences in electronegativity between the atoms are large.

37. A is correct.

Boyle's Law:

$$(P_1V_1) = (P_2V_2)$$

Solve for the final pressure:

$$P_2 = (P_1V_1) / V_2$$

$$P_2 = [(360 \text{ mmHg}) \times (440 \text{ mL})] / 820 \text{ mL}$$

$$P_2 = 193.2 \text{ mmHg}$$

38. D is correct.

Ba	C_2	O_4
+2	$(2 \times ?)$	(4×-2)

The sum of charges in a neutral molecule is zero:

$$2 + (2 \times \text{oxidation number of C}) + (4 \times -2) = 0$$

$$2 + (2 \times \text{oxidation number of C}) + (-8) = 0$$

$$2 \times (\text{oxidation number of C}) = -2 + 8$$

$$2 \times (\text{oxidation number of C}) = +6$$

$$\text{oxidation number of C} = +3$$

39. E is correct.

Heat capacity is amount of heat required to increase temperature of *the whole sample* by 1 °C.

Specific heat capacity is the heat required to increase temperature of *1 gram* of sample by 1 °C.

$$\text{Heat capacity} = \text{mass} \times \text{specific heat capacity}$$

$$\text{Heat capacity} = (68.0 \text{ g}) \times (4.184 \text{ J/g·°C})$$

$$\text{Heat capacity} = 285 \text{ J/°C}$$

40. A is correct.

For a reaction to occur, the molecules must have enough energy during a collision and strike each other with the proper spatial orientation to overcome the energy barrier (activation energy).

41. A is correct.

Mass of KCl = mass % × mass of solution

Mass of KCl = (18%) × (28 g)

Mass of KCl = 5.04 g

42. E is correct.

For a conjugate pair (e.g., formic acid and the formate ion), the product of K_a of the acid and the K_b of the base is equal to 10^{-14}:

$$K_a K_b = 10^{-14}$$

Therefore:

$$pK_a + pK_b = 14$$

Rearrange to solve for pK_b:

$$pK_b = 14 - pK_a$$

$$pK_b = 14 - [-\log(1.7 \times 10^{-4})]$$

$$pK_b = 14 + \log(1.7 \times 10^{-4})$$

43. B is correct.

Determine the oxidation numbers of each atom in both sides of the reaction.

Cu has an oxidation number of +1 on the left and 0 on the right, so Cu was reduced.

44. C is correct.

The properties of the elements on the periodic table repeat at regular intervals, creating "groups" or "families" of elements. Each column on the periodic table is a group, and elements within groups have similar physical and chemical characteristics (due to the orbital location of their outermost electron). These column groups would only exist if the elements of the periodic table were listed by increasing atomic number.

45. E is correct.

Hydrogens, bonded directly to F, O or N, participate in hydrogen bonds. The hydrogen is partial positive (i.e., $\partial+$) due to the bond to these electronegative atoms. The lone pair of electrons on the F, O or N interacts with the partial positive ($\partial+$) hydrogen to form a hydrogen bond.

46. E is correct.

For most substances, the solid form is denser than the liquid phase. Therefore, a block of most solids sinks in the liquid. With regards to pure water though, a block of ice (solid phase) floats in liquid water because ice is less dense.

Like other substances, when liquid water is cooled from room temperature, it becomes increasingly dense. However, at approximately 4 °C (39 °F), water reaches its maximum density, and as it's cooled further, it expands and becomes less dense. This phenomenon is known as negative thermal expansion and is attributed to strong intermolecular interactions that are orientation-dependent.

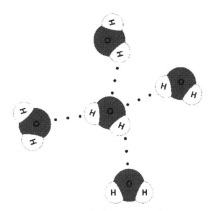

Ice with 4 hydrogen bonds between the water molecules

The density of water is about 1 g/cm^3 and depends on the temperature. When frozen, the density of water is decreased by about 9%. This is due to the decrease in intermolecular vibrations, which allows water molecules to form stable hydrogen bonds with other water molecules around. As these hydrogen bonds form, molecules are locking into positions similar to the hexagonal structure.

Even though hydrogen bonds are shorter in the crystal than in the liquid, this position locking decreases the average coordination number of water molecules as the liquid reaches the solid phase.

47. C is correct. Balanced reaction:

$$4\ NH_3 + 5\ O_2 \rightarrow 4\ NO + 6\ H_2O$$

48. B is correct.

Because the sample in this problem absorbs heat and undergoes a phase change, calculation of the heat has to be done in steps:

a) Ice temperature increases from –8 °C to 0 °C

$$q = m \times c \times \Delta T$$

$q = 15 \text{ g} \times 2.09 \text{ J/g·°C} \times 8 \text{ °C}$

$q = 250.8 \text{ J}$

b) Ice reaches melting point and starts melting to form water at 0 °C

$q = m \times \text{heat of fusion}$

$q = 15 \text{ g} \times 334 \text{ J/g}$

$q = 5,010 \text{ J}$

c) Water temperature increases from 0 °C to 15 °C

$q = m \times c \times \Delta T$

$q = 15 \text{ g} \times 4.18 \text{ J/g·°C} \times 15 \text{ °C}$

$q = 940.5 \text{ J}$

Sum the results to obtain total required heat = (250.8 J + 5,010 J + 940.5 J)

$q = 6,201 \text{ J}$

49. B is correct. The rate-determining step of a reaction is the slowest step (i.e., takes the most time).

50. D is correct. Fluorine salts often dissociate into anions and cations and are soluble in water.

Sulfide salts are generally insoluble in water.

Acetic acid is a short chain carboxylic acid compounds that is soluble in water.

51. E is correct.

Amphoteric compounds act as Brønsted-Lowry acids (i.e., donate protons) and as bases (i.e., accept protons).

Examples of amphoteric molecules include amino acids (i.e., an amine and carboxylic acid group), and self-ionizable compounds such as water.

HSO_4^- acts as both a proton donor and a proton acceptor.

52. E is correct. The elements Li, Na, K, Rb and Cs are Group IA / 1 elements.

Within a group, the radius of an atom increases from top to bottom.

The atom with the largest radius (size) is the lowest atom in the group (i.e., largest principal quantum number), which is Cs.

53. B is correct.

Bond angles in a tetrahedral molecule are approximately 109.5°.

The exact value depends on the relative size (i.e., steric hindrance) of the substituents bonded to the central atom and is measured experimentally.

The bond angle of 104.5° (i.e., bent) is observed in water due to the two lone pairs of electrons on the oxygen, which decrease the bond angle from the predicted 109.5°.

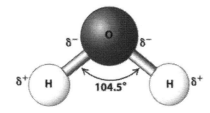

The bond angle of 109.5° (i.e., tetrahedral) is observed in sp^3 hybridized atoms (e.g., CH_4).

54. E is correct.

Charles' law explains how, at constant pressure, gases behave when heated.

Charles' law:

V α T or V / T = constant

or

$(V_1 / T_1) = (V_2 / T_2)$

Volume and temperature are proportional. Therefore, an increase in one term results in an increase in the other.

55. A is correct. Determine the oxidation numbers of each atom on both sides of the reaction.

Cr has an oxidation number of 0 on the left and +3 on the right, which means Cr was oxidized.

Cl has oxidation number of 0 on the left and −1 on the right, which means that Cl was reduced.

56. A is correct.

Negative ΔH_f^o indicates the release of energy upon formation of a certain molecule.

The molecule's energy level is lower than the sum of energies for the reactants.

Molecules with lower energy levels tend to be more stable.

The total enthalpy (i.e., internal energy) of a system cannot be measured directly; the *enthalpy change* of a system is measured instead.

Enthalpy change is defined by the following equation:

$$\Delta H = H_f - H_i$$

If the standard enthalpy of the products is less than the standard enthalpy of the reactants, the standard enthalpy of reaction is negative and the reaction is exothermic (i.e., releases heat).

If the standard enthalpy of the products are more than the standard enthalpy of the reactants, the standard enthalpy of reaction is positive and the reaction is endothermic (i.e., absorbs heat).

57. E is correct. All are important conditions for chemical reactions to occur.

58. D is correct. Molarity is defined as the number of moles of solute per liter of solution. Molarity is based on a specified volume of solution.

Molality (molal concentration), is a measure of the concentration of a solute in a solution in terms of amount of substance in a specified amount of mass of the solvent.

59. A is correct. The Brønsted-Lowry acid-base theory focuses on the ability to accept and donate protons (H^+).

A Brønsted-Lowry acid is the term for a substance that donates a proton (H^+) in an acid-base reaction, while a Brønsted-Lowry base is the term for a substance that accepts a proton.

60. E is correct. A cathode is the electrode from which conventional current leaves a polarized electric device (i.e., cathode current departs).

Positively charged cations always move towards the cathode and negatively charged anions move away.

Cathode polarity (with respect to the anode) can be positive or negative and depends on the type of device.

If the device provides energy (e.g., discharging a battery), the cathode is positive.

If the device takes energy (e.g., recharging a battery), the cathode is negative.

In a discharging battery or galvanic cell, the cathode is always positively charged.

In electrolysis, reduction occurs at the cathode, while oxidation occurs at the anode.

Explanations: Diagnostic Test #3

1. B is correct.

The anion has the largest radius because it has the greatest number of electrons occupying the valence orbitals around the nucleus.

2. C is correct.

Valence electrons are those electrons of the outermost electron shell that can participate in a chemical bond.

Lone pairs are those valence electrons that do not participate in bonding within the compound.

3. D is correct.

Hydrocarbons are nonpolar molecules, which means that the dominant intermolecular force is London dispersion (i.e., van der Waals). This force gets stronger as the number of atoms in each molecule increases.

Stronger intermolecular forces result in a higher boiling point.

C_2H_6 has the least number of atoms and therefore has the lowest boiling point.

4. C is correct.

Assume that hydrogen and oxygen have their most common oxidation states, which is +1 and –2, respectively.

Because the sum of oxidation numbers in a neutral molecule is zero:

0 = (oxidation state of H) + (oxidation state of Br) + [4 × (oxidation state of O)]

0 = 1 + oxidation state of Br + 4(–2)

oxidation state of Br = +7

5. A is correct.

In a chemical reaction, bonds within reactants are broken and new bonds form.

Therefore, in bond dissociation problems:

$\Delta H_{reaction}$ = sum of bond energy in reactants – sum of bond energy in products.

This is the opposite of ΔH_f problems, where:

$\Delta H_{reaction}$ = sum of ΔH_f product – sum of ΔH_f reactant

For $N_2 + 3 H_2 \rightarrow 2 NH_3$

$\Delta H_{reaction}$ = sum of bond energy in reactants – sum of bond energy in products

$\Delta H_{reaction} = [(N\equiv N) + 3(H\text{–}H)] - [2 \times 3(N\text{–}H)]$

$\Delta H_{reaction} = [(946 \text{ kJ}) + (3 \times 436 \text{ kJ}) - (2 \times (3 \times 389 \text{ kJ}))]$

$\Delta H_{reaction} = -80 \text{ kJ}$

6. C is correct.

Usually, to solve this kind of problem, determine the order of all reactants (X, Y, Z).

However, if you look at the answer choices, all of them pertain to the order of X. Therefore, calculate the order of X.

Find 2 experiments where the concentrations of other reactants (Y and Z) are constant: experiments 3 and 4.

Notice that when the concentration of X is reduced from 0.600 M to 0.200 M (i.e., a factor of 3), the rate also decreases by a factor of 3 (from 15 to 5). Therefore, the reaction is first order in respect to X.

7. E is correct.

$3 \text{ AgNO}_3 \, (aq) + \text{Li}_3\text{PO}_4 \, (aq) \rightarrow \text{Ag}_3\text{PO}_4 + 3 \text{ LiNO}_3$

For double-replacement reactions, one of the prerequisites is having at least one product molecule precipitating (e.g., AgCl or Ag_3PO_4, in this example).

Be familiar with the solubility for various salts.

8. C is correct.

H_2O lost a proton (H^+) to form ^-OH.

The proton is taken by CO_3^{2-} (base) and it becomes HCO_3^- (conjugate acid).

H_2O acts as the donor and transfers a proton to CO_3^{2-}, which acts as the acceptor.

9. A is correct.

$Cl_2 \rightarrow 2 \, Cl^-$

Balance the charges by adding electrons:

$Cl_2 + 2 \, e^- \rightarrow 2 \, Cl^-$

According to the balanced reaction, Cl_2 gains 2 electrons to form Cl^- ions.

10. B is correct.

There are six alkaline earth metals located in group II (i.e., column) of the periodic table. The six elements are beryllium (Be), magnesium (Mg), calcium (Ca), strontium (Sr), barium (Ba) and radium (Ra).

They have very similar properties: all shiny, silvery-white, somewhat reactive metals at STP (standard temperature and pressure).

11. D is correct.

Nitrogen has a valence number of 5 electrons. With three substituents (e.g., 3 chlorines), the lone pair on the nitrogen atom interconverts and adopts the geometry of trigonal pyramidal (similar to NH_3, ammonia).

12. D is correct.

Ideal gas equation:

$$PV = nRT$$

where P is pressure, V is volume, n is the number of moles, R is the universal gas constant and T is temperature.

13. C is correct.

Balanced equation (decomposition):

$$3\ NO \rightarrow N_2O + NO_2$$

14. D is correct.

Decreasing external pressure increases the distance between gas molecules.

Therefore, the phase change is likely from liquid → gas.

15. A is correct.

Endothermic reactions are nonspontaneous with heat as a reactant. The products are less stable than the reactants and ΔG is positive.

Exothermic reactions are spontaneous with heat as a product. The products are more stable than the reactants and ΔG is negative.

16. E is correct.

Carbonates (CO_3), nitrates (NO_3) and acetates ($C_2H_3O_2$) tend to be soluble in water.

Most silver salts are insoluble. $AgNO_3$ and $Ag(C_2H_3O_2)$ are common soluble salts of silver; virtually all others insoluble.

17. A is correct.

The formula for pH is:

$$pH = -\log[H^+]$$

Rearrange to solve for $[H^+]$:

$$[H^+] = 10^{-pH}$$

$$[H^+] = 10^{-6.35}$$

$$[H^+] = 4.5 \times 10^{-7} \text{ M}$$

18. E is correct. Electrons become excited when gaining energy from absorbing a photon.

A valence electron can absorb energy and enter an excited state. The excited state can often occurs when an electron absorbs energy and jumps from its original energy level or orbital (i.e., the ground state), to an empty orbital of a higher energy shell, further from the nucleus.

19. E is correct. Formulas of ionic compounds are written with the cation first, followed by the anion.

A common example is NaCl (e.g., Na^+Cl^-), which is the formula for sodium chloride.

Na^+ is the symbol for the positively-charged sodium cation.

Cl^- is the symbol for the negatively-charged chloride anion.

All the other statements are true of ionic compounds.

20. C is correct. Kinetic Molecular Theory of Gas Molecules defines temperature in terms of the *average* speed of the molecules and assumes differences in speed for individual gas molecules.

The kinetic theory of gases describes a gas as a large number of small particles in constant rapid motion. These particles collide with each other and with the walls of the container.

Their average kinetic energy depends only on the absolute temperature of the system.

21. C is correct.   Calculations:

% nitrogen = (molecular weight N) / (wt of compound)

% nitrogen 14 g/mol / [14 g/mol + (2 × 16 g/mol)]

% nitrogen = 14 g/mol / (46 g/mol)

% nitrogen = 0.304 = 30.4%

22. A is correct.

Endothermic reactions are nonspontaneous with heat as a reactant. The products are less stable than the reactants and ΔG is positive.

Exothermic reactions are spontaneous with heat as a product. The products are more stable than the reactants and ΔG is negative.

Isothermal means the same amount of heat.

Spontaneous refers to a reaction with products more stable than reactants (i.e., ΔG is negative).

Exergonic refers to a reaction with a negative ΔG (i.e., products are more stable than reactants).

23. B is correct.

Increased temperature means the molecules have more kinetic energy. Kinetic energy (i.e., energy of motion) is needed for the molecules to collide (i.e., frequency of collision, force of impact and collision angle).

The energy barrier for the reaction to yield products is the energy of activation.

Heating (i.e., adding energy) causes the molecules to increase their average kinetic energy.

24. E is correct.

When a solution is diluted, the moles of solute (n) is constant.

However, the molarity and volume change because n = MV:

$n_1 = n_2$

$M_1V_1 = M_2V_2$

$M_2 = (M_1V_1) / V_2$

$M_2 = [1.00 \text{ M} \times (500.0 \text{ mL} \times 0.001 \text{ L/mL})] / 3.50 \text{ L}$

$M_2 = 0.143 \text{ M}$

25. D is correct.

Start by calculating the moles of HCl:

Moles HCl = molarity HCl × volume HCl

Moles HCl = 0.1 M × (25 mL × 0.001 L/mL)

Moles HCl = 0.0025 mole

Use the coefficients in the reaction equation to determine the moles of $Ba(OH)_2$:

Moles of $Ba(OH)_2$ = (coefficient $Ba(OH)_2$ / coefficient HCl) × moles HCl

Moles of $Ba(OH)_2$ = (½) × 0.0025 mole

Moles of $Ba(OH)_2$ = 0.00125 mole

Divide moles by molarity to calculate volume:

Volume of $Ba(OH)_2$ = moles of $Ba(OH)_2$ / molarity of $Ba(OH)_2$

Volume of $Ba(OH)_2$ = 0.00125 mole / 0.15 M

Volume of $Ba(OH)_2$ = 0.00833 L

Convert volume to milliliters:

0.00833 L × 1,000 mL/L = 8.33 mL

26. B is correct.

The net reaction:

$$Cu + Li^+ \rightarrow Cu^{2+} + Li$$

Reverse the sign of potential values for the oxidation reaction.

Arrange the provided equations to end up with the net reaction upon addition:

$Cu \rightarrow Cu^{2+} + 2\ e^-$ $E° = -0.337$ V

$Li^+ + e^- \rightarrow Li$ $E° = -3.03$ V

Multiply the second equation by 2 to match the number of electrons from 1st reaction:

$2\ Li^+ + 2\ e^- \rightarrow 2\ Li$ $E° = -3.03$ V

($E°$ values are constant and not affected by change in coefficients)

Now, add those equations together to obtain the net reaction and $E°$:

$Cu \rightarrow Cu^{2+} + 2\ e^-$ $E° = -0.337$ V

$\underline{2\ Li^+ + 2\ e^- \rightarrow 2\ Li}$ $E° = -3.03$ V

$Cu + 2\ Li^+ \rightarrow Cu^{2+} + 2\ Li$ $E° = -3.367$ V

27. E is correct. Noble gas electronic configurations are characterized by filled valence *s* and *p* subshells.

The *s* shell can accommodate 2 electrons and the *p* shell 6 electrons.

28. C is correct. Polar molecules have dipole moments due to non-uniform distributions of charge.

A partial positive charge may be on one side of the atom, while a partial negative charge is on the other side.

29. C is correct. London dispersion forces are the weakest of the intermolecular forces (e.g., hydrogen bonding, dipole-dipole, dipole-induced dipole).

The molecule that lacks electronegative atoms will not have partial positive and partial negative regions necessary for dipoles (and the other forms of intermolecular bonding).

30. A is correct. The ClO^- and Cl^- combine to form Cl_2.

The oxidation state of chlorine in Cl_2 is defined as 0.

The oxidation state of chlorine in ClO^- is +1 and Cl^- is –1.

Because chlorine is being oxidized and reduced in the same reaction, this reaction is an example of disproportionation.

31. B is correct. Heat is energy that is transferred to the molecules and increases their kinetic energy.

Temperature is a measure of the average kinetic energy of the molecules.

32. D is correct. The rate of a reaction depends on the reactants being transformed into products, which requires reactants to overcome the barrier to the reaction (i.e., energy of activation).

Increasing the concentration of the reactants allows more reactants to collide and proceed in the forward direction.

Increasing the pressure effectively increases the concentration because the molecules are closer together.

Increasing the temperature would increase the rate of the reaction because molecules can overcome the energy of activation barrier. Decreasing the temperature of the reaction decreases the reaction rate.

33. D is correct.

A "solution" is a homogeneous mixture. Therefore, a mixture is a homogeneous structure considered to be a solution, since it is composed of more than one chemical compound.

34. A is correct.

$C_1V_1 = C_2V_2$

moles H^+ = moles ^-OH

$(x$ ml)·(0.25 M)·(2 moles H^+ / 1 mole H_2SO_4)

   = (40 ml)·(0.3 M)·(1 mole ^-OH / 1 mole NaOH)

x = 24 ml

35. E is correct.

Seventeen elements are generally classified as nonmetals. Eleven are gases: hydrogen (H), helium (He), nitrogen (N), oxygen (O), fluorine (F), neon (Ne), chlorine (Cl), argon (Ar), krypton (Kr), xenon (Xe) and radon (Rn). One nonmetal is a liquid – bromine (Br) – and a five are solids: carbon (C), phosphorus (P), sulfur (S), selenium (Se) and iodine (I).

Nonmetals tend to be highly volatile (i.e., easily vaporized), have low elasticity and are good insulators of heat and electricity.

Nonmetals tend to have high ionization energy and electronegativity and share (or gain) an electron when bonding with other elements.

36. D is correct.

A carbonate (resonance forms shown below) is a salt of carbonic acid and is characterized by the presence of the carbonate ion, CO_3^{-2}

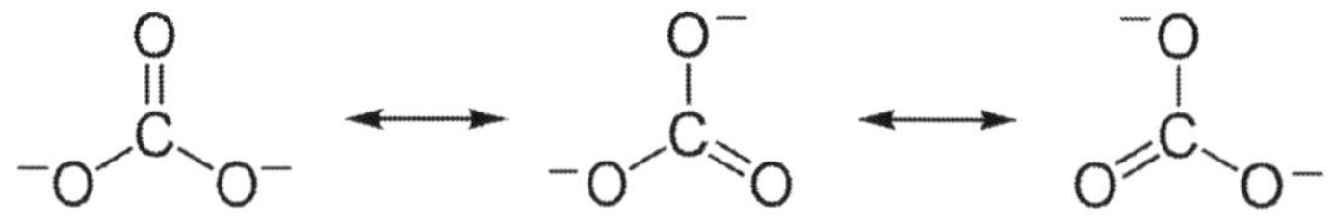

Carbonic acid (shown below) has the chemical formula H_2CO_3.

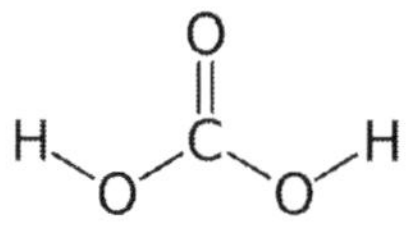

37. D is correct.

Convert the initial temperature from Celsius to Kelvin:

27 °C = 273 + 27 = 300 K

Charles' Law:

$(V_1 / T_1) = (V_2 / T_2)$

Solve for the final volume:

$V_2 = (V_1 / T_1) / T_2$

$V_2 = (50 K) \times [(1.00 L) / (300 K)]$

$V_2 = 0.167 L = 167 mL$

38. A is correct.

Calculate the molecular mass (MW) of K_2CrO_4:

MW of K_2CrO_4:

(2 × atomic mass of K) + atomic mass of Cr + (4 × atomic mass of O)

(2 × 39.10 g/mole) + 52.00 g/mole + (4 × 16.00 g/mole)

MW of K_2CrO_4 = 194.20 g/mole

To obtain percent by mass composition of chromium, divide the mass of a Cr atom by the molecular mass, and multiply with 100%.

% mass of Cr = (mass of Cr in molecule / molecular mass of K_2CrO_4) × 100%

% mass of Cr = (52.00g / 194.20 g/mole) × 100%

% mass of Cr = 26.8%

39. B is correct.

Change in temperature is equivalent when measured in either Celsius or Kelvin.

40. E is correct.

The equilibrium constant of a chemical reaction is the value of the reaction quotient when the reaction has reached equilibrium.

An equilibrium constant value is independent of the analytical concentrations of the reactant and product species in a mixture, but depends on temperature and on ionic strength (i.e., dissociation into ions in solution).

For a general chemical equilibrium of the reaction $aA + bB \rightarrow cC + dD$:

$$K_{eq} = [C]^c \times [D]^d / [A]^a \times [B]^b$$

An equilibrium constant is related to the standard Gibbs free energy change for the reaction.

$$\Delta G = -RT \ln K_{eq}$$

41. B is correct.

A suspension is a heterogeneous mixture containing solid particles that are sufficiently large to precipitate; usually they must be larger than one micrometer in size.

Unlike colloids, suspensions eventually settle (e.g., sand in water). The suspended particles are visible under a microscope and settle over time, which distinguishes a suspension from a colloid, in which the suspended particles are smaller and do not settle.

Colloidal particles are too small to be extracted by simple filtration.

Colloids and suspensions are different from solutions, in which the dissolved substance (solute) does not exist as a solid, and solvent and solute are homogeneously mixed.

42. C is correct.

An acid donates hydrogen ions (H^+) in water. It is important to differentiate the hydrogen ion from a hydrogen atom (H), because a hydrogen ion refers to a hydrogen atom that has donated its one electron and thus consists of only a nucleus (i.e., proton and neutron). A hydrogen ion H^+ is thus equivalent to a proton.

43. D is correct.

Calculate moles of chromium:

moles Cr = mass Cr / molecular mass of Cr

moles Cr = 40.0 g / 52.0 g/mol

moles Cr = 0.769 mol

The solution is aqueous $CrCl_3$, which dissociates into the following ions:

$$CrCl_3 \rightarrow Cr^{3+} + 3\ Cl^-$$

Half reaction of chromium reduction:

$$Cr^{3+}(aq) + 3\ e^- \rightarrow Cr\ (s)$$

In order to calculate charge required to deposit metal, calculate the moles of electron:

moles of electron = (coefficient e⁻ / coefficient Cr) × moles Cr

moles of electron = (3 / 1) × 0.769 mol

moles of electron = 2.31 mol

Calculate total charge:

charge = moles of electron × Faraday's constant

charge = 2.31 mol × 96,500 C/mol

charge = 222,692 C ≈ 2.23 × 10⁵ C

44. D is correct.

The atomic number (represented by the symbol *Z*) is the number of protons for an atom of a given element. In the periodic table, the elements are listed by order of increasing atomic number.

45. B is correct.

The hydrogens and oxygen in water molecule are held together by covalent bonds.

However, the electrons are closer to the oxygen nucleus than the hydrogen nucleus, due to the geometry of the molecule and the electronegativity difference between oxygen and hydrogen.

Dipole in a water molecule

Oxygen has a partial negative charge and each hydrogen has a partial positive charge.

46. D is correct.

Vapor pressure is the pressure of a vapor in thermodynamic equilibrium with its condensed phases (solid or liquid) in a closed container. Vapor pressure is dependent on temperature only.

$$P = Ae^{(-\Delta Hvap / RT)}$$

The relationship between vapor pressure and temperature is exponential, and as temperature increases, vapor pressure increases.

47. A is correct.

Use the molecular mass of H = 1 g/mol and for O = 16 g/mol.

HO has a hydrogen fraction 1 / (1 g + 16 g) = 0.06 = 6%.

H_2O has a hydrogen fraction 2 / (2 g + 16 g) = 0.11 = 11%.

The others choices are not empirical formulae.

48. D is correct.

The Second law implies irreversible reactions. If a statement describes a process as in only one direction, it could be a consequence of the Second law.

49. E is correct.

A catalyst increases the rate of a reaction by lowering the activation energy (i.e., the energy of the reaction's transition state) by providing an alternative chemical pathway for the reaction.

There are many different mechanisms that the catalyst can use to provide this alternative pathway, including changing the proximity and orientation of the reactants, forming ionic bonds with the intermediates and creating bond strain.

50. B is correct.

The *–ate* ending indicates the species with more oxygen than the species ending in *–ite*.

However, it does not indicate a specific number of oxygens.

51. C is correct.

In the Brønsted–Lowry theory, acids and bases are defined by the way they react.

The definition is expressed in terms of an equilibrium expression:

acid + base $\leftrightarrow$ conjugate base + conjugate acid.

With an acid, HA, the equation can be written symbolically as:

$HA + B \leftrightarrow A^- + HB^+$

The Brønsted-Lowry acid is the species that donates a proton (H^+).

The Brønsted-Lowry base is the species that accepts the proton (H^+).

The acid forms its conjugate base, and the base forms its conjugate acid by exchange of a proton.

52. B is correct.

The electron configuration is the arrangement of electrons by sublevels (i.e., shells) according to increasing energy. An electron shell represents the orbit of the electrons in that energy level.

Each shell can hold a maximum number of electrons, and the outermost shell contains electrons of the highest energy.

A continuous spectrum refers to an uninterrupted spectrum of waves or frequencies.

Atomic number is the number of protons in an atom of a particular element, and atomic notation refers to the way that a chemical symbol is written, with the mass number as a superscript and the atomic number as a subscript.

Excited state is a quantum state of a system whereby an atom (or molecule or nucleus) has a higher energy than the ground state (i.e. higher energy orbital).

53. D is correct.

Bond energy is related to bond dissociation energy (i.e., energy required to break a bond).

Bond length is inversely related to bond strength.

Longer bonds have lower bond energy and are weaker.

54. C is correct.

Since both samples of He and Ne are at the same temperature, pressure, and volume, both have equal moles of gas.

Even though there are equal moles of each gas of He and Ne, use the molar masses given in the periodic table and notice that the samples contain different masses of each sample.

55. C is correct.

Oxidation number for Br is –1 on the left and 0 on the right; increase in oxidation number means that Br is oxidized in this reaction.

56. C is correct.

The total enthalpy (i.e., internal energy) of a system cannot be measured directly; the *enthalpy change* of a system is measured instead.

Enthalpy change is defined by the following equation:

$$\Delta H = H_f - H_i$$

If the standard enthalpy of the products is less than the standard enthalpy of the reactants, the standard enthalpy of reaction is negative and the reaction is exothermic (i.e., releases heat).

If the standard enthalpy of the products is greater than the standard enthalpy of the reactants, the standard enthalpy of reaction is positive and the reaction is endothermic (i.e., absorbs heat).

Since the entropy change is negative, it cannot be determined from the information given if the reaction is spontaneous under standard conditions.

57. D is correct.

Check the K_{eq} of the new equilibrium state:

$$K_{eq} = [A]\cdot[B] / [AB]$$

$$K_{eq} = (2 \times 1) / 64$$

$$K_{eq} = 1 / 32$$

Because K_{eq} has changed, it can only mean that the temperature has changed, which would also change K_{eq}.

58. A is correct. Start by calculating the number of moles:

Moles of Na_2CO_3 = mass Na_2CO_3 / moles of Na_2CO_3

Moles of Na_2CO_3 = 0.500 g / 105.99 g/mol

Moles of Na_2CO_3 = 4.717×10^{-3} mol

Check the reaction to obtain coefficients of HCl and Na_2CO_3.

Moles of HCl required = (coefficient of HCl / coefficient of Na_2CO_3) × moles Na_2CO_3

Moles of HCl required = (2/1) × 4.717×10^{-3} mol

Moles of HCl required = 9.434×10^{-3} mol

Use the number of moles and the molarity to calculate volume:

volume of HCl = moles of HCl / molarity of HCl

volume of HCl = 9.434×10^{-3} mol / 0.1 M

volume of HCl = 0.0943 L

Convert to milliliters:

0.0943 L × (1,000 mL / L) = 94.3 mL

59. B is correct.

Complete reaction:

2 HNO_3 (*aq*) + $Ba(OH)_2$ (*aq*) → $Ba(NO_3)_2$ and 2 H_2O

60. D is correct.

Oxidation always occurs at the anode, while reduction always occurs at the cathode.

Mg^{2+} does not lose any more electrons and Cl^- does not gain any more electrons.

This page is intentionally left blank

Explanations: Diagnostic Test #4

1. E is correct.

A metallic element is typically shiny, opaque and hard. They have good electrical and thermal conductivity. Generally, metallic elements are malleable (i.e., able to be pressed into shapes without breaking), fusible (i.e., able to be melted) and ductile (i.e., able to be drawn into a thin wire).

2. D is correct.

In PO_4^{3-}, the central atom is P and it has 5 electrons. To reach stability (i.e., complete octet with 8 electrons), it needs 3 more electrons.

Three oxygen atoms donate one electron each to create a single covalent bond with phosphate. After creating those bonds, phosphate has 8 total electrons and is stable. It still has a free electron pair, which is used to form a coordinate covalent bond with the fourth oxygen atom. The other 3 oxygen atoms gain an electron each to reach stability, resulting in a negatively-charged phosphate ion.

Calculate the formal charges: electrons in covalent coordinate bonds are treated as free electrons.

Phosphate:

(5 valence e^-) – (3 bonding pairs) – (2 e^- in covalent coordinate bond) = 0

For each of the 3 oxygens that gained an electron:

(6 valence e^-) – (5 free e^-) – (1 bonding pair) – (1 gained e^-) = –1

Oxygen with coordinate covalent bond:

(6 valence e^-) – (6 free e^-) = 0

Oxygen did not contribute any electrons to the coordinate bond.

Total charge of ion: –3

Because there are 4 oxygen atoms, there are 4 possible combinations whereby one of the oxygen atoms has covalent coordinate bond with phosphate and the remaining 3 atoms are attached to phosphate.

Four resonance structures of the PO_4^{3-} ion

3. E is correct.

STP (i.e., standard temperature and pressure) conditions are temperature of 0 °C (273 K) and pressure of 1 atm.

4. B is correct.

Pure elements always have an oxidation number 0.

For $ZnSO_4$, the sulfate ion (SO_4) always has oxidation number of –2.

Therefore, the Zn ion is +2.

5. D is correct.

Heat = mass × specific heat × change in temperature.

$$q = m \times c \times \Delta T$$

Rearrange the equation to solve for ΔT:

$$\Delta T = q / (m \times c)$$

Convert the energy to joules:

$$6.90 \times 10^2 \text{ calories} \times 4{,}180 \text{ J/calorie} = 2{,}884{,}200 \text{ J}$$

Often, heat is expressed in kilojoules (kJ).

Because the specific heat is in joules, convert kilojoules into joules:

$$57.4 \text{ kg} \times 1{,}000 \text{ g/kg} = 57{,}400 \text{ g}$$

Use those values in the rearranged heat equation to obtain ΔT:

$$\Delta T = q / (m \times c)$$
$$\Delta T = 2{,}884{,}200 \text{ J} / (57{,}400 \text{ g} \times 4.18 \text{ J/g·°C})$$
$$\Delta T = 12.0 \text{ °C}$$

6. D is correct.

The rate of a reaction depends on the energy of activation (E_{act}), which is the highest barrier in the energy profile diagram.

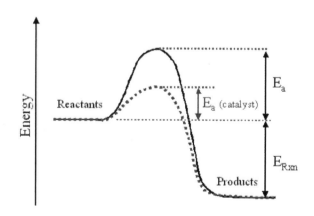

7. C is correct.

The "like dissolves like" rule applies when a solvent is miscible with a solute that has similar properties.

A polar solute is miscible with a polar solvent (e.g., via hydrogen bonding) and the rule applies for nonpolar solute / solvent (e.g., via hydrophobic interactions).

8. C is correct.

Acetic acid (CH_3COOH) is a proton (H^+) donor and a weak acid, which are a property of a Brønsted-Lowry acid.

9. A is correct.

A reducing agent causes another substance to be oxidized.

Oxidation is defined as an increase in the oxidation number and is the loss of electrons.

10. D is correct.

All atoms of a given element have the same number of protons (i.e., atomic number). Elements may have different numbers of neutrons, forming isotopes of the same elements. They may also have different numbers of electrons, forming charged particles called ions (anions and cations).

11. C is correct.

Valence electrons are those of the outermost electron shell that can participate in a chemical bond. The number of valence electrons for an element can be determined by its group (i.e., vertical column) on the periodic table. With the exception of the transition metals (i.e., groups 3-12), the group number identifies how many valence electrons are associated with a particular element: all elements of the same group have the same number of valence electrons.

Chlorine belongs to group VIIA/17 in the periodic table and has 7 valence electrons.

To reach stability, chlorine needs 8 electrons and the chloride ion gains an electron to achieve 8 electrons.

12. B is correct.

Boyle's Law:

$$(P_1V_1) = (P_2V_2)$$

Solve for the final volume:

$$V_2 = (P_1V_1) / (P_2)$$

$$V_2 = [(0.96 \text{ atm}) \times (4.8 \text{ L})] / (1.4 \text{ atm})$$

$$V_2 = 3.29 \text{ L} \approx 3.3 \text{ L}$$

13. A is correct.

Salts of group 1A metals and all nitrate salts completely dissociate in water and have no equilibrium constant.

The salt can be identified by the (*aq*) notation, which means it dissociates.

Ag_2SO_4 is a salt that precipitates out of solution hence the (*s*) notation.

14. E is correct.

Balanced equation:

$$Zn(HCO_3)_2(s) \rightarrow ZnCO_3 + H_2O + CO_2$$

Decomposition to form water and carbon dioxide is a characteristic reaction of bicarbonate (HCO_3^-).

15. E is correct.

The rate-determining step has the highest activation energy (energy barrier to product formation).

16. C is correct. A colloidal suspension contains microscopically dispersed insoluble particles (i.e., colloid) suspended throughout the liquid.

The colloid particles are larger than those of the solution, but not large enough to precipitate due to gravity.

17. A is correct.

$$K_a = [H^+] \cdot [F^-] / [HF]$$

$$K_a = (5 \times 10^{-2}) \cdot (5 \times 10^{-5}) / (2.5 \times 10^{-1})$$

$$K_a = 1 \times 10^{-5}$$

18. E is correct. Selenium (element 34) is a nonmetal.

19. A is correct. CH_2O is an aldehyde (i.e., formaldehyde).

The carbonyl carbon is double bonded to the oxygen and is sp^2 hybridized.

20. B is correct.

Hydrocarbons are nonpolar molecules, which means that the dominant intermolecular force is London dispersion. This force gets stronger as the number of atoms in each molecule increases. Stronger forces result in a higher boiling point.

21. B is correct.

$CH_4 + 2 O_2 \rightarrow CO_2 + 2 H_2O$ is a combustion reaction.

A single-replacement reaction results in the production of a compound and an element, but this reaction results in the production of two compounds. This reaction is a combustion reaction where methane (CH_4) reacts with oxygen.

A: $AgNO_3 + KCl \rightarrow KNO_3 + AgCl$ is correctly classified as a double-replacement reaction, where parts of two ionic compounds ($AgNO_3$ and KCl) are exchanged to make two new compounds (KNO_3 and $AgCl$).

C: $Zn + H_2SO_4 \rightarrow ZnSO_4 + H_2$ is correctly classified as a single-replacement reaction, where one element is substituted for another element in a compound, making a new compound ($ZnSO_4$) and an element (H_2).

D: $2 KClO_3 \rightarrow 2 KCl + 3 O_2$ is correctly classified as a decomposition reaction, where one chemical compound ($2 KClO_3$) is split into two or more products ($2 KCl$ and $3 O_2$).

22. E is correct.

Balanced synthesis reaction:

$$4 Li(s) + O_2(g) = 2 Li_2O$$

In ionic form, oxygen has an oxidation number of –2.

Because Li is in Group IA, its oxidation number is +1.

The compound of these elements is Li_2O.

23. C is correct.

The definition of one molar is one mol per liter of solution (mol L^{-1}).

Reaction rate is measured in molarity per second (mol L^{-1} s^{-1}).

24. E is correct.

When a solution is diluted, the moles of solute (n) is constant but the molarity and volume change.

$n = MV$

$n_1 = n_2$

$M_1V_1 = M_2V_2$

Solve for V_2:

$M_2 = (M_1V_1) / V_2$

$M_2 = (4 \text{ M} \times 1 \text{ mL}) / 20 \text{ mL}$

$M_2 = 0.20 \text{ M}$

Usually, in molarity calculations, volumes are expressed in liters.

However, this problem involves a volume comparison so both can be in mL because the units cancel.

25. B is correct.

According to the Brønsted-Lowry definition of acids and bases (independently discovered by Brønsted and Lowry in 1923), a hydrogen ion (H^+ or proton) is removed from the acid and transferred to the base.

After deprotonation, the acid becomes the conjugate base while, the base becomes the conjugate acid.

26. E is correct.

Oxidation is defined as a loss of electrons and an increase in oxidation number (increase in the number of bonds to oxygen or to electronegative atoms).

Reduction is defined as a gain of electrons and a decrease in oxidation number (often involves the increase in the number of bonds to hydrogens).

27. E is correct.

The series of alkali metals (group IA) includes lithium (Li), potassium (K), sodium (Na), rubidium (Rb), cesium (Cs) and francium (Fr).

The alkali metals have low electronegativity and react violently with water (e.g., the violent reaction of metallic sodium with water).

Alkali metals (group IA) lose one electron to become +1 cations and the resulting ion has a complete octet of valence electrons.

28. A is correct.

The oxygen and two hydrogens within a water molecule are held together by covalent bonds, which involve the sharing of electron pairs between the atoms. It is a polar covalent bond because the electrons are closer to the oxygen than the hydrogen.

Water molecules participate in hydrogen bonding with other water molecules due to this polar nature (i.e., intermolecular for neighboring water molecules). However, the hydrogen bond is not the bond holding the water molecule together (i.e., intramolecular covalent bonds between the 2 H and O of a single water molecule).

29. E is correct.

Apply the ideal-gas equation:

$$PV = nRT$$

Set the total and partial mole/pressure conditions of Ar equal:

$$(n_T / P_T) = (n_{Ar} / P_{Ar})$$

Solve for the partial-pressure of Ar:

$$P_{Ar} = n_{Ar} / (n_T / P_T)$$

$$P_{Ar} = (0.40 \text{ moles Ar}) / [(1.00 \text{ moles total}) / (1.20 \text{ atm total})]$$

$$P_{Ar} = 0.48 \text{ atm}$$

30. C is correct. Balanced equation:

$$N_2\ (g) + 3\ H_2\ (g) \rightarrow 2\ NH_3\ (g)$$

31. B is correct.

Determine the moles of N_2:

moles N_2 = mass N_2 / molecular mass N_2

moles N_2 = 60.0g / (2 × 14.01 g/mol)

moles N_2 = 2.14 moles

ΔH is positive so energy is consumed by the reaction.

ΔH value provided in the question is for one mole of N_2 (or one mole of O_2 / 2 moles of NO).

Calculate the heat consumed by 2.13 moles of N_2:

2.14 × 43 kcal = 92.0 kcal

32. B is correct.

Relationship between constant units and reaction order:

zero order = mol $L^{-1}s^{-1}$

first order = s^{-1}

second order = L $mol^{-1}s^{-1}$

Because the constant (k) unit is s^{-1}, this is a first order reaction.

Integrated rate equation for a first order reaction:

$\ln[A_t] - \ln[A_o] = -k$t

where A_t = concentration at t, A_o = initial concentration, k = rate constant, t = time

Partial pressure can be substituted for concentration:

$\ln[A_t] = -k$t + $\ln[A_o]$

$\ln[A_t] = -1 × 10^{-4}$ s^{-1} × 23,000 s + $\ln[100]$

$\ln[A_t] = -2.3 + 4.6$

$\ln[A_t] = 2.3$

$[A_t] = e^{2.3} = 9.97 \approx 10$ torr

Alternatively, use the equation:

$\log[A]_t = -k$t / 2.303 + $\log[A]_0$

$\log[A]_0 = \log[100] = 2$

$-k$t/2.303 = $-1 × 10^{-4}$ × 23,000 / 2.3 = -1

Thus, $\log[A]_t = 1$ or $[A]_t = 10$

33. E is correct.

The solvent is the component with the largest proportion in the mixture.

34. D is correct.

By the Brønsted-Lowry definition, a base accepts H^+ (hydrogen) ions.

By the Arrhenius definition, a base donates ^-OH (hydroxide) ions in water.

By the Lewis definition, a base donates electrons.

A hydronium ion is the aqueous cation of H_3O^+ and is present when an Arrhenius acid is dissolved in water.

35. C is correct.

Metalloids are semimetallic elements (i.e., between metals and nonmetals). The metalloids are boron (B), silicon (Si), germanium (Ge), arsenic (As), antimony (Sb) and tellurium (Te). Some literature reports polonium (Po) and astatine (At) as metalloids.

They have properties between metals and nonmetals. They typically have a metallic appearance, but are only fair conductors of electricity (as opposed to metals which are excellent conductors), which makes them useable in the semi-conductor industry.

Metalloids tend to be brittle, and chemically they behave more like nonmetals.

36. E is correct. The representative example would be ammonia (NH_3), which is not trigonal planar (e.g., carbocation, carbanion or radical) due to the interconversion of the molecule's lone pair of electrons on the nitrogen.

37. C is correct.

P, n and R are constants.

Ideal gas law: $PV = nRT$ means V is proportional to T.

Since the absolute temperature decreased by a factor of 3 (from 300 K to 100 K), the volume decreases by a factor of 3.

New volume: (300 cm^3) / 3 = 100 cm^3

38. C is correct.

A reducing agent donates an electron to another compound in a redox chemical reaction. The reducing agent is losing electrons; therefore, it is oxidized.

39. C is correct.

Intensive properties do not depend on the amount of the material present. Density (i.e., mass / volume) is an intensive property, because if a container of liquid is reduced by a percentage, the density is the same as the density of the original liquid sample.

40. B is correct.

The rate (k) of formation/consumption of all species in a reaction is proportional to their coefficients.

If k of a species is known, the k of other species can be calculated using simple proportions.

k consumption of CH_4O / k consumption of O_2 = coefficient of CH_4O / coefficient of O_2

k consumption of CH_4O = (coefficient of CH_4O / coefficient of O_2) × k of consumption of O_2

k consumption of CH_4O = (2/3) × 0.450 mol L^{-1} s^{-1}

k consumption of CH_4O = 0.30 mol L^{-1} s^{-1}

41. E is correct.

$HC_2H_3O_2$ is an acid and NH_3 is a base. Therefore, the acid will donate a proton (H^+) to the base.

$$HC_2H_3O_2 \, (aq) + NH_3 \, (aq) \rightarrow NH_4^+ \, (aq) + C_2H_3O_2^- \, (aq)$$

This is different from most acid-base reactions, where the net ionic reaction is usually:

$$H^+ \, (aq) + OH^- \, (aq) \rightarrow H_2O \, (l)$$

42. C is correct.

Ashes is the powder residue after the combustion of wood. Ashes are basic, so they react with the oils from a person's skin and convert them into fatty acids. This produces solutions of soap that can be used as a cleaning agent, which is why a person might wash their hands with ashes.

43. C is correct. Since E° is negative and G is positive, the reaction is not spontaneous as written and proceeds in the opposite direction (i.e., towards reactants).

44. B is correct.

Electron shells represent the orbit that electrons follow around an atom's nucleus. Each shell is composed of one or more subshells, which are named using lowercase letters (e.g., *s*, *p*, *d*, *f*). The number before the lowercase letter represents the number of the shell.

The *s* subshell is the lowest energy subshell and the *f* subshell is the highest energy subshell.

There is no 6*s* subshell because the largest shell is the n=5 shell.

45. D is correct.

Beryllium has two valence electrons and BeF_2 is a linear molecule, therefore it has no net dipole moment (the vectors from each electronegative fluorine cancel).

46. E is correct.

Gay-Lussac's Law:

$$(P_1 / T_1) = (P_2 / T_2) \text{ or } (P_1T_2) = (P_2T_1)$$

Solve for the final pressure:

$$P_2 = (P_1T_2) / T_1$$

$$P_2 = [(9.50 \text{ atm}) \times (440 \text{ K})] / (220 \text{ K})$$

$$P_2 = 19.0 \text{ atm}$$

47. E is correct.

It is important to know some of the most common ions and their charges (e.g., –1 for nitrate and –3 for phosphate).

Use the periodic table to determine the oxidation numbers of calcium and sodium.

$$Ca(NO_3)_2 \text{ } (aq) + Na_3PO_4 \text{ } (aq) \rightarrow Ca_3(PO_4)_2 \text{ } (s) + NaNO_3 \text{ } (aq)$$

Start by balancing the number of calcium atoms, put 3 on calcium nitrate on the left.

Now, there are 6 nitrate ions on the left, so add 6 on sodium nitrate (on product side).

Finally, add 2 on sodium phosphate to balance the reaction.

$$3 \text{ } Ca(NO_3)_2 \text{ } (aq) + 2 \text{ } Na_3PO_4 \text{ } (aq) \rightarrow Ca_3(PO_4)_2 \text{ } (s) + 6 \text{ } NaNO_3 \text{ } (aq)$$

48. B is correct.

49. B is correct.

Increasing the temperature of a system is the average kinetic energy (KE) of particles. As the average kinetic energy increases, the particles move faster and collide more frequently, possessing greater energy when they collide. These factors increase the reaction rate.

50. A is correct.

Mass % NaCl = (mass of NaCl / total mass) × 100%

Mass % NaCl = [(16.5 g) / (16.5 g + 172 g)] × 100%

Mass % NaCl = [(16.5 g) / (188.5 g)] × 100%

Mass % NaCl = 8.8%

51. C is correct. Acids have protons (H^+) and bases have ^-OH (hydroxide), so they react to produce H_2O.

52. B is correct.

A sulfur atom contains 16 electrons.

$1s^2 2s^2 2p^6 3s^2 3p^4$ is the electronic configuration of a ground-state sulfur atom.

53. C is correct.

A coordinate bond is a covalent bond (i.e., shared pair of electrons) in which both electrons come from the same atom.

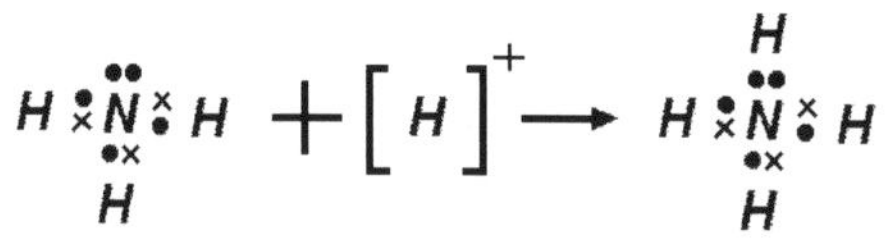

The coordinate bond forms with nitrogen donating its lone pair to H+

54. C is correct.

Ideal gas equation:

PV = nRT

Convert the given temperature units from Celsius to Kelvin:

$T_1 = 24.5 \,°C + 273 = 297.5 \,K$

$T_2 = 186 \,°C + 273 = 459 \,K$

Set the initial and final P/V/T conditions equal:

$(P_1 V_1 / T_1) = (P_2 V_2 / T_2)$

Solve for the final pressure:

$(P_2 V_2 / T_2) = (P_1 V_1 / T_1)$

$P_2 = (P_1 V_1 T_2) / (V_2 T_1)$

$P_2 = (770 \,torr \times 16.5 \,L \times 459 \,K) / (16.8 \,L \times 297.5 \,K)$

$P_2 = 1{,}166.79 \,torr \approx 1{,}167 \,torr$

55. A is correct.

To determine the empirical formula, assume 100 g of a compound.

C: $15.8 \,g \times (1 \,mole / 12 \,g) = 1.3 \,moles$

N: $36.8 \,g \times (1 \,mole / 14 \,g) = 2.6 \,moles$

S: $42.1 \,g \times (1 \,mole / 32 \,g) = 1.3 \,moles$

H: $5.3 \,g \times (1 \,mole / 1 \,g) = 5.3 \,moles$

Therefore, the ratio of atoms in the compound: $C_{1.3}S_{1.3}N_{2.6}H_{5.3}$

Divide each by 1.3: $C_1 S_1 N_2 H_4$

Empirical formula: $N_2 H_4 CS$

56. C is correct.

$\Delta H_{rxn} = (\Delta H_f \text{ of the products}) - (\Delta H_f \text{ of the reactants})$

$\Delta H_{rxn} = (\Delta H_{f,\,products}) - (\Delta H_{f,\,reactants})$

$\Delta H_{rxn} = [(-635.5 \,kJ/mol) + (-395.5 \,kJ/mol)] - (-1{,}206.5 \,kJ/mol)$

$\Delta H_{rxn} = (-1{,}031 \,kJ/mol) - (-1{,}206.5 \,kJ/mol)$

$\Delta H_{rxn} = 177.5 \,kJ/mol$

57. E is correct.

Catalysts lower the activation energy of a reaction, which is the minimum amount of energy that must be input to cause a chemical reaction. By doing this, catalysts cause a reaction to proceed faster, thus increasing the rate of the reaction.

A catalyst is neither created nor consumed in a reaction, but this is not why the rate of the reaction is increased.

58. A is correct.

Henry's Law:

k_H = concentration / pressure

where k_H = Henry's law constant, c = concentration of gas in solution, and p = partial pressure of gas

Rearrange to solve for c:

c = k_H × p

c = 6.8 × 10^{-4} mol/L·atm × 0.78 atm

c = 5.3 × 10^{-4} M

59. B is correct.

NH_3 accepts a proton to form ammonium: $NH_3 + H^+ \rightarrow NH_4^+$

NH_3 (charge = 0) and proton (charge = +1); the product molecule has a charge of 0 + 1 = +1.

Additionally, since NH_3 has eight valence electrons and H^+ has zero, NH_4^+ molecule has 8 electrons.

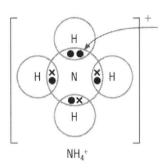

NH_4^+

From the Lewis dot structure, when NH_3 donates a lone pair to H^+ to form the coordinate covalent bond, both of the electrons involved in forming the new N-H bond come from the lone pair on the nitrogen atom in the NH_3 molecule (since there are no electrons at all in a bare proton).

The nitrogen shares its lone pair of electrons with the proton, resulting in a formal charge of +1 on the nitrogen.

60. A is correct.

In Vessel I, iron (Fe) forms iron ions (Fe^{2+}) and electrons (e^-).

In Vessel II, copper ion (Cu^{2+}) and electron (e^-) combine to form copper metal (Cu).

Therefore, the electrons flow from Vessel I to Vessel II.

Explanations:
Topical
Practice Question

Atomic and Molecular Structure; Periodic Table: Explanations

==

Practice Set 1: Questions 1–20

==

1. B is correct.

Ionization energy (IE) is the amount of energy required to remove the most loosely bound electron of an isolated gaseous atom to form a cation. This is an endothermic process.

Ionization energy is expressed as:

$$X + \text{energy} \rightarrow X^+ + e^-$$

where X is any atom (or molecule) capable of being ionized (i.e., having an electron removed), X^+ is that atom or molecule after an electron is removed, and e^- is the removed electron.

The principal quantum number (n) describes the size of the orbital and the energy of an electron and the most probable distance of the electron from the nucleus. It refers to the size of the orbital and the energy level of an electron.

The elements with larger shell sizes (n is large) listed at the bottom of the periodic table have low ionization energies. This is due to the shielding (by the inner shell electrons) from the positive charge of the nucleus. The greater the distance between the electrons and the nucleus, the less energy is needed to remove the outer valence electrons.

2. C is correct.

Accepting electrons to form anions is a characteristic of non-metals to obtain the electron configuration of the noble gases (i.e., complete octet).

With the exception of helium (which has a complete octet with 2 electrons, $1s^2$), the noble gases have complete octets with ns^2 and np^6 orbitals.

Donating electrons to form cations (e.g., Ca^{2+}, Fr^+, Na^+) is a characteristic of metals to obtain the electron configuration of the noble gases (i.e., complete octet).

3. E is correct.

Metalloids are semimetallic elements (i.e., between metals and nonmetals). The metalloids are boron (B), silicon (Si), germanium (Ge), arsenic (As), antimony (Sb) and tellurium (Te). Some literature reports polonium (Po) and astatine (At) as metalloids.

Seventeen elements are generally classified as nonmetals. Eleven are gases: hydrogen (H), helium (He), nitrogen (N), oxygen (O), fluorine (F), neon (Ne), chlorine (Cl), argon (Ar), krypton (Kr), xenon (Xe) and radon (Rn). One nonmetal is a liquid – bromine (Br) – and five are solids: carbon (C), phosphorus (P), sulfur (S), selenium (Se) and iodine (I).

4. B is correct.

An element is a pure chemical substance that consists of a single type of atom, distinguished by its atomic number (Z) (i.e. the number of protons that it contains). There are 118 elements that have been identified, of which the first 94 occur naturally on Earth, with the remaining 24 being synthetic elements.

The properties of the elements on the periodic table repeat at regular intervals, creating "groups" or "families" of elements. Each column on the periodic table is a group, and elements within each group have similar physical and chemical characteristics due to the orbital location of their outermost electron. These groups only exist because the elements of the periodic table are listed by increasing atomic number.

5. C is correct.

For $n = 2$ shell, it has 2 orbitals: *s, p*

Each orbital can hold two electrons.

Maximum number of electrons in each shell:

The *s* subshell has 1 spherical orbital and can accommodate 2 electrons.

The *p* subshell has 3 dumbell-shaped orbitals and can accommodate 6 electrons.

Maximum number of electrons in $n = 2$ shell is:

2 (for *s*) + 6 (for *p*) = 8 electrons

6. B is correct.

Groups IVA, VA and VIA each contain at least one metal and one nonmetal.

Group IVA has three metals (tin, lead and flerovium) and one nonmetal (carbon).

Group VA has two metals (bismuth and ununpentium) and two nonmetals (nitrogen and phosphorous).

Group VIA has one metal (livermonium) and three nonmetals (oxygen, sulfur and selenium).

All three groups are part of the *p*-block of the periodic table.

7. C is correct. The majority of elements on the periodic table (over 100 elements) are metals. Currently, there are 84 metal elements on the Periodic Table.

Seventeen elements are generally classified as nonmetals. Eleven are gases: hydrogen (H), helium (He), nitrogen (N), oxygen (O), fluorine (F), neon (Ne), chlorine (Cl), argon (Ar), krypton (Kr), xenon (Xe) and radon (Rn). One nonmetal is a liquid – bromine (Br) – and five are solids: carbon (C), phosphorus (P), sulfur (S), selenium (Se) and iodine (I).

Therefore, with the ratio of 84:17, there are about five times more metals than nonmetals.

8. D is correct.

English chemist John Dalton is known for his Atomic Theory, which states that *elements are made of small particles called atoms, which cannot be created or destroyed.*

9. B is correct.

Isotopes are variants of a particular element, which differ in the number of neutrons. All isotopes of the element have the same number of protons and occupy the same position on the periodic table.

The number of protons within the atom's nucleus is the atomic number (Z) and is equal to the number of electrons in the neutral (non-ionized) atom. Each atomic number identifies a specific element, but not the isotope; an atom of a given element may have a wide range in its number of neutrons.

The number of both protons and neutrons (i.e., nucleons) in the nucleus is the atom's mass number (A), and each isotope of an element has a different mass number.

The atomic mass unit (amu) was designed using ^{12}C isotope as the reference.

1 amu = 1/12 mass of a ^{12}C atom.

Masses of other elements are measured against this standard.

If the mass of an atom 55.43 amu, the atom's mass is 55.43 × (1/12 mass of ^{12}C).

10. A is correct.

The three coordinates that come from Schrodinger's wave equations are the principal (n), angular (l) and magnetic (m) quantum numbers. These quantum numbers describe the size, shape and orientation in space of the orbitals on an atom.

The principal quantum number (n) describes the size of the orbital and the energy of an electron and the most probable distance of the electron from the nucleus. It refers to the size of the orbital and the energy level of an electron.

The angular momentum quantum number (*l*) describes the shape of the orbital within the subshells.

The magnetic quantum number (*m*) determines the number of orbitals and their orientation within a subshell. Consequently, its value depends on the orbital angular momentum quantum number (*l*). Given a certain *l*, *m* is an interval ranging from –*l* to +*l* (i.e., it can be zero, a negative integer or a positive integer).

The *s* is the spin quantum number (e.g., +½ or –½).

11. B is correct.

Electron shells represent the orbit that electrons allow around an atom's nucleus. Each shell is composed of one or more subshells, which are named using lowercase letters (*s*, *p*, *d*, *f*).

The first shell has one subshell (1*s*), the second shell has two subshells (2*s*, 2*p*), the third subshell has three subshells (3*s*, 3*p*, 3*d*), etc.

An *s* subshell holds 2 electrons, and each subsequent subshell in the series can hold 4 more (*p* holds 6, *d* holds 10, *f* holds 14).

The shell number (i.e., principal quantum number) before the *s* (i.e., 4 in this example) does not affect how many electrons can occupy the subshell.

Subshell name	Subshell max electrons	Shell max electrons
1s	2	2
2s	2	2 + 6 = 8
2p	6	
3s	2	2 + 6 + 10 = 18
3p	6	
3d	10	
4s	2	2 + 6 + + 10 + 14 = 32
4p	6	
4d	10	
4f	14	

12. E is correct.

The specific, characteristic line spectra for atoms result from photons being emitted when excited electrons drop to lower energy levels.

13. A is correct.

In general, the size of neutral atoms increases down a group (i.e., increasing shell size) and decreases from left to right across the periodic table.

Negative ions (anions) are *much larger* than their neutral element, while positive ions (cations) are *much smaller*. All examples are isoelectronic because of the same number of electrons.

Atomic numbers:

Br = 35; K = 19; Ar = 18; Ca = 20 and Cl = 17

The general trend for atomic radius is to decrease from left to right and increase from top to bottom in the periodic table. When the ion gains or loses an electron to create a new charged ion, its radius would change slightly, but the general trend of radius still applies.

The ions K^+, Ca^{2+}, Cl^-, and Ar have identical numbers of electrons.

However, Br is located below Cl (larger principal quantum number, n) and its atomic number is almost twice the others. This indicates that Br has more electrons and its radius must be significantly larger than the other atoms.

14. C is correct. The ground state configuration of sulfur is $[Ne]3s^23p^4$.

According to Hund's rule, the p orbitals are filled separately, and then pair the electrons by $+\frac{1}{2}$ or $-\frac{1}{2}$ spin.

The first three p electrons fill separate orbitals and then the fourth electron pairs with two remaining unpaired electrons.

15. E is correct.

There are two ways to obtain the proper answer to this problem:

1. Using atomic number.

   Calculate the atomic number by adding all the electrons:

   $2 + 2 + 6 + 2 + 6 + 1 = 19$

Find element number 19 in the periodic table.

Check the group where it is located to see other elements that belong to the same group.

Element number 19 is potassium (K), so the element that belong to the same group (IA) is lithium (Li).

2. Using subshells.

   Identify the outermost subshell and use it to identify its group in the periodic table:

   In this problem, the outermost subshell is $4s^1$.

Relationship between outermost subshell and group:

   s^1 = Group IA

   s^2 = Group IIA

   p^1 = Group IIIA

   p^2 = Group IVA

   …

p^6 = Group VIII A

d = transition element

f = lanthanide/actinide element

16. C is correct.

The number of valence electrons for an element can be determined by its group (i.e., vertical column) on the periodic table. With the exception of the transition metals (i.e., groups 3-12), the group number identifies how many valence electrons are associated with a particular element: all elements of the same group have the same number of valence electrons.

Atoms are most stable when they contain 8 electrons (i.e., complete octet) in the valance shell.

17. D is correct. The principal quantum number (n) describes the size of the orbital and the energy of an electron and the most probable distance of the electron from the nucleus. It refers to the size of the orbital and the energy level of an electron.

The elements with larger shell sizes (n is large) listed at the bottom of the periodic table have low ionization energies. This is due to the shielding (by the inner shell electrons) from the positive charge of the nucleus. The greater the distance between the electrons and the nucleus, the less energy is needed to remove the outer valence electrons.

Ionization energy decreases with increasing shell size (i.e., n value) and generally increases to the right across a period (i.e., row) in the periodic table.

18. C is correct.

The f subshell has 7 orbitals.

Each orbital can hold two electrons.

The capacity of an f subshell is 7 orbitals × 2 electrons/orbital = 14 electrons.

19. C is correct. The term "electron affinity" does not use the word energy as a reference, it is one of the measurable energies just like ionization energy.

20. E is correct. The attraction of the nucleus on the outermost electrons determines the ionization energy, which increases towards the right and increases up on the periodic table.

==

Practice Set 2: Questions 21–40

==

21. C is correct.

The mass number (A) is the sum of protons and neutrons in an atom.

The mass number is an approximation of the atomic weight of the element as amu (grams per mole).

The problem only specifies the atomic mass (A) of Cl: 35 amu.

The atomic number (Z) is not given, but the information is available in the periodic table (atomic number = 17).

> number of neutrons = atomic weight – atomic number
>
> number of neutrons = 35 – 17
>
> number of neutrons = 18

22. D is correct. An element is a pure chemical substance that consists of a single type of atom, distinguished by its atomic number (Z) (i.e., the number of protons that it contains). There are 118 elements that have been identified, of which the first 94 occur naturally on Earth, with the remaining 24 being synthetic elements.

The properties of the elements on the periodic table repeat at regular intervals, creating "groups" or "families" of elements. Each column on the periodic table is a group, and elements within each group have similar physical and chemical characteristics due to the orbital location of their outermost electron. These groups only exist because the elements of the periodic table are listed by increasing atomic number.

23. E is correct. Metals are the elements that form positive ions by losing electrons during chemical reactions. Thus metals are electropositive elements.

Metals are characterized by bright luster, hardness, ability to resonate sound and are excellent conductors of heat and electricity.

Metals, except mercury, are solids under normal conditions. Potassium has the lowest melting point of the solid metals at 146 °F.

24. C is correct.

Electron affinity is defined as the energy liberated when an electron is added to a gaseous neutral atom converting it to an anion.

---

25. D is correct.

Metalloids are semimetallic elements (i.e., between metals and nonmetals). The metalloids are boron (B), silicon (Si), germanium (Ge), arsenic (As), antimony (Sb) and tellurium (Te). Some literature reports polonium (Po) and astatine (At) as metalloids.

They have properties between metals and nonmetals. They typically have a metallic appearance but are only fair conductors of electricity (as opposed to metals which are excellent conductors), which makes them useable in the semi-conductor industry.

Metalloids tend to be brittle, and chemically they behave more like nonmetals.

26. D is correct. Halogens (group VIIA) include fluorine (F), chlorine (Cl), bromine (Br), iodine (I) and astatine (At).

Halogens gain one electron to become a –1 anion, and the resulting ion has a complete octet of valence electrons.

27. C is correct. Dalton's Atomic Theory, developed in the early 1800s, states that atoms of a given element are identical in mass and properties.

The masses of atoms of a particular element may be not identical, although all atoms of an element must have the same number of protons; they can have different numbers of neutrons (i.e., isotopes).

28. D is correct.

Elements are defined by the number of protons (i.e., atomic number).

The isotopes are neutral atoms: # electrons = # protons.

Isotopes are variants of a particular element which differ in the number of neutrons. All isotopes of the element have the same number of protons and occupy the same position on the periodic table.

The number of protons is denoted by the subscript on the left.

The number of protons and neutrons is denoted by the superscript on the left.

The charge of an ion is denoted by the superscript on the right.

The number of protons within the atom's nucleus is the atomic number (Z) and is equal to the number of electrons in the neutral (non-ionized) atom. Each atomic number identifies a specific element, but not the isotope; an atom of a given element may have a wide range in its number of neutrons.

The number of both protons and neutrons (i.e., nucleons) in the nucleus is the atom's mass number (A), and each isotope of an element has a different mass number.

29. E is correct.

A cathode ray particle is a different name for an electron.

Those particles (i.e., electrons) are attracted to the positively charged cathode, which implies that they are negatively charged.

30. B is correct.

The three coordinates that come from Schrodinger's wave equations are the principal (n), angular (l) and magnetic (m) quantum numbers. These quantum numbers describe the size, shape and orientation in space of the orbitals on an atom.

The principal quantum number (n) describes the size of the orbital, the energy of an electron and the most probable distance of the electron from the nucleus. It refers to the size of the orbital and the energy level of an electron.

The angular momentum quantum number (l) describes the shape of the orbital of the subshells.

Carbon has an atomic number of 6 and an electron configuration of $1s^2, 2s^2, 2p^2$.

Therefore, electrons are in the second shell of $n = 2$ and two subshells are in the outermost shell of $l = 1$.

The values of l are 0 and 1 whereby, only the largest value of l, ($l = 1$) is reported.

31. A is correct. The alkaline earth metals (group IIA), in the ground state, have a filled s subshell with 2 electrons.

32. D is correct. The 3rd shell consists of s, p and d subshells.

Each orbital can hold two electrons.

   The s subshell has 1 spherical orbital and can accommodate 2 electrons

   The p subshell has 3 dumbbell-shaped orbitals and can accommodate 6 electrons

   The d subshell has 5 lobe-shaped orbitals and can accommodate 10 electrons

   1s
   2s 2p
   3s 3p 3d
   4s 4p 4d 4f
   5s 5p 5d 5f ...
   6s 6p 6d ... ...

   Order of filling orbitals

The $n = 3$ shell can accommodate a total of 18 electrons.

The element with the electron configuration terminating in $3p^4$ is sulfur (i.e., total of 16 electrons).

33. B is correct.

Ions typically form with the same electron configuration as the noble gases. With the exception of helium (which has a complete octet with 2 electrons, $1s^2$), the noble gases have complete octets with ns^2 and np^6 orbitals.

Halogens (group VIIA) include fluorine (F), chlorine (Cl), bromine (Br), iodine (I) and astatine (At).

Halogens gain one electron to become –1 anion and the resulting ion has a complete octet of valence electrons.

34. C is correct.

A continuous spectrum refers to a broad uninterrupted spectrum of radiant energy.

The visible spectrum refers to the light that humans can see and includes the colors of the rainbow.

The ultraviolet spectrum refers to electromagnetic radiation with wavelength shorter than visible light but longer than X-rays.

The radiant energy spectrum refers to electromagnetic (EM) waves of all wavelengths, but the bands of frequency in an EM signal may be sharply defined with interruptions, or they may be broad.

35. A is correct.

In general, the size of neutral atoms increases down a group (i.e., increasing shell size) and decreases from left to right across the periodic table.

Positive ions (cations) are *much smaller* than the neutral element (due to greater effective nuclear charge), while negative ions (anions) are *much larger* (due to smaller effective nuclear charge and repulsion of valence electrons).

36. C is correct.

In the ground state, the $3p$ orbitals fill before the $3d$ orbitals.

The lowest energy orbital completely fills before an orbital of a higher energy level.

Aufbau principle to determine the order of energy levels in subshells:

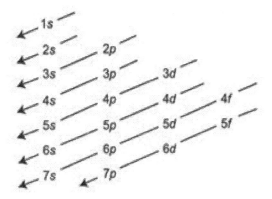

From the table above, the orbitals increase in energy from: $1s < 2s < 2p < 3s < 3p < 4s < 3d < 4p < 5s < 4d < 5p < 6s < 4f < 5d < 6p < 7s < 5f < 6d < 7p$

37. B is correct.

Ionization energy is defined as the energy needed to remove an electron from a neutral atom of the element in the gas phase.

The principal quantum number (n) describes the size of the orbital and the energy of an electron and the most probable distance of the electron from the nucleus. It refers to the size of the orbital and the energy level of an electron.

The elements with larger shell sizes (n is large) listed at the bottom of the periodic table have low ionization energies. This is due to the shielding (by the inner shell electrons) from the positive charge of the nucleus. The greater the distance between the electrons and the nucleus, the less energy is needed to remove the outer valence electrons.

Ionization energy decreases with increasing shell size (i.e., n value) and generally increases to the right across a period (i.e., row) in the periodic table.

Neon (Ne) has an atomic number of 10 and a shell size of $n = 2$.

Rubidium (Rb) has an atomic number of 37 and a shell size of $n = 5$.

Potassium (K) has an atomic number of 19 and a shell size of $n = 4$.

Calcium (Ca) has an atomic number of 20 and a shell size is $n = 4$.

Magnesium (Mg) has an atomic number of 12 and a shell size of $n = 3$.

38. B is correct.

Seventeen elements are generally classified as nonmetals. Eleven are gases: hydrogen (H), helium (He), nitrogen (N), oxygen (O), fluorine (F), neon (Ne), chlorine (Cl), argon (Ar), krypton (Kr), xenon (Xe) and radon (Rn). One nonmetal is a liquid – bromine (Br) – and five are solids: carbon (C), phosphorus (P), sulfur (S), selenium (Se) and iodine (I).

Alkali metals (group IA) include lithium (Li), potassium (K), sodium (Na), rubidium (Rb), cesium (Cs) and francium (Fr).

Alkali metals lose one electron to become +1 cations, and the resulting ion has a complete octet of valence electrons.

Alkaline earth metals (group IIA) include beryllium (Be), magnesium (Mg), calcium (Ca), strontium (Sr), barium (Ba) and radium (Ra). Alkaline earth metals lose two electrons to become +2 cations and the resulting ion has a complete octet of valence electrons.

39. C is correct.

The atom has 47 protons, 47 electrons and 60 neutrons.

Because the periodic table is arranged by atomic number (Z), the fastest way to identify an element is to determine its atomic number. The atomic number is equal to the number of protons or electrons, which means that this atom's atomic number is 47. Use this information to locate element #47 in the table, which is Ag (silver).

Check the atomic mass (A), which is equal to atomic number + number of neutrons.

For this atom, the mass is 60 + 47 = 107.

The mass of Ag on the periodic table is listed as 107.87, which is the average mass of all Ag isotopes.

Usually all isotopes of an element have similar masses (within 1-3 amu to each other).

40. D is correct.

The three coordinates that come from Schrodinger's wave equations are the principal (n), angular (l) and magnetic (m) quantum numbers.

These quantum numbers describe the size, shape and orientation in space of the orbitals in an atom.

The principal quantum number (n) describes the size of the orbital, the energy of an electron and the most probable distance of the electron from the nucleus.

===

Practice Set 3: Questions 41–60

===

41. B is correct.

The atomic number (Z) is the sum of protons in an atom which determines the chemical properties of an element and its location on the periodic table.

The mass number (A) is the sum of protons and neutrons in an atom.

The mass number is an approximation of the atomic weight of the element as amu (grams per mole).

Atomic mass – atomic number = number of neutrons

9 – 4 = 5 neutrons

42. A is correct. Electrons are the negatively-charged particles (charge –1) located in the electron cloud, orbiting around the nucleus of the atom. Electrons are extremely tiny particles, much smaller than protons and neutrons, and they have a mass of about 5×10^{-4} amu.

43. D is correct.

A compound consists of two or more different atoms which associate via chemical bonds.

Calcium chloride ($CaCl_2$) is an ionic compound of calcium and chloride.

Dichloromethane has the molecular formula of CH_2Cl_2

Dichlorocalcium exists as a hydrate with the molecular formula of $CaCl_2 \cdot (H_2O)_2$.

Carbon chloride (i.e., carbon tetrachloride) has the molecular formula of CCl_4.

Dicalcium chloride is not the proper IUPAC name for calcium chloride ($CaCl_2$).

44. A is correct.

Congeners are chemical substances related by origin, structure or function. In regards of the periodic table, congeners are the elements of the same group which share similar properties (e.g., copper, silver and gold are congeners of Group 11).

Stereoisomers, diastereomers and epimers are terms commonly used in organic chemistry.

Stereoisomers: are chiral molecules (attached to 4 different substituents and are non-superimposable mirror images. They have the same molecular formula and the same sequence of bonded atoms, but are oriented differently in 3-D space (e.g., *R* / *S* enantiomers).

Diastereomers are chiral molecules that are not mirror images. The most common form is a chiral molecule with more than 1 chiral center. Additionally, *cis / trans* (*E / Z*) geometric isomers are also diastereomers.

Epimers: diastereomers that differ in absolute configuration at only one chiral center.

Anomers: is a type of stereoisomer used in carbohydrate chemistry to describe the orientation of the glycosidic bond of adjacent saccharides (e.g., α and β linkage of sugars). A refers to the hydroxyl group – of the anomeric carbon – pointing downward while β points upward.

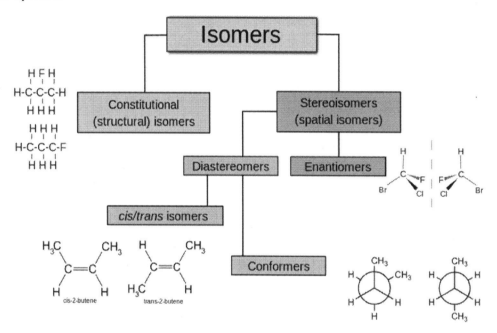

Summary of isomers

45. D is correct.

A group (or family) is a vertical column, and elements within each group share similar properties.

A period is a horizontal row in the periodic table of elements.

46. A is correct.

Metals, except mercury, are solids under normal conditions.

Potassium has the lowest melting point of the solid metals at 146 °F.

The relatively low melting temperature for potassium is due to its fourth shell ($n = 4$), which means its valence electrons are further from the nucleus; therefore, there is less attraction between its electrons and protons.

47. E is correct.

Alkaline earth metals (group IIA) include beryllium (Be), magnesium (Mg), calcium (Ca), strontium (Sr), barium (Ba) and radium (Ra). Alkaline earth metals lose two electrons to become +2 cations and the resulting ion has a complete octet of valence electrons.

Transition metals (or transition elements) are defined as elements that have a partially-filled *d* or *f* subshell in a common oxidative state.

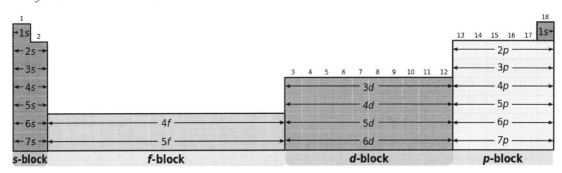

Transition metals occur in groups (vertical columns) 3–12 of the period table. They occur in periods (horizontal rows) 4–7. This group of elements includes silver, iron and copper.

The *f*-block lanthanides (i.e., rare earth metals) and actinides (i.e., radioactive elements) are also considered transition metals and are known as inner transition metals.

Noble gases (group VIIIA) include helium (He), neon (Ne), argon (Ar), krypton (Kr) xenon (Xe), radon (Rn) and ununoctium (Uuo).

Alkali metals (group IA) include lithium (Li), potassium (K), sodium (Na), rubidium (Rb), cesium (Cs) and francium (Fr). Alkali metals lose one electron to become +1 cations, and the resulting ion has a complete octet of valence electrons.

Halogens (group VIIA) includes fluorine (F), chlorine (Cl), bromine (Br), iodine (I) and astatine (At). Halogens gain one electron to become a –1 anion, and the resulting ion has a complete octet of valence electrons.

48. D is correct. The metalloids have some properties of metals and some properties of nonmetals.

Metalloids are semimetallic elements (i.e., between metals and nonmetals). The metalloids are boron (B), silicon (Si), germanium (Ge), arsenic (As), antimony (Sb) and tellurium (Te). Some literature reports polonium (Po) and astatine (At) as metalloids.

They have properties between metals and nonmetals. They typically have a metallic appearance but are only fair conductors of electricity (as opposed to metals which are excellent conductors), which makes them useable in the semi-conductor industry.

Metalloids tend to be brittle, and chemically they behave more like nonmetals.

However, the elements in the IIIB group are transition metals, not metalloids.

49. B is correct. Halogens (group VIIA) include fluorine (F), chlorine (Cl), bromine (Br), iodine (I) and astatine (At).

Halogens gain one electron to become a –1 anion and the resulting ion has a complete octet of valence electrons.

50. A is correct. Isotopes are variants of a particular element which differ in the number of neutrons. All isotopes of the element have the same number of protons and occupy the same position on the periodic table.

The number of protons within the atom's nucleus is the atomic number (Z) and is equal to the number of electrons in the neutral (non-ionized) atom. Each atomic number identifies a specific element, but not the isotope; an atom of a given element may have a wide range in its number of neutrons.

The number of both protons and neutrons (i.e., nucleons) in the nucleus is the atom's mass number (A), and each isotope of an element has a different mass number.

From the periodic table, the atomic mass of a natural sample of Si is 28.1 which is less than the mass of ^{29}Si or ^{30}Si. Therefore, ^{28}Si is the most abundant isotope.

51. E is correct. The initial explanation was that the ray was present in the gas and the cathode activated it.

The ray was observed even when gas was not present, so the conclusion was that the ray must have been coming from the cathode itself.

52. E is correct.

The choices correctly describe the spin quantum number (*s*).

The three coordinates that come from Schrodinger's wave equations are the principal (*n*), angular (*l*) and magnetic (*m*) quantum numbers. These quantum numbers describe the size, shape and orientation in space of the orbitals of an atom.

The principal quantum number (*n*) describes the size of the orbital and the energy of an electron and the most probable distance of the electron from the nucleus. It refers to the size of the orbital and the energy level of an electron.

The angular momentum quantum number (*l*) describes the shape of the orbitals of the subshells.

The magnetic quantum number (*m*) determines the number of orbitals and their orientation within a subshell. Consequently, its value depends on the orbital angular momentum quantum number (*l*).

Given a certain *l*, *m* is an interval ranging from –*l* to +*l* (i.e., it can be zero, a negative integer, or a positive integer).

The *s* is the spin quantum number (e.g., +½ or –½).

53. D is correct. The three coordinates that come from Schrodinger's wave equations are the principal (*n*), angular (*l*), and magnetic (*m*) quantum numbers. These quantum numbers describe the size, shape and orientation in space of the orbitals on an atom.

The principal quantum number (*n*) describes the size of the orbital and the energy of an electron and the most probable distance of the electron from the nucleus. It refers to the size of the orbital and the energy level of an electron.

The angular momentum quantum number (*l*) describes the shape of the orbital of the subshells.

The magnetic quantum number (*m*) determines the number of orbitals and their orientation within a subshell. Consequently, its value depends on the orbital angular momentum quantum number (*l*). Given a certain *l*, *m* is an interval ranging from –*l* to +*l* (i.e., it can be zero, a negative integer, or a positive integer).

The fourth quantum number is *s*, which is the spin quantum number (e.g., +½ or –½).

Electrons cannot be precisely located in space at any point in time, and orbitals describe probability regions for finding the electrons.

The values needed to locate an electron are *n*, *m* and *l*. The spin can be either +½ or –½, so four values are needed to describe a single electron.

54. A is correct.

The lowest energy orbital completely fills before an orbital of a higher energy level.

Aufbau principle to determine the order of energy levelσ in subshells:

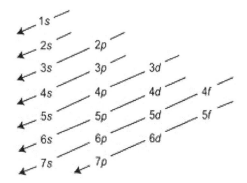

From the table above, the orbitals increase in energy from: $1s < 2s < 2p < 3s < 3p < 4s < 3d < 4p < 5s < 4d < 5p < 6s < 4f < 5d < 6p < 7s < 5f < 6d < 7p$

55. D is correct.

In general, the size of neutral atoms increases down a group (i.e., increasing shell size) and decreases from left to right across the periodic table.

Positive ions (cations) are *much smaller* than the neutral element (due to greater effective nuclear charge), while negative ions (anions) are *much larger* (due to smaller effective nuclear charge and repulsion of valence electrons).

56. D is correct. Boron's atomic number is 5, therefore it contains 5 electrons.

Use the Aufbau principle to determine the order of filling orbitals.

Remember that each electron shell (principal quantum number, *n*) starts with a new *s* orbital.

57. A is correct. Identify an element using the periodic table is its atomic number.

The atomic number is equal to the number of protons or electrons.

The total number of electrons can be determined by adding all the electrons in the provided electron configuration:

$$2 + 2 + 6 + 2 + 6 + 2 + 10 + 6 + 2 + 10 + 2 = 50.$$

Element #50 in the periodic table is tin (Sn).

58. A is correct. Ionization energy (IE) is the amount of energy required to remove the most loosely bound electron of an isolated gaseous atom to form a cation. This is an endothermic process.

Ionization energy is expressed as:

$$X + energy \rightarrow X^+ + e^-$$

where X is any atom (or molecule) capable of being ionized (i.e., having an electron removed), X^+ is that atom or molecule after an electron is removed, and e^- is the removed electron.

The principal quantum number (*n*) describes the size of the orbital and the energy of an electron and the most probable distance of the electron from the nucleus. It refers to the size of the orbital and the energy level of an electron.

The elements with larger shell sizes (*n* is large) listed at the bottom of the periodic table have low ionization energies. This is due to the shielding (by the inner shell electrons) from the positive charge of the nucleus. The greater the distance between the electrons and the nucleus, the less energy is needed to remove the outer valence electrons.

Ionization energy decreases with increasing shell size (i.e., *n* value) and generally increases to the right across a period (i.e., row) in the periodic table.

Argon (Ar) has an atomic number of 18 and a shell size of *n* = 3.

Strontium (Sr) has an atomic number of 38 and a shell size of *n* = 5.

Bromine (Br) has an atomic number of 35 and a shell size of *n* = 4.

Indium (In) has an atomic number of 49 and a shell size is *n* = 5.

Tin (Sn) has an atomic number of 50 and a shell size of *n* = 5.

59. A is correct.

Electronegativity is defined as the ability of an atom to attract electrons when it bonds with another atom. The most common use of electronegativity pertains to polarity along the sigma (single) bond.

The trend for increasing electronegativity within the periodic table is up and toward the right. The most electron negative atom is fluorine (F), while the least electronegative atom is francium (Fr).

The greater the difference in electronegativity between two atoms, the more polar of a bond these atoms form, whereby the atom with the higher electronegativity is the partial (delta) negative end of the dipole.

60. C is correct.

Seventeen elements are generally classified as nonmetals. Eleven are gases: hydrogen (H), helium (He), nitrogen (N), oxygen (O), fluorine (F), neon (Ne), chlorine (Cl), argon (Ar), krypton (Kr), xenon (Xe) and radon (Rn). One nonmetal is a liquid – bromine (Br) – and five are solids: carbon (C), phosphorus (P), sulfur (S), selenium (Se) and iodine (I).

Metals, except mercury, are solids under normal conditions. Potassium has the lowest melting point of the solid metals at 146 °F.

==

Practice Set 4: Questions 61–80

==

61. D is correct. When an electron absorbs energy, it moves temporarily to a higher energy level. It then drops back to its initial state (also known as ground state), while emitting the excess energy. This emission can be observed as visible spectrum lines.

The protons do not move between energy levels, so they can't absorb or emit energy.

62. B is correct. The three coordinates that come from Schrodinger's wave equations are the principal (n), angular (l) and magnetic (m) quantum numbers. These quantum numbers describe the size, shape and orientation in space of the orbitals on an atom.

The principal quantum number (n) describes the size of the orbital, the energy of an electron and the most probable distance of the electron from the nucleus.

The angular momentum quantum number (l) describes the shape of the orbital of the subshells.

The magnetic quantum number (m) determines the number of orbitals and their orientation within a subshell. Consequently, its value depends on the orbital angular momentum quantum number (l). Given a certain l, m is an interval ranging from $-l$ to $+l$ (i.e., it can be zero, a negative integer, or a positive integer).

l must be less than n, while m_l must be less than or equal to l.

63. C is correct. The mass number (A) is the total number of nucleons (i.e., protons and neutrons) in an atom.

The atomic number (Z) is the number of protons in an atom.

The number of neutrons in an atom can be calculated by subtracting the atomic number (Z) from the mass number (A).

      Mass number – atomic number = number of neutrons

64. B is correct. A compound consists of two or more different types of atoms which associate via chemical bonds.

An element is a pure chemical substance that consists of a single type of atom, defined by its atomic number (Z) which is the number of protons.

There are 118 elements that have been identified, of which the first 94 occur naturally on Earth.

65. E is correct. Alkali metals (group IA) include lithium (Li), potassium (K), sodium (Na), rubidium (Rb), cesium (Cs) and francium (Fr).

Alkaline earth metals (group IIA) include beryllium (Be), magnesium (Mg), calcium (Ca), strontium (Sr), barium (Ba) and radium (Ra).

Halogens (group VIIA) include fluorine (F), chlorine (Cl), bromine (Br), iodine (I) and astatine (At). Halogens gain one electron to become –1 anion and the resulting ion has a complete octet of valence electrons.

Noble gases (group VIIIA) include helium (He), neon (Ne), argon (Ar), krypton (Kr) xenon (Xe), radon (Rn) and ununoctium (Uuo). With the exception of helium (which has a complete octet with 2 electrons, $1s^2$), the noble gases have complete octets with ns^2 and np^6 orbitals.

Representative elements on the periodic table are groups IA and IIA (on the left) and groups IIIA – VIIIA (on the right).

Polonium (Po) is element 84 is a highly radioactive, with no stable isotopes, and is classified as either a metalloid or a metal.

66. B is correct.

Metalloids are semimetallic elements (i.e. between metals and nonmetals). The metalloids are boron (B), silicon (Si), germanium (Ge), arsenic (As), antimony (Sb) and tellurium (Te). Some literature reports polonium (Po) and astatine (At) as metalloids.

They have properties between metals and nonmetals. They typically have a metallic appearance but are only fair conductors of electricity (as opposed to metals which are excellent conductors), which makes them useable in the semi-conductor industry.

Metalloids tend to be brittle, and chemically they behave more like nonmetals.

Alkali metals (group IA) include lithium (Li), potassium (K), sodium (Na), rubidium (Rb), cesium (Cs) and francium (Fr).

Alkaline earth metals (group IIA) include beryllium (Be), magnesium (Mg), calcium (Ca), strontium (Sr), barium (Ba) and radium (Ra).

Seventeen elements are generally classified as nonmetals. Eleven are gases: hydrogen (H), helium (He), nitrogen (N), oxygen (O), fluorine (F), neon (Ne), chlorine (Cl), argon (Ar), krypton (Kr), xenon (Xe) and radon (Rn). One nonmetal is a liquid – bromine (Br) – and five are solids: carbon (C), phosphorus (P), sulfur (S), selenium (Se) and iodine (I).

Nonmetals tend to be highly volatile (i.e., easily vaporized), have low elasticity and are good insulators of heat and electricity.

Nonmetals tend to have high ionization energy and electronegativity and share (or gain) an electron when bonding with other elements.

Halogens (group VIIA) include fluorine (F), chlorine (Cl), bromine (Br), iodine (I) and astatine (At). Halogens gain one electron to become a –1 anion and the resulting ion has a complete octet of valence electrons.

67. D is correct.

In general, the size of neutral atoms increases down a group (i.e., increasing shell size) and decreases from left to right across the periodic table.

Positive ions (cations) are *much smaller* than the neutral element (due to greater effective nuclear charge), while negative ions (anions) are *much larger* (due to smaller effective nuclear charge and repulsion of valence electrons).

Sulfur (S, atomic number = 16) is smaller than aluminum (Al, atomic number = 13) due to the increase in the number of protons (effective nuclear charge) from left to right across a period (i.e., horizontal rows).

Al^{3+} has the same electronic configuration as Ne ($1s^2 2s^2 2p^6$) compared to Al ($1s^2 2s^2 2p^6 3s^2 3p^1$).

68. A is correct. The valence shell is the outermost shell (i.e., highest principal quantum number, *n*) of an atom.

Valence electrons are those electrons of the outermost electron shell that can participate in a chemical bond.

The number of valence electrons for an element can be determined by its group (i.e., vertical column) on the periodic table. With the exception of the transition metals (i.e., groups 3-12), the group number identifies how many valence electrons are associated with a particular element: all elements of the same group have the same number of valence electrons.

Lewis dot structures showing valence electrons for elements

69. B is correct. The semimetallic elements are arsenic (As), antimony (Sb), bismuth (Bi) and graphite (crystalline form of carbon). Arsenic and antimony are also considered metalloids (along with boron, silicon, germanium and tellurium), but the terms semimetal and metalloid are not synonymous. Semimetals, in contrast to metalloids, can also be chemical compounds.

70. C is correct.

Noble gases (group VIIIA) include helium (He), neon (Ne), argon (Ar), krypton (Kr) xenon (Xe), radon (Rn) and ununoctium (Uuo).

With the exception of helium (which has a complete octet with 2 electrons, $1s^2$), the noble gases have complete octets with ns^2 and np^6 orbitals.

The metalloids are boron (B), silicon (Si), germanium (Ge), arsenic (As), antimony (Sb) and tellurium (Te). Some literature reports polonium (Po) and astatine (At) as metalloids.

71. D is correct.

Isotopes are variants of a particular element which differ in the number of neutrons. All isotopes of the element have the same number of protons and occupy the same position on the periodic table.

The experimental results should depend on the mass of the gas molecules.

Deuterium (D or ^2H) is known as heavy hydrogen. It is one of two stable isotopes of hydrogen. The nucleus of deuterium contains one proton and one neutron, compared to H which has 1 proton and 0 neutrons. The mass of deuterium is 2.0141 daltons, compared to 1.0079 daltons for hydrogen.

Based on difference of mass between the isotopes, the density, rate of gas effusion and atomic vibrations would be different.

72. E is correct.

Elements are defined by the number of protons (i.e., atomic number).

The isotopes are neutral atoms: # electrons = # protons.

Isotopes are variants of a particular element which differ in the number of neutrons. All isotopes of the element have the same number of protons and occupy the same position on the periodic table.

The number of protons and neutrons is denoted by the superscript on the left.

Since naturally occurring lithium has a mass of 6.9 g/mol and both protons and neutrons have a mass of approximately 1 g/mol, ^{7}lithium is the predominant isotope.

73. A is correct.

The charge on 1 electron is negative.

One mole of electrons:

Avogadro's number × e⁻.

---

74. E is correct.

Each orbital can hold two electrons.

The *f* subshell has 7 orbitals and can accommodate 14 electrons.

The *d* subshell has 5 lobed orbitals and can accommodate 10 electrons.

The $n = 3$ shell contains only *s*, *p* and *d* subshells.

75. B is correct.

Ionization energy (IE) is the amount of energy required to remove the most loosely bound electron of an isolated gaseous atom to form a cation. This is an endothermic process.

Ionization energy is expressed as:

$$X + energy \rightarrow X^+ + e^-$$

where X is any atom (or molecule) capable of being ionized (i.e., having an electron removed), X^+ is that atom or molecule after an electron is removed, and e^- is the removed electron.

The principal quantum number (*n*) describes the size of the orbital and the energy of an electron and the most probable distance of the electron from the nucleus. It refers to the size of the orbital and the energy level of an electron.

The elements with larger shell sizes (*n* is large) listed at the bottom of the periodic table have low ionization energies. This is due to the shielding (by the inner shell electrons) from the positive charge of the nucleus. The greater the distance between the electrons and the nucleus, the less energy is needed to remove the outer valence electrons.

Ionization energy decreases with increasing shell size (i.e., *n* value) and generally increases to the right across a period (i.e., row) in the periodic table.

Chlorine (Cl) has an atomic number of 10 and a shell size of $n = 3$.

Francium (Fr) has an atomic number of 87 and a shell size of $n = 7$.

Gallium (Ga) has an atomic number of 31 and a shell size of $n = 4$.

Iodine (I) has an atomic number of 53 and a shell size is $n = 5$.

Cesium (Cs) has an atomic number of 55 and a shell size of $n = 6$.

76. D is correct.

Electrons are electrostatically (i.e., negative and positive charge) attracted to the nucleus and an atom's electrons generally occupy outer shells only if the more inner shells have already been completely filled by other electrons. However, there are exceptions to this rule with some atoms having two or even three incomplete outer shells.

The Aufbau (German for building up) principle is based on the Madelung rule for the order of filling the subshells based on lowest energy levels.

1s
2s 2p
3s 3p 3d
4s 4p 4d 4f
5s 5p 5d 5f ...
6s 6p 6d ... ...

Order of filling electron's orbitals

77. C is correct.

In Bohr's model of the atom, electrons can jump to higher energy levels, gaining energy, or drop to lower energy levels, releasing energy. When electric current flows through an element in the gas phase, a glowing light is produced.

By directing this light through a prism, a pattern of lines known as the atomic spectra can be seen.

These lines are produced by excited electrons dropping to lower energy levels. Since the energy levels in each element are different, each element has a unique set of lines it produces, which is why the spectrum is called the "atomic fingerprint" of the element.

78. E is correct.

Obtain the atomic number of Mn from the periodic table.

Mn is a transition metal and it is located in Group VIIB/7; its atomic number is 25.

Use the Aufbau principle to fill up the orbitals of Mn: $1s^22s^22p^63s^23p^64s^23d^5$

The transition metals occur in groups 3–12 (vertical columns) of the period table. They occur in periods 4–7 (horizontal rows).

Transition metals are defined as elements that have a partially-filled d or f subshell in a common oxidative state. This group of elements includes silver, iron and copper.

The transition metals are elements whose atom has an incomplete d sub-shell, or which can give rise to cations with an incomplete d sub-shell. By this definition, all of the elements in groups 3–11 (or 12 by some literature) are transition metals.

The transition elements have characteristics that are not found in other elements, which result from the partially filled *d* shell. These include: the formation of compounds whose color is due to *d–d* electronic transitions, the formation of compounds in many oxidation states, due to the relatively low reactivity of unpaired *d* electrons.

The transition elements form many paramagnetic (i.e., attracted to an externally applied magnetic field) compounds due to the presence of unpaired *d* electrons. By exception to their unique traits, a few compounds of main group elements are also paramagnetic (e.g., nitric oxide and oxygen).

79. E is correct.

Electronegativity is defined as the ability of an atom to attract electrons when it bonds with another atom. The most common use of electronegativity pertains to polarity along the sigma (single) bond.

The trend for increasing electronegativity within the periodic table is up and toward the right. The most electron negative atom is fluorine (F), while the least electronegative atom is francium (Fr).

80. C is correct.

Alkali metals (group IA) include lithium (Li), potassium (K), sodium (Na), rubidium (Rb), cesium (Cs) and francium (Fr). Alkali metals lose one electron to become +1 cations and the resulting ion has a complete octet of valence electrons.

Alkaline earth metals (group IIA) include beryllium (Be), magnesium (Mg), calcium (Ca), strontium (Sr), barium (Ba) and radium (Ra). Alkaline earth metals lose two electrons to become +2 cations and the resulting ion has a complete octet of valence electrons.

Chemical Bonding: Explanations

==

Practice Set 1: Questions 1–20

==

1. D is correct.

The valence shell is the outermost shell (i.e., highest principal quantum number, n) of an atom.

Valence electrons are those electrons of the outermost electron shell that can participate in a chemical bond.

The number of valence electrons for an element can be determined by its group (i.e., vertical column) on the periodic table. With the exception of the transition metals (i.e., groups 3-12), the group number identifies how many valence electrons are associated with a particular element: all elements of the same group have the same number of valence electrons.

2. A is correct.

Three degenerate p orbitals exist for any atom with an electron configuration in the second shell or higher. The first shell only has access to s orbitals.

The d orbitals become available from n = 3 (third shell).

3. C is correct. The valence shell is the outermost shell (i.e., highest principal quantum number, n) of an atom.

Valence electrons are those electrons of the outermost electron shell that can participate in a chemical bond.

The number of valence electrons for an element can be determined by its group (i.e., vertical column) on the periodic table. With the exception of the transition metals (i.e., groups 3-12), the group number identifies how many valence electrons are associated with a particular element: all elements of the same group have the same number of valence electrons.

To find the total number of valence electrons in a sulfite ion, SO_3^{2-}, start by adding the valence electrons of each atom:

Sulfur = 6; Oxygen = $(6 \times 3) = 18$

Total = 24

This ion has a net charge of –2, which indicates that it has 2 extra electrons. Therefore, the total number of valence electrons would be $24 + 2 = 26$ electrons.

4. E is correct. London dispersion forces result from the momentary flux of valence electrons and are present in all compounds; they are the attractive forces that hold molecules together.

They are the weakest of all the intermolecular forces, and their strength increases with increasing size (i.e., surface area contact) and polarity of the molecules involved.

5. B is correct.

Each hydroxyl group (alcohol or ~OH) has an oxygen with 2 lone pairs and one attached hydrogen.

Therefore, each hydroxyl group can participate in 3 hydrogen bonds:

5 hydroxyl groups × 3 bonds = 15 hydrogen bonds.

The oxygen of the ether group (C–O–C) in the ring has 2 lone pairs for an additional 2 H–bonds.

6. B is correct. The valence shell is the outermost shell (i.e., highest principal quantum number, n) of an atom.

Valence electrons are those electrons of the outermost electron shell that can participate in a chemical bond.

The number of valence electrons for an element can be determined by its group (i.e., vertical column) on the periodic table. With the exception of the transition metals (i.e., groups 3-12), the group number identifies how many valence electrons are associated with a particular element: all elements of the same group have the same number of valence electrons.

$$\begin{matrix} & H & H & \\ H: & \ddot{C} & \ddot{C} & :H \\ & H & H & \end{matrix}$$

Lewis dot structure for methane

7. A is correct.

Calculate potential energy for each molecule of NaCl:

$E = q_1 q_2 / k \cdot r$

$E = [(1.602 \times 10^{-19}\,C)\cdot(-1.602 \times 10^{-19}\,C)] / [(1.11 \times 10^{-10}\,C^2\,J^{-1}\,m^{-1})\cdot(282 \times 10^{-12}\,m)]$

$E = -8.20 \times 10^{-19}\,J$ per molecule of NaCl

Calculate the energy released for one mole of NaCl:

$[(-8.20 \times 10^{-19}\,J) \times (6.02 \times 10^{23}\,mol^{-1})] = -493{,}640\,J \approx -494\,kJ/mol$

8. A is correct.

Hydrogen bonds are the strongest intermolecular forces (i.e., between molecules), followed by dipole–dipole, dipole–induced dipole and van der Waals forces (i.e., London dispersion).

Van der Waals forces involve nonpolar (hydrophobic) molecules, such as hydrocarbons. The van der Waals force is the sum total of attractive or repulsive forces between molecules, and therefore can be either attractive or repulsive. It can include the force between two permanent dipoles, the force between a permanent dipole and a temporary dipole, or the force between two temporary dipoles.

Hydrogens, bonded directly to F, O or N, participate in hydrogen bonds. The hydrogen is partial positive (i.e., delta plus or $\partial+$) due to the bond to these electronegative atoms. The lone pair of electrons on the F, O or N interacts with the $\partial+$ hydrogen to form a hydrogen bond.

9. D is correct.

Representative structures include:

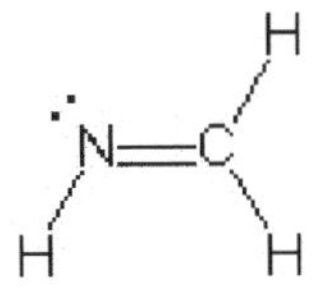

$HNCH_2$: one single and one double bond

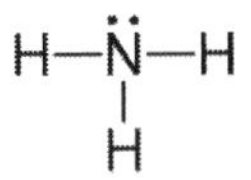

NH_3 : three single bonds

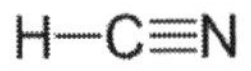

HCN : one triple bond and one single bond

10. E is correct.

The valence shell is the outermost shell (i.e., highest principal quantum number, *n*) of an atom.

Valence electrons are those electrons of the outermost electron shell that can participate in a chemical bond.

H·							He:
Li·	·Be·	·B·	·C·	·N·	:O·	:F·	:Ne:
Na·	·Mg·	·Al·	·Si·	·P·	:S·	:Cl·	:Ar:
K·	·Ca·	·Ga·	·Ge·	·As·	:Se·	:Br·	:Kr:
Rb·	·Sr·	·In·	·Sn·	·Sb·	:Te·	:I·	:Xe:

Sample Lewis dot structures for some elements

The number of valence electrons for an element can be determined by its group (i.e., vertical column) on the periodic table. With the exception of the transition metals (i.e., groups 3-12), the group number identifies how many valence electrons are associated with a particular element: all elements of the same group have the same number of valence electrons.

11. B is correct.

The nitrite ion has the chemical formula NO_2^- with the negative charge distributed between the two oxygen atoms.

Two resonance structures of the nitrite ion

12. E is correct.

Nitrogen has 5 valence electrons. In ammonia, nitrogen has 3 bonds to hydrogen and a lone pair remains on the central nitrogen atom.

The ammonium ion (NH_4^+) has 4 hydrogens and the lone pair of the nitrogen has been used to bond to the H^+ that has added to ammonia.

Formal charge shown on the hydronium ion

13. E is correct.

In atoms or molecules that are ions, the number of electrons is not equal to the number of protons, which gives the molecule a charge (either positive or negative).

Ionic bonds form when the difference in electronegativity of atoms in a compound is greater than 1.7 Pauling units.

Ionic bonds involve the transfer of an electron from the electropositive element (along the left-hand column/group) to the electronegative element (along the right-hand column/groups) on the periodic table.

Oppositely charged ions are attracted to each other and this attraction results in ionic bonds.

In an ionic bond, electron(s) are transferred from a metal to a nonmetal, giving both molecules a full valence shell and causing the molecules to closely associate with each other.

14. A is correct.

Electronegativity is a chemical property that describes an atom's tendency to attract electrons to itself.

The most electronegative atom is F, while the least electronegative atom is Fr. The trend for increasing electronegativity within the periodic table is up and toward the right (i.e., fluorine).

15. D is correct.

Hydrogen bonds are the strongest intermolecular forces (i.e., between molecules), followed by dipole–dipole, dipole–induced dipole and van der Waals forces (i.e., London dispersion).

London dispersion forces are present in all compounds; they are the attractive forces that hold molecules together. They are the weakest of all the intermolecular forces, and their strength increases with increasing size and polarity of the molecules involved.

16. C is correct.

CO_2 does not have any non-bonding electrons on the central carbon atom and it is symmetrical, so it is non-polar and has zero dipole moment.

Both SO_2^- and H_2O have non-bonding electrons, which means that they have dipole magnitude.

When comparing the dipole of molecules, use the difference of electronegativity values between the atoms. H is much more electropositive than S, so the dipole moment between H and O in H_2O molecule is greater than the dipole moment between S and O in SO_2^- molecule.

17. C is correct.

Cohesion is the property of like molecules sticking together. Water molecules are joined by hydrogen bonds.

Adhesion is the attraction between unlike molecules (e.g., the meniscus observed from water molecules adhering to the graduated cylinder).

Polarity is the differences in electronegativity between bonded molecules. Polarity gives rise to the delta plus (on H) and the delta minus (on O), which permits hydrogen bonds to form between water molecules.

18. A is correct.

With little or no difference in electronegativity between the elements (i.e., Pauling units < 0.4), it is a nonpolar covalent bond, whereby the electrons are shared between the two bonding atoms.

Among the answer choices, the atoms of H, C and O are closest in magnitude for Pauling units for electronegativity.

19. D is correct.

Positively charged nuclei repel each other while each attracts the bonding electrons. These opposing forces reach equilibrium at the bond length.

20. C is correct.

In a carbonate ion (CO_3^{2-}), the carbon atom is bonded to 3 oxygen atoms. Two of those bonds are single covalent bonds and the oxygen atoms each have an extra (third) lone pair of electron, which imparts a negative formal charge. The remaining oxygen has a double bond with carbon.

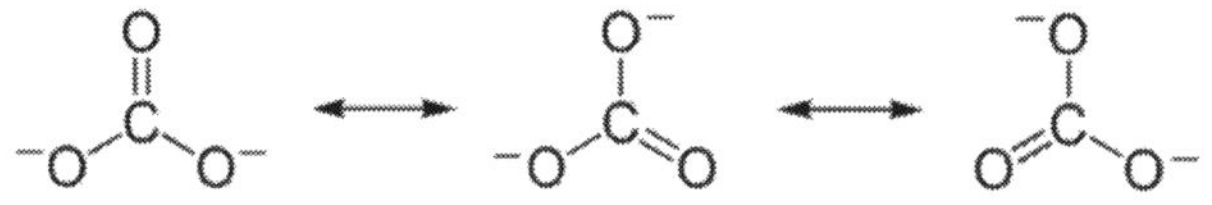

Three resonance structures for the carbonate ion CO_3^{2-}

===

Practice Set 2: Questions 21–40

===

21. D is correct. A dipole is a separation of full (or partial) positive and negative charges due to differences in electronegativity of atoms.

22. C is correct.

Ionic bonds involve the transfer of an electron from the electropositive element (along the left-hand column/group) to the electronegative atom (along the right-hand column/groups) on the periodic table.

Ca is a group II element with 2 electrons in its valence shell.

I is a group VII element with 7 electrons in its valence shell.

Ca becomes Ca^{2+}, and each of the two electrons is joined to I, which becomes I^-.

23. B is correct. An atom with 4 valence electrons can make a maximum of 4 bonds. 1 double and 1 triple bond equals 5 bonds, which exceeds the maximum allowable bonds.

24. D is correct.

Water molecules stick to each other (i.e., cohesion) due to the collective action of hydrogen bonds between individual water molecules. These hydrogen bonds are constantly breaking and reforming, a large portion of the molecules are held together by these bonds.

Water also sticks to surfaces (i.e., adhesion) because of water's polarity. On an extremely smooth surface (e.g., glass) the water may form a thin film because the molecular forces between glass and water molecules (adhesive forces) are stronger than the cohesive forces between the water molecules.

25. D is correct.

Hydrogen bonds are the strongest intermolecular forces (i.e., between molecules), followed by dipole–dipole, dipole–induced dipole and van der Waals forces (i.e., London dispersion).

When ionic compounds are dissolved, each ion is surrounded by more than one water molecule. The combined force ion–dipole interactions of several water molecules is stronger than a single ionic bond.

26. E is correct.

Hydrogens, bonded directly to F, O or N, participate in hydrogen bonds. The hydrogen is partial positive (i.e., delta plus or $\partial+$) due to the bond to these electronegative atoms. The lone pair of electrons on the F, O or N interacts with the $\partial+$ hydrogen to form a hydrogen bond.

The two lone pairs of electrons on the oxygen atom can each participate as a hydrogen bond acceptor. The molecule does not have a hydrogen bonded directly to an electronegative atom (F, O or N) and cannot be a hydrogen bond donor.

27. A is correct.

28. C is correct. The molecule H_2CO (formaldehyde) is shown below and has one C=O bond and two C–H bonds.

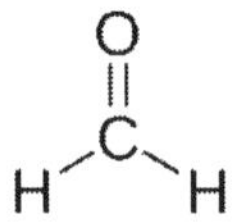

Because the bonds are between different atoms, there is a dipole moment and this results in three polar bonds.

29. A is correct.

The valence shell is the outermost shell (i.e., highest principal quantum number, *n*) of an atom.

Valence electrons are those electrons of the outermost electron shell that can participate in a chemical bond.

The number of valence electrons for an element can be determined by its group (i.e., vertical column) on the periodic table. With the exception of the transition metals (i.e., groups 3-12), the group number identifies how many valence electrons are associated with a particular element: all elements of the same group have the same number of valence electrons.

30. D is correct.

Group IA elements (e.g., Li, Na and K) have a tendency to lose 1 electron to achieve a complete octet to be cations with a +1 charge.

Group IIA elements (e.g., Mg and Ca) have a tendency to lose 2 electrons to achieve a complete octet to be cations with a +2 charge.

Group VIIA elements (halogens such as F, CL, Br and I) have a tendency to gain 1 electron to achieve a complete octet to be anions with a –1 charge.

31. B is correct.

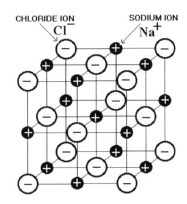

Lattice structure of sodium chloride

32. E is correct. Each positively charged nuclei attracts the bonding electrons.

33. E is correct. Electronegativity is a measure of how strongly an element attracts electrons within a bond.

Electronegativity is the relative attraction of the nucleus for bonding electrons. It increases from left to right (i.e., periods) and from bottom to top along a group (similar to the trend for ionization energy). The most electronegative atom is F, while the least electronegative atom is Fr.

The greater the difference in electronegativity between two atoms in a compound, the more polar of a bond these atoms form whereby the atom with the higher electronegativity is the partial (delta) negative end of the dipole.

34. A is correct. Hydrogen bonds are the strongest intermolecular forces (i.e., between molecules), followed by dipole–dipole, dipole–induced dipole and van der Waals forces (i.e., London dispersion).

Hydrogens, bonded directly to F, O or N, participate in hydrogen bonds. H–bonding is a polar interaction involving hydrogen forming bonds to the electronegative atoms such of F, O or N, which accounts for the high boiling points of water. The hydrogen is partial positive (i.e., delta plus or ∂+) due to the bond to these electronegative atoms. The lone pair of electrons on the F, O or N interacts with the ∂+ hydrogen to form a hydrogen bond.

Molecular geometry of H_2S

Polar molecules have high boiling points because of polar interaction. H_2S is a polar molecule but does not form hydrogen bonds; it forms dipole–dipole interactions.

35. D is correct.

With a total of 4 electron pairs, the starting shape of this element is a tetrahedral.

After the removal of 2 of the 4 groups surrounding the central atom, the central atom has two groups bound (e.g., H_2O). The molecule has the hybridization (and original angles) from a tetrahedral shape, so it is bent rather than linear.

36. D is correct.

Salt crystals are held together by ionic bonds. Salts are composed of cations and anions and are electrically neutral. When salts are dissolved in solution, they separate into their constituent ions by breaking of noncovalent interactions.

Water: the hydrogen atoms in the molecule are covalently bonded to the oxygen atom.

Hydrogen peroxide: the molecule has one more oxygen atom than water molecule does, and is also held together by covalent bonds.

Ester (RCOOR'): undergo hydrolysis and breaks covalent bonds to separate into its constituent carboxylic acid (RCOOH) and alcohol (ROH).

37. B is correct.

An ionic compound consists of a metal ion and a nonmetal ion.

Ionic bonds are formed between elements with an electronegativity difference greater than 1.7 Pauling units (e.g., a metal atom and a non-metal atom).

(K and I) form ionic bonds because K is a metal and I is a nonmetal.

(C and Cl) and (H and O) only have nonmetals, while (Fe and Mg) has only metals.

(Ga and Si) has a metal (Ga) and a metalloid (Si); they *might* form weak ionic bonds.

38. A is correct.

A coordinate bond is a covalent bond (i.e., shared pair of electrons) in which both electrons come from the same atom.

$$H \times \overset{\bullet\bullet}{\underset{H}{\overset{\bullet}{N}}} \times H \ + \ [H]^+ \ \longrightarrow \ H \times \overset{H}{\underset{H}{\overset{\bullet\bullet}{N}}} \times H$$

The lone pair of the nitrogen is donated to form the fourth N–H bond

39. B is correct.

Dipole moment depends on the overall shape of the molecule, the length of the bond, and whether the electrons are pulled to one side of the bond (or the molecule overall).

For a large dipole moment, one element pulls electrons more strongly (i.e. differences in electronegativity).

Electronegativity is a measure of how strongly an element attracts electrons within a bond.

Electronegativity is the relative attraction of the nucleus for bonding electrons. It increases from left to right (i.e., periods) and from bottom to top along a group (similar to the trend for ionization energy). The most electronegative atom is F, while the least electronegative atom is Fr.

The greater the difference in electronegativity between two atoms in a compound, the more polar of a bond these atoms form whereby the atom with the higher electronegativity is the partial (delta) negative end of the dipole.

40. A is correct.

The valence shell is the outermost shell (i.e., highest principal quantum number, *n*) of an atom.

The noble gas configuration simply refers to eight electrons in the atom's outermost valence shell, referred to as a complete octet.

Depending on how many electrons it starts with, an atom may have to lose, gain or share an electron to obtain the noble gas configuration.

Practice Set 3: Questions 41–60

41. E is correct.

The bond between the oxygens is nonpolar, while the bonds between the oxygens and hydrogens are polar (due to the differences in electronegativity).

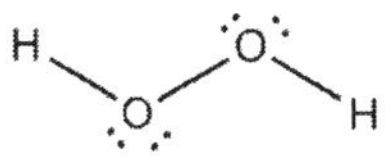

Line bond structure of H_2O_2 with lone pairs shown

42. A is correct.

The octet rule states that atoms of main-group elements tend to combine in a way that each atom has eight electrons in its valence shell. This occurs because electron arrangements involving eight valence electrons are extremely stable, as is the case with the noble gasses.

Selenium (Se) is in group VI and has 6 valence electrons. By gaining two electrons, it has a complete octet (i.e., stable).

43. C is correct.

44. D is correct.

Hydrogen bonds are the strongest intermolecular forces (i.e., between molecules), followed by dipole–dipole, dipole–induced dipole and van der Waals forces (i.e., London dispersion).

45. C is correct.

An ion is an atom (or a molecule) in which the total number of electrons is not equal to the total number of protons. Therefore, the atom (or molecule) has a net positive or negative electrical charge.

If a neutral atom loses one or more electrons, it has a net positive charge (i.e., cation).

If a neutral atom gains one or more electrons, it has a net negative charge (i.e., anion).

Aluminum is a group III atom and has proportionally more protons per electron once the cation forms.

All other elements listed are from group I or II.

46. A is correct. Dipole–dipole (e.g., CH_3Cl...CH_3Cl) attraction occurs between neutral molecules, while ion–dipole interaction involves dipole interactions with charged ions (e.g., CH_3Cl...$^-OOCCH_3$).

Hydrogen bonds are the strongest intermolecular forces (i.e., between molecules), followed by dipole–dipole, dipole–induced dipole and van der Waals forces (i.e., London dispersion).

47. E is correct.

When more than two H_2O molecules are present (e.g., liquid water), more bonds (between 2 and 4) are possible because the oxygen of one water molecule has two lone pairs of electrons, each of which can form a hydrogen bond with a hydrogen on another water molecule.

This bonding can repeat such that every water molecule is H–bonded with up to four other molecules (two through its two lone pairs of O, and two through its two hydrogen atoms).

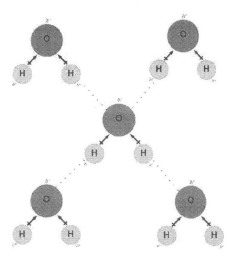

Ice with 4 hydrogen bonds between the water molecules

Hydrogen bonding affects the crystal structure of ice (hexagonal lattice). The density of ice is less than the density of water at the same temperature. Thus, the solid phase of water (ice) floats on the liquid. The creation of the additional H–bonds (up to 4 for ice) forces the individual molecules further from each other which gives it less density, unlike most other substances in the solid phase.

For most substances, the solid form is denser than the liquid phase. Therefore, a block of most solids sinks in the liquid. With regards to pure water though, a block of ice (solid phase) floats in liquid water because ice is less dense.

Like other substances, when liquid water is cooled from room temperature, it becomes increasingly dense. However, at approximately 4 °C (39 °F), water reaches its maximum density, and as it's cooled further, it expands and becomes less dense. This phenomenon is known as *negative thermal expansion* and is attributed to strong intermolecular interactions that are orientation-dependent.

The density of water is about 1 g/cm^3 and depends on the temperature. When frozen, the density of water is decreased by about 9%. This is due to the decrease in intermolecular vibrations, which allows water molecules to form stable hydrogen bonds with other water molecules around. As these hydrogen bonds form, molecules are locking into positions similar to the hexagonal structure.

Even though hydrogen bonds are shorter in the crystal than in the liquid, this position locking decreases the average coordination number of water molecules as the liquid reaches the solid phase.

48. A is correct.

The phrase "from its elements" in the question stem implies the need to create the formation reaction of the compound from its elements.

Chemical equation:

$$3\ Na^+ + N^{3-} \rightarrow Na_3N$$

Each sodium ion loses one electron to form Na$^+$ ions.

Nitrogen gains 3 electrons to form the N^{3-} ion.

Schematic of ionic compound

49. D is correct.

The valence shell is the outermost shell (i.e., highest principal quantum number, *n*) of an atom.

Valence electrons are those electrons of the outermost electron shell that can participate in a chemical bond.

The number of valence electrons for an element can be determined by its group (i.e., vertical column) on the periodic table. With the exception of the transition metals (i.e., groups 3-12), the group number identifies how many valence electrons are associated with a particular element: all elements of the same group have the same number of valence electrons.

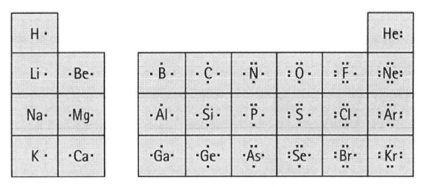

Sample Lewis dot structures for some elements

Ga^+ has two valance electrons (same electronic configuration as Ca).

S^{2-} has eight valance electrons (same electronic configuration as Ar).

Mg^{2+} has eight valance electrons (same electronic configuration as Ne).

Ar^+ has seven valance electrons (same electronic configuration as Cl).

F^- has eight valance electrons (same electronic configuration as Ne).

50. B is correct. The octet rule states that atoms of main-group elements tend to combine in a way that each atom has eight electrons in its valence shell.

51. D is correct.

52. D is correct.

Hydrogen sulfide (i.e., sewer gas) is H_2S.

Hydrosulfide (bisulfide) ion is HS^-.

Sulfide ion is S^{2-}

53. D is correct.

An ionic compound consists of a metal ion and a nonmetal ion.

Ionic bonds are formed between elements with an electronegativity difference greater than 1.7 Pauling units (e.g., a metal atom and a non-metal atom).

The charge on bicarbonate ion (HCO_3) is −1, while the charge on Mg is +2.

The proper formula is $Mg(HCO_3)_2$

54. C is correct.

Lattice: crystalline structure – consists of unit cells

Unit cell: smallest unit of solid crystalline pattern

Covalent unit and *ionic unit* are not valid terms.

55. D is correct.

Formula to calculate dipole moment:

$$\mu = qr$$

where μ is dipole moment (coulomb-meter or C·m), q is charge (coulomb or C), and r is radius (meter or m)

Convert the unit of dipole moment from Debye to C·m:

$$0.16 \times 3.34 \times 10^{-30} = 5.34 \times 10^{-31} \text{ C·m}$$

Convert the unit of radius to meter:

$$115 \text{ pm} \times 1 \times 10^{-12} \text{ m/pm} = 115 \times 10^{-12} \text{ m}$$

Rearrange the dipole moment equation to solve for q:

$$q = \mu / r$$

$$q = (5.34 \times 10^{-31} \text{ C·m}) / (115 \times 10^{-12} \text{ m})$$

$$q = 4.65 \times 10^{-21} \text{ C}$$

Express the charge in terms of electron charge (e).

$$(4.65 \times 10^{-21} \text{ C}) / (1.602 \times 10^{-19} \text{ C/e}) = 0.029 \text{ e}$$

In this NO molecule, oxygen is the more electronegative atom.

Therefore, the charge experienced by the oxygen atom is negative: –0.029e.

56. A is correct.

The greater the difference in electronegativity between two atoms in a compound, the more polar of a bond these atoms form, whereby the atom with the higher electronegativity is the partial (delta) negative end of the dipole.

57. C is correct.

Hybridization of the central atom and the corresponding molecular geometry:

Examples of *sp³* hybridized atoms with 4 substituents (CH4),

3 substituents (NH3) and two substituents (H2O)

<u>Hybridization - Shape</u>

sp – linear

sp² – trigonal planar

sp³ – tetrahedral

sp³d – trigonal bipyramid

58. C is correct.

Hydrogen bonds are the strongest intermolecular forces (i.e., between molecules), followed by dipole–dipole, dipole–induced dipole and van der Waals forces (i.e., London dispersion).

Hydrogen is a very electropositive element and O is a very electronegative element. Therefore, these elements will be attracted to each other, both within the same water molecule and between water molecules.

Ionic or covalent bonding can only form within a molecule and not between adjacent molecules.

59. E is correct. In a compound, the sum of ionic charges must equal to zero.

For the charges of K^+ and CO_3^{2-} to even out, there has to be 2 K^+ ions for every CO_3^{2-} ion.

The formula of this balanced molecule is K_2CO_3.

60. C is correct. The substantial difference between the two forms of carbon (i.e., graphite and diamonds) is mainly due to their crystal structure, which is hexagonal for graphite and cubic for diamond.

The conditions to convert graphite into diamond are high pressure and high temperature. That is why creating synthetic diamonds is time-consuming, energy-intensive and expensive, since carbon is forced to change its bonding structure

Practice Set 4: Questions 61–89

61. E is correct. Lewis acids are defined as electron pair acceptors, whereas Lewis bases are electron pair donors.

Boron has an atomic number of five and has a vacant $2p$ orbital to accept electrons.

62. D is correct. Hydrogen bonds are the strongest intermolecular forces (i.e., between molecules), followed by dipole–dipole, dipole–induced dipole and van der Waals forces (i.e., London dispersion).

63. A is correct.

In carbon–carbon double bonds there is overlap of sp^2 orbitals and a p orbital on the adjacent carbon atoms. The sp^2 orbitals overlap head-to-head as a *sigma* (σ) bond, whereas the p orbitals overlap sideways as a *pi* (π) bond.

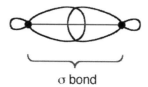

σ bond

Sigma bond formation showing electron density along the internucleus axis

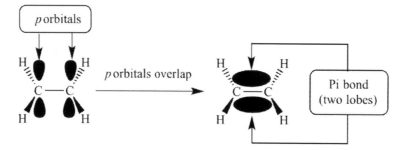

Two *pi* orbitals showing the *pi* bond formation during sideways overlap – note the absence of electron density (i.e., node) along the internucleus axis.

Bond lengths and strengths (σ or π) depends on the size and shape of the atomic orbitals and the density of these orbitals to overlap effectively.

The σ bonds are stronger than π bonds because head-to-head orbital overlap involves more shared electron density than sideways overlap. The σ bonds formed from two $2s$ orbitals are shorter than those formed from two $2p$ orbitals or two $3s$ orbitals.

Carbon, oxygen and nitrogen are in the second period ($n = 2$), while sulfur (S), phosphorus (P) and silicon (Si) are in the third period. Therefore, S, P and Si use $3p$ orbitals to form π bonds, while C, N and O use $2p$ orbitals. The $3p$ orbitals are much larger than $2p$ orbitals and therefore there is a reduced probability for an overlap of the $2p$ orbital of C and the $3p$ orbital of S, P and Si.

B: S, P, and Si can hybridize, but these elements can combine s and p orbitals and (unlike C, O and N) have d orbitals.

C: S, P and Si (in their ground state electron configurations) have partially occupied p orbitals which form bonds.

D: carbon combines with elements below the second row of the periodic table. For example, carbon forms bonds with higher principal quantum number ($n > 2$) halogens (e.g., F, Cl, Br and I).

64. E is correct. The magnesium atom has a +2 charge and the sulfur atom has a –2 charge.

65. C is correct. Hydrogen bonds are the strongest intermolecular forces (i.e., between molecules), followed by dipole–dipole, dipole–induced dipole and van der Waals forces (i.e., London dispersion).

Larger atoms have more electrons, which means that they are capable of exerting stronger induced dipole forces compared to smaller atoms.

Bromine is located under chlorine on the periodic table, which means it has more electrons and stronger induced dipole forces.

66. A is correct. Hydrogen bonds are the strongest intermolecular forces (i.e., between molecules), followed by dipole–dipole, dipole–induced dipole and van der Waals forces (i.e., London dispersion).

Hydrogens, bonded directly to F, O or N, participate in hydrogen bonds. The hydrogen is partially positive (i.e., delta plus: $\partial+$) due to the bond to these electronegative atoms. The lone pair of electrons on the F, O or N interacts with the partial positive ($\partial+$) hydrogen to form a hydrogen bond.

When ~NH or ~OH groups are present in a molecule, they form hydrogen bonds with other molecules.

Hydrogen bonding is the strongest intermolecular force and it is the major intermolecular force in this substance.

67. B is correct.

Potassium oxide (K_2O) contains a metal and nonmetal, which form a salt.

Salts contain ionic bonds and dissociate in aqueous solutions, and are therefore strong electrolytes.

A polyatomic (i.e., molecular) ion is a charged chemical species composed of two or more atoms covalently bonded or composed of a metal complex acting as a single unit. An example is the hydroxide ion consisting of one oxygen atom and one hydrogen atom; hydroxide has a charge of -1.

A polyatomic ion does bond with other ions.

A polyatomic ion has various charges.

A polyatomic ion might contain only metals or nonmetals.

A polyatomic ion is not neutral.

oxidation state	-1	$+1$	$+3$	$+5$	$+7$
anion name	chloride	hypochlorite	chlorite	chlorate	perchlorate
formula	$Cl-$	ClO^-	ClO^{2-}	ClO^{3-}	ClO^{4-}

68. D is correct.

The valence shell is the outermost shell (i.e., highest principal quantum number, n) of an atom.

Valence electrons are those electrons of the outermost electron shell that can participate in a chemical bond.

69. B is correct.

Nitrogen (NH_3) is neutral with three bonds, negative with two bonds ($^-NH_2$) and positive with 4 bonds ($^+NH_4$)

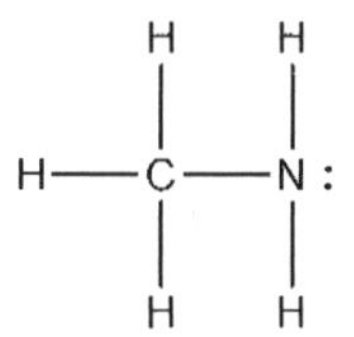

Line bond structure of methylamine with the lone pair on nitrogen shown

70. B is correct. Sulfide ion is S^{2-}.

Hydrogen sulfide (i.e., sewer gas) is H_2S.

Hydrosulfide (bisulfide) ion is HS^-.

Sulfite ion is the conjugate base of bisulfite and has the molecular formula of SO_3^{2-}

Sulfur (S) is a chemical element with an atomic number of 16.

Sulfate ion is polyatomic anion (i.e., two or more atoms covalently bonded or metal complex) with the molecular formula of SO_4^{2-}

Sulfur acid (HSO_3^-) results from the combination of sulfur dioxide (SO_2) and H_2O.

71. E is correct. Ionic bonds involve electrostatic interactions between oppositely charged atoms.

Electrons from the metallic atom are transferred to the nonmetallic atom, giving both atoms a full valence shell.

72. B is correct. If the charge of O is −1, the proper formula of its compound with K (+1) should be KO.

73. C is correct. The lattice energy of a crystalline solid is usually defined as the energy of formation of the crystal from infinitely-separated ions (i.e., an exothermic process and hence the negative sign).

Some older textbooks define lattice energy with the opposite sign. The older notation was referring to the energy required to convert the crystal into infinitely separated gaseous ions in vacuum (i.e., an endothermic process and hence the positive sign).

Lattice energy decreases downward for a group.

Lattice energy increases with charge.

Because both NaCl and LiF contain charges of +1 and −1, they would have smaller lattice energy than the higher-charged ions on other options.

Na is lower than Li and Cl is lower than F in their respective groups, so NaCl would have lower lattice energy than LiF.

The lattice energy of a crystalline solid is usually defined as the energy of formation of the crystal from infinitely-separated ions (i.e., an exothermic process and hence the negative sign).

Some older textbooks define lattice energy with the opposite sign. The older notation was referring to the energy required to convert the crystal into infinitely separated gaseous ions in vacuum (i.e., an endothermic process and hence the positive sign).

The bond between ions of opposite charge is strongest when the ions are small.

The force of attraction between oppositely charged particles is directly proportional to the product of the charges on the two objects (q_1 and q_2), and inversely proportional to the square of the distance between the objects (r^2):

$$F = q_1 \times q_2 / r^2$$

Therefore, the strength of the bond between the ions of opposite charge in an ionic compound depends on the charges on the ions and the distance between the centers of the ions when they pack to form a crystal.

For NaCl, the lattice energy is the energy released by the reaction:

$$Na^+ (g) + Cl^- (g) \rightarrow NaCl (s), \text{ lattice energy} = -786 \text{ kJ/mol}$$

Other examples:

Al_2O_3, lattice energy $= -15,916$ kJ/mol

KF, lattice energy $= -821$ kJ/mol

LiF, lattice energy $= -1,036$ kJ/mol

NaOH, lattice energy $= -900$ kJ/mol

74. C is correct. Formula to calculate dipole moment:

$$\mu = qr$$

where μ is dipole moment (coulomb per meter or C/m), q is charge (coulomb or C), and r is radius (meter or m)

Convert the unit of radius to meters:

$$154 \text{ pm} \times 1 \times 10^{-12} \text{ m/pm} = 154 \times 10^{-12} \text{ m}$$

Convert the charge to coulombs:

$$0.167 \, e \times 1.602 \times 10^{-19} \text{ C/e}^- = 2.68 \times 10^{-20} \text{ C}$$

Use these values to calculate dipole moment:

$$\mu = qr$$
$$\mu = 2.68 \times 10^{-20} \text{ C} \times 154 \times 10^{-12} \text{ m}$$
$$\mu = 4.13 \times 10^{-30} \text{ C·m}$$

Finally, convert the dipole moment to Debye:

$$4.13 \times 10^{-30} \text{ C·m} / 3.34 \times 10^{-30} \text{ C·m·D}^{-1} = 1.24 \text{ D}$$

75. B is correct.

The greater the difference in electronegativity between two atoms in a compound, the more polar of a bond these atoms form whereby the atom with the higher electronegativity is the partial (delta) negative end of the dipole.

Although each C–Cl bond is very polar, the dipole moments of each of the four bonds in CCl_4 (carbon tetrachloride) cancel because the molecule is a symmetric tetrahedron.

76. C is correct.

The pK_a of the carboxylic acid is about 5 and is deprotonated (exists as an anion) at pH of 10.

The pK_a of the alcohol is about 15 and is protonated (neutral) at pH of 10.

77. E is correct.

Hybridization of the central atom and the corresponding molecular geometry:

Hybridization - Shape

sp – linear

sp^2 – trigonal planar

sp^3 – tetrahedral

sp^3d – trigonal bipyramid

BF_3 is sp^2 hybridized and has a trigonal planar molecular geometry

78. B is correct.

The valence shell is the outermost shell (i.e., highest principal quantum number, n) of an atom.

The octet rule states that atoms of main-group elements tend to combine in a way that each atom has eight electrons in its valence shell. This occurs because electron arrangements involving eight valence electrons are extremely stable, as is the case with the noble gasses.

79. D is correct.

80. D is correct.

Electronegativity is defined as the ability of an atom to attract electrons when it bonds with another atom.

The most electron negative atom is F, while the least electronegative atom is Fr. The trend for increasing electronegativity within the periodic table is up and toward the right (i.e., fluorine).

Chlorine has the highest electronegativity of the elements listed.

Electronegativity is a characteristic of non-metals.

States of Matter: Gases, Liquids, Solids: Explanations

1. A is correct.

Solids, liquids and gases all have a vapor pressure which increases from solid to gas.

Vapor pressure is the pressure exerted by a vapor in equilibrium with its condensed phases (i.e., solid or liquid) in a closed system, at a given temperature.

Vapor pressure is a colligative property of a substance and depends only on the quantity of solutes present, not on their identity.

2. C is correct.

Charles' law (i.e., law of volumes) explains how, at constant pressure, gases behave when temperature changes:

$$V \propto T$$

or

$$V \, / \, T = \text{constant}$$

or

$$(V_1 \, / \, T_1) = (V_2 \, / \, T_2)$$

Volume and temperature are proportional.

Doubling the temperature at constant pressure doubles the volume.

3. C is correct.

Colligative properties include: lowering of vapor pressure, elevation of boiling point, depression of freezing point and increased osmotic pressure.

Addition of solute to a pure solvent lowers the vapor pressure of the solvent; therefore, a higher temperature is required to bring the vapor pressure of the solution in an open container up to the atmospheric pressure. This increases the boiling point.

Because adding solute lowers the vapor pressure, the freezing point of the solution decreases (e.g., automobile antifreeze).

4. A is correct.

At a pressure and temperature corresponding to the triple point (point D on the graph) of a substance, all three states (gas, liquid and solid) exist in equilibrium.

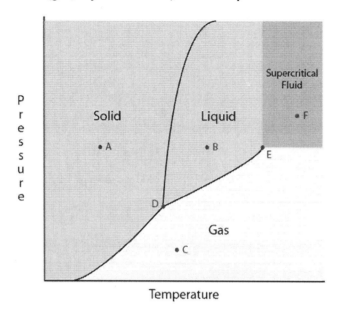

Phase diagram of pressure vs. temperature

The critical point (point E on the graph) is the end point of the phase equilibrium curve where the liquid and its vapor become indistinguishable.

5. A is correct.

In the van der Waals equation, *a* is the negative deviation due to attractive forces and *b* is the positive deviation due to molecular volume.

6. B is correct.

R is the symbol for the ideal gas constant.

R is expressed in (L × atm) / mole × K and the value = 0.0821.

Convert to different units (torr and mL)

$$0.0821[(L \times atm) / (mole \times K)] \times (760 \text{ torr/atm}) \times (1{,}000 \text{ mL/L})$$

$$R = 62{,}396 (torr \times mL) / mole \times K$$

7. B is correct.

Ideal gas law:

$$PV = nRT$$

where P is pressure, V is volume, n is the number of molecules, R is the ideal gas constant and T is the temperature of the gas.

R and n are constant.

From this equation, if both pressure and temperature are halved, there would be no effect on the volume.

8. B is correct.

Kinetic molecular theory of gas molecules states that the average kinetic energy per molecule in a system is proportional to the temperature of the gas.

Since it is given that containers X and Y are both at the same temperature and pressure, then molecules of both gases must possess the same amount of average kinetic energy.

9. E is correct.

Barometer and manometer are used to measure pressure.

Barometers are designed to measure atmospheric pressure, while a manometer can measure pressure that is lower than atmospheric pressure.

A manometer has both ends of the tube open to the outside (while some may have one end closed), whereas a barometer is a type of closed-end manometer with one end of the glass tube closed and sealed with a vacuum.

The atmospheric pressure is 760 mmHg, so the barometer should be able to accommodate that.

10. D is correct. Vapor pressure is the pressure exerted by a vapor in equilibrium with its condensed phases (i.e., solid or liquid) in a closed system, at a given temperature.

Raoult's law states the partial vapor pressure of each component of an ideal mixture of liquids is equal to the vapor pressure of the pure component multiplied by its mole fraction in the mixture.

In exothermic reactions, the vapor pressure deviates negatively for Raoult's law.

Depending on the ratios of the liquids in a solution, the vapor pressure could be lower than either or just lower than X, because X is a higher boiling point, thus a lower vapor pressure.

The boiling point increases from adding of Y to the mixture because the vapor pressure decreases.

11. B is correct.

$$2\text{ Na }(s) + \text{Cl}_2\,(g) \rightarrow 2\text{ NaCl }(s)$$

In its elemental form, chlorine exists as a gas.

In its elemental form, Na exists as a solid.

12. C is correct.

The molecules of an ideal gas do not occupy a significant amount of space and exert no intermolecular forces, while the molecules of a real gas do occupy space and do exert (weak attractive) intermolecular forces.

However, both an ideal gas and a real gas have pressure, which is created from molecular collisions with the walls of the container.

13. A is correct.

Boyle's law (i.e., pressure-volume law) states that pressure and volume are inversely proportional:

$$(P_1V_1) = (P_2V_2)$$

Solve for the final pressure:

$$P_2 = (P_1V_1) / V_2$$

$$P_2 = [(0.95\text{ atm}) \times (2.75\text{ L})] / (0.45\text{ L})$$

$$P_2 = 5.80\text{ atm}$$

14. D is correct.

Avogadro's law is an experimental gas law relating volume of a gas to the amount of substance of gas present.

Avogadro's law states that equal volumes of all gases, at the same temperature and pressure, have the same number of molecules.

For a given mass of an ideal gas, the volume and amount (i.e., moles) of the gas are directly proportional if the temperature and pressure are constant:

$$V \,\alpha\, n$$

where V = volume and n = number of moles of the gas.

Charles' law (i.e., law of volumes) explains how, at constant pressure, gases behave when temperature changes:

$$V \,\alpha\, T$$

or

V / T = constant

or

$(V_1 / T_1) = (V_2 / T_2)$

Volume and temperature are proportional. Therefore, an increase in one term results in an increase in the other.

Gay-Lussac's law (i.e., pressure-temperature law) states that pressure is proportional to temperature:

$P \alpha T$

or

$(P_1 / T_1) = (P_2 / T_2)$

or

$(P_1 T_2) = (P_2 T_1)$

or

P / T = constant

If the pressure of a gas increases, the temperature also increases.

Boyle's law (i.e., pressure-volume law) states that pressure and volume are inversely proportional:

15. C is correct.

Ideal gas law:

$PV = nRT$

where P is pressure, V is volume, n is the number of molecules, R is the ideal gas constant and T is the temperature of the gas.

R and n are constant.

If T is constant, the equations becomes PV = constant.

They are inversely proportional: if one of the values is reduced, the other increases.

16. A is correct.

Vaporization refers to the change of state from a liquid to a gas. There are two types of vaporization: boiling and evaporation, which are differentiated based on the temperature at which they occur.

Evaporation occurs at a temperature below the boiling point, while boiling occurs at a temperature at or above the boiling point.

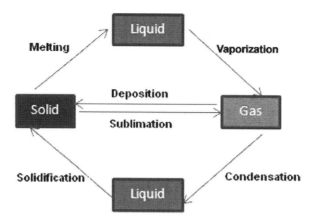

Interconversion of states of matter

17. C is correct.

Ideal gas law:

$PV = nRT$

from which simpler gas laws such as Boyle's, Charles' and Avogadro's laws are derived.

The value of n and R are constant.

The common format of the combined gas law:

$(P_1 V_1) / T_1 = (P_2 V_2) / T_2$

Try modifying the equations to recreate all the formats of the equation provided by the problem.

$T_2 = T_1 \times P_1 / P_2 \times V_2 / V_1$ should be written as $T_2 = T_1 \times V_1/V_2 \times P_1/P_2$

18. C is correct.

Intermolecular forces act between neighboring molecules. Examples include hydrogen bonding, dipole-dipole, dipole-induced dipole and van der Waals (i.e. London dispersion) forces.

A dipole-dipole attraction involves asymmetric, polar molecules (based on differences in electronegativity between atoms) that create a dipole moment (i.e., net vector indicating the force).

Sulfur dioxide with indicated bond angle

19. C is correct.

Increasing the pressure of the gas above the liquid puts stress on the equilibrium of the system. Gas molecules start to collide with the liquid surface more often, which increases the rate of gas molecules entering the solution, thus increasing the solubility.

20. E is correct.

Avogadro's law states the correlation between volume and moles (n).

Avogadro's law is an experimental gas law relating volume of a gas to the amount of substance of gas present. A modern statement of Avogadro's law is:

At the same pressure and temperature, equal volumes of all gases have the same number of molecules.

$$V \propto n$$

or

$$V / n = k$$

where V is the volume of the gas, n is the number of moles of the gas and k is a constant equal to RT/P (where R is the universal gas constant, T is the temperature in Kelvin and P is the pressure).

For comparing the same substance under two sets of conditions, the law is expressed as:

$$V_1 / n_1 = V_2 / n_2$$

===

Practice Set 2: Questions 21–40

===

21. E is correct.

Colligative properties of solutions depend on the ratio of the number of solute particles to the number of solvent molecules in a solution, and not on the type of chemical species present.

Colligative properties include: lowering of vapor pressure, elevation of boiling point, depression of freezing point and increased osmotic pressure.

Boiling point (BP) elevation:

$$\Delta BP = iKm$$

where i = the number of particles produced when the solute dissociates, K = boiling elevation constant and m = molality (moles/kg solvent).

In this problem, acid molality is not known.

22. A is correct.

An ideal gas has no intermolecular forces, indicating that its molecules have no attraction to each other. The molecules of a real gas, however, do have intermolecular forces, although these forces are extremely weak.

Therefore, the molecules of a real gas are slightly attracted to one another, although the attraction is nowhere near as strong as the attraction in liquids and solids.

23. E is correct.

Standard temperature and pressure (STP) has a temperature of 273.15 K (0 °C, 32 °F) and a pressure of 760 mmHg (100 kPa, 1 bar, 14.504 psi, 0.98692 atm).

The mm of Hg was defined as the pressure generated by a column of mercury one millimeter high. The pressure of mercury depends on temperature and gravity.

This variation in mmHg is a difference in units of about of 0.000015%.

In general, 1 torr = 1 mm of Hg.

760 mmHg = 1 atm

The torr is defined as 1/760 of an atmosphere (i.e., 1 atm = 760 torr).

24. D is correct.

At lower temperatures, the potential energy due to the intermolecular forces is more significant compared to the kinetic energy; this causes the pressure to be reduced because the gas molecules are attracted to each other.

25. D is correct.

Dalton's law (i.e., law of partial pressures) states that *the pressure exerted by a mixture of gases is equal to the sum of the individual gas pressures*.

The pressure due to N_2 and CO_2:

(320 torr + 240 torr) = 560 torr

The partial pressure of O_2 is:

740 torr – 560 torr = 180 torr

180 torr / 740 torr = 24%

26. A is correct.

Ideal gas law:

PV = nRT

where P is pressure, V is volume, n is the number of molecules, R is the ideal gas constant and T is the temperature of the gas.

If the volume is reduced by ½, the number of moles is reduced by ½.

Pressure is reduced to 90%, so the number of moles is reduced by 90%.

Therefore, the total reduction in moles is (½ × 90%) = 45%.

Mass is proportional to number of moles for a given gas, so the mass reduction can be calculated directly:

New mass is 45% of 40 grams = (0.45 × 40 g) = 18 grams

27. D is correct.

Evaporation describes the phase change from liquid to gas.

The mass of the molecules and the attraction of the molecules with their neighbors (to form intermolecular attractions) determine their kinetic energy.

The increase in kinetic energy is required for individual molecules to move from the liquid to the gaseous phase.

28. B is correct.

The molecules of an ideal gas exert no attractive forces. Therefore, a real gas behaves most nearly like an ideal gas when it is at high temperature and low pressure, because under these conditions the molecules are far apart from each other and exert little or no attractive forces on each other.

29. E is correct.

Hydroxyl (~OH) groups greatly increase the boiling point because they form hydrogen bonds with ~OH groups of neighboring molecules.

Hydrocarbons are nonpolar molecules, which means that the dominant intermolecular force is London dispersion. This force gets stronger as the number of atoms in each molecule increases. Stronger force increases the boiling point.

Branching of the hydrocarbon also affects the boiling point. Straight molecules have slightly higher boiling points than branched molecules with the same number of atoms. The reason is that straight molecules can align parallel against each other and all atoms in the molecules are involved in the London dispersion forces.

Another factor is the presence of other heteroatoms (i.e., atoms other than carbon and hydrogen). For example, the electronegative oxygen atom between carbon groups or in an ether (C–O–C) slightly increases the boiling point.

30. A is correct.

Kinetic theory explains macroscopic properties of gases (e.g., temperature, volume and pressure) by their molecular composition and motion.

The gas pressure is due to the collisions on the walls of a container from molecules moving at different velocities.

Temperature = $\frac{1}{2}mv^2$

31. B is correct.

Methanol (CH_3OH) is an alcohol that participates in hydrogen bonding.

Therefore, this gas experiences the strongest intermolecular forces.

32. D is correct.

Density = mass / volume

Gas molecules have a large amount of space between them, therefore they can be pushed together and thus gases are very compressible. Because there is such a large amount of space between each molecule in a gas, the extent to which the gas molecules can be pushed together is much greater than the extent to which liquid molecules can be pushed together. Therefore, gases have a greater compressibility than liquids.

Gas molecules are further apart than liquid molecules, which is why gases have a smaller density.

33. C is correct. Vapor pressure is the pressure exerted by a vapor in equilibrium with its condensed phases (i.e., solid or liquid) in a closed system, at a given temperature.

Vapor pressure is inversely correlated with the strength of intermolecular force.

With stronger intermolecular forces, the molecules are more likely to stick together in the liquid form and fewer of them participate in the liquid-vapor equilibrium.

The vapor pressure of a liquid decreases when a nonvolatile substance is dissolved into a liquid.

The decrease in the vapor pressure of a substance is proportional to the number of moles of the solute dissolved in a definite weight of the solvent. This is known as Raoult's law.

34. B is correct. Dalton's law (i.e., law of partial pressures) states that *the pressure exerted by a mixture of gases is equal to the sum of the individual gas pressures.* It is an empirical law that was observed by English chemist John Dalton, and is related to the ideal gas laws.

35. C is correct. Solids have a definite shape and volume. For example, a block of granite does not change its shape or its volume regardless of the container in which it is placed.

Molecules in a solid are very tightly packed due to the strong intermolecular attractions, which prevents the molecules from moving around.

36. E is correct. Ideal gas law: $PV = nRT$

where P is pressure, V is volume, n is the number of molecules, R is the ideal gas constant and T is the temperature of the gas.

At STP (standard conditions for temperature and pressure), it is known that the pressure and temperature for all three flasks are the same. It is also known that the volume is the same in each case – 2.0 L.

Therefore, since R is a constant, the number of molecules "n" must be the same for the ideal gas law to hold true.

37. A is correct.

Hydrogens, bonded directly to F, O or N, participate in hydrogen bonds. The hydrogen is partially positive (i.e., delta plus: $\partial+$) due to the bond to these electronegative atoms. The lone pair of electrons on the F, O or N interacts with the partial positive ($\partial+$) hydrogen to form a hydrogen bond.

D: the hydrogen on the methyl carbon and that carbon is not attached to N, O, or F. Therefore, that particular hydrogen can't form a hydrogen bond, even though there is an available oxygen on the other methanol to form hydrogen bond.

38. C is correct.

Boyle's law (Mariotte's law or the Boyle-Mariotte law) is an experimental gas law that describes how the volume of a gas increases as the pressure decreases (i.e., they are inversely proportional), if the temperature is constant.

Boyle's law (i.e., pressure-volume law) states that pressure and volume are inversely proportional:

$$P_1V_1 = P_2V_2$$

or $P \times V = $ constant

If the volume of a gas increases, its pressure decreases proportionally.

Dalton's law (i.e., law of partial pressures) states that *the pressure exerted by a mixture of gases is equal to the sum of the individual gas pressures*.

Charles' law (i.e., law of volumes) explains how, at constant pressure, gases behave when temperature changes:

$$V \alpha T$$

or $V / T = $ constant

or $(V_1 / T_1) = (V_2 / T_2)$

Volume and temperature are proportional: an increase in one results in an increase in the other.

Gay-Lussac's law (i.e., pressure-temperature law) states that pressure is proportional to temperature:

$$P \alpha T$$

or $(P_1 / T_1) = (P_2 / T_2)$

or $(P_1T_2) = (P_2T_1)$

or $P / T = $ constant

If the pressure of a gas increases, the temperature also increases.

Avogadro's law is an experimental gas law relating volume of a gas to the amount of substance of gas present. It states that, *equal volumes of all gases, at the same temperature and pressure, have the same number of molecules.*

39. B is correct.

As the automobile travels the highway, friction is generated between the road and its tires. The heat energy increases the temperature of the air inside the tires, causing the molecules to have more velocity. These fast-moving molecules collide with the walls of the tire at a higher rate, and thus pressure is increased.

Gay-Lussac's law (i.e., pressure-temperature law) states that pressure is proportional to temperature:

$$P \propto T$$

or

$$(P_1 / T_1) = (P_2 / T_2)$$

or

$$(P_1 T_2) = (P_2 T_1)$$

or

$$P / T = \text{constant}$$

If the temperature of a gas is increases, the pressure also increases.

40. C is correct.

The balanced chemical equation:

$$N_2 + 3 H_2 \rightarrow 2 NH_3$$

Use the balanced coefficients from the written equation, apply dimensional analysis to solve for the volume of H_2 needed to produce 10.6 L NH_3:

$$V_{H2} = V_{NH3} \times (\text{mol } H_2 / \text{mol } NH_3)$$

$$V_{H2} = (12.5 \text{ L}) \times (3 \text{ mol} / 2 \text{ mol})$$

$$V_{H2} = 18.8 \text{ L}$$

===

Practice Set 3: Questions 41–60

===

41. C is correct.

Dalton's law (i.e., law of partial pressures) states that *the pressure exerted by a mixture of gases is equal to the sum of the individual gas pressures.*

Convert the masses of the gases into moles:

Moles of O_2:

16 g of O_2 × 32 g/mole = 0.5 mole

Moles of N_2:

14 g of N_2 × 28 g/mole = 0.5 mole

Mole of CO_2:

88 g of CO_2 × 44 g/mole = 2 moles

Total moles:

(0.5 mol + 0.5 mole + 2 mol) = 3 moles

The total pressure of 1 atm (or 760 mmHg) has 38 mmHg contributed as H_2O vapor.

Total pressure due to N_2:

(760 mmHg – 38 mmHg) = 722 mmHg

$O_2 = CO_2$

The partial pressure of CO_2:

mole fraction × (total pressure of the gas mixture – H_2O vapor)

(2 moles CO_2 / 3 moles total gas)] × (760 mmHg – 38 mmHg)

partial pressure of CO_2 = 481 mmHg

42. E is correct.

Colligative properties are properties of solutions that depend on the ratio of the number of solute particles to the number of solvent molecules in a solution, and not on the type of chemical species present.

Colligative properties include: lowering of vapor pressure, elevation of boiling point, depression of freezing point and increased osmotic pressure

Dissolving a solute into a solvent alters the solvent's freezing point, melting point, boiling point and vapor pressure.

43. B is correct.

Boyle's law (i.e., pressure-volume law) states that pressure and volume are inversely proportional:

$$(P_1V_1) = (P_2V_2)$$

or

$$P \times V = constant$$

If the volume of a gas increases, its pressure decreases proportionally.

44. E is correct.

Gases form homogeneous mixtures, regardless of the identities or relative proportions of the component gases. There is a relatively large distance between gas molecules (as opposed to solids or liquids where the molecules are much closer together).

When a pressure is applied to gas, its volume readily decreases, and thus gases are highly compressible.

There are no attractive forces between gas molecules, which is why molecules of a gas can move about freely.

45. E is correct.

Solids have a definite shape and volume. For example, a block of granite does not change its shape or its volume regardless of the container in which it is placed.

Molecules in a solid are very tightly packed due to the strong intermolecular attractions, which prevents the molecules from moving around.

46. A is correct.

Standard temperature and pressure (STP) has a temperature of 273.15 K (0 °C, 32 °F) and a pressure of 760 mmHg (100 kPa, 1 bar, 14.504 psi, 0.98692 atm).

The mm of Hg was defined as the pressure generated by a column of mercury one millimeter high. The pressure of mercury depends on temperature and gravity.

This variation in mmHg is a difference in units of about of 0.000015%.

In general, 1 torr = 1 mm of Hg.

760 mmHg = 1 atm

The torr is defined as 1/760 of an atmosphere (i.e., 1 atm = 760 torr).

47. C is correct.

Intermolecular forces act between neighboring molecules. Examples include hydrogen bonding, dipole-dipole, dipole-induced dipole and van der Waals (i.e. London dispersion) forces.

Stronger force results in a higher boiling point.

CH_3COOH is a carboxylic acid that can from two hydrogen bonds. Therefore, it has the highest boiling point.

Ethanoic acid with the two hydrogen bonds indicated on the structure

48. C is correct.

Molecules in solids have the most attraction their neighbors, followed by liquids (significant motion between the individual molecules) and then gas.

A molecule in an ideal gas have no attractions to other gas molecules. For a gas experiencing low pressure, the particles are far enough apart for no attractive forces to exist between the individual gas molecules.

49. C is correct.

Ideal gas law:

$$PV = nRT$$

where P is pressure, V is volume, n is the number of molecules, R is the ideal gas constant and T is the temperature of the gas.

Set the initial and final P, V and T conditions equal:

$$(P_1V_1 / T_1) = (P_2V_2 / T_2)$$

Solve for the final volume of N_2:

$$(P_2V_2 / T_2) = (P_1V_1 / T_1)$$

$$V_2 = (T_2 P_1 V_1) / (P_2 T_1)$$

$$V_2 = [(295 \text{ K}) \times (760 \text{ mmHg}) \times (0.190 \text{ L N}_2)] / [(660 \text{ mmHg}) \times (273 \text{ K})]$$

$$V_2 = 0.236 \text{ L}$$

50. B is correct.

Volatility is the tendency of a substance to vaporize (phase change from liquid to vapor).

Volatility is directly related to a substance's vapor pressure. At a given temperature, a substance with higher vapor pressure vaporizes more readily than a substance with a lower vapor pressure.

Molecules with weak intermolecular attraction are able to increase their kinetic energy with the transfer of less heat due to a smaller molecular mass. The increase in kinetic energy is required for individual molecules to move from the liquid to the gaseous phase.

51. B is correct.

Barometer and manometer are used to measure pressure.

Barometers are designed to measure atmospheric pressure, while a manometer can measure pressure that is lower than atmospheric pressure.

A manometer has both ends of the tube open to the outside (while some may have one end closed), whereas a barometer is a type of closed-end manometer with one end of the glass tube closed and sealed with a vacuum.

Difference of mercury height on both necks indicates the capacity of a manometer.

820 mm – 160 mm = 660 mm

Historically, the pressure unit of torr is set to equal 1 mmHg, or the rise/dip of 1 mm of mercury in a manometer.

Because the manometer uses mercury, the height difference (660 mm) is equal to its measuring capacity in torr (660 torr).

52. C is correct.

The conditions of the ideal gases are the same, so the number of moles (i.e., molecules) is equal.

At STP, temperature is the same, so the kinetic energy of the molecules is the same.

However, the molar mass of oxygen and nitrogen are different. Therefore, the density is different.

53. A is correct. Vapor pressure is the pressure exerted by a vapor in equilibrium with its condensed phases (i.e., solid or liquid) in a closed system, at a given temperature.

The compound exists as a liquid if the external pressure > compound's vapor pressure.

A substance boils when vapor pressure = external pressure.

54. D is correct.

Gas molecules have a large amount of space between them, therefore they can be pushed together and gases are thus very compressible.

Molecules in solids and liquids are already close together, therefore they cannot get significantly closer, and are thus nearly incompressible.

55. C is correct.

Charles' law (i.e., law of volumes) explains how, at constant pressure, gases behave when temperature changes:

$$V \alpha T$$

or

$$V / T = \text{constant}$$

or

$$(V_1 / T_1) = (V_2 / T_2)$$

Volume and temperature are proportional. Therefore, an increase in one results in an increase in the other.

Gay-Lussac's law (i.e., pressure-temperature law) states that pressure is proportional to temperature:

$$P \alpha T$$

or

$$(P_1 / T_1) = (P_2 / T_2)$$

or

$$(P_1 T_2) = (P_2 T_1)$$

or

$$P / T = \text{constant}$$

If the pressure of a gas increases, the temperature also increases.

Dalton's law (i.e., law of partial pressures) states that *the pressure exerted by a mixture of gases is equal to the sum of the individual gas pressures*

Boyle's law (i.e., pressure-volume law) states that pressure and volume are inversely proportional:

$$(P_1 V_1) = (P_2 V_2)$$

or

$$P \times V = \text{constant}$$

If the volume of a gas increases, its pressure decreases proportionally.

Avogadro's law is an experimental gas law relating volume of a gas to the amount of substance of gas present. It states that, *equal volumes of all gases, at the same temperature and pressure, have the same number of molecules.*

56. B is correct.

Sublimation is the direct change of state from a solid to a gas, skipping the intermediate liquid phase.

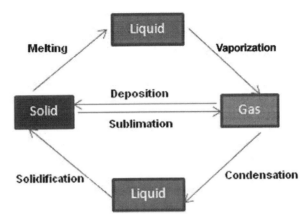

Interconversion of states of matter

An example of a compound that undergoes sublimation is solid carbon dioxide (i.e., dry ice). CO_2 changes phases from solid to gas (i.e., bypasses the liquid phase) and is often used as a cooling agent.

57. B is correct.

Graham's law of effusion states that the rate of effusion (i.e., escaping through a small hole) of a gas is inversely proportional to the square root of the molar mass of its particles.

Rate 1 / Rate 2 = √(molar mass gas 1 / molar mass gas 2)

The diffusion rate is the inverse root of the molecular weights of the gases.

Therefore, the rate of effusion is:

O_2 / H_2 = √(2 / 32)

rate of diffusion = 1 : 4

58. B is correct.

To calculate number of molecules, calculate the moles of gas using the ideal gas law:

$PV = nRT$

$n = PV / RT$

Because the gas constant R is in L·atm K^{-1} mol^{-1}, pressure must be converted into atm:

320 mmHg × (1 / 760 atm/mmHg) = 320 mmHg / 760 atm

(Leave it in this fraction form because the answer choices are in this format.)

Convert the temperature to Kelvin:

10 °C + 273 = 283 K

Substitute those values into the ideal gas equation:

$n = PV / RT$

n = (320 mmHg / 760 atm) × 6 L / (0.0821 L·atm K^{-1} mol^{-1} × 283 K)

This expression represents the number of gas moles present in the container.

Calculate the number of molecules:

number of molecules = moles × Avogadro's number

number of molecules = (320 mmHg / 760 atm) × 6 / (0.0821 × 283) × 6.02 × 10^{23}

number of molecules = (320 / 760)·(6)·(6 × 10^{23}) / (0.0821)·(283)

59. A is correct. At STP (standard conditions for temperature and pressure), the pressure and temperature are the same regardless of the gas.

The ideal gas law:

$PV = nRT$

where P is pressure, V is volume, n is the number of molecules, R is the ideal gas constant and T is the temperature of the gas.

Therefore, one molecule of each gas occupies the same volume at STP. Since CO_2 molecules have the largest mass, CO_2 gas has a greater mass in the same volume, and thus it has the greatest density.

60. C is correct. Hydrogens, bonded directly to F, O or N, participate in hydrogen bonds. The hydrogen is partially positive (i.e., delta plus: $\partial+$) due to the bond to these electronegative atoms. The lone pair of electrons on the F, O or N interacts with the partial positive ($\partial+$) hydrogen to form a hydrogen bond.

===

Practice Set 4: Questions 61–80

===

61. D is correct.

Calculate the moles of each gas:

moles = mass / molar mass

moles H_2 = 9.50 g / (2 × 1.01 g/mole)

moles H_2 = 4.70 moles

moles Ne = 14.0 g / (20.18 g/mole)

moles Ne = 0.694 moles

Calculate the mole fraction of H:

Mole fraction of H = moles of H / total moles in mixture

Mole fraction of H = 4.70 moles / (4.70 moles + 0.694 moles)

Mole fraction of H = 4.70 moles / (5.394 moles)

Mole fraction of H = 0.87 moles

62. E is correct.

Vapor pressure is the pressure exerted by a vapor in equilibrium with
its condensed phases (i.e., solid or liquid) in a closed system, at a given temperature.

Boiling occurs when the vapor pressure of a liquid equals atmospheric pressure.

Vapor pressure always increases as the temperature increases.

Liquid A boils at a lower temperature than B because the vapor pressure of Liquid A is
closer to the atmospheric pressure.

63. B is correct.

Colligative properties of solutions depend on the ratio of the number of solute particles to
the number of solvent molecules in a solution, and not on the type of chemical species
present.

Colligative properties include: lowering of vapor pressure, elevation of boiling point,
depression of freezing point and increased osmotic pressure.

Freezing point (FP) depression:

ΔFP = –iKm

347

where i = the number of particles produced when the solute dissociates, K = freezing point depression constant and m = molality (moles/kg solvent).

$$-iKm = -2 \text{ K}$$

$$-(1)\cdot(40)\cdot(x) = -2$$

$$x = -2 / -1(40)$$

$$x = 0.05 \text{ molal}$$

Assume that compound *x* does not dissociate.

$$0.5 \text{ mole compound } (x) / \text{kg camphor} = 25 \text{ g} / \text{kg camphor}$$

Therefore, if 0.05 mole = 25 g

$$1 \text{ mole} = 500 \text{ g}$$

64. E is correct.

Boiling occurs when the vapor pressure of a liquid equals atmospheric pressure.

Vapor pressure is the pressure exerted by a vapor in equilibrium with its condensed phases (i.e., solid or liquid) in a closed system, at a given temperature.

Atmospheric pressure is the pressure exerted by the weight of air in the atmosphere.

Vapor pressure is inversely correlated with the strength of intermolecular force.

With stronger intermolecular forces, the molecules are more likely to stick together in the liquid form and fewer of them participate in the liquid-vapor equilibrium; therefore, the molecule would boil at a higher temperature.

65. D is correct.

Van der Waals equation describes factors that must be accounted for when the ideal gas law is used to calculate values for nonideal gases.

The terms that affect the pressure and volume of the ideal gas law are intermolecular forces and volume of nonideal gas molecules.

66. E is correct.

Ideal gas law:

$$PV = nRT$$

where P is pressure, V is volume, n is the number of molecules, R is the ideal gas constant and T is the temperature of the gas.

Units of R can be calculated by rearranging the expression:

$R = PV/nT$

$R = 1 \cdot atm/mol \cdot K$

67. A is correct.

Ideal-gas law:

$PV = nRT$

where P is pressure, V is volume, n is the number of molecules, R is the ideal gas constant and T is the temperature of the gas.

Set the initial and final P/V/T conditions equal:

$(P_1 V_1 / T_1) = (P_2 V_2 / T_2)$

STP condition are temperature of 0 °C (273 K) and pressure of 1 atm.

Solve for the final temperature:

$(P_2 V_2 / T_2) = (P_1 V_1 / T_1)$

$T_2 = (P_2 V_2 T_1) / (P_1 V_1)$

$T_2 = [(0.80 \text{ atm}) \times (0.155 \text{ L}) \times (273 \text{ K})] / [(1.00 \text{ atm}) \times (0.120 \text{ L})]$

$T_2 = 282.1 \text{ K}$

Then convert temperature units to degrees Celsius:

$T_2 = (282.1 \text{ K} - 273 \text{ K})$

$T_2 = 9.1 \text{ °C}$

68. C is correct.

Atmospheric pressure is the pressure exerted by the weight of air in the atmosphere.

Boiling occurs when vapor pressure of the liquid is higher than the atmospheric pressure.

At standard atmospheric pressure and 22 °C, the vapor pressure of water is less than the atmospheric pressure, and it does not boil.

However, when a vacuum pump is used, the atmospheric pressure is reduced until it has a lower vapor pressure than water, which allows water to boil at a much lower temperature.

69. E is correct.

The kinetic theory of gases describes a gas as a large number of small particles in constant rapid motion. These particles collide with each other and with the walls of the container.

Their average kinetic energy depends only on the absolute temperature of the system.

$$\text{temperature} = \tfrac{1}{2}mv^2$$

At high temperatures, the particles are moving greater velocity, and at a temperature of absolute zero (i.e., 0 K), there is no movement of gas particles.

Therefore, as temperature decreases, kinetic energy decreases, and so does the velocity of the gas molecules.

70. A is correct.

Dalton's law (i.e., law of partial pressures) states that *the pressure exerted by a mixture of gases is equal to the sum of the individual gas pressures*.

Partial pressure of molecules in a mixture is proportional to their molar ratios.

Use the coefficients of the reaction to determine molar ratio.

Based on that information, calculate the partial pressure of O_2:

(coefficient O_2) / (sum of coefficients in mixture) × total pressure

$[1 / (2 + 1)] \times 1{,}250$ torr

417 torr = partial pressure of O_2

71. D is correct.

$$2\ Na\ (s) + Cl_2\ (g) \rightarrow 2\ NaCl\ (s)$$

In its elemental form, Na exists as a solid.

In its elemental form, chlorine exists as a gas.

72. B is correct.

Charles' law (i.e., law of volumes) explains how, at constant pressure, gases behave when temperature changes:

$$V \alpha T$$

or

$$V / T = \text{constant}$$

or

$$(V_1 / T_1) = (V_2 / T_2)$$

Volume and temperature are proportional.

Therefore, an increase in one term results in an increase in the other.

73. E is correct.

Gay-Lussac's law (i.e., pressure-temperature law) states that pressure is proportional to temperature:

$P \propto T$

or

$(P_1 / T_1) = (P_2 / T_2)$

or

$(P_1 T_2) = (P_2 T_1)$

or

$P / T = \text{constant}$

If the pressure of a gas increases, the temperature is increased proportionally.

Quadrupling the temperature increases the pressure fourfold.

Boyle's law (i.e., pressure-volume law) states that pressure and volume are inversely proportional:

$(P_1 V_1) = (P_2 V_2)$

or

$P \times V = \text{constant}$

Reducing the volume by half increases the pressure twofold.

Therefore, the total increase in pressure would be by a factor of $4 \times 2 = 8$.

74. C is correct.

Scientists found that the relationships between pressure, temperature and volume of a sample of gas hold true for all gases, and the gas laws were developed.

Boyle's law (i.e., pressure-volume law) states that pressure and volume are inversely proportional:

$(P_1 V_1) = (P_2 V_2)$

or

$P \times V = \text{constant}$

If the volume of a gas increases, its pressure decreases proportionally.

Charles' law (i.e., law of volumes) explains how, at constant pressure, gases behave when temperature changes:

$$(V_1 / T_1) = (V_2 / T_2)$$

Gay-Lussac's law (i.e., pressure-temperature law) states that pressure is proportional to temperature:

$$P \, \alpha \, T$$

or

$$(P_1 / T_1) = (P_2 / T_2) \text{ or } (P_1 T_2) = (P_2 T_1)$$

or

$$P / T = \text{constant}$$

If the pressure of a gas increases, the temperature also increases.

75. A is correct.

Sublimation is the direct change of state from a solid to a gas, skipping the intermediate liquid phase.

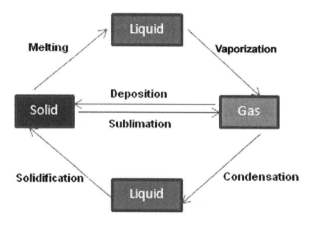

Interconversion of states of matter

An example of a compound that undergoes sublimation is solid carbon dioxide (i.e., dry ice). CO_2 changes phases from solid to gas (i.e., bypasses the liquid phase) and is often used as a cooling agent.

76. B is correct.

Graham's law of effusion states that the rate of effusion (i.e., escaping through a small hole) of a gas is inversely proportional to the square root of the molar mass of its particles.

$$\text{Rate 1 / Rate 2} = \sqrt{(\text{molar mass gas 1 / molar mass gas 2})}$$

Set the rate of effusion of krypton over the rate of effusion of methane:

$Rate_{Kr} / Rate_{CH4} = \sqrt{[(M_{Kr}) / (M_{CH4})]}$

Solve for the ratio of effusion rates:

$Rate_{Kr} / Rate_{CH4} = \sqrt{[(83.798 \text{ g/mol}) / (16.04 \text{ g/mol})]}$

$Rate_{Kr} / Rate_{CH4} = 2.29$

Larger gas molecules must effuse at a slower rate; the effusion rate of Kr gas molecules must be slower than methane molecules:

$Rate_{Kr} = [Rate_{CH4} / (2.29)]$

$Rate_{Kr} = [(631 \text{ m/s}) / (2.29)]$

$Rate_{Kr} = 276 \text{ m/s}$

77. C is correct.

Observe information about gas C. Temperature, pressure and volume of the gas is indicated.

Substitute these values into the ideal gas law equation to determine the number of moles:

$PV = nRT$

$n = PV / RT$

Convert all units to the units indicated in the gas constant:

volume = 668.5 mL × (1 L / 1,000 mL)

volume = 0. 669 L

pressure = 745.5 torr × (1 atm / 760 torr)

pressure = 0.981 atm

temperature = 32.0 °C + 273.15 K

temperature = 305.2 K

$n = PV / RT$

$n = (0.981 \text{ atm} \times 0.669 \text{ L}) / (0.0821 \text{ L·atm K}^{-1} \text{ mol}^{-1} \times 305.2 \text{ K})$

$n = 0.026 \text{ mole}$

Law of mass conservation states that total mass of products = total mass of reactants.

Based on this law, mass of gas C can be determined:

mass product = mass reactant

mass A = mass B + mass C

$$5.2 \text{ g} = 3.8 \text{ g} + \text{mass C}$$

$$\text{mass C} = 1.4 \text{ g}$$

Calculate molar mass of C:

$$\text{molar mass} = 1.4 \text{ g} / 0.026 \text{ mole}$$

$$\text{molar mass} = 53.9 \text{ g} / \text{mole}$$

78. E is correct.

Liquids take the shape of the container that they are in (i.e., they have an indefinite shape). This can be visualized by considering of a liter of water poured into a cylindrical bucket or a square box. In both cases, it takes up the shape of the container.

However, liquids have definite volume. The volume of water in the given example is 1 L, regardless of the container it is in.

79. D is correct.

Intermolecular forces act between neighboring molecules. Examples include hydrogen bonding, dipole-dipole, dipole-induced dipole and van der Waals (i.e. London dispersion) forces.

Hydrogens, bonded directly to F, O or N, participate in hydrogen bonds. The hydrogen is partially positive (i.e., delta plus: $\partial+$) due to the bond to these electronegative atoms. The lone pair of electrons on the F, O or N interacts with the partial positive ($\partial+$) hydrogen to form a hydrogen bond.

80. D is correct.

When the balloon is placed in a freezer, the temperature of the helium in the balloon decreases because the surroundings are colder than the balloon, and heat is transferred from the balloon to the surrounding air until thermal equilibrium is reached.

When temperature of a gas decreases, the molecules move more slowly and become closer together, causing the volume of the balloon to decrease.

From the ideal gas law,

$$PV = nRT$$

If temperature decreases, volume must also decrease (assuming that pressure remains constant).

Stoichiometry: Explanations

===

Practice Set 1: Questions 1–20

===

1. C is correct.

One mole of an ideal gas occupies 22.4 L at STP.

3 mole × 22.4 L = 67.2 L

2. C is correct.

Use the mnemonic OIL RIG: <u>O</u>xidation <u>I</u>s <u>L</u>oss, <u>R</u>eduction <u>I</u>s <u>G</u>ain (of electrons).

Oxidation is the loss of electrons, while reduction is the gain of electrons.

An oxidizing agent undergoes reduction, while a reducing agent undergoes oxidation.

Check the oxidation numbers of each atom.

Oxidation number for S is +6 as a reactant and +4 as a product, which means that it is reduced.

If a substance is reduced in a redox reaction, it is the oxidizing agent, because it causes the other reagent (HI) to be oxidized.

3. C is correct.

Balanced equation (combustion):

$2\ C_6H_{14} + 19\ O_2 \rightarrow 12\ CO_2 + 14\ H_2O$

4. E is correct.

An oxidation number is the charge on an atom that is not present in the elemental state when the element is neutral.

Electronegativity refers to the attraction an atom has for additional electrons.

5. C is correct.

CH_3COOH has 2 carbons, 4 hydrogens and 2 oxygens: $C_2O_2H_4$

Reduce to the smallest coefficients by dividing by two: COH_2

6. B is correct.

Oxidation numbers of Cl in each compound:

$NaClO_2$	+3
$Al(ClO_4)_3$	+7
$Ca(ClO_3)_2$	+5
$LiClO_3$	+5

7. A is correct.

Formula mass is a synonym for molecular mass/molecular weight (MW).

Molecular mass = (atomic mass of C) + (2 × atomic mass of O)

Molecular mass = (12.01 g/mole) + (2 × 16.00 g/mole)

Molecular mass = 44.01 g/mole

Note: 1 amu = 1 g/mole

8. C is correct.

Cadmium is located in group II, so its oxidation number is +2.

Sulfur tends to form sulfide ion (oxidation number –2).

The net oxidation number is zero and therefore, the compound is CdS.

9. B is correct.

Balanced reaction (single replacement):

$$Cl_2 \ (g) + 2 \ NaI \ (aq) \rightarrow I_2 \ (s) + 2 \ NaCl \ (aq)$$

10. C is correct.

Use the mnemonic OIL RIG: <u>O</u>xidation <u>I</u>s <u>L</u>oss, <u>R</u>eduction <u>I</u>s <u>G</u>ain (of electrons).

Oxidation is the loss of electrons, while reduction is the gain of electrons.

An oxidizing agent undergoes reduction, while a reducing agent undergoes oxidation.

When there are 2 reactants in a redox reaction, one will be oxidized and the other will be reduced. The oxidized species is the reducing agent, and vice versa.

Determine the oxidation number of all atoms:

I changes its oxidation state from –1 as a reactant to 0 as a product.

I is oxidized, therefore the compound that contains I (NaI) is the reducing agent. Species in their elemental state have an oxidation number of 0.

Since the reaction is spontaneous, NaI is the *strongest* reducing agent in the reaction, because it is capable of reducing another species spontaneously without needing any external energy for the reaction to proceed.

11. C is correct.

To determine remainder of a reactant, calculate how many moles of that reactant are required to produce the specified amount of product.

Use the coefficients to calculate the moles of the reactant:

$$\text{moles } N_2 = (1 / 2) \times 18 \text{ moles} = 9 \text{ moles } N_2$$

Therefore, the remainder is:

$$(14.5 \text{ moles } N_2) - (9 \text{ moles } N_2) = 5.5 \text{ moles } N_2 \text{ remaining}$$

12. D is correct.

$CaCO_3 \rightarrow CaO + CO_2$ is a decomposition reaction because one complex compound is being broken down into two or more parts. However, the redox part is incorrect, because the reactants and products are all compounds (no single elements) and there is no change in oxidation state (i.e., no gain or loss of electrons).

A: $AgNO_3 + NaCl \rightarrow AgCl + NaNO_3$ is correctly classified as a double-replacement reaction (sometimes referred to as double-displacement) because parts of two ionic compounds are exchanged to make two new compounds. It is also a non-redox reaction because the reactants and products are all compounds (no single elements) and there is no change in oxidation state (i.e., no gain or loss of electrons).

B: $Cl_2 + F_2 \rightarrow 2 \ ClF$ is correctly classified as a synthesis reaction because two species are combining to form a more complex chemical compound as the product. It is also a redox reaction because the F atoms in F_2 are reduced (i.e., gain electrons) and the Cl atoms in Cl_2 are oxidized (i.e., lose electrons) forming a covalent compound.

C: $H_2O + SO_2 \rightarrow H_2SO_3$ is correctly classified as a synthesis reaction because two species are combining to form a more complex chemical compound as the product. It is also a non-redox reaction because the reactants and products are all compounds (no single elements) and there is no change in oxidation state (i.e., no gain or loss of electrons).

13. C is correct. Hydrogen is being oxidized (or ignited) to produce water.

The balanced equation that describes the ignition of hydrogen gas in air to produce water is:

$$½ O_2 + H_2 \rightarrow H_2O$$

This equation suggests that for every mole of water that is produced in the reaction, 1 mole of hydrogen and ½ mole of oxygen gas is needed.

The maximum amount of water that can be produced in the reaction is determined by the amount of limited reactant available. This requires identifying which reactant is the limiting reactant and can be done by comparing the number of moles of oxygen and hydrogen.

From the question, there are 10 grams of oxygen gas and 1 gram of hydrogen gas. This is equivalent to 0.3125 moles of oxygen and 0.5 moles of hydrogen.

Because the reaction requires twice as much hydrogen as oxygen gas, the limiting reactant is hydrogen gas (0.3215 moles of O_2 requires 0.625 moles of hydrogen, but only 0.5 moles of H_2 are available).

Since one equivalent of water is produced for every equivalent of hydrogen that is burned, the amount of water produced is:

$$(18 \text{ grams/mol } H_2O) \times (0.5 \text{ mol } H_2O) = 9 \text{ grams of } H_2O$$

14. D is correct. Calculate the moles of Cl^- ion:

Moles of Cl^- ion = number of Cl^- atoms / Avogadro's number

Moles of Cl^- ion = 6.8×10^{22} atoms / 6.02×10^{23} atoms/mole

Moles of Cl^- ion = 0.113 moles

In a solution, $BaCl_2$ dissociates:

$$BaCl_2 \rightarrow Ba^{2+} + 2 Cl^-$$

The moles of from Cl^- previous calculation can be used to calculate the moles of Ba^{2+}:

Moles of Ba^{2+} = (coefficient of Ba^{2+} / coefficient Cl^-) × moles of Cl^-

Moles of Ba^{2+} = (½) × 0.113 moles

Moles of Ba^{2+} = 0.0565 moles

Calculate the mass of Ba^{2+}:

Mass of Ba^{2+} = moles of Ba^{2+} × atomic mass of Ba

Mass of Ba^{2+} = 0.0565 moles × 137.33 g/mole

Mass of Ba^{2+} = 7.76 g

15. D is correct.

Na	Br	O_3
+1	x	(3×-2)
+1	x	-6

The sum of charges in a neutral molecule is zero:

1 + oxidation number of Br:

$$1 + x + (-6) = 0$$

$$-5 + x = 0$$

$$x = +5$$

oxidation number of Br = +5

16. E is correct.

Balanced equation:

$$2\ Al + Fe_2O_3 \rightarrow 2\ Fe + Al_2O_3$$

The sum of the coefficients of the products = 3.

17. B is correct.

$2\ H_2O_2\ (s) \rightarrow 2\ H_2O\ (l) + O_2\ (g)$ is incorrectly classified. The decomposition part of the classification is correct, because one complex compound (H_2O_2) is being broken down into two or more parts (H_2O and O_2).

However, it is a redox reaction because oxygen is being lost from H_2O_2, which is one of the three indicators of a redox reaction (i.e., electron loss/gain, hydrogen loss/gain, oxygen loss/gain). Additionally, one of the products is a single element (O_2), which is also a clue that it is a redox reaction.

$AgNO_3\ (aq) + KOH\ (aq) \rightarrow KNO_3\ (aq) + AgOH\ (s)$ is correctly classified as a non-redox reaction because the reactants and products are all compounds (no single elements) and there is no change in oxidation state (i.e., no gain or loss of electrons). It is also a precipitation reaction, because the chemical reaction occurs in aqueous solution and one of the products formed (AgOH) is insoluble, which makes it a precipitate.

$Pb(NO_3)_2\ (aq) + 2\ Na\ (s) \rightarrow Pb\ (s) + 2\ NaNO_3\ (aq)$ is correctly classified as a redox reaction because the nitrate (NO_3^-), which dissociates, is oxidized (loses electrons), the Na^+ is reduced (gains electrons), and the two combine to form the ionic compound $NaNO_3$. It is a single-replacement reaction because one element is substituted for another element in a compound, making a new compound ($2NaNO_3$) and an element (Pb).

HNO_3 (*aq*) + LiOH (*aq*) → $LiNO_3$ (*aq*) + H_2O (*l*) is correctly classified as a non-redox reaction because the reactants and products are all compounds (no single elements) and there is no change in oxidation state (i.e., no gain or loss of electrons). It is also a double-replacement reaction because parts of two ionic compounds are exchanged to make two new compounds.

18. C is correct.

At STP, 1 mole of gas has a volume of 22.4 L.

Calculate moles of O_2:

> moles of O_2 = (15.0 L) / (22.4 L/mole)

> moles of O_2 = 0.67 mole

Calculate the moles of O_2, using the fact that 1 mole of O_2 has 6.02×10^{23} O_2 molecules:

> molecules of O_2 = 0.67 mole × (6.02×10^{23} molecules/mole)

> molecules of O_2 = 4.03×10^{23} molecules

19. E is correct.

20. D is correct.

Use the mnemonic OIL RIG: <u>O</u>xidation <u>I</u>s <u>L</u>oss, <u>R</u>eduction <u>I</u>s <u>G</u>ain (of electrons).

Oxidation is the loss of electrons, while reduction is the gain of electrons.

An oxidizing agent undergoes reduction, while a reducing agent undergoes oxidation.

Co^{2+} is the starting reactant because it has to lose electrons and produce an ion with a higher oxidation number.

Copyright © 2017 Sterling Test Prep. Any duplication is illegal.

==

Practice Set 2: Questions 21–40

==

21. D is correct.

Double replacement reaction:

HCl has a molar mass of 36.5 g/mol:

       365 grams HCl = 10 moles HCl

       10 moles are 75% of the total yield.

       10 moles PCl_3 / 0.75 = 13.5 moles of HCl.

Apply the mole ratios:

       Coefficients: 3 HCl = PCl_3

       13.5 / 3 = moles of PCl_3

       13.5 moles of HCl is produced by 4.5 moles of PCl_3

22. A is correct. All elements in their free state will have oxidation number of zero.

23. B is correct. Balanced chemical equation:

       $C_3H_8 + 5\ O_2 \rightarrow 3\ CO_2 + 4\ H_2O$

By using the coefficients from the balanced equation, apply dimensional analysis to solve for the volume of H_2O produced from the 2.6 L C_3H_8 reacted:

       $V_{H2O} = V_{C3H8} \times$ (mol H_2O / mol C_3H_8)

       V_{H2O} = (2.6 L) × (4 mol / 1 mol)

       V_{H2O} = 10.4 L

24. C is correct.

Use the mnemonic OIL RIG: Oxidation Is Loss, Reduction Is Gain (of electrons).

Oxidation is the loss of electrons, while reduction is the gain of electrons.

An oxidizing agent undergoes reduction, while a reducing agent undergoes oxidation.

The oxidation number of Hg decreases (i.e., reduction) from +2 as a reactant ($HgCl_2$) to +1 as a product (Hg_2Cl_2). This means that Hg gained one electron.

25. C is correct.

Balanced equation (synthesis):

$$4 \text{ P } (s) + 5 \text{ O}_2 \text{ } (g) \rightarrow 2 \text{ P}_2\text{O}_5 \text{ } (s)$$

26. E is correct.

27. A is correct. Formula mass is a synonym for molecular mass/molecular weight (MW).

Start by calculating the mass of the formula unit (CH_2O)

$$CH_2O = (12.01 \text{ g/mol} + 2.02 \text{ g/mol} + 16.00 \text{ g/mol}) = 30.03 \text{ g/mol}$$

Divide the molar mass with the formula unit mass:

$$180 \text{ g/mol} / 30.03 \text{ g/mol} = 5.994$$

Round to the closest whole number: 6

Multiply the formula unit by 6:

$$(CH_2O)_6 = C_6H_{12}O_6$$

28. E is correct.

Calculate the moles of LiI present. The molecular weight of LiI is 133.85 g/mol.

Moles of LiI:

$$6.45 \text{ g} / 133.85 \text{ g/mole} = 0.0482 \text{ moles}$$

Each mole of LiI contains 6.02×10^{23} molecules.

Number of molecules:

$$0.0482 \times 6.02 \times 10^{23} = 2.90 \times 10^{22} \text{ molecules}$$

1 molecule is equal to 1 formula unit.

29. E is correct. A combustion engine creates various nitrogen oxide compounds often referred to as NOx gases, because each gas would have a different value of x in their formula.

30. C is correct.

Balanced equation (synthesis):

$$4 \text{ P } (s) + 3 \text{ O}_2 \text{ } (g) \rightarrow 2 \text{ P}_2\text{O}_3 \text{ } (s)$$

31. A is correct.

Use the mnemonic OIL RIG: <u>O</u>xidation <u>I</u>s <u>L</u>oss, <u>R</u>eduction <u>I</u>s <u>G</u>ain (of electrons).

Oxidation is the loss of electrons, while reduction is the gain of electrons.

An oxidizing agent undergoes reduction, while a reducing agent undergoes oxidation.

Because the forward reaction is spontaneous, the reverse reaction is not spontaneous.

Sn cannot reduce Mg^{2+}; therefore, Sn is the weakest oxidizing agent.

32. C is correct.

Balancing Redox Equations

From the balanced equation, the coefficient for the proton can be determined. Balancing a redox equation not only requires balancing the atoms that are in the equation, but the charges must be balanced as well.

The equations must be separated into two different half-reactions. One of the half-reactions addresses the oxidizing component, and the other addresses the reducing component.

Magnesium is being oxidized, therefore the unbalanced oxidation half-reaction will be:

$$Mg\ (s) \rightarrow Mg^{2+}\ (aq)$$

Furthermore, the nitrogen is being reduced, therefore the unbalanced reduction half-reaction will be:

$$NO_3^-\ (aq) \rightarrow NO_2\ (aq)$$

At this stage, each half reaction needs to be balanced for each atom, and the net electric charge on each side of the equations must be balanced as well.

Order of operations for balancing half-reactions:

1) Balance atoms except for oxygen and hydrogen.

2) Balance the oxygen atom count by adding water.

3) Balance the hydrogen atom count by adding protons.

   a) If in basic solution, add equal amounts of hydroxide to each side to cancel the protons.

4) Balance the electric charge by adding electrons.

5) If necessary, multiply the coefficients of one half-reaction equation by a factor that cancels the electron count when both equations are combined.

6) Cancel any ions or molecules that appear on both sides of the overall equation.

After determining the balanced overall redox reaction, the stoichiometry indicates the moles of protons that are involved.

For magnesium:

$$Mg\ (s) \rightarrow Mg^{2+}\ (aq)$$

The magnesium is already balanced with a coefficient of 1. There are no hydrogen or oxygen atoms present in the equation. The magnesium cation has a +2 charge, so to balance the charge, 2 moles of electrons should be added to the right side.

The balanced half-reaction for oxidation:

$$Mg\ (s) \rightarrow Mg^{2+}\ (aq) + 2\ e^-$$

For nitrogen:

$$NO_3^-\ (aq) \rightarrow NO_2\ (aq)$$

The equation is already balanced for nitrogen because one nitrogen atom appears on both sides of the reaction. The nitrate reactant has three oxygen atoms, while the nitrite product has two oxygen atoms.

To balance the oxygen, one mole of water should be added to the right side:

$$NO_3^-\ (aq) \rightarrow NO_2\ (aq) + H_2O$$

Adding water to the right side of the equation introduces hydrogen atoms to that side. Therefore, the hydrogen atom count needs to be balanced. Water possesses two hydrogen atoms, therefore, two protons need to be added to the left side of the reaction:

$$NO_3^-\ (aq) + 2\ H^+ \rightarrow NO_2\ (aq) + H_2O$$

The reaction is occurring in acidic conditions. If the reaction was basic, then OH^- would need to be added to both sides to cancel the protons.

Next, the net charge will need to be balanced. The left side has a net charge of +1 (+2 from the protons and –1 from the electron), while the right side is neutral. Therefore, one electron should be added to the left side:

$$NO_3^-\ (aq) + 2\ H^+ + e^- \rightarrow NO_2\ (aq) + H_2O$$

When half reactions are recombined, the electrons in the overall reaction must cancel.

The reduction half-reaction will contribute one electron to the left side of the overall equation, while the oxidation half-reaction will contribute two electrons to the product side.

Therefore, the coefficients of the reduction half-reaction should be doubled:

$$2 \times [NO_3^-\ (aq) + 2\ H^+ + e^- \rightarrow NO_2\ (aq) + H_2O]$$
$$= 2\ NO_3^-\ (aq) + \mathbf{4\ H^+} + 2\ e^- \rightarrow 2\ NO_2\ (aq) + 2\ H_2O$$

The answer will be 4 at this step.

Combining both half reactions gives:

$$Mg\ (s) + 2\ NO_3^-\ (aq) + \mathbf{4\ H^+} + 2\ e^- \rightarrow Mg^{2+}\ (aq) + 2\ e^- + 2\ NO_2\ (aq) + 2\ H_2O$$

Cancel the electrons that appear on both sides of the reaction in the following balanced net equation:

$$Mg\ (s) + 2\ NO_3^-\ (aq) + \textbf{4 H}^+ \rightarrow Mg^{2+}\ (aq) + 2\ NO_2\ (aq) + 2\ H_2O$$

This equation is now fully balanced for mass, oxygen, hydrogen and electric charge.

33. E is correct. To obtain moles, divide sample mass by the molecular mass.

Because all of the options have the same mass, a comparison of molecular mass provides the answer without performing the actual calculation.

The molecule with the smallest molecular mass has the greatest number of moles.

34. A is correct. The law of constant composition states that *all samples of a given chemical compound have the same chemical composition by mass.*

This is true for all compounds, including ethyl alcohol.

This law is also referred to as the law of definite proportions or Proust's Law because this observation was first made by the French chemist Joseph Proust.

35. A is correct.

The coefficients in balanced reactions refer to moles (or molecules) but not grams.

1 mole of N_2 gas reacts with 3 moles of H_2 gas to produce 2 moles of NH_3 gas.

36. C is correct.

Calculate the number of moles of Al_2O_3:

$$2\ Al\ /\ 1\ Al_2O_3 = 0.2\ moles\ Al\ /\ x\ moles\ Al_2O_3$$

$$x\ moles\ Al_2O_3 = 0.2\ moles\ Al \times 1\ Al_2O_3\ /\ 2\ Al$$

$$x = 0.1\ moles\ Al_2O_3$$

Therefore:

$$(0.1\ mole\ Al_2O_3)\cdot(102\ g/mole\ Al_2O_3) = 10.2\ g\ Al_2O_3$$

37. D is correct.

Because Na is a metal, Na is more electropositive than H.

Therefore, the positive charge is on Na (i.e., +1), which means that charge on H is −1.

38. A is correct. $PbO + C \rightarrow Pb + CO$ is a single replacement reaction because only one element is being transferred from one reactant to another.

However, it is a redox reaction because the lead (Pb^{2+}), which dissociates, is reduced (gains electrons), the oxygen (O^{2-}) is oxidized (loses electrons). Additionally, one of the products is a single element (Pb), which is also a clue that it is a redox reaction.

C: the reaction is double-replacement and not the combustion because the combustion reactions must always have a hydrocarbon and O_2 as reactants. Double-replacement reactions often result in formation of a solid, water and gas.

39. B is correct.

The sum of all the oxidation numbers in any neutral molecule must be zero.

The oxidation number of each H is +1 and the oxidation number of each O is –2.

If x denotes the oxidation number of S in H_2SO_4, then:

$$2(+1) + x + 4(-2) = 0$$

$$+2 + x + -8 = 0$$

$$x = +6$$

In H_2SO_4, the oxidation sate of sulfur is +6.

40. A is correct. To calculate number of molecules, start by calculating the moles of gas using the ideal gas equation:

$$PV = nRT$$

Rearrange to isolate the number of moles:

$$n = PV / RT$$

Because the gas constant R is in L·atm K^{-1} mol^{-1}, the pressure has to be converted into atm:

780 torr × (1 atm / 760 torr) = 1.026 atm

Convert the volume to liters:

500 mL × 0.001 L/mL = 0.5 L

Substitute into the ideal gas equation:

$$n = PV / RT$$

$$n = 1.026 \text{ atm} \times 0.5 \text{ L} / (0.08206 \text{ L·atm } K^{-1} mol^{-1} \times 320 \text{ K})$$

$$n = 0.513 \text{ L·atm} / (26.259 \text{ L·atm } mol^{-1})$$

$$n = 0.0195 \text{ mol}$$

==

Practice Set 3: Questions 41–60

==

41. B is correct.

Use the mnemonic OIL RIG: <u>O</u>xidation <u>I</u>s <u>L</u>oss, <u>R</u>eduction <u>I</u>s <u>G</u>ain (of electrons).

The oxidizing and reducing agents are always reactants, not products, in a redox reaction.

The oxidizing agent is the species that gets reduced (i.e., gains electrons) and causes oxidation of the other species.

The reducing agent is the species that gets oxidized (i.e., loses electrons) and causes reduction of the other species.

42. E is correct.

Balancing a redox equation in acidic solution by the half-reaction method involves each of the steps described.

43. D is correct.

Formula mass is a synonym for molecular mass/molecular weight (MW).

$$MW \text{ of } C_6H_{12}O_6 = (6 \times \text{atomic mass C}) + (12 \times \text{atomic mass H}) + (6 \times \text{atomic mass O})$$

$$MW \text{ of } C_6H_{12}O_6 = (6 \times 12.01 \text{ g/mole}) + (12 \times 1.01 \text{ g/mole}) + (6 \times 16.00 \text{ g/mole})$$

$$MW \text{ of } C_6H_{12}O_6 = (72.06 \text{ g/mole}) + (12.12 \text{ g/mole}) + (96.00 \text{ g/mole})$$

$$MW \text{ of } C_6H_{12}O_6 = 180.18 \text{ g/mole}$$

44. E is correct.

The molecular mass of oxygen is 16 g/mole.

The atomic mass unit (amu) or dalton (Da) is the standard unit for indicating mass on an atomic or molecular scale (atomic mass). One amu is approximately the mass of one nucleon (either a single proton or neutron) and is numerically equivalent to 1 g/mol.

45. D is correct.

Balanced equation (combustion):

$$2 \, C_2H_6 + 7 \, O_2 \rightarrow 4 \, CO_2 + 6 \, H_2O$$

46. E is correct.

Use the mnemonic OIL RIG: <u>O</u>xidation <u>I</u>s <u>L</u>oss, <u>R</u>eduction <u>I</u>s <u>G</u>ain (of electrons).

Oxidation is the loss of electrons, while reduction is the gain of electrons.

An oxidizing agent undergoes reduction, while a reducing agent undergoes oxidation.

Evaluate the oxidation number in each atom.

S changes from +6 as a reactant to –2 as a product so it is reduced because the oxidation number decreases.

47. C is correct.

Balanced equation (double replacement):

$$C_2H_5OH\ (g) + 3\ O_2\ (g) \rightarrow 2\ CO_2\ (g) + 3\ H_2O\ (g)$$

48. E is correct.

Note: 1 amu (atomic mass unit) = 1 g/mole.

Moles of C = mass of C / atomic mass of C

Moles of C = (4.50 g) / (12.01 g/mole)

Moles of C = 0.375 mole

49. C is correct.

According to the law of mass conservation, there should be equal amounts of carbon in the product (CO_2) and reactant (the hydrocarbon sample).

Start by calculating the amount of carbon in the product (CO_2).

First calculate the mass % of carbon in CO_2:

Molecular mass of CO_2 = atomic mass of carbon + (2 × atomic mass of oxygen)

Molecular mass of CO_2 = 12.01 g/mole + (2 × 16.00 g/mole)

Molecular mass of CO_2 = 44.01 g/mole

Mass % of carbon in CO_2 = (mass of carbon / molecular mass of CO_2) × 100%

Mass % of carbon in CO_2 = (12.01 g/mole / 44.01 g/mole) × 100%

Mass % of carbon in CO_2 = 27.3%

Calculate the mass of carbon in the CO_2:

Mass of carbon = mass of CO_2 × mass % of carbon in CO_2

Mass of carbon = 8.98 g × 27.3%

Mass of carbon = 2.45 g

The mass of carbon in the starting reactant (the hydrocarbon sample) should also be 2.45 g.

Mass % carbon in hydrocarbon = (mass carbon in sample / total mass sample) × 100%

Mass % of carbon in hydrocarbon = (2.45 g / 6.84 g) × 100%

Mass % of carbon in hydrocarbon = 35.8%

50. E is correct.

The number of each atom on the reactants side must be the same and equal in number to the number of atoms on the product side of the reaction.

51. D is correct.

Using ½ reactions, the balanced reaction is:

$$6 \ (Fe^{2+} \rightarrow Fe^{3} + 1 \ e^-)$$

$$Cr_2O_7^{2-} + 14 \ H^+ + 6 \ e^- \rightarrow 2 \ Cr^{3+} + 7 \ H_2O$$

$$\overline{Cr_2O_7^{2-} + 4 \ H^+ + 6 \ Fe^{2+} \rightarrow 2 \ Cr^{3+} + 6 \ Fe^{3+} + 7 \ H_2O}$$

The sum of coefficients in the balanced reaction is 36.

52. E is correct.

Balanced reaction:

$$4 \ RuS \ (s) + 9 \ O_2 + 4 \ H_2O \rightarrow 2 \ Ru_2O_3 \ (s) + 4 \ H_2SO_4$$

Calculate the moles of H_2SO_4:

49 g × 1 mol / 98 g = 0.5 mole H_2SO_4

If 0.5 mole H_2SO_4 is produced, set a ratio for O_2 consumed.

9 O_2 / 4 H_2SO_4 = x moles O_2 / 0.5 mole H_2SO_4

x moles O_2 = 9 O_2 / 4 H_2SO_4 × 0.5 mole H_2SO_4

x = 1.125 moles O_2 × 22.4 liters / 1 mole

x = 25.2 liters of O_2

53. C is correct.

Identify the limiting reactant:

Al is the limiting reactant because 2 atoms of Al combine with 1 molecule of ferric oxide to produce the products. If the reaction starts with equal numbers of moles of each reactant, Al is depleted.

Use moles of Al and coefficients to calculate moles of other products/reactant.

Coefficient of Al = coefficient of Fe

Moles of iron produced = 0.20 moles.

54. B is correct.

$S_2 \qquad O_8$

$2x \qquad (8 \times -2)$

The sum of charges on the molecule is –2:

$2x + (8 \times -2) = -2$

$2x + (-16) = -2$

$2x = +14$

oxidation number of S = +7

55. D is correct.

Na is in group IA, so its oxidation number is always +1.

Oxygen is usually –2, with some exceptions, such as peroxide (H_2O_2), where it is –1.

Cr is a transition metal and could have more than one possible oxidation number.

To determine Cr's oxidation number, use the known oxidation numbers:

$2(+1) + Cr + 4(-2) = 0$

$2 + Cr - 8 = 0$

$Cr = 6$

56. B is correct. The net charge of $H_2SO_4 = 0$

Hydrogen has a common oxidation number of +1 whereas each oxygen atom has an oxidation number of –2.

$$H_2 \qquad\qquad S \qquad\qquad O_4$$
$$(2 \times 1) \qquad\qquad x \qquad\qquad (4 \times -2)$$
$$2 + x + -8 = 0$$
$$x = +6$$

In H_2SO_4, the oxidation of sulfur is +6.

57. C is correct.

Use the mnemonic OIL RIG: <u>O</u>xidation <u>I</u>s <u>L</u>oss, <u>R</u>eduction <u>I</u>s <u>G</u>ain (of electrons).

Oxidation is the loss of electrons, while reduction is the gain of electrons.

An oxidizing agent undergoes reduction, while a reducing agent undergoes oxidation.

Oxidation number for Sn is +2 as a reactant and +4 as a product; increase in oxidation number means that Sn^{2+} is oxidized in this reaction.

58. D is correct. Na_2Cl_2 and 2 NaCl are not the same.

Na_2Cl_2 is a molecule of 2 Na and 2 Cl.

NaCl is a compound that consists of 1 Na and 1 Cl.

59. E is correct.

I: represents the volume of 1 mol of gas at STP

II: mass of 1 mol of PH_3

III: number of molecules in 1 mol of PH_3

60. D is correct.

Use the mnemonic OIL RIG: <u>O</u>xidation <u>I</u>s <u>L</u>oss, <u>R</u>eduction <u>I</u>s <u>G</u>ain (of electrons).

Oxidation is the loss of electrons, while reduction is the gain of electrons.

An oxidizing agent undergoes reduction, while a reducing agent undergoes oxidation.

Co^{2+} is the starting reactant because it has to lose electrons and produce an ion with a higher oxidation number.

==

Practice Set 4: Questions 61–80

==

61. E is correct.

Use the mnemonic OIL RIG: <u>O</u>xidation <u>I</u>s <u>L</u>oss, <u>R</u>eduction <u>I</u>s <u>G</u>ain (of electrons).

The oxidizing and reducing agents are always reactants, not products, in a redox reaction.

The oxidizing agent is the species that is reduced (i.e., gains electrons).

The reducing agent is the species that is oxidized (i.e., loses electrons).

62. D is correct.

Calculations:

% mass Cl = (molecular mass Cl) / (molecular mass of compound) × 100%

% mass Cl = 4(35.5 g/mol) / [12 g/mol + 4(35.5 g/mol)] × 100%

% mass Cl = (142 g/mol) / (154 g/mol) × 100%

% mass Cl = 0.922 × 100% = 92%

63. E is correct.

I: total ionic charge of reactants must equal total ionic charge of products, which means that no electrons can "disappear" from the reaction, they can only be transferred from one atom to another. Therefore, the total charge will always be the same.

II: atoms of each reactant must equal atoms of product, which is true for all chemical reactions, because atoms in chemical reactions cannot be created or destroyed.

III: any electrons that are gained by one atom must be lost by another atom.

64. B is correct.

The molecular weight is approximately 99.

Determine the molecular weight of each compound.

Note, unlike % by mass, there is no division.

$Cl_2C_2H_4$ = 2(35.5 g/mol) + 2(12 g/mol) + 4(1 g/mol)

$Cl_2C_2H_4$ = 71 g/mol + 24 g/mol + 4 g/mol)

$Cl_2C_2H_4$ = 99 g/mol

65. E is correct.

Formula mass is a synonym for molecular mass/molecular weight (MW).

Start by calculating the mass of the formula unit (CH):

CH = (12.01 g/mol + 1.01 g/mol) = 13.02 g/mol

Divide the molar mass by the formula unit mass:

78 g/mol / 13.02 g/mol = 5.99

Round to the closest whole number: 6

Multiply the formula unit by 6:

$(CH)_6 = C_6H_6$

66. D is correct.

There is 1 oxygen atom from GaO plus 6 oxygen atoms from $(NO_3)_2$, so the total is 7.

67. B is correct.

Ethanol (C_2H_5OH) undergoes combination with oxygen to produce carbon dioxide and water.

68. C is correct.

Balanced reaction (combustion):

$2 C_3H_7OH + 9 O_2 \rightarrow 6 CO_2 + 8 H_2O$

69. C is correct.

Balanced equation (double replacement):

$Co_2O_3 (s) + 3 CO (g) \rightarrow 2 Co (s) + 3 CO_2 (g)$

70. B is correct.

The molar volume (V_m) is the volume occupied by one mole of a substance (i.e., element or compound) at a given temperature and pressure.

71. A is correct.

Use the mnemonic OIL RIG: Oxidation Is Loss, Reduction Is Gain (of electrons).

Oxidation is the loss of electrons, while reduction is the gain of electrons.

An oxidizing agent undergoes reduction, while a reducing agent undergoes oxidation.

Because the forward reaction is spontaneous, the reverse reaction is not spontaneous.

Mg^{2+} cannot oxidize Sn; therefore, Mg^{2+} is the weakest oxidizing agent.

72. D is correct.

H_2 is the limiting reactant.

24 moles of H_2 should produce: $24 \times (2 / 3) = 16$ moles of NH_3

If only 13.5 moles are produced, the yield:

13.5 moles / 16 moles $\times$ 100% = 84%

73. B is correct.

Balanced reaction:

$H_2 + \frac{1}{2} O_2 \rightarrow H_2O$

Multiply all the equations by 2 to remove the fraction:

$2 H_2 + O_2 \rightarrow 2 H_2O$

Find the limiting reactant by calculating the moles of each reactant:

Moles of hydrogen = mass of hydrogen / (2 $\times$ atomic mass of hydrogen)

Moles of hydrogen = 25 g / (2 $\times$ 1.01 g/mole)

Moles of hydrogen = 12.38 moles

Moles of oxygen = mass of oxygen / (2 $\times$ atomic mass of oxygen)

Moles of oxygen = 225 g / (2 $\times$ 16.00 g/mole)

Moles of oxygen = 7.03 moles

Divide the number of moles of each reactant by its coefficient.

The reactant with the smaller number of moles is the limiting reactant.

Hydrogen = 12.38 moles / 2

Hydrogen = 6.19 moles

Oxygen = 7.03 moles / 1

Oxygen = 7.03 moles

Because hydrogen has a smaller number of moles after the division, hydrogen is the limiting reactant and all hydrogen will be depleted in the reaction.

$$2 H_2 + O_2 \rightarrow 2 H_2O$$

Both hydrogen and water have coefficients of 2, therefore, these have the same number of moles.

There are 12.38 moles of hydrogen, which means there are 12.38 moles of water produced by this reaction.

Molecular mass of H_2O = (2 × molecular mass of hydrogen) + atomic mass of oxygen

Molecular mass of H_2O = (2 × 1.01 g/mole) + 16.00 g/mole

Molecular mass of H_2O = 18.02 g/mole

Mass of H_2O = moles of H_2O × molecular mass of H_2O

Mass of H_2O = 12.38 moles × 18.02 g/mole

Mass of H_2O = 223 g

74. C is correct.

Li	Cl	O_2
+1	x	(2 × –2)

The sum of charges in a neutral molecule is zero:

$$1 + x + (2 \times -2) = 0$$

$$1 + x + (-4) = 0$$

$$x = -1 + 4$$

oxidation number of Cl = +3

75. D is correct. Using half reactions, the balanced reaction is:

To balance hydrogen   To balance oxygen

↓   ↓

$$4[5 e^- + 8 H^+ + MnO_4^- \rightarrow Mn^{2+} + 4 (H_2O)]$$

$$5[(H_2O) + C_3H_7OH \rightarrow C_2H_5CO_2H + 4 H^+ + 4 e^-]$$

$$\overline{12 H^+ + 4 MnO_4^- + 5 C_3H_7OH \rightarrow 11 H_2O + 4 Mn^{2+} + 5 C_2H_5CO_2H}$$

Multiply by a common multiple of 4 and 5:

The sum of the product's coefficients: $11 + 4 + 5 = 20$.

76. A is correct.

PbO (*s*) + C (*s*) → Pb (*s*) + CO (*g*) is a single-replacement reaction because only one element (i.e., oxygen) is being transferred from one reactant to another.

77. E is correct. The reactants in a chemical reaction are always on the left side of the reaction arrow, while the products are on the right side.

In this reaction, the reactants are $C_6H_{12}O_6$, H_2O and O_2.

There is a distinction between the terms *reactant* and *reagent*.

A reactant is a substance consumed in the course of a chemical reaction.

A reagent is a substance (e.g., solvent) added to a system to cause a chemical reaction.

78. C is correct. Determine the number of moles of He:

4 g × 4.0 g/mol = 1 mole

Each mole of He has 2 electrons since He has atomic number 2 (# electrons = # protons for neutral atoms).

Therefore, 1 mole of He × 2 electrons / mole = 2 mole of electrons

79. D is correct. In this molecule, Br has the oxidation number of −1 because it is a halogen, and the gaining of one electron results in a complete octet for bromine.

The sum of charges in a neutral molecule = 0

0 = (oxidation state of Fe) + (3 × oxidation state of Br)

0 = (oxidation state of Fe) + (3 × −1)

0 = oxidation state of Fe − 3

oxidation state of Fe = +3

80. B is correct. A mole is a unit of measurement used to express amounts of a chemical substance.

The number of molecules in a mole is 6.02×10^{23}, which is Avogadro's number.

However, Avogadro's number relates to the number of molecules, not the amount of substance.

Molar mass refers to the mass per mole of a substance.

Formula mass is a term that is sometimes used to mean molecular mass or molecular weight, and it refers to the mass of a certain molecule.

Explanations: Thermochemistry

==

Practice Set 1: Questions 1–20

==

1. A is correct.

A reaction's enthalpy is specified by ΔH (not ΔG). ΔH determines whether a reaction is exothermic (releases heat to surroundings) or endothermic (absorbs heat from surroundings).

To predict spontaneity of reaction, use the Gibbs free energy equation:

$$\Delta G = \Delta H° - T\Delta S$$

The reaction is spontaneous (i.e., exergonic) if ΔG is negative.

The reaction is nonspontaneous (i.e., endergonic) if ΔG is positive.

2. B is correct.

Heat is energy and the energy from the heat is transferred to the gas molecules which increases their movement (i.e., kinetic energy).

Temperature is a measure of the average kinetic energy of the molecules.

3. E is correct.

Heat capacity is amount of heat required to increase temperature of *the whole sample* by 1 °C.

Specific heat is the heat required to increase temperature of *1 gram* of sample by 1 °C.

Heat = mass × specific heat × change in temperature:

$$q = m \times c \times \Delta T$$

$$q = 21.0 \text{ g} \times 0.382 \text{ J/g·°C} \times (68.5 °C - 21.0 °C)$$

$$q = 21.0 \text{ g} \times 0.382 \text{ J/g·°C} \times (47.5 °C)$$

$$q = 381 \text{ J}$$

4. E is correct.

This is a theory/memorization question.

However, problem can be solved by comparing the options for the most plausible.

Kinetic energy is correlated with temperature, so the formula that involves temperature would be a good choice.

Another approach is to analyze the units. Apply the units to the variables and evaluate them to obtain the answer.

For example, choices A and B have moles, pressure (Pa, bar or atm) and area (m^2), so it is not possible for them to result in energy (J) when multiplied.

Options C and D have molarity (moles/L) and volume (L or m^3); it's also impossible for them to result in energy (J) when multiplied.

Option E is nRT: mol × (J/mol K) × K; all units but J cancel, so this is a plausible formula for kinetic energy.

Additionally, for questions using formulas, dimensional analysis limits the answer choices on these type of question.

5. A is correct.

ΔH refers to enthalpy (or heat).

Endothermic reactions have heat as a reactant.

Exothermic reactions have heat as a product.

Exothermic reactions release heat, and cause the temperature of the immediate surroundings to rise (i.e., net loss of energy) while an endothermic process absorbs heat and cools the surroundings (i.e., net gain of energy).

Endothermic reactions absorb energy to break strong bonds to form a less stable state (i.e., positive enthalpy).
Exothermic reaction release energy during the formation of stronger bonds to produce the more stable state (i.e., negative enthalpy).

6. D is correct. Endothermic reactions absorb energy to break strong bonds to form a less stable state (i.e., positive enthalpy).
Exothermic reaction release energy during the formation of stronger bonds to produce the more stable state (i.e., negative enthalpy).

Spontaneity of a reaction is determined by the calculation of ΔG using:

$$\Delta G = \Delta H - T\Delta S$$

Reaction is spontaneous when the value of ΔG is negative.

In this problem, the reaction is endothermic, which means that ΔH is positive.

Also, the reaction decreases ΔS, which means that ΔS value is negative.

Substituting these values into the equation:

ΔG = ΔH – T(–ΔS)

ΔG = ΔH + TΔS, with ΔH and ΔS both positive values

For this problem, the value of ΔG is always positive.

The reaction does not occur because ΔG needs to be negative for a spontaneous reaction to proceed, the products are more stable than the reactants.

7. E is correct. Chemical energy is potential energy stored in molecular bonds.

Electrical energy is the kinetic energy associated with the motion of electrons (e.g., in wires, circuits, lightening). The potential energy stored in a flashlight battery is also electrical energy.

Heat is the spontaneous transfer of energy from a hot object to a cold one with no displacement or deformation of the objects (i.e., no work done).

8. A is correct.

Entropy is higher for states that are less organized (i.e., more random or disordered).

9. C is correct. ΔH refers to enthalpy (or heat). Endothermic reactions have heat as a reactant. Exothermic reactions have heat as a product.

Exothermic reactions release heat, and cause the temperature of the immediate surroundings to rise (i.e., net loss of energy) while an endothermic process absorbs heat and cools the surroundings (i.e., net gain of energy).

Endothermic reactions absorb energy to break strong bonds to form a less stable state (i.e., positive enthalpy).
Exothermic reaction release energy during the formation of stronger bonds to produce the more stable state (i.e., negative enthalpy).

The reaction is nonspontaneous (i.e., endergonic) if the products are less stable than the reactants and ΔG is positive.

The reaction is spontaneous (i.e., exergonic) if the products are more stable than the reactants and ΔG is negative.

10. E is correct.

This cannot be determined because when the given $\Delta G = \Delta H - T\Delta S$, both terms cancel.

The system is at equilibrium when $\Delta G = 0$, but in this question both sides of the equation cancel:

$$\underbrace{X - RY}_{\Delta G \text{ term}} = \underbrace{X - RY}_{\substack{\Delta H - T\Delta S \\ \text{term}}}, \quad \text{so } 0 = 0$$

11. C is correct.

Gibbs free energy:

$$\Delta G = \Delta H - T\Delta S$$

Stable molecules are non-spontaneous because they have a negative (or relatively low) ΔG.

ΔG is most negative (most stable) when ΔH is smallest and ΔS is largest.

12. A is correct.

ΔH refers to enthalpy (or heat).

Endothermic reactions have heat as a reactant.

Exothermic reactions have heat as a product.

The reaction is nonspontaneous (i.e., endergonic) if the products are less stable than the reactants and ΔG is positive.

The reaction is spontaneous (i.e., exergonic) if the products are more stable than the reactants and ΔG is negative.

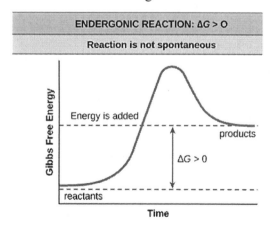 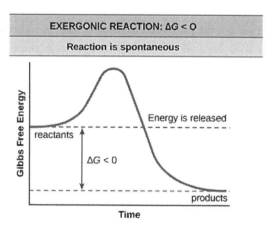

Exothermic reactions release heat, and cause the temperature of the immediate surroundings to rise (i.e., net loss of energy) while an endothermic process absorbs heat and cools the surroundings (i.e., net gain of energy).

Endothermic reactions absorb energy to break strong bonds to form a less stable state (i.e., positive enthalpy).

Exothermic reaction release energy during the formation of stronger bonds to produce the more stable state (i.e., negative enthalpy).

13. B is correct. Gibbs free energy:

$$\Delta G = \Delta H - T\Delta S$$

Entropy (ΔS) determines the favorability of chemical reactions.

If entropy is large, the reaction is more likely to proceed.

14. D is correct. In a chemical reaction, bonds within reactants are broken down and new bonds will be formed to create products. Therefore, in bond dissociation problems,

ΔH reaction = sum of bond energy in reactants – sum of bond energy in products

For $H_2C=CH_2 + H_2 \rightarrow CH_3–CH_3$:

$\Delta H_{reaction}$ = sum of bond energy in reactants – sum of bond energy in products

$\Delta H_{reaction} = [(C=C) + 4(C–H) + (H–H)] – [(C–C) + 6(C–H)]$

$\Delta H_{reaction} = [612 \text{ kJ} + (4 \times 412 \text{ kJ}) + 436 \text{ kJ}] – [348 \text{ kJ} + (6 \times 412 \text{ kJ})]$

$\Delta H_{reaction} = -124 \text{ kJ}$

Remember that this is the opposite of ΔH_f problems, where:

$\Delta H_{reaction}$ = (sum of ΔH_f products) – (sum of ΔH_f reactants)

15. C is correct. Bond dissociation energy is the energy required to break a bond between two gaseous items and is useful in estimating the enthalpy change in a reaction.

16. B is correct.

The ΔH value is positive, which means the reaction is endothermic and absorbs energy from the surroundings.

ΔH value is always expressed as energy released/absorbed per mole (for species with coefficient of 1).

If the coefficient is 2 then it is the energy transferred per 2 moles. For example, for the stated reaction, 2 moles of NO are produced from 1 mole for each reagent. Therefore, 43.2 kcal are produced when 2 moles of NO are produced.

17. A is correct.

State function depend only on the initial and final states of the system, and are independent of the paths taken to reach the final state.

Common examples of a state function in thermodynamics include internal energy, enthalpy, entropy, pressure, temperature and volume.

Work and heat relate to the change in energy of a system when it moves from one state to another which depends on how a system changes between states.

18. B is correct. The temperature (i.e., average kinetic energy) of a substance remains constant during a phase change (e.g., solid to liquid or liquid to gas).

For example, the heat (i.e., energy) breaks bonds between the ice molecules as they change phases into the liquid phase. Since the average kinetic energy of the molecules does not change at the moment of the phase change (i.e., melting), the temperature of the molecules does not change.

19. C is correct. In a chemical reaction, bonds within reactants are broken and new bonds form to create products.

Bond dissociation:

$\Delta H_{reaction}$ = (sum of bond energy in reactants) – (sum of bond energy in products)

$O=C=O + 3 H_2 \rightarrow CH_3-O-H + H-O-H$

$\Delta H_{reaction}$ = (sum of bond energy in reactants) – (sum of bond energy in products)

$\Delta H_{reaction} = [2(C=O) + 3(H-H)] - [3(C-H) + (C-O) + (O-H) + 2(O-H)]$

$\Delta H_{reaction} = [(2 \times 743 \text{ kJ}) + (3 \times 436 \text{ kJ})] - [(3 \times 412 \text{ kJ}) + 360 \text{ kJ} + 463 \text{ kJ} + (2 \times 463 \text{ kJ})]$

$\Delta H_{reaction} = -191 \text{ kJ}$

This is the reverse of ΔH_f problems, where:

$\Delta H_{reaction}$ = (sum of $\Delta H_{f \ product}$) – (sum of $\Delta H_{f \ reactant}$)

20. C is correct.

Entropy indicates how a system is organized; increased entropy means less order.

The entropy of universe is always increasing because a system moves towards more disorder unless energy is added to the system.

The second law of thermodynamics states that entropy of interconnected systems, without the addition of energy, always increases.

==

Practice Set 2: Questions 21–40

==

21. A is correct.

Gibbs free energy:

$$\Delta G = \Delta H - T\Delta S$$

The value that is the largest positive value is the most endothermic while the value that is the largest negative value is the most exothermic.

ΔH refers to enthalpy (or heat).

Endothermic reactions have heat as a reactant.

Exothermic reactions have heat as a product.

Exothermic reactions release heat, and cause the temperature of the immediate surroundings to rise (i.e., net loss of energy) while an endothermic process absorbs heat and cools the surroundings (i.e., net gain of energy).

Endothermic reactions absorb energy to break strong bonds to form a less stable state (i.e., positive enthalpy).
Exothermic reaction release energy during the formation of stronger bonds to produce the more stable state (i.e., negative enthalpy).

22. C is correct.

Potential Energy **Stored energy and the energy of position (gravitational)**	**Kinetic Energy** **Energy of motion: motion of waves, electrons, atoms, molecules and substances.**
Chemical Energy Chemical energy is the energy stored in the bonds of atoms and molecules. Examples of stored chemical energy: biomass, petroleum, natural gas, propane, coal.	**Thermal Energy** Thermal energy is an internal energy in substances; it is the vibration and movement of atoms and molecules within substances. Geothermal energy is an example of thermal energy.

23. A is correct.

By convention, the ΔG for an element in its standard state is 0.

---

24. B is correct. Test strategy: when given a choice among similar explanations, carefully evaluate the most descriptive one.

However, always check the statement because sometimes the most descriptive option is not accurate.

Here, the longest option is also accurate, so that would be the best choice among all options.

25. C is correct. ΔG is always negative for spontaneous reactions.

26. C is correct. Conduction (i.e., transfer of thermal energy through matter) is reduced by an insulator.

Air and vacuum are the excellent insulators. Storm windows, which have air wedged between two glass panes, work by utilizing this principle of conduction.

27. A is correct. ΔH refers to enthalpy (or heat).

Endothermic reactions have heat as a reactant.

Exothermic reactions have heat as a product.

Exothermic reactions release heat, and cause the temperature of the immediate surroundings to rise (i.e., net loss of energy) while an endothermic process absorbs heat and cools the surroundings (i.e., net gain of energy).

The reaction is nonspontaneous (i.e., endergonic) if the products are less stable than the reactants and ΔG is positive.

The reaction is spontaneous (i.e., exergonic) if the products are more stable than the reactants and ΔG is negative.

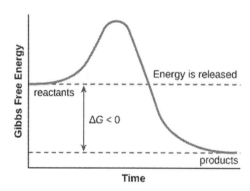

Exergonic reactions are spontaneous and have reactants with more energy than the products.

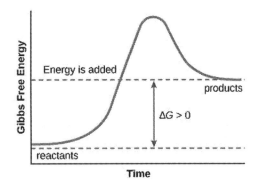

Endergonic reactions are nonspontaneous and have products with more energy than the reactants.

28. D is correct.

Heat capacity is amount of heat required to increase temperature of *the whole sample* by 1 °C.

Specific heat is the heat required to increase temperature of *1 gram* of sample by 1 °C.

q = mass × heat of condensation

q = 16 g × 1,380 J/g

q = 22,080 J

29. A is correct.

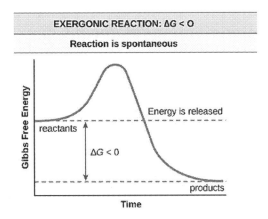
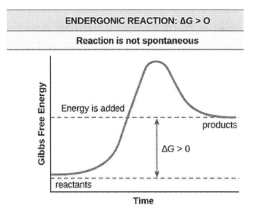

$\Delta G = \Delta H - T\Delta S$ refers to exergonic when ΔG is negative and endergonic when ΔG is positive.

If ΔS is 0 then $\Delta G = \Delta H$ because the $T\Delta S$ term cancels because it equals zero).

ΔH refers to exothermic when ΔH is negative and endothermic when ΔH is positive.

30. E is correct. Heat of formation is defined as the heat required or released upon creation of one mole of the substance from its elements.

If the given reaction is reversed and divided by two, it would be the formation reaction of NH_3:

$$½ N_2 + 3/2 H_2 \rightarrow NH_3$$

ΔH of this reaction would also be reversed (i.e., plus to minus sign) and divided by two:

$$\Delta H = -(92.4 \text{ kJ/mol}) / 2$$

$$\Delta H = -46.2 \text{ kJ/mol}$$

31. B is correct. Gibbs free energy:

$$\Delta G = \Delta H - T\Delta S$$

With a positive ΔH and negative ΔS, ΔG is positive, so the reaction is nonspontaneous.

32. C is correct. Entropy (ΔS) measures the degree of disorder in a system.

When a change causes the components of a system to transform into higher energy phase (solid $\rightarrow$ liquid, liquid $\rightarrow$ gas), entropy of the system increases.

33. D is correct. During phase changes, only the mass and heat of specific phase change is required to calculate energy released or absorbed.

Because water is turning into ice, the specific heat required is the heat of solidification.

34. B is correct. Nuclear energy is considered energy because splitting or combining atoms results in enormous amounts of energy, which is used in atomic bombs and nuclear power plants.

Potential Energy **Stored energy and the energy of position (gravitational)**	**Kinetic Energy** **Energy of motion: motion of waves, electrons, atoms, molecules and substances.**
Nuclear Energy Nuclear energy is the energy stored in the nucleus of an atom. It is the energy that holds the nucleus together. The nucleus of the uranium atom is an example of nuclear energy.	**Electrical Energy** Electrical energy is the movement of electrons. Lightning and electricity are examples of electrical energy.

35. D is correct.

Entropy is a measurement of disorder.

Gases contain more energy than liquids of the same element and have a higher degree of randomness.

Entropy is the unavailable energy which cannot be converted into mechanical work.

36. A is correct. There are two different methods available to solve this problem. Both methods are based on the definition of ΔH formation as energy consumed/released when one mole of molecule is produced from its elemental atoms.

Method 1.

Rearrange and add all the equations together to create the formation reaction of C_2H_5OH.

Information provided by the problem:

$$C_2H_5OH + 3\ O_2 \rightarrow 2\ CO_2 + 3\ H_2O \qquad \Delta H = 327 \text{ kcal}$$

$$H_2O \rightarrow H_2 + \tfrac{1}{2}\ O_2 \qquad \Delta H = 68.3 \text{ kcal}$$

$$C + O_2 \rightarrow CO_2 \qquad \Delta H = -94.1 \text{ kcal}$$

Place C_2H_5OH on the product side. For the other two reactions, arrange them so the elements are on the left and the molecules are on the right (remember that the goal is to create a formation reaction: elements forming a molecule).

When reversing the direction of a reaction, change the positive/negative sign of ΔH.

Multiplying the whole reaction by a coefficient would also multiply ΔH by the same ratio.

$$2\ CO_2 + 3\ H_2O \rightarrow C_2H_5OH + 3\ O_2 \qquad \Delta H = -327 \text{ kcal}$$

$$3\ H_2 + 3/2\ O_2 \rightarrow 3\ H_2O \qquad \Delta H = -204.9 \text{ kcal}$$

$$\underline{2\ C + 2\ O_2 \rightarrow 2\ CO_2} \qquad \underline{\Delta H = -188.2 \text{ kcal}}$$

$$2\ C + 3\ H_2 + 1/2\ O_2 \rightarrow C_2H_5OH \qquad \Delta H = -720.1 \text{ kcal}$$

ΔH formation of C_2H_5OH is −720.1 kcal.

Method 2.

Heat of formation (ΔH_f) data can be used to calculate ΔH of a reaction:

$$\Delta H_{reaction} = \text{sum of } \Delta H_{f \ product} - \text{sum of } \Delta H_{f \ reactant}$$

Apply the formula on the first equation:

$$C_2H_5OH + 3\ O_2 \rightarrow 2\ CO_2 + 3\ H_2O \qquad \Delta H = 327 \text{ kcal}$$

$$\Delta H_{reaction} = \text{sum of } \Delta H_{f \ product} - \text{sum of } \Delta H_{f \ reactant}$$

$$327 \text{ kcal} = [(\Delta H_f\ CO_2) + 3(\Delta H_f\ H_2O)] - (\Delta H_f\ C_2H_5OH) + 3(\Delta H_f\ O_2)]$$

Oxygen (O_2) is an element, so $\Delta H_f = 0$

For CO_2 and H_2O, ΔH_f information can be obtained from the other 2 reactions:

$$H_2O \rightarrow H_2 + \tfrac{1}{2}\,O_2 \qquad \Delta H = 68.3 \text{ kcal}$$

$$C + O_2 \rightarrow CO_2 \qquad \Delta H = -94.1 \text{ kcal}$$

The CO_2 reaction is already a formation reaction – creation of one mole of a molecule from its elements. Therefore, ΔH_f of $CO_2 = -94.1$ kcal

If the H_2O reaction is reversed, it will also be a formation reaction.

$$H_2 + \tfrac{1}{2}\,O_2 \rightarrow H_2O \qquad \Delta H = -68.3 \text{ kcal}$$

Using those values, calculate ΔH_f of C_2H_5OH:

$$327 \text{ kcal} = [2(\Delta H_f\, CO_2) + 3(\Delta H_f\, H_2O)] - [(\Delta H_f\, C_2H_5OH) + 3(\Delta H_f\, O_2)]$$

$$327 \text{ kcal} = [2(-94.1 \text{ kcal}) + 3(-68.3 \text{ kcal})] - [(\Delta H_f\, C_2H_5OH) + 3(0 \text{ kcal})]$$

$$327 \text{ kcal} = [(-188.2 \text{ kcal}) + (-204.9 \text{ kcal})] - (\Delta H_f\, C_2H_5OH)$$

$$327 \text{ kcal} = (-393.1 \text{ kcal}) - (\Delta H_f\, C_2H_5OH)$$

$$\Delta H_f\, C_2H_5OH = -720.1 \text{ kcal}$$

37. B is correct.

$$S + O_2 \rightarrow SO_2 + 69.8 \text{ kcal}$$

The reaction indicates that 69.8 kcal of energy is released (i.e., on the product side).

All species in this reaction have the coefficient of 1, which means that the ΔH value is calculated by reacting 1 mole of each reagent to create 1 mole of product.

The atomic mass of sulfur is 32.1 g, which means that this reaction uses 32.1 g of sulfur.

38. D is correct.

The disorder of the system is decreasing, as more complex and ordered molecules are forming from the reaction of H_2 and O_2 gases.

3 moles of gas are combining to form 2 moles of gas.

Additionally, two molecules are joining to form one molecule.

39. D is correct. In thermodynamics, an isolated system is a system enclosed by rigid immovable walls through which neither matter nor energy pass.

Temperature is a measure of energy and is not a form of energy. Therefore, temperature cannot be exchanged between system and surroundings.

A closed system can exchange energy (as heat or work) with its surroundings, but not matter.

An isolated system cannot exchange energy (as heat or work) or matter with the surroundings.

An open system can exchange energy and matter with the surroundings.

40. E is correct. State function depends only on the initial and final states of the system, and is independent of the paths taken to reach the final state.

Common examples of a state function in thermodynamics include internal energy, enthalpy, entropy, pressure, temperature and volume.

==

Practice Set 3: Questions 41–60

==

41. A is correct.

When comparing various fuels in varying forms (e.g., solid, liquid or gas), it's easiest to compare energy released in terms of mass, because matter has mass regardless of its state (as opposed to volume, which is convenient for a liquid or gas, but not for a solid).

Moles are more complicated because they have to be converted to mass before a direct comparison can be made between the fuels.

42. C is correct.

Convection is heat carried by fluids (i.e., liquids and gases). Heat is prevented from leaving the system through convection when the lid is placed on the cup.

43. B is correct.

For a reaction to be spontaneous, the total entropy ($\Delta S_{system} + \Delta S_{surrounding}$) has to be positive (i.e., greater than 0).

44. E is correct.

Explosion of gases: chemical $\rightarrow$ heat energy

Heat converting into steam, which in turn moves a turbine: heat $\rightarrow$ mechanical energy

Generator creates electricity: mechanical $\rightarrow$ electrical energy

Potential Energy **Stored energy and the energy of position (gravitational)**	**Kinetic Energy** **Energy of motion: motion of waves, electrons, atoms, molecules and substances.**
Chemical Energy Chemical energy is the energy stored in the bonds of atoms and molecules. Examples of stored chemical energy: biomass, petroleum, natural gas, propane, coal.	**Radiant Energy** Radiant energy is electromagnetic energy that travels in transverse waves. Radiant energy includes visible light, x-rays, gamma rays and radio waves. Solar energy is an example of radiant energy.

Nuclear Energy	**Thermal Energy**
Nuclear energy is the energy stored in the nucleus of an atom. It is the energy that holds the nucleus together. The nucleus of the uranium atom is an example of nuclear energy.	Thermal energy is an internal energy in substances; it is the vibration and movement of atoms and molecules within substances. Geo-thermal energy is an example of thermal energy.
Stored Mechanical Energy	**Motion**
Stored mechanical energy is energy stored in objects by the application of a force. Compressed springs and stretched rubber bands are examples of stored mechanical energy.	The movement of objects or substances from one place to another is motion. Wind and hydropower are examples of motion.
	Sound
Gravitational Energy	Sound is the movement of energy through substances in longitudinal (compression/rarefaction) waves.
Gravitational Energy is the energy of place or position. Water in a reservoir behind a hydropower dam is an example of gravitational potential energy. When the water is released to spin the turbines, it becomes kinetic energy.	**Electrical Energy**
	Electrical energy is the movement of electrons. Lightning and electricity are examples of electrical energy.

45. A is correct.

Relationship between enthalpy (ΔH) and internal energy (ΔE):

Enthalpy = Internal energy + work (for gases, work = PV)

$$\Delta H = \Delta E + \Delta(PV)$$

Solving for ΔE:

$$\Delta E = \Delta H - \Delta(PV)$$

According to ideal gas law:

$$PV = nRT$$

Substitute ideal gas law to the previous equation:

$$\Delta E = \Delta H - \Delta(nRT)$$

R and T are constant, which leaves Δn as the variable.

The reaction is C_2H_2 (g) + $2H_2$ (g) → C_2H_6 (g).

There are three gas molecules on the left and one on the right, which means $\Delta n = 1 - 3 = -2$.

In this problem, the temperature is not provided. However, the presence of degree symbols ($\Delta G°$, $\Delta H°$, $\Delta S°$) indicates that those are standard values, which are measured at 25 °C or 298.15 K.

Always double check the units before performing calculations; ΔH is in kilojoules, while the gas constant (R) is 8.314 J/mol K. Convert ΔH to joules before calculating.

Use the Δn and T values to calculate ΔE:

$$\Delta E = \Delta H - \Delta nRT$$

$$\Delta E = -311,500 \text{ J/mol} - (-2 \times 8.314 \text{ J/mol K} \times 298.15 \text{ K})$$

$$\Delta E = -306,542 \text{ J} \approx -306.5 \text{ kJ}$$

46. B is correct. All thermodynamic functions in $\Delta G = \Delta H - T\Delta S$ refer to the system.

47. C is correct. Increase in entropy indicates increase in disorder; find a reaction that creates higher number of molecules on the product side compared to the reactant side.

48. C is correct.

When enthalpy is calculated, work done by gases is not taken into account; however, the energy of the reaction includes the work done by gases.

The largest difference between the energy of the reaction and enthalpy would be for reactions with the largest difference in the number of gas molecules between the product and reactants.

49. B is correct. ΔH refers to enthalpy (or heat).

Endothermic reactions have heat as a reactant.

Exothermic reactions have heat as a product.

Endothermic reactions absorb energy to break strong bonds to form a less stable state (i.e., positive enthalpy).
Exothermic reaction release energy during the formation of stronger bonds to produce the more stable state (i.e., negative enthalpy).

The reaction is nonspontaneous (i.e., endergonic) if the products are less stable than the reactants and ΔG is positive.

The reaction is spontaneous (i.e., exergonic) if the products are more stable than the reactants and ΔG is negative.

50. B is correct.

All thermodynamic functions in $\Delta G = \Delta H - T\Delta S$ refer to the system.

51. C is correct. To predict spontaneity of reaction, use the Gibbs free energy equation:

$$\Delta G = \Delta H° - T\Delta S$$

The reaction is spontaneous if ΔG is negative.

Substitute the given values to the equation:

$$\Delta G = -113.4 \text{ kJ/mol} - [T \times (-145.7 \text{ J/K mol})]$$

$$\Delta G = -113.4 \text{ kJ/mol} + (T \times 145.7 \text{ J/K mol})$$

Important: note that the units aren't identical, $\Delta H°$ is in kJ and $\Delta S°$ is in J. Convert kJ to J (1 kJ = 1,000 J):

$$\Delta G = -113,400 \text{ J/mol} + (T \times 145.7 \text{ J/K mol})$$

It can be predicted that the value of ΔG would be negative if the value of T is small.

If T goes higher, ΔG approaches a positive value and the reaction would be nonspontaneous.

52. E is correct.

Enthalpy:

$$U + PV$$

53. C is correct. State function depend only on the initial and final states of the system, and are independent of the paths taken to reach the final state.

Common examples of a state function in thermodynamics include internal energy, enthalpy, entropy, pressure, temperature and volume.

Extensive property is a property that changes when the size of the sample changes. Examples include mass, volume, length and total charge.

Entropy has no absolute zero value and a substance at zero Kelvin has zero entropy (i.e., no motion).

54. C is correct.

In an exothermic reaction, the bonds formed are stronger than the bonds broken.

55. D is correct. Calculate the value of $\Delta H_f = \Delta H_{f\ product} - \Delta H_{f\ reactant}$

$$\Delta H_f = -436.8 \text{ kJ mol}^{-1} - (-391.2 \text{ kJ mol}^{-1})$$

$$\Delta H_f = -45.6 \text{ kJ mol}^{-1}$$

To determine spontaneity, calculate the Gibbs free energy:

$\Delta G = \Delta H° - T\Delta S$

The reaction is spontaneous if ΔG is negative:

$\Delta G = -45.6 \text{ kJ} - T\Delta S$

Typical ΔS values are around 100–200 J.

If the ΔH value is –45.6 kJ or –45,600 J, the value of ΔG would still be negative unless $T\Delta S$ is less than –45,600.

Therefore, the reaction would be spontaneous over a broad range of temperatures.

56. E is correct. Enthalpy is an extensive property: it varies with quantity of the matter.

Reaction 1 : $P_4 + 6 \text{ Cl}_2 \rightarrow 4 \text{ PCl}_3$ $\Delta H = -1,289 \text{ kJ}$

Reaction 2 : $3 P_4 + 18 \text{ Cl}_2 \rightarrow 12 \text{ PCl}_3$ $\Delta H = ?$

The only difference between reactions 1 and 2 are the coefficients.

In reaction 2, all coefficients are three times reaction 1. Reaction 2 consumes three times as much reactants as reaction 1, and correspondingly reaction 2 releases three times as much energy as reaction 1.

$\Delta H = 3 \times -1,289 \text{ kJ} = -3,837 \text{ kJ}$

57. C is correct.

ΔH refers to enthalpy (or heat).

Endothermic reactions have heat as a reactant.

Exothermic reactions have heat as a product.

Endothermic reactions absorb energy to break strong bonds to form a less stable state (i.e., positive enthalpy).

Exothermic reaction release energy during the formation of stronger bonds to produce the more stable state (i.e., negative enthalpy).

The reaction is nonspontaneous (i.e., endergonic) if the products are less stable than the reactants and ΔG is positive.

The reaction is spontaneous (i.e., exergonic) if the products are more stable than the reactants and ΔG is negative.

Endothermic reactions consume energy, which means that there should be heat on the reactants' side.

58. D is correct. According to the second law of thermodynamics, the entropy gain of the universe must always be positive (i.e., increased disorder).

The entropy of a system, however, can be negative if the surroundings experience an increase in entropy greater than the negative entropy change experienced by the system.

59. E is correct.

In thermodynamics, an isolated system is a system enclosed by rigid immovable walls through which neither matter nor energy pass.

Bell jars are designed to not let air or other materials in or out. Insulated means that heat cannot get in or out.

Evaporation indicates a phase change (vaporization) from liquid to gaseous phase; however, it does not imply that the matter has escaped its system.

A closed system can exchange energy (as heat or work) with its surroundings, but not matter.

An isolated system cannot exchange energy (as heat or work) or matter with the surroundings.

An open system can exchange energy and matter with the surroundings.

60. E is correct. The Law of Conservation of Energy states that the total energy (e.g., potential or kinetic) of an isolated system remains constant and is conserved. Energy can be neither created nor destroyed, but is transformed from one form to another. For instance, chemical energy can be converted to kinetic energy in the explosion of a firecracker.

The Law of Conservation of Mass states that for any system closed to all transfers of matter and energy, the mass of the system must remain constant over time.

Law of Definite Proportions (Proust's law) states that a chemical compound always contains exactly the same proportion of elements by mass. The law of definite proportions forms the basis of stoichiometry (i.e., from the known amounts of separate reactants, the amount of the product can be calculated).

Avogadro's Law is an experimental gas law relating volume of a gas to the amount of substance of gas present. It states that equal volumes of all gases, at the same temperature and pressure, have the same number of molecules.

Boyle's law is an experimental gas law that describes how the pressure of a gas tends to increase as the volume of a gas decreases. It states that the absolute pressure exerted by a given mass of an ideal gas is inversely proportional to the volume it occupies, if the temperature and amount of gas remain unchanged within a closed system.

Practice Set 4: Questions 61–80

61. C is correct.

ΔH refers to enthalpy (or heat).

Endothermic reactions have heat as a reactant.

Exothermic reactions have heat as a product.

Exothermic reactions release heat, and cause the temperature of the immediate surroundings to rise (i.e., net loss of energy) while an endothermic process absorbs heat and cools the surroundings (i.e., net gain of energy).

Endothermic reactions absorb energy to break strong bonds to form a less stable state (i.e., positive enthalpy).
Exothermic reaction release energy during the formation of stronger bonds to produce the more stable state (i.e., negative enthalpy).

The reaction is nonspontaneous (i.e., endergonic) if the products are less stable than the reactants and ΔG is positive.

The reaction is spontaneous (i.e., exergonic) if the products are more stable than the reactants and ΔG is negative.

62. C is correct. Temperature is a measure of the average kinetic energy of the molecules.

Kinetic energy is proportional to temperature.

In most thermodynamic equations, temperatures are expressed in Kelvin, so convert the Celsius temperatures to Kelvin:

25 °C + 273.15 = 298.15 K

50 °C + 273.15 = 323.15 K

Calculate the kinetic energy using simple proportions:

KE = (323.15 K / 298.15 K) × 500 J

KE = 540 J

63. C is correct.

The equation relates the change in entropy (ΔS) at different temperatures.

Entropy increases at higher temperatures (i.e., increased kinetic energy).

64. B is correct.

A change is exothermic when energy is released to the surroundings.

Energy loss occurs when a substance changes to a more rigid phase (e.g., gas → liquid or liquid → solid).

65. A is correct.

Potential Energy Stored energy and the energy of position (gravitational)	Kinetic Energy Energy of motion: motion of waves, electrons, atoms, molecules and substances.
Chemical Energy	**Electrical Energy**
Chemical energy is the energy stored in the bonds of atoms and molecules. Examples of stored chemical energy: biomass, petroleum, natural gas, propane, coal.	Electrical energy is the movement of electrons. Lightning and electricity are examples of electrical energy.

66. B is correct.

At equilibrium, there is no potential and therefore neither direction of the reaction is favored.

Reaction potential (E) indicates the tendency of reaction to be spontaneous in either direction.

Because the solution is in equilibrium, no further reactions occurs in either direction. Therefore, $E = 0$.

67. D is correct.

The transformation from solid to gas is accompanied by an increase in entropy (i.e., disorder).

The molecules of gas have greater kinetic energy than the molecules of solids.

68. C is correct.

The reaction is nonspontaneous (i.e., endergonic) if the products are less stable than the reactants and ΔG is positive.

The reaction is spontaneous (i.e., exergonic) if the products are more stable than the reactants and ΔG is negative.

69. E is correct.

Spontaneity of a reaction is determined by evaluating the Gibbs free energy, or ΔG.

$$\Delta G = \Delta H - T\Delta S$$

A reaction is spontaneous if $\Delta G < 0$ (or ΔG is negative).

For ΔG to be negative, ΔH has to be less than $T\Delta S$.

A reaction is nonspontaneous if $\Delta G > 0$ (or ΔG is positive and ΔH is greater than $T\Delta S$).

70. B is correct.

The reaction is nonspontaneous (i.e., endergonic) if the products are less stable than the reactants and ΔG is positive.

The reaction is spontaneous (i.e., exergonic) if the products are more stable than the reactants and ΔG is negative.

Entropy (ΔS) is determined by the relative number of molecules (compounds):

The reactants have one molecule (with a coefficient total of 2).

The products have two molecules (with a coefficient total of 7).

The number of molecules has increased from reactants to products. Therefore, the entropy (i.e., disorder) has increased.

71. D is correct. ΔG indicates the energy made available to do non P–V work.

This is a useful quantity for processes like batteries and living cells which do not have expanding gases.

72. C is correct.

Internal energy of a system is the energy contained within the system, excluding the kinetic energy of motion of the system as a whole and the potential energy of the system as a whole due to external force fields.

The internal energy of a system can be changed by transfers of matter and by work and heat transfer. When matter transfer is prevented by impermeable container walls, the system is said to be closed. The First law of thermodynamics states that the increase in internal energy is equal to the total heat added plus the work done on the system by its surroundings. If the container walls don't pass energy or matter, the system is isolated and its internal energy remains constant.

Bond energy is internal potential energy (PE), while thermal energy is internal kinetic energy (KE).

73. D is correct.

Endothermic reactions absorb energy to break strong bonds to form a less stable state (i.e., positive enthalpy).

Exothermic reaction release energy during the formation of stronger bonds to produce the more stable state (i.e., negative enthalpy).

To predict spontaneity of reaction, use the Gibbs free energy equation:

$$\Delta G = \Delta H° - T\Delta S$$

The reaction is nonspontaneous (i.e., endergonic) if the products are less stable than the reactants and ΔG is positive.

The reaction is spontaneous (i.e., exergonic) if the products are more stable than the reactants and ΔG is negative.

It is the total amount of energy that is determinative. Some bonds are stronger than others, so there is a net gain or net loss of energy when formed.

74. E is correct.

The starting material is ice at −25 °C, which means that its temperature has to be raised to 0 °C before it can melt.

The first term in the heat calculation is:

specific heat of ice (A) × mass × change of temperature

75. C is correct.

The heat of formation of water vapor is similar to the highly exothermic process for the heat of combustion of hydrogen.

Heat is required to convert H_2O (*l*) into vapor, therefore the heat of formation of water vapor must be less exothermic than of H_2O (*l*).

Solid → liquid → gas: endothermic because the reaction absorbs energy to break strong bonds to form a less stable state (i.e., positive enthalpy).
Gas → liquid → solid: exothermic because the reaction releases energy during the formation of stronger bonds to produce the more stable state (i.e., negative enthalpy).

76. E is correct.

77. B is correct.

Einstein established the equivalence of mass and energy, whereby the energy equivalent of mass is given by $E = mc^2$.

Energy can be converted to mass, and mass can be converted to energy as long as the total energy, including mass energy, is conserved.

In nuclear fission, the mass of the parent nucleus is greater than the sum of the masses of the daughter nuclei. This deficit in mass is converted into energy.

78. D is correct.

A closed system can exchange energy (as heat or work) but not matter, with its surroundings.

An isolated system cannot exchange energy (as heat or work) or matter with the surroundings.

An open system can exchange energy and matter with the surroundings.

79. A is correct.

Gases have the highest entropy (i.e., disorder or randomness).

Solutions have higher entropy than pure phases since the molecules are more scattered.

The liquid phase has less entropy than the aqueous phase.

80. D is correct.

A closed system can exchange energy (as heat or work) but not matter, with its surroundings.

An isolated system cannot exchange energy (as heat or work) or matter with the surroundings.

An open system can exchange energy and matter with the surroundings.

Explanations: Equilibrium and Reaction Rates

==

Practice Set 1: Questions 1–20

==

1. A is correct.

General formula for the equilibrium constant of a reaction:

$$aA + bB \leftrightarrow cC + dD$$

$$K_{eq} = ([C]^c \times [D]^d) / ([A]^a \times [B]^b)$$

For the reaction above:

$$K_{eq} = [C] / [A]^2 \times [B]^3$$

2. B is correct.

Two gases having the same temperature have the same average molecular kinetic energy.

Therefore,

$$(\tfrac{1}{2})m_A v_A^2 = (\tfrac{1}{2})m_B v_B^2$$

$$m_A v_A^2 = m_B v_B^2$$

$$(m_B / m_A) = (v_A / v_B)^2$$

$$(v_A / v_B) = 2$$

$$(m_B / m_A) = 2^2 = 4$$

The only gases listed with a mass ratio of about 4 to 1 are iron (55.8 g/mol) and nitrogen (14 g/mol).

3. A is correct.

The slowest reaction would be the reaction with the highest activation energy and the lowest temperature.

4. A is correct.

The rate law is calculated experimentally by comparing trials and determining how changes in the initial concentrations of the reactants affect the rate of the reaction.

$$\text{rate} = k[A]^x \cdot [B]^y$$

where k is the rate constant and the exponents x and y are the partial reaction orders (i.e., determined experimentally). They are not equal to the stoichiometric coefficients.

To determine order of reactant A, find two experiments where the concentrations of B are identical and concentrations of A are different.

Use data from experiments 2 and 3 to calculate order of A:

$$\text{Rate}_3 / \text{Rate}_2 = ([A]_3 / [A]_2)^{\text{order of A}}$$

$$0.500 / 0.500 = (0.060 / 0.030)^{\text{order of A}}$$

$$1 = (2)^{\text{order of A}}$$

Order of A = 0

5. C is correct.

The balanced equation:

$$C_2H_6O + 3\ O_2 \rightarrow 2\ CO_2 + 3\ H_2O$$

Rate of reaction/consumption is proportional to the coefficients.

The rate of carbon dioxide production is twice the rate of ethanol consumption:

$$2 \times 4.0\ M\ s^{-1} = 8.0\ M\ s^{-1}$$

6. D is correct. General formula for the equilibrium constant of a reaction:

$$aA + bB \leftrightarrow cC + dD$$

$$K_{eq} = ([C]^c \times [D]^d) / ([A]^a \times [B]^b)$$

For equilibrium constant calculation, only include species in aqueous or gas phases.

$$K_{eq} = 1 / [Cl_2]$$

7. B is correct.

$$K_{eq} = [\text{products}] / [\text{reactants}]$$

If the K_{eq} is less than 1 (e.g., 6.3×10^{-14}), then the numerator (i.e., products) is smaller than the denominator (i.e., reactants) and fewer products have formed relative to the reactants.

If the reaction favors reactants compared to products, the equilibrium lies to the left.

8. A is correct.

The higher the energy of activation, the slower is the reaction. The height of this barrier is independent from the determination of spontaneous (ΔG is negative with products more stable than reactants) or nonspontaneous reactions (ΔG is positive with products less stable than reactants).

9. E is correct.

The main function of catalysts is lowering the reaction's activation energy (energy barrier), thus increasing its rate (k).

Temperature is a measure of the average kinetic energy (i.e., KE = ½mv^2) of the molecules.

Increased concentration of reactants increases the probability that the reactants collide with sufficient energy and orientation to overcome the energy of activation barrier and proceed toward products.

10. D is correct.

Every reaction has activation energy: amount of energy required by the reactant to start reacting.

On the graph, activation energy can be estimated by calculating the distance between initial energy level (i.e., reactant) and the peak (i.e., transition state) on the graph. Activation energy is *not* the difference between energy levels of initial and final state (reactant and product).

A catalyst provides an alternative pathway for the reaction to proceed to product formation. It lowers the energy of activation (i.e., relative energy between reactants and transition state) and therefore speed the rate of the reaction.

Catalysts have no effect on the Gibbs free energy (ΔG: stability of products vs. reactants) or the enthalpy (ΔH: bond breaking in reactants or bond making in products).

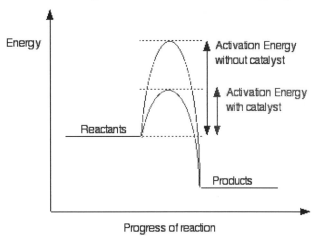

11. D is correct.

The activation energy is the energy barrier that must be overcome for the transformation of reactant(s) into product(s).

A reaction with a higher activation energy (energy barrier), has a decreased rate (k).

12. B is correct.

The activation energy is the energy barrier that must be overcome for the transformation of reactant(s) into product(s).

A reaction with a lower activation energy (energy barrier), has an increased rate (k).

13. D is correct.

The activation energy is the energy barrier that must be overcome for the transformation of reactant(s) into product(s).

A reaction with a higher activation energy (energy barrier), has a decreased rate (k).

If the graphs are at the same scale, the height of the activation energy (R to highest peak on the graph) is greatest in graph d.

14. B is correct.

If the graphs are at the same scale, the height of the activation energy (R to highest peak on the graph) is smallest in graph b.

The main function of catalysts is lowering the reaction's activation energy (energy barrier), thus increasing its rate (k).

Although catalysts do decrease the amount of energy required to reach the rate-limiting transition state, they do *not* decrease the relative energy of the products and reactants. Therefore, a catalyst has no effect on ΔG.

A catalyst provides an alternative pathway for the reaction to proceed to product formation. It lowers the energy of activation (i.e., relative energy between reactants and transition state) and therefore speed the rate of the reaction.

Catalysts have no effect on the Gibbs free energy (ΔG: stability of products vs. reactants) or the enthalpy (ΔH: bond breaking in reactants or bond making in products).

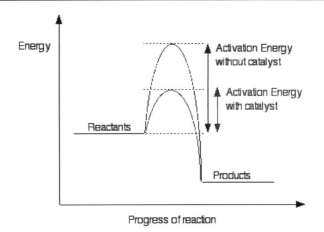

Catalysts have no effect on ΔG (relative levels of R and P. Graph D shows an endergonic reaction with products less stable than reactants. All other graphs show an exergonic reaction with the same relative difference between the more stable products and the less stable reactants; only the energy of activation is different on the graphs.

15. B is correct.

A reaction is at equilibrium when the rate of the forward reaction equals the rate of the reverse reaction. Achieving equilibrium is common for reactions.

Catalysts, by definition, are regenerated during the course of a reaction and are not consumed by the reaction.

16. D is correct.

The molecules must collide with sufficient energy, frequency of collision and the proper orientation to overcome the barrier of the activation energy.

17. B is correct.

A catalyst lowers the energy of activation, which increases the rate of the reaction.

The main function of catalysts is lowering the reaction's activation energy (energy barrier), thus increasing its rate (k).

Although catalysts do decrease the amount of energy required to reach the rate-limiting transition state, they do *not* decrease the relative energy of the products and reactants. Therefore, a catalyst has no effect on ΔG.

18. E is correct.

When changing the conditions of a reaction, Le Châtelier's principle states that the position of equilibrium shifts to counteract the change. If the concentration of reactants or products changes, the position of the equilibrium changes.

Adding reactants or removing products shifts the equilibrium to the right.

19. A is correct.

When changing the conditions of a reaction, Le Châtelier's principle states that the position of equilibrium shifts to counteract the change. If the reaction temperature, pressure or volume changes, the position of equilibrium changes.

Adding reactants or removing products shifts the equilibrium to the right.

Heat (i.e., energy related to temperature) is a reactant and increasing its value drives the reaction toward product formation.

Decreasing the pressure on the reaction vessel drives the reaction toward reactants (i.e., to the left). The relative molar concentration of the reactants (i.e., 2 + 6) is greater than the products (i.e., 4 + 3).

The other choices listed drive the reaction toward reactants (i.e., to the left).

20. C is correct.

First, calculate the concentration/molarity of each reactant:

H_2 : 0.20 moles / 4.00 L = 0.05 M

X_2 : 0.20 moles / 4.00 L = 0.05 M

HX: 0.800 moles / 4.00L = 0.20 M

Use the concentrations to calculate Q:

$Q = [HX]^2 / [H_2] \cdot [X_2]$

$Q = (0.20)^2 / (0.05 \times 0.05)$

$Q = 16$

Because $Q < K_c$ (i.e., $16 < 24.4$), the reaction shifts to the right.

For Q to increase and match K_c, the numerator (i.e., $[HX]^2$) which is the product (right side) of the equation needs to be increased.

===

Practice Set 2: Questions 21–40

===

21. E is correct.

General formula for the equilibrium constant of a reaction:

$$a\text{A} + b\text{B} \leftrightarrow c\text{C} + d\text{D}$$

$$K_{eq} = ([\text{C}]^c \times [\text{D}]^d) / ([\text{A}]^a \times [\text{B}]^b)$$

For equilibrium constant (K_c) calculation, only include species in aqueous or gas phases:

$$K_c = [CO_2] [H_2O]^2 / [CH_4]$$

22. A is correct.

The rate law is calculated by determining how changes in concentrations of the reactants affect the initial rate of the reaction.

$$\text{rate} = k[\text{A}]^x \cdot [\text{B}]^y$$

where k is the rate constant and the exponents x and y are the partial reaction orders. They are not equal to the stoichiometric coefficients.

Whenever the fast (i.e., second) step follows the slow (i.e., first) step, the fast step is assumed to reach equilibrium and the equilibrium concentrations are used for the rate law of the slow step.

23. E is correct.

The main function of catalysts is lowering the reaction's activation energy (energy barrier), thus increasing its rate (k).

Although catalysts do decrease the amount of energy required to reach the rate-limiting transition state, they do *not* decrease the relative energy of the products and reactants. Therefore, a catalyst has no effect on ΔG.

A catalyst provides an alternative pathway for the reaction to proceed to product formation. It lowers the energy of activation (i.e., relative energy between reactants and transition state) and therefore speed the rate of the reaction.

Catalysts have no effect on the Gibbs free energy (ΔG: stability of products vs. reactants) or the enthalpy (ΔH: bond breaking in reactants or bond making in products).

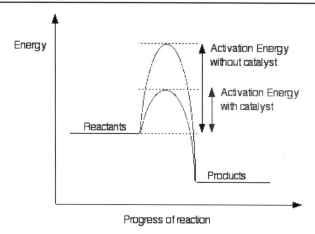

24. B is correct.

In equilibrium reactions, the state of equilibrium can vary between conditions, so any proportion of product/reactant mass is possible.

The question refers to the state *after* a reaction reached equilibrium.

For an endergonic reaction ($\Delta G < 1$), the grams of product would be less than reactants.

For an exergonic reaction ($\Delta G > 1$), the grams of product would be more than reactants.

When $\Delta G = 1$, the mass of products and reactants would be equal.

25. C is correct.

The rate law is calculated experimentally by comparing trials and determining how changes in the initial concentrations of the reactants affect the rate of the reaction.

$$\text{rate} = k[A]^x \cdot [B]^y$$

where k is the rate constant and the exponents x and y are the partial reaction orders (i.e., determined experimentally). They are not equal to the stoichiometric coefficients.

Rate laws cannot be determined from the balanced equation (i.e., used to determine equilibrium) unless the reaction occurs in a single step.

From the data, when the concentration doubles, the rate quadrupled.

Since 4 is 2^2, the rate law is second order, therefore the rate = $k[H_2]^2$.

26. A is correct. Calculate the change in Gibbs free energy:

$$\Delta G = -RT \ln K_{eq}$$

$$-68.4 \text{ kJ} = -8.314 \text{ J/mol·K} \times 299.15 \text{ K} \times \ln K_{eq}$$

$$-68.4 \text{ kJ} / -8.314 \text{ J/mol·K} \times 299.15 \text{ K} = \ln K_{eq}$$

$$-68,400 \text{ J} / -2,487.13 \text{ J/mol} = \ln K_{eq}$$

$$\ln K_{eq} = 27.50$$

$$K_{eq} = e^{27.50}$$

$$K_{eq} = 8.77 \times 10^{11}$$

27. B is correct. The order of the reaction has to be determined experimentally.

It is possible for a reaction's order to be identical with its coefficients. For example, in a single-step reaction or during the slow step of a multi-step reaction, the coefficients correlate to the rate law.

28. A is correct. General formula for the equilibrium constant of a reaction:

$$a\text{A} + b\text{B} \leftrightarrow c\text{C} + d\text{D}$$

$$K_{eq} = ([\text{C}]^c \times [\text{D}]^d) / ([\text{A}]^a \times [\text{B}]^b)$$

For equilibrium constant calculation, only include species in aqueous or gas phases:

$$K_{eq} = 1 / [\text{CO}] \times [\text{H}_2]^2$$

29. E is correct. Two peaks in this reaction indicate two energy-requiring steps with one intermediate (i.e., C) and each peak (i.e., B and D) as an activated complex (i.e., transition states). The activated complex (i.e., transition state) is undergoing bond breaking/bond making events.

30. A is correct. Activation energy for the slow step of a reaction is the distance from the starting material (or an intermediate) to the activated complex (i.e., transition state) with the absolute highest energy (i.e., highest point on the graph).

31. C is correct. Activation energy for the slow step of a reverse reaction is the distance from an intermediate (or product) to the activated complex (i.e., transition state) with the absolute highest energy (i.e., highest point on the graph). The slow step may not have the greatest magnitude for activation energy (e.g., E→ D on the graph).

---

32. B is correct.

The change in energy for this reaction (or ΔH) is the difference between energy contents of the reactants and the products.

33. A is correct.

As the temperature (i.e., average kinetic energy) increases, the particles move faster (i.e., increased kinetic energy) and collide more frequently per unit time. This increases the reaction rate.

34. A is correct.

When changing the conditions of a reaction, Le Châtelier's principle states that the position of equilibrium will shift to counteract the change. If the reaction temperature, pressure or volume is changed, the position of equilibrium will change.

According Le Châtelier's principle, endothermic (+ΔH) reactions increase the formation of products at higher temperatures.

Since both sides of the reaction have 2 gas molecules, a change in pressure has no effect on equilibrium.

35. B is correct.

All chemical reactions eventually reach equilibrium, the state at which the reactants and products are present in concentrations that have no further tendency to change with time. Therefore, the rate of production of each of the products (i.e., forward reaction) equals the rate of their consumption by the reverse reaction.

36. E is correct.

Chemical equilibrium refers to a dynamic process whereby the *rate* at which a reactant molecule is being transformed into product is the same as the *rate* for a product molecule to be transformed into a reactant.

All chemical reactions eventually reach equilibrium, the state at which the reactants and products are present in concentrations that have no further tendency to change with time.

37. A is correct.

Expression for equilibrium constant:

$$K = [H_2O]^2[Cl_2]^2 / [HCl]^4 \cdot [O_2]$$

Solve for $[Cl_2]$:

$$[Cl_2]^2 = (K \times [HCl]^4 \cdot [O_2]) / [H_2O]^2$$

$$[Cl_2]^2 = [46.0 \times (0.150)^4 \times 0.395] / (0.625)^2$$

$$[Cl_2]^2 = 0.0235$$

$$[Cl_2] = 0.153 \text{ M}$$

38. A is correct.

To determine the amount of each compound at equilibrium, consider the chemical reaction written in the form:

$$aA + bB \leftrightarrow cC + dD$$

The equilibrium constant (K_c) is defined as:

$$K_c = ([C]^c \times [D]^d) / ([A]^a \times [B]^b)$$

or

$$K_c = [\text{products}] / [\text{reactants}]$$

If the K_{eq} is greater than 1, the numerator (i.e., products) is larger than the denominator (i.e., reactants) and more products have formed relative to the reactants.

If the reaction favors products compared to reactants, the equilibrium lies to the right.

39. D is correct.

Increasing the pressure increases the rate of a reaction because there is an increased probability that any two reactant molecules collide with sufficient energy to overcome the energy of activation and form products.

40. E is correct.

When changing the conditions of a reaction, Le Châtelier's principle states that the position of equilibrium will shift to counteract the change. If the reaction temperature, pressure, volume or concentration changes, the position of the equilibrium changes.

CO is a reactant and increasing its concentration shifts the equilibrium toward product formation (i.e., to the right).

Practice Set 3: Questions 41–60

41. A is correct.

General formula for the equilibrium constant of a reaction:

$$aA + bB \leftrightarrow cC + dD$$

$$K_{eq} = ([C]^c \times [D]^d) / ([A]^a \times [B]^b)$$

For equilibrium constant calculation, only include species in aqueous or gas phases:

$$K_{eq} = [NO]^4 \times [H_2O]^6 / [NH_3]^4 \times [O_2]^5$$

42. E is correct.

The high levels of CO_2 cause a person to hyperventilate in an attempt to reduce the amount of CO_2 (reactant). Hyperventilating has the effect of driving the reaction toward products.

Removing products (i.e., HCO_3^- and H^+) or intermediates (H_2CO_3) drives the reaction toward products.

43. B is correct.

The units of the rate constants:

Zero order reaction: $M \, sec^{-1}$

First order reaction: sec^{-1}

Second order reaction: $L \, mole^{-1} \, sec^{-1}$

44. E is correct.

A reaction proceeds when the reactant(s) have sufficient energy to overcome the energy of activation and proceed to products. Increasing the temperature increases the kinetic energy of the molecule and increases the frequency of collision and increases the probability that the reactants will overcome the barrier (energy of activation) to form products.

45. B is correct.

Low activation energy increases the rate because the energy required for the reaction to proceed is lower.

High temperature increases the rate because faster-moving molecules have greater probability of collision, which facilitates the reaction.

Combined together, lower activation energy and a higher temperature results in the highest relative rate for the reaction.

46. C is correct.

The rate law is calculated by comparing trials and determining how changes in the initial concentrations of the reactants affect the rate of the reaction.

$$\text{rate} = k[A]^x \cdot [B]^y$$

where k is the rate constant and the exponents x and y are the partial reaction orders (i.e., determined experimentally). They are not equal to the stoichiometric coefficients.

Start by identifying two reactions where the concentration of XO is constant and O_2 is different: experiments 1 and 2. When the concentration of O_2 is doubled, the rate is also doubled. This indicates that the order of the reaction for O_2 is 1.

Now, determine the order for XO.

Find 2 reactions where the concentration of O_2 is constant and XO is different: experiments 2 and 3. When the concentration of XO is tripled, the rate is multiplied by a factor of 9. 3^2 = 9, which means the order of the reaction with respect to XO is 2.

Therefore, the expression of rate law is:

$$\text{rate} = k[XO]^2 \cdot [O_2]$$

47. B is correct.

General formula for the equilibrium constant of a reaction:

$$a\text{A} + b\text{B} \leftrightarrow c\text{C} + d\text{D}$$

$$K_{eq} = ([C]^c \times [D]^d) / ([A]^a \times [B]^b)$$

For equilibrium constant calculation, only include species in aqueous or gas phases.

$$K_{eq} = 1 / [CO_2]$$

48. D is correct.

$$K_{eq} = [\text{products}] / [\text{reactants}]$$

If the numerator (i.e., products) is smaller than the denominator (i.e., reactants), and fewer products have formed relative to the reactants. Therefore, K_{eq} is less than 1.

49. C is correct.

The activation energy is the energy barrier for a reaction to proceed. For the forward reaction, it is measured from the reactants to the highest energy level in the reaction.

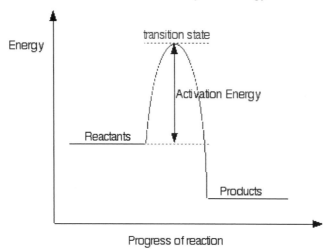

A reaction mechanism with a low energy of activation proceeds faster than a reaction with a high energy of activation.

50. E is correct. As the average kinetic energy (i.e., KE = $\frac{1}{2}mv^2$) increases, the particles move faster and collide more frequently per unit time and possess greater energy when they collide. This increases the reaction rate. Hence the reaction rate of most reactions increases with increasing temperature.

For reversible reactions, it is common for the rate law to depend on the concentration of the products. The overall rate is negative (except autocatalytic reactions). As the concentration of products decreases, their collision frequency decreases and the rate of the reverse reaction decreases. Therefore, the overall rate of the reaction increases.

The main function of catalysts is lowering the reaction's activation energy (energy barrier), thus increasing its rate (k).

51. C is correct.

General formula for the equilibrium constant of a reaction:

$$a\text{A} + b\text{B} \leftrightarrow c\text{C} + d\text{D}$$

$$K_{eq} = ([\text{C}]^c \times [\text{D}]^d) / ([\text{A}]^a \times [\text{B}]^b)$$

For the ionization equilibrium (K_i) constant calculation, only include species in aqueous or gas phases (which, in this case, is all):

$$K_i = [\text{H}^+] \cdot [\text{HS}^-] / [\text{H}_2\text{S}]$$

52. B is correct.

As the temperature (i.e., average kinetic energy) increases, the particles move faster and collide more frequently per unit time and possess greater energy when they collide. This increases the reaction rate. Hence the reaction rate of most reactions
increases with increasing temperature.

53. B is correct.

Reactions are spontaneous when Gibbs free energy (ΔG) is negative and the reaction is described as exergonic; the products are more stable than the reactants.

Reactions are nonspontaneous when Gibbs free energy (ΔG) is positive and the reaction is described as endergonic; the products are less stable than the reactants.

54. C is correct.

When changing the conditions of a reaction, Le Châtelier's principle states that the position of equilibrium will shift to counteract the change. If the reaction temperature, pressure or volume is changed, the position of equilibrium will change.

There are 2 moles on each side, so changes in pressure (or volume) do not shift the equilibrium.

55. A is correct. All of the choices are possible events of chemical reactions, but they do not need to happen for a reaction to occur, except that reactant particles must collide (i.e., make contact) with each other.

56. D is correct.

The enthalpy or heat of reaction (ΔH) is not a function of temperature.

Since the reaction is exothermic, Le Châtelier's principle states that increasing the temperature decreases the forward reaction.

57. E is correct.

When changing the conditions of a reaction, Le Châtelier's principle states that the position of equilibrium shifts to counteract the change. If the reaction's concentration changes, the position of the equilibrium changes.

Adding solid $KC_2H_3O_2$ is equivalent to adding K^+ and $C_2H_3O_2^-$ (i.e., product). The increased concentration of products shifts the equilibrium toward reactants (i.e., to the left).

58. E is correct.

When changing the conditions of a reaction, Le Châtelier's principle states that the position of equilibrium shifts to counteract the change. If the reaction temperature, pressure or volume is changed, the position of equilibrium will change.

The $K_{eq} = 2.8 \times 10^{-21}$ which indicates a low concentration of products compared to reactants:

$$K_{eq} = [\text{products}] \, / \, [\text{reactants}]$$

59. E is correct.

Chemical equilibrium refers to a dynamic process whereby the rate at which a reactant molecule is being transformed into product is the same as the rate for a product molecule to be transformed into a reactant. The rate of the forward reaction is equal to the rate of the reverse reaction.

60. C is correct.

All chemical reactions eventually reach equilibrium, the state at which the reactants and products are present in concentrations that have no further tendency to change with time.

Catalysts speed up reactions, and therefore increase the rate at which equilibrium is reached, but they never alter the thermodynamics of a reaction and therefore do not change free energy ΔG.

Catalysts do not alter the equilibrium constant.

===

Practice Set 4: Questions 61–80

===

61. E is correct.

To determine the order with respect to W, compare the data for trials 2 and 4.

The concentrations of X and Y do not change when comparing trials 2 and 4, but the concentration of W changes from 0.015 to 0.03, which corresponds to an increase by a factor of 2. However, the rate did not increase (0.08 remains 0.08), therefore the order with respect to W is 0.

The order for X is determined by comparing the data for trials 1 and 3.

The concentrations for W and Z are constant, and the concentration for X increases by a factor of 3 (from 0.5 to 0.15). The rate of the reaction increased by a factor of 9 (0.04 to 0.36). Since $3^2 = 9$, the order of the reaction with respect to X is two.

The order with respect to Y is found by comparing the data from trials 1 and 5. [W] and [X] do not change but [Y] goes up by a factor of 4. The rate from trial 1 to 5 goes up by a factor of 2. Since $4^{1/2} = 2$, the order of the reaction with respect to Y is ½.

The overall order is found by the sum of the orders for X, Y, and Z: $0 + 2 + ½ = 2½$.

62. B is correct.

Since the order with respect to W is zero, the rate of formation of Z does not depend on the concentration of W.

63. D is correct.

The rate law is calculated by comparing trials and determining how changes in the initial concentrations of the reactants affect the rate of the reaction.

$$\text{rate} = k[A]^x \cdot [B]^y$$

where k is the rate constant and the exponents x and y are the partial reaction orders (i.e., determined experimentally). They are not equal to the stoichiometric coefficients.

Use the partial orders determined in question **61** to express the rate law:

$$\text{rate} = k[W]^0[X]^2[Z]^{½}$$

Substitute the values for trial #1:

$$0.04 = k\,[0.01]^0[0.05]^2[0.04]^{½}$$
$$0.04 = (k)\cdot(1)\cdot(2.5 \times 10^{-3})\cdot(2 \times 10^{-1})$$

$$k = 80$$

64. A is correct.

When changing the conditions of a reaction, Le Châtelier's principle states that the position of the equilibrium shifts to counteract the change. If the reaction temperature, pressure or volume changes, the position of the equilibrium changes.

Decreasing the temperature of the system favors the production of more heat. It shifts the reaction towards the exothermic side. Because $\Delta H > 0$ (i.e., heat is a reactant), the reaction is endothermic. Therefore, decreasing the temperature shifts the equilibrium toward the reactants.

65. D is correct.

General formula for the equilibrium constant of a reaction:

$$a\text{A} + b\text{B} \leftrightarrow c\text{C} + d\text{D}$$

$$K_{eq} = ([\text{C}]^c \times [\text{D}]^d) / ([\text{A}]^a \times [\text{B}]^b)$$

For the equilibrium constant (K_i), only include species in aqueous phases:

$$K_i = [\text{H}^+] \times [\text{H}_2\text{PO}_4^-] / [\text{H}_3\text{PO}_4]$$

66. C is correct. Catalysts speed up reactions, and therefore increase the rate at which equilibrium is reached, but they never alter the thermodynamics of a reaction and therefore do not change free energy ΔG.

A catalyst provides an alternative pathway for the reaction to proceed to product formation. It lowers the energy of activation (i.e., relative energy between reactants and transition state) and therefore speed the rate of the reaction.

Catalysts have no effect on the Gibbs free energy (ΔG: stability of products vs. reactants) or the enthalpy (ΔH: bond breaking in reactants or bond making in products).

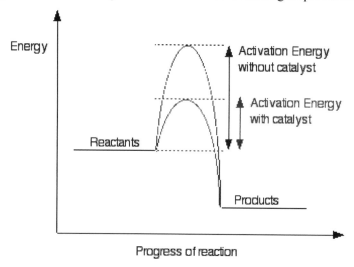

67. D is correct.

General formula for the equilibrium constant of a reaction:

$$a\text{A} + b\text{B} \leftrightarrow c\text{C} + d\text{D}$$

$$K_{eq} = ([\text{C}]^c \times [\text{D}]^d) / ([\text{A}]^a \times [\text{B}]^b)$$

For the ionization equilibrium constant (K_i) calculation, only include species in aqueous or gas phases (which, in this case, is all of them):

$$K_i = [\text{H}^+]\cdot[\text{HSO}_3^-] / [\text{H}_2\text{SO}_3]$$

68. D is correct.

$$K_{eq} = [\text{products}] / [\text{reactants}]$$

If the K_{eq} is greater than 1, then the numerator (i.e., products) is greater than the denominator (i.e., reactants) and more products have formed relative to the reactants.

69. B is correct.

The activation energy is the energy barrier for a reaction to proceed. For the forward reaction, it is measured from the energy of the reactants to the highest energy level in the reaction.

70. A is correct.

Lowering the temperature decreases the rate of a reaction because the molecules involved in the reaction move and collide more slowly, so the reaction occurs at a slower speed.

Increasing the concentration of reactants due to the increased the probability that the reactants collide with sufficient energy and orientation to overcome the energy of activation barrier and proceed toward products.

The main function of catalysts is lowering the reaction's activation energy (energy barrier), thus increasing its rate (k).

71. B is correct.

The activation energy is the energy barrier that must be overcome for the transformation of reactant(s) into product(s). The molecules must collide with the proper orientation and energy (i.e., kinetic energy is the average temperature) to overcome the energy of activation barrier.

72. B is correct.

The activation energy is the energy barrier that must be overcome for the transformation of reactant(s) into product(s). The molecules must collide with the proper orientation and energy (i.e., kinetic energy is the average temperature) to overcome the energy of activation barrier.

Solids describe molecules with limited relative motion. Liquids are molecules with more relative motion than solids while gases exhibit the most relative motion.

73. B is correct.

The rate law is calculated experimentally by comparing trials and determining how changes in the initial concentrations of the reactants affect the rate of the reaction.

$$\text{rate} = k[A]^x \cdot [B]^y$$

where k is the rate constant and the exponents x and y are the partial reaction orders (i.e., determined experimentally). They are not equal to the stoichiometric coefficients.

Comparing Trials 1 and 3, [A] increased by a factor of 3 as did the reaction rate; thus, the reaction is first order with respect to A.

Comparing Trials 1 and 2, [B] increased by a factor of 4 and the reaction rate increased by a factor of $16 = 4^2$. Thus, the reaction is second order with respect to B.

Therefore, the rate $= k[A] \cdot [B]^2$

74. D is correct.

The molecules must collide with sufficient energy, frequency of collision and the proper orientation to overcome the barrier of the activation energy.

75. D is correct.

When changing the conditions of a reaction, Le Châtelier's principle states that the position of equilibrium shifts to counteract the change. If the reaction temperature, pressure or volume is changed, the position of equilibrium changes.

Removing NH_3 and adding N_2 shifts the equilibrium to the right.

Removing N_2 or adding NH_3 shifts the equilibrium to the left.

76. B is correct.

Increasing [$HC_2H_3O_2$] and increasing [H^+] will affect the equilibrium because both of the species added are part of the equilibrium equation.

K_{eq} = [products] / [reactants]

K_{eq} = [$C_2H_3O_2^-$] / [$HC_2H_3O_2$]·[H^+]

Adding solid $NaC_2H_3O_2$: in aqueous solutions, $NaC_2H_3O_2$ dissociates into Na^+ (*aq*) and $C_2H_3O_2^-$ (*aq*). Therefore, the overall concentration of $C_2H_3O_2^-$ (*aq*) increases and it affects the equilibrium.

Adding solid $NaNO_3$: this is a salt and does not react with any of the reactant or product molecules, therefore it will not affect the equilibrium.

Adding solid $NaOH$: the reactant is an acid because it dissociates into hydrogen ions and anions in aqueous solutions. It reacts with bases (e.g., $NaOH$) to create water and salt. Thus, $NaOH$ reduces the concentration of the reactant, which will affect the equilibrium.

Increasing [$HC_2H_3O_2$] and [H^+] increases reactants and drives the reaction toward product formation.

77. D is correct.

Calculate the value of the equilibrium expression: hydrogen iodide concentration decreases for equilibrium to be reached.

K = [products] / [reactants]

K = [HI]^2 / [H_2]·[I_2]

To determine the state of a reaction, calculate its reaction quotient (Q). Q has the same method of calculation as equilibrium constant (K); the difference is K has to be calculated at point of equilibrium, whereas Q can be calculated at any time.

If $Q > K$, reaction shifts towards reactants (more reactants, less products)

If $Q = K$, reaction is at equilibrium

If $Q < K$, reaction shifts towards products (more products, less reactants)

Q = [HI]^2 / [H_2]·[I_2]

Q = (3)^2 / 0.4 × 0.6

Q = 37.5

Because $Q > K$ (i.e., (37.5 > 35), the reaction shifts toward reactants (larger denominator) and the amount of product (HI) decreases.

78. C is correct.

Decreasing the concentration of reactants (or decreasing pressure) decreases the rate of a reaction because there is a decreased probability that any two reactant molecules collide with sufficient energy to overcome the energy of activation and form products.

79. B is correct.

Chemical equilibrium expression is dependent on the stoichiometry of the reaction, more specifically, the coefficients of each species involved in the reaction.

The mechanism refers to the pathway of product formation (e.g., S_N1 or S_N2) but has no effect on the relative energies of the reactants and products (i.e., position for the equilibrium).

The rate refers to the time needed to achieve equilibrium but has no effect on the position of the equilibrium.

80. E is correct.

$$K = [\text{products}] / [\text{reactants}]$$

$$K = [CH_3OH] / [H_2O]^2 \cdot [CO]$$

None of the stated changes tend to decrease the *magnitude* of the equilibrium constant K.

For exothermic reactions ($\Delta H < 0$), decreasing the temperature increases the magnitude of K.

Changes in volume, pressure or concentration do not affect the magnitude of K.

Explanations: Solution Chemistry

Practice Set 1: Questions 1–20

1. E is correct.

Solubility is proportional to pressure. Use simple proportions to compare solubility in different pressures:

$P_1 / S_1 = P_2 / S_2$

$S_2 = P_2 / (P_1 / S_1)$

$S_2 = 4.5 \text{ atm} / (1.00 \text{ atm} / 1.90 \text{ cc}/100 \text{ mL})$

$S_2 = 8.55 \text{ cc} / 100 \text{ mL}$

2. E is correct.

The correct interpretation of molarity is moles of solute per liter of solvent.

3. A is correct.

NaCl is a charged, ionic salt (Na^+ and Cl^-) and therefore is extremely water soluble.

Hexanol can hydrogen bond with water due to the hydroxyl group, but the long hydrocarbon chain reduces its solubility, and the chains interact via hydrophobic interactions forming micelles.

Aluminum hydroxide has poor solubility in water and requires the addition of Brønsted-Lowry acids to completely dissolve.

4. A is correct.

Spectator ions appear on both sides of the net ionic equation.

Ionic equation of the reaction:

$Ba^{2+}(aq) + 2\ Cl^-(aq) + 2\ K^+(aq) + CrO_4^-(aq) \rightarrow BaCrO_4(s) + 2\ K^+(aq) + 2\ Cl^-(aq)$

5. D is correct.

Higher pressure exerts more pressure on the solution, which allows more molecules to dissolve in the solvent.

Lower temperature also increases gas solubility.

As the temperature increases, both solvent and solute molecules move faster, and it is more difficult for the solvent molecules to bond with the solute.

6. A is correct.

Solutes dissolve in the solvent to form a solution.

7. B is correct.

When the compound is dissolved in water, the attached hydrate/water crystals dissociate and become part of the water solvent.

Therefore, the only ions left are 1 Co^{2+} and 2 NO_3^-.

8. D is correct.

The mass of a solution is always calculated by taking the total mass of the solution and container and subtracting the mass of the container.

9. A is correct. An insoluble compound is incapable of being dissolved (especially with reference to water).

Hydroxide salts of Group I elements are soluble, while hydroxide salts of Group II elements (Ca, Sr and Ba) are slightly soluble.

Salts containing nitrate ion (NO_3^-) are generally soluble.

Most sulfate salts are soluble. Important exceptions: $BaSO_4$, $PbSO_4$, Ag_2SO_4 and $SrSO_4$.

Hydroxide salts of transition metals and Al^{3+} are insoluble.

Thus, $Fe(OH)_3$, $Al(OH)_3$ and $Co(OH)_2$ are not soluble.

10. C is correct.

% v/v solution = (volume of acetone / volume of solution) × 100%

% v/v solution = {25 mL / (25 mL + 75 mL)} × 100%

% v/v solution = 25%

11. C is correct.

The van der Waals forces in the hydrocarbons are relatively weak, while hydrogen bonds between H_2O molecules are strong intermolecular bonds.

Bonds between polar H_2O and nonpolar octane are weaker than the bonds between two polar H_2O molecules (i.e., hydrogen bonds).

12. A is correct.

To find the K_{sp}, take the molarities (or concentrations) of the products (cC and dD) and multiply them.

For K_{sp}, only aqueous species are included in the calculation.

If any of the products have coefficients in front of them, raise the product to that coefficient power and multiply the concentration by that coefficient:

$$K_{sp} = [C]^c \cdot [D]^d$$
$$K_{sp} = [Cu^{2+}]^3 \cdot [PO_4^{3-}]^2$$

The reactant (aA) is a solid and is not included in the K_{sp} equation.

Solids are not included when calculating equilibrium constant expressions, because their concentrations do not change the expression. Any change in their concentrations is insignificant, and is thus omitted.

13. C is correct.

The *like dissolves like* rule applies when a solvent is miscible with a solute that has similar properties.

A polar solute (e.g., ethanol) is miscible with a polar solvent (e.g., water).

14. C is correct.

In a net ionic equation, substances that do not dissociate in aqueous solutions are written in their molecular form (not broken down into ions).

Gases, liquids and solids are written in molecular form.

Some solutions do not dissociate into ions in water, or do so in very little amounts (e.g., weak acids such as HF, CH_3COOH). They are also written in molecular form.

15. B is correct. A supersaturated solution contains more of the dissolved material than could be dissolved by the solvent under normal conditions. Increased heat allows for a solution to become supersaturated. The term also refers to the vapor of a compound that has a higher partial pressure than the vapor pressure of that compound.

A supersaturated solution forms a precipitate if seed crystals are added as the solution reaches a lower energy state when solutes precipitate from the solution.

16. E is correct.

Mass % = mass of solute / mass of solution

Rearrange that equation to solve for mass of solution:

mass of solution = mass of solute / mass %

mass of solution = 122 g / 7.50%

mass of solution = 122 g / 0.075

mass of solution = 1,627 g

17. B is correct.

Determine moles of NaH_3:

Moles of NH_3 = mass of NH_3 / molecular weight of NH_3

Moles of NH_3 = 15.0 g / (14.01 g/mol + 3 × 1.01 g/mol)

Moles of NH_3 = 15.0 g / (17.04 g/mol)

Moles of NH_3 = 0.88 mol

Determine the volume of the solution:

Volume of solution = mass / density

Volume of solution = 250 g / 0.974 g/mL

Volume of solution = 256.7 mL

Convert volume to liters:

Volume = 256.7 mL × 0.001 L / mL

Volume = 0.2567 L

Divide moles by the volume to calculate molarity:

Molarity = moles / volume

Molarity = 0.88 mol / 0.2567 L

Molarity = 3.42 M

18. A is correct.

Solutions with the highest concentration of ions have the highest boiling point.

Calculate the concentration of ions in each solution:

0.2 M $Al(NO_3)_3 = 0.2$ M $\times$ 4 ions $= 0.8$ M

0.2 M $MgCl_2 = 0.2$ M $\times$ 3 ions $= 0.6$ M

0.2 M glucose $= 0.2$ M $\times$ 1 ion $= 0.2$ M (glucose does not dissociate into ions in solution)

0.2 M $Na_2SO_4 = 0.2$ M $\times$ 3 ions $= 0.6$ M

Water $= 0$ M

19. A is correct.

Calculate the number of ions in each option:

A: $Li_3PO_4 \rightarrow 3\ Li^+ + PO_4^{3-}$ (4 ions)

B: $Ca(NO_3)_2 \rightarrow Ca^{2+} + 2\ NO_3^-$ (3 ions)

C: $MgSO_4 \rightarrow Mg^{2+} + SO_4^{2-}$ (2 ions)

D: $(NH_4)_2SO_4 \rightarrow 2\ NH_4^+ + SO_4^{2-}$ (3 ions)

E: $(NH_4)_4Fe(CN)_6 \rightarrow 4\ NH_4^+ + Fe(CN)_6^{4-}$ (5 ions)

20. D is correct.

An electrolyte is a substance that produces an electrically conducting solution when dissolved in a polar solvent (e.g., water).

The dissolved electrolyte separates into positively-charged cations and negatively-charged anions.

Strong electrolytes dissociate completely (or almost completely), because the resulting ions are stable in the solution.

Practice Set 2: Questions 21–40

21. B is correct.

Note that carbonate salts help remove 'hardness' in water.

Generally, SO_4, NO_3 and Cl salts tend to be soluble in water, while CO_3 salts are less soluble.

22. A is correct.

A *spectator ion* is an *ion* that exists in the same form on both the reactant and product sides of a chemical reaction.

Balanced equation:

$$Pb(NO_3)_2 \ (aq) + H_2SO_4 \ (aq) \rightarrow PbSO_4 \ (s) + 2 \ HNO_3 \ (aq)$$

23. C is correct.

A polar solute is miscible with a polar solvent.

Ascorbic acid is polar and is therefore miscible in water.

24. E is correct.

Apply the formula for the molar concentration of a solution:

$$M_1V_1 = M_2V_2$$

Substitute the given volume and molar concentrations of HCl, solve for the final volume of HCl of the resulting dilution:

$$V_2 = [M_1V_1] / (M_2)$$

$$V_2 = [(2.00 \ M \ HCl) \times (0.125 \ L \ HCl)] / (0.400 \ M \ HCl)$$

$$V_2 = 0.625 \ L \ HCl$$

Solve for the volume of water needed to be added to the initial volume of HCl in order to obtain the final diluted volume of HCl:

$$V_{H_2O} = V_2 - V_1$$

$$V_{H_2O} = (0.625 \ L \ HCl) - (0.125 \ L \ HCl)$$

$$V_{H_2O} = 0.500 \ L = 500 \ mL$$

25. A is correct.

The *–ate* ending indicates the species with more oxygen than species ending in *–ite*.

However, it does not indicate a specific number of oxygen molecules.

26. C is correct.

Solubility is the property of a solid, liquid, or gaseous substance (i.e., solute) by which it dissolves in a solid, liquid, or gaseous solvent to form a solution (i.e., solute in the solvent).

The solubility of a substance depends on the physical and chemical properties of the solute and solvent as well as on the temperature, pressure and pH of the solution.

Gaseous solutes (e.g., oxygen) exhibit complex behavior with temperature. As the temperature rises, gases usually become less soluble in water but more soluble in organic solvents.

27. A is correct. A saturated solution contains the maximum amount of dissolved material in the solvent under normal conditions. Increased heat allows for a solution to become supersaturated. The term also refers to the vapor of a compound that has a higher partial pressure than the vapor pressure of that compound.

A saturated solution forms a precipitate as more solute is added to the solution.

28. D is correct.

Immiscible refers to the property (of solutions) of when two or more substances (e.g., oil and water) are mixed together and eventually separate into two layers.

Miscible is when two liquids are mixed together, but do not necessarily interact chemically.

In contrast to miscibility, *soluble* means the substance (solid, liquid or gas) can *dissolve* in another solid, liquid or gas. In other words, a substance *dissolves* when it becomes incorporated into another substance. Also, in contrast to miscibility, solubility involves a *saturation point*, at a substance cannot dissolve any further and a mass, the *precipitate*, begins to form.

29. D is correct.

In this case, hydration means dissolving in water rather than reacting with water.

Therefore, the compound dissociates into its ions (without involving water in the actual chemical reaction).

30. A is correct.

Depending on the solubility of a solute, there are three possible results:

1) a dilute solution has less solute than the maximum amount that it is able to dissolve;

2) a saturated solution has exactly the same amount as its solubility;

3) a precipitate forms if there is more solute than is able to be dissolved, so the excess solute separates from the solution (i.e., crystallization).

Precipitation lowers the concentration of the solute to the saturation level in order to increase the stability of the solution.

Gas solubility is inversely proportional to temperature and proportional to pressure.

31. E is correct.

Like dissolves like means that polar substances tend to dissolve in polar solvents and nonpolar substances in nonpolar solvents.

Molecules that can form hydrogen bonds with water are soluble.

Salts are ionic compounds.

The anion and cation bond with the polar molecule of water and are both soluble.

32. B is correct.

Like dissolves like means that polar substances tend to dissolve in polar solvents and nonpolar substances in nonpolar solvents.

Methanol (CH_3OH) is a polar molecule. Therefore, methanol is soluble in water because it can hydrogen bond with the water.

33. B is correct.

To find the K_{sp}, take the molarities or concentrations of the products (cC and dD) and multiply them.

For K_{sp}, only aqueous species are included in the calculation.

If any of the products have coefficients in front of them, raise the product to that coefficient power and multiply the concentration by that coefficient:

$$K_{sp} = [C]^c \cdot [D]^d$$

$$K_{sp} = [Au^{3+}] \cdot [Cl^-]^3$$

The reactant (aA) is a solid and is not included in the K_{sp} equation.

Solids are not included when calculating equilibrium constant expressions, because their concentrations do not change the expression. Any change in their concentrations is insignificant, and is thus omitted.

34. B is correct.

Break down the molecules into their constituent ions:

$$CaCO_3 + 2 H^+ + 2 NO_3^- \rightarrow Ca^{2+} + 2 NO_3^- + CO_2 + H_2O$$

Remove all species that appear on both sides of the reaction:

$$CaCO_3 + 2 H^+ \rightarrow Ca^{2+} + CO_2 + H_2O$$

35. D is correct.

According to the problem, there are 0.950 moles of nitrate ion in a $Fe(NO_3)_3$ solution.

Because there are three nitrate (NO_3) ions for each $Fe(NO_3)_3$ molecule, the moles of $Fe(NO_3)_3$ can be calculated:

(1 mole / 3 mole) × 0.950 moles = 0.317 moles

Calculate the volume of solution:

Volume of solution = moles of solute / molarity

Volume of solution = 0.317 moles / 0.550 mol/L

Volume of solution = 0.576 L

Convert the volume into milliliters:

0.576 L × 1,000 mL/L = 576 mL

36. A is correct.

Divide the given concentration of Ca^{2+} by 2:

$[Ca^{2+}] = [48 \text{ mEq } Ca^{2+}] / 2 = 24 \text{ mM } Ca^{2+}$

$[Ca^{2+}] = 24 \text{ mM } Ca^{2+}$

mEq is equivalent to milimolar (mM).

Divide the concentration of Ca^{2+} by 1,000 to obtain the concentration of Ca^{2+} in units of molarity:

$[Ca^{2+}] = 24 \text{ mM } Ca^{2+} \times [(1 \text{ M}) / (1,000 \text{ mM})]$

$[Ca^{2+}] = 0.024 \text{ M } Ca^{2+}$

37. A is correct.

Start by calculating the number of moles:

Moles of LiOH = mass of LiOH / molar mass of LiOH

Moles of LiOH = 36.0 g / (24.0 g/mol)

Moles of LiOH = 1.50 moles

Divide moles by volume to calculate molarity:

Molarity = moles / volume

Molarity = 1.50 moles / (975 mL × 0.001 L/mL)

Molarity = 1.54 M

38. A is correct.

When a substance is dissolved in water, the boiling point of the solution increases.

The increase in boiling point is proportional to the amount of ions present.

39. D is correct.

When AgCl dissociates, equal amounts of Ag^+ and Cl^- are produced. If the concentration of Cl^- is *B*, this must also be the concentration of Ag^+.

Therefore, *B* can be the concentration of Ag.

The concentration of silver ion can also be determined by dividing the K_{sp} by the concentration of chloride ion:

$K_{sp} = [Ag^+]\cdot[Cl^-]$.

Therefore, the concentration of Ag can be *A/B* moles/liter.

40. B is correct.

Strong electrolytes dissociate completely (or almost completely) in water. Strong acids and bases both dissociate almost completely, but weak acids and bases dissociate only slightly.

==

Practice Set 3: Questions 41–60

==

41. E is correct.

Solute-solute and solvent-solvent attractions are important in establishing bonding amongst themselves, both for solvent and solute.

Once they are mixed in a solution, solute-solvent attraction becomes the major attraction force, but the other two forces (solute-solute and solvent-solvent attractions) are still present.

42. B is correct.

Since the empirical formula for magnesium iodide is MgI_2, two moles of dissolved I^- result from each mole of dissolved MgI_2.

Therefore, if $[MgI_2] = 0.40$ M, then $[I^-] = 2(0.40$ M$) = 0.80$ M.

43. B is correct. Ammonia forms hydrogen bonds, and SO_2 is polar.

44. A is correct.

The chlorite ion (chlorine dioxide anion) is ClO_2^-. A chlorite is a compound that contains this group, with chlorine in an oxidation state of +3.

Formula	Cl^-	ClO^-	ClO_2^-	ClO_3^-	ClO_4^-
Anion name	chloride	hypochlorite	chlorite	chlorate	perchlorate
Oxidation state	−1	+1	+3	+5	+7

45. D is correct.

Water softeners cannot remove ions from the water without replacing them.

The process replaces the ions that cause scaling (precipitation) with non-reactive ions.

46. B is correct.

These compounds are rarely encountered in most chemistry problems and are part of the very long list of exceptions to the solubility rule.

Salts containing nitrate ion (NO_3^-) are generally soluble.

---

47. A is correct.

Hydration involves the interaction of water molecules to the solute. The water molecules exchange bonding relationships with the solute, whereby water-water bonds break and water-solute bonds form.

When an ion is hydrated, it is surrounded and bonded by water molecules. The average number of water molecules bonding to an ion is known as its hydration number.

Hydration numbers can vary, but often are either 4 or 6.

48. E is correct.

Solvation describes the process whereby the solute molecules are surrounded by the solvent.

49. D is correct. Miscible refers to the property (of solutions) when two or more substances (e.g., water and alcohol) are mixed together without separating.

50. C is correct.

The *like dissolves like* rule applies when a solvent is miscible with a solute that has similar properties.

A nonpolar solute is immiscible with a polar solvent.

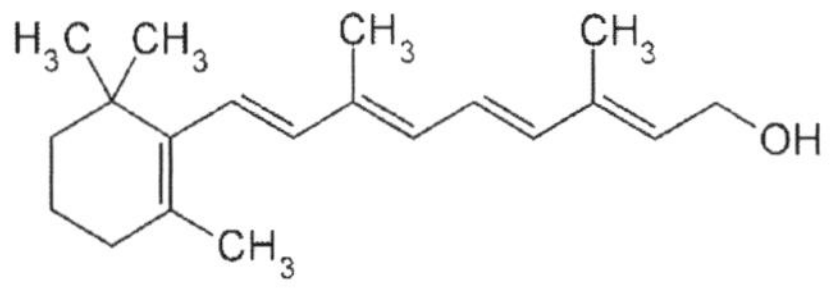

Retinol (animal of vitamin A)

51. B is correct. Only aqueous (*aq*) species are broken down into their ions for ionic equations. Solids, liquids, and gases stay the same.

52. E is correct.

For K_{sp}, only aqueous species are included in the calculation.

The decomposition of $PbCl_2$:

$$PbCl_2 \rightarrow Pb^{2+} + 2\ Cl^-$$

$$K_{sp} = [Pb^{2+}] \cdot [Cl^-]^2$$

When x moles of $PbCl_2$ fully dissociate, x moles of Pb and $2x$ moles of Cl^- are produced:

$K_{sp} = (x)\cdot(2x)^2$

$K_{sp} = 4x^3$

53. B is correct. Strong electrolytes dissociate completely (or almost completely) in water.

Strong acids and bases both dissociate nearly completely (i.e., form stable anions), but weak acids and bases dissociate only slightly (i.e., form unstable anions).

54. A is correct. A *spectator ion* is an *ion* that exists in the same form on both the reactant and product sides of a chemical reaction.

Balanced equation for nitrous oxide and potassium chloride:

KOH and $HNO_3 \rightarrow KNO_3 + H_2O$

55. A is correct.

When a solution is diluted, the moles of solute (n) are constant.

However, the molarity and volume will change because n = MV:

$n_1 = n_2$

$M_1V_1 = M_2V_2$

$V_2 = (M_1V_1) / M_2$

$V_2 = (0.20 \text{ M} \times 6.0 \text{ L}) / 14 \text{ M}$

$V_2 = 0.086 \text{ L}$

Convert to milliliters:

$0.086 \text{ L} \times (1,000 \text{ mL} / \text{L}) = 86 \text{ mL}$

56. B is correct.

When a solution is diluted, the moles of solute are constant.

Use this formula to calculate the new molarity:

$M_1V_1 = M_2V_2$

$160 \text{ mL} \times 4.50 \text{ M} = 595 \text{ mL} \times M_2$

$M_2 = (160 \text{ mL} / 595 \text{ mL}) \times 4.50 \text{ M}$

$M_2 = 1.21 \text{ M}$

57. B is correct.

Like dissolves like means that polar substances tend to dissolve in polar solvents and nonpolar substances in nonpolar solvents.

Since benzene is nonpolar, look for a nonpolar substance.

Silver chloride is ionic, while CH_2Cl_2, H_2S and SO_2 are polar.

58. B is correct.

Molarity can vary based on temperature because it involves the volume of solvent.

At different temperatures, the volume of water varies slightly, which affects the molarity.

59. D is correct.

Concentration:

solute / volume

For example: 10 g / 1 liter = 10 g/liter

2 g / 1 liter = 2 g/liter

60. E is correct.

The NaOH content is 5.0% (m/v). It means that the solute (NaOH) is measured in grams, but the solution volume is measured in milliliters. Therefore, in this problem, the mass and volume of the solution are interchangeable (1 g = 1 mL).

mass of NaOH = % NaOH × volume of solution

mass of NaOH = 5.0% × 75.0 mL

mass of NaOH = 3.75 g

===

Practice Set 4: Questions 61–80

===

61. D is correct. Adding NaCl increases [Cl⁻] in solution (i.e., common ion effect), which increases the precipitation of $PbCl_2$, because the ion product increases. This increase causes lead chloride to precipitate and the concentration of free chloride in solution to decrease.

62. A is correct.

AgCl has a stronger tendency to form than $PbCl_2$ because of its smaller K_{sp}.

Therefore, as AgCl forms, an equivalent amount of $PbCl_2$ dissolves.

63. A is correct.

For the dissolution of $PbCl_2$:

$$PbCl_2 \rightarrow Pb^{2+} + 2\ Cl^-$$

$$K_{sp} = [Pb^{2+}] \cdot [2\ Cl^-]^2 = 10^{-5}$$

$$K_{sp} = (x) \cdot (2x)^2 = 10^{-5}$$

$$4x^3 = 10^{-5}$$

$$x \approx 0.014$$

$$[Cl^-] = 2(0.014)$$

$$[Cl^-] = 0.028$$

For the dissolution of AgCl:

$$AgCl \rightarrow Ag^+ + Cl^-$$

$$K_{sp} = [Ag^+] \cdot [Cl^-]$$

$$K_{sp} = (x) \cdot (x)$$

$$10^{-10} = x^2$$

$$x = 10^{-5}$$

$$[Cl^-] = 10^{-5}$$

64. A is correct.

The intermolecular bonding (i.e., van der Waals) in all alkanes is similar.

---

65. C is correct.

Ideally, dilute solutions are so dilute that solute molecules do not interact.

Therefore, the mole fraction of the solvent approaches one.

66. D is correct.

Henry's law states that, at a constant temperature, the amount of gas that dissolves in a volume of liquid is directly proportional to the partial pressure of that gas in equilibrium with that liquid.

Tyndall effect is light scattering by particles in a colloid (or particles in a very fine suspension).

A colloidal suspension contains microscopically dispersed insoluble particles (i.e., colloid) suspended throughout the liquid. The colloid particles are larger than those of the solution, but not large enough to precipitate due to gravity.

67. C is correct.

Miscible refers to the property (of solutions) when two or more substances (e.g., water and alcohol) are mixed together without separating.

68. B is correct.

Start by calculating moles of glucose:

Moles of glucose = mass of glucose / molar mass of glucose

Moles of glucose = 10.0 g / (180.0 g/mol)

Moles of glucose = 0.0555 mol

Then, divide moles by volume to calculate molarity:

Molarity of glucose = moles of glucose / volume of glucose

Molarity of glucose = 0.0555 mol / (100 mL × 0.001 L/mL)

Molarity = 0.555 M

69. E is correct.

An insoluble compound is incapable of being dissolved (especially with reference to water).

Hydroxide salts of Group I elements are soluble.

Hydroxide salts of Group II elements (Ca, Sr and Ba) are slightly soluble.

Hydroxide salts of transition metals and Al^{3+} are insoluble. Thus, $Fe(OH)_3$, $Al(OH)_3$, $Co(OH)_2$ are not soluble.

Most sulfate salts are soluble. Important exceptions are: $BaSO_4$, $PbSO_4$, Ag_2SO_4 and $SrSO_4$.

Salts containing Cl^-, Br^- and I^- are generally soluble. Exceptions are halide salts of Ag^+, Pb^{2+} and $(Hg_2)^{2+}$. $AgCl$, $PbBr_2$ and Hg_2Cl_2 are all insoluble.

Chromates are frequently insoluble. Examples: $PbCrO_4$, $BaCrO_4$

70. C is correct.

The overall reaction is:

$$Zn\ (s) + 2HCl\ (aq) \rightarrow ZnCl_2\ (aq) + H_2\ (g)$$

Because HCl and $ZnCl_2$ are ionic, they both dissociate into ions in aqueous solutions:

$$Zn\ (s) + 2\ H^+\ (aq) + 2\ Cl^-\ (aq) \rightarrow Zn^{2+}\ (aq) + 2\ Cl^-\ (aq) + H_2\ (g)$$

The common ion (Cl) cancels to yield the net ionic reaction:

$$Zn\ (s) + 2\ H^+\ (aq) \rightarrow Zn^{2+}\ (aq) + H_2\ (g)$$

71. E is correct.

The *like dissolves like* rule applies when a solvent is miscible with a solute that has similar properties.

A polar solute (e.g., ketone, alcohols or carboxylic acids) is miscible with a polar (water) solvent.

The three molecules are polar and are therefore soluble in water.

72. A is correct.

Calculation of the solubility constant (K_{sp}) is similar to the equilibrium constant.

The concentration of each species is raised to the power of their coefficients and multiplied with each other.

For K_{sp}, only aqueous species are included in the calculation.

$$CaF_2\ (s) \rightarrow Ca^{2+}\ (aq) + 2F^-\ (aq)$$

The concentration of fluorine ions can be determined using concentration of calcium ions:

$$[F^-] = 2 \times [Ca^{2+}]$$

$$[F^-] = 2 \times 0.00021\ M$$

$$[F^-] = 4.2 \times 10^{-4}\ M$$

Then, K_{sp} can be determined:

$$K_{sp} = [Ca^{2+}] \cdot [F^-]^2$$

$$K_{sp} = (2.1 \times 10^{-4} \text{ M}) \times (4.2 \times 10^{-4} \text{ M})^2$$

$$K_{sp} = 3.7 \times 10^{-11}$$

73. E is correct.

To determine the number of equivalents:

(4 moles / liter) × (3 equivalents / mole) × (1/3 liter)

= 4 equivalents

74. A is correct.

An electrolyte is a substance that produces an electrically conducting solution when dissolved in a polar solvent (e.g., water).

The dissolved electrolyte separates into positively-charged cations and negatively-charged anions.

Electrolytes conduct electricity.

75. A is correct.

This is a frequently encountered insoluble salt in chemistry problems.

Most sulfate salts are soluble. Important exceptions are: $BaSO_4$, $PbSO_4$, Ag_2SO_4 and $SrSO_4$.

76. C is correct.

When the ion product is equal to or greater than K_{sp}, precipitation of the salt occurs.

If the ion product value is less than K_{sp}, precipitation does not occur.

77. C is correct.

Gas solubility is inversely proportional to temperature, so a low temperature increases solubility.

High pressure of O_2 above the solution increases both pressure of solution (which improves solubility) and amount of O_2 available for dissolving.

78. C is correct.

Molality is the number of solute moles dissolved in 1,000 grams of solvent.

The total mass of the solution is 1,000 g + mass of solute.

Mass of solute (CH_3OH) = moles CH_3OH × molecular mass of CH_3OH

Mass of solute (CH_3OH) = 8.60 moles × [12.01 g/mol + (4 × 1.01 g/mol) + 16 g/mol]

Mass of solute (CH_3OH) = 8.60 moles × (32.05 g/mol)

Mass of solute (CH_3OH) = 275.63 g

Total mass of solution: 1,000 g + 275.63 g = 1,275.63 g

Volume of solution = mass / density

Volume of solution = 1,275.63 g / 0.94 g/mL

Volume of solution = 1,357.05 mL

Divide moles by volume to calculate molarity:

Molarity = number of moles / volume

Molarity = 8.60 moles / 1,357.05 mL

Molarity = 6.34 M

79. E is correct.

By definition, a 15.0% aqueous solution of KI contains 15% KI and the remainder (100 % – 15% = 85%) is water.

If there are 100 g of KI solution, it has 15 g of KI and 85 g of water.

The answer choice of 15 g KI / 100 g water is incorrect because 100 g is the mass of the solution; the actual mass of water is 85 g.

80. D is correct.

Molarity equals moles of solute divided by liters of solution.

$1 \ cm^3$ = 1 mL

Molarity:

(0.75 mol) / (0.075 L) = 10 M

This page is intentionally left blank

Explanations: Acids and Bases

===

Practice Set 1: Questions 1–20

===

1. A is correct. An acid dissociates a proton to form the conjugate base, while a conjugate base accepts a proton to form the acid.

2. B is correct.

$$pH = -\log[H^+]$$

$$pH = -\log(0.10)$$

$$pH = 1$$

3. A is correct. A salt is a combination of an acid and a base.

Its pH will be determined by the acid and base that created the salt.

Combination include:

Weak acid and strong base: salt is basic

Strong acid and weak base: salt is acidic

Strong acid and strong base: salt is neutral

Weak acid and weak base: could be anything (acidic, basic, or neutral)

Examples of strong acids and bases that commonly appear in chemistry problems:

Strong acids: HCl, HBr, HI, H_2SO_4, $HClO_4$ and HNO_3

Strong bases: $NaOH$, KOH, $Ca(OH)_2$ and $Ba(OH)_2$

The hydroxides of Group I and II metals are considered strong bases. Examples include $LiOH$ (lithium hydroxide), $NaOH$ (sodium hydroxide), KOH (potassium hydroxide), $RbOH$ (rubidium hydroxide), $CsOH$ (cesium hydroxide), $Ca(OH)_2$ (calcium hydroxide), $Sr(OH)_2$ (strontium hydroxide) and $Ba(OH)_2$ (barium hydroxide).

4. C is correct.

The Brønsted-Lowry acid–base theory focuses on the ability to accept and donate protons (H^+).

A Brønsted-Lowry acid is the term for a substance that donates a proton (H^+) in an acid–base reaction, while a Brønsted-Lowry base is the term for a substance that accepts a proton.

---

5. C is correct. A solution's conductivity is correlated to the amount of ions present in a solution. The fact that the bulb is shining brightly implies that the solution is an excellent conductor, which means that the solution has a high concentration of ions.

6. C is correct. An amphoteric compound can react both as an acid (i.e., donates protons) as well as a base (i.e., accepts protons).

One type of amphoteric species are amphiprotic molecules, which can either accept or donate a proton (H^+). Examples of amphiprotic molecules include amino acids (i.e., an amine and carboxylic acid group) and self-ionizable compounds such as water.

7. E is correct. Strong acids completely dissociate protons into the aqueous solution. The resulting anion is stable, which accounts for the ~100% ionization of the strong acid.

Weak acids do not completely (or appreciably) dissociate protons into the aqueous solution. The resulting anion is unstable which accounts for a small ionization of the weak acid.

Each of the listed strong acids form an anion stabilized by resonance.

$HClO_4$ (perchloric acid) has a pK_a of –10.

H_2SO_4 (sulfuric acid) is a diprotic acid and has a pK_a of –3 and 1.99.

HNO_3 (nitrous acid) has a pK_a of –1.4.

8. E is correct.

To find the pH of strong acid and strong base solutions (where $[H^+] > 10^{-6}$), use the equation:

$$pH = -\log[H_3O^+]$$

Given that $[H^+] < 10^{-9}$, the pH = 8. This means that the $[H^+]$ comes from H_2O and not from the acid, because the solution is very dilute. Therefore, it can be deduced that the pH of the solution is that of neutral H_2O, which is 7.

Note that this approach only applies to strong acids and strong bases.

9. B is correct.

The self-ionization (autoionization) of water is an ionization reaction in pure water or an aqueous solution, in which a water molecule, H_2O, deprotonates (loses the nucleus of one of its hydrogen atoms) to become a hydroxide ion, (^-OH).

10. B is correct. An electrolyte is a substance that dissociates into cations (i.e., positive ions) and anions (i.e., negative ions) when placed in solution.

NH_3 is a weak acid with a pK_a of 38. Therefore, it does not readily dissociate into H^+ and $^-NH_2$.

$HC_2H_3O_2$ (bicarbonate) has a pK_a of about 10.3 and is considered a weak acid because it does not dissociate completely. Therefore, it does not readily dissociate into H^+ and $^-C_2H_3O_2$.

HCN (nitrile) is a weak acid with a pK_a of 9.3. Therefore, it does not readily dissociate into H^+ and ^-CN (i.e., cyanide).

11. B is correct. If the $[H_3O^+] = [^-OH]$, it has a pH of 7 and the solution is neutral.

12. E is correct. The Arrhenius acid–base theory states that acids produce H^+ ions (protons) in H_2O solution and bases produce ^-OH ions (hydroxide) in H_2O solution.

13. C is correct. The Brønsted-Lowry acid–base theory focuses on the ability to accept and donate protons (H^+).

A Brønsted-Lowry acid is the term for a substance that donates a proton in an acid–base reaction, while a Brønsted-Lowry base is the term for a substance that accepts a proton.

The definition is expressed in terms of an equilibrium expression

acid + base ↔ conjugate base + conjugate acid.

14. B is correct.

According to the Brønsted-Lowry acid–base theory:

An acid (reactant) dissociates a proton to become the conjugate base (product).

A base (reactant) gains a proton to become the conjugate acid (product).

The definition is expressed in terms of an equilibrium expression

acid + base ↔ conjugate base + conjugate acid.

15. C is correct.

The pH scale has a range from 1 to 14, with 7 being a neutral pH.

Acidic solutions have a pH below 7, while basic solutions have a pH above 7.

The pH scale is a log scale where 7 has a 50% deprotonated: 50% protonated (neutral) species.

At pH of 5, there are 1 deprotonated : 100 protonated species. The ratio is 1:100.

A pH change of 1 unit changes the ration by 10×.

Lower pH (< 7) results in more protonated species, while an increase in pH (> 7) results in more deprotonated (anion) species.

16. A is correct.

pI is the symbol for isoelectric point: the pH where a protein ion has zero net charge.

To calculate pI of amino acids with 2 pK_a values, take the average of the pK_a's:

pI = $(pK_{a1} + pK_{a2})$ / 2

pI = (2.2 + 4.2) / 2

pI = 3.2

17. D is correct.

Acidic solutions contain hydronium ions (H_3O^+). These ions are in the aqueous form because they are dissolved in water. Although chemists often write H^+ (*aq*), referring to a single hydrogen nucleus (a proton), it actually exists as the hydrogen proton (H^+).

18. C is correct.

The equivalence point is the point at which chemically equivalent quantities of acid and base have been mixed. The moles of acid are equivalent to the moles of base.

The endpoint (related to, but not the same as the equivalence point) refers to the point at which the indicator changes color in a colorimetric titration. The endpoint can be found by an indicator, such as phenolphthalein (i.e., it turns colorless in acidic solutions and pink in basic solutions).

A buffer is an aqueous solution that consists of a weak acid and its conjugate base, or vice versa. Buffered solutions resist changes in pH, and are often used to keep the pH at a nearly constant value in many chemical applications. It does this by readily absorbing or releasing protons (H^+) and ^-OH.

When an acid is added to the solution, the buffer releases ^-OH and accepts H^+ ions from the acid.

When a base is added, the buffer accepts ^-OH ions from the base and releases protons (H^+).

Using the Henderson-Hasselbalch equation:

pH = pK_a + log([A^-] / [HA]),

where [HA] = concentration of the weak acid, in units of molarity; [A⁻] = concentration of the conjugate base, in units of molarity.

$$pK_a = -\log(K_a)$$

where K_a = acid dissociation constant.

From the question, the concentration of the conjugate base equals the concentration of the weak acid. This equates to the following expression:

$$[HA] = [A^-]$$

Rearranging: $[A^-] / [HA]$, like in the Henderson-Hasselbalch equation:

$$[A^-] / [HA] = 1$$

Substituting the value into the Henderson-Hasselbalch equation:

$$pH = pK_a + \log(1)$$

$$pH = pK_a + 0$$

$$pH = pK_a$$

When $pH = pK_a$, the titration is in the buffering region.

19. D is correct.

The ionic product constant of water:

$$K_w = [H_3O^+] \cdot [^-OH]$$

$$[^-OH] = K_w / [H_3O^+]$$

$$[^-OH] = [1 \times 10^{-14}] / [7.5 \times 10^{-9}]$$

$$[^-OH] = 1.3 \times 10^{-6}$$

20. C is correct.

Consider the K_a presented in the question – which species is more acidic or basic than NH_3?

NH_4^+ is correct because it is NH_3 after absorbing one proton. The concentration of H^+ in water is proportional to K_a. NH_4^+ is the conjugate acid of NH_3.

A: H^+ is definitely acidic.

B: NH_2^- is NH_3 with one less proton. If a base loses a proton, it would be an even stronger base with a higher affinity for proton, so this is not a weaker base than NH_3.

D: Water is neutral.

E: NH_3 will have the same K_a (1.8×10^{-5}).

===

Practice Set 2: Questions 21–40

===

21. E is correct.

An acid as a reactant produces a conjugate base, while a base as a reactant produces a conjugate acid.

The conjugate base of a chemical species is that species after H^+ has dissociated.

Therefore, the conjugate base of HSO_4^- is SO_4^{2-}.

The conjugate base of H_3O^+ is H_2O.

22. A is correct.

Start by calculating the moles of $Ca(OH)_2$:

Moles of $Ca(OH)_2$ = molarity $Ca(OH)_2$ × volume of $Ca(OH)_2$

Moles of $Ca(OH)_2$ = 0.1 M × (30 mL × 0.001 L/mL)

Moles of $Ca(OH)_2$ = 0.003 mol

Use the coefficients from the reaction equation to determine moles of HNO_3:

Moles of HNO_3 = (coefficient of HNO_3) / [coefficient $Ca(OH)_2$ × moles of $Ca(OH)_2$]

Moles of HNO_3 = (2 / 1) × 0.003 mol

Moles of HNO_3 = 0.006 mol

Divide moles by molarity to calculate volume:

Volume of HNO_3 = moles of HNO_3 / molarity of HNO_3

Volume of HNO_3 = 0.006 mol / 0.2 M

Volume of HNO_3 = 0.03 L

Convert volume to milliliters:

0.03 L × 1000 mL / L = 30 mL

23. D is correct.

Acidic solutions have a pH less than 7 due to a higher concentration of H^+ ions relative to ^-OH ions.

Basic solutions have a pH greater than 7 due to a higher concentration of ^-OH ions relative to H^+ ions.

24. D is correct.

An amphoteric compound can react both as an acid (i.e., donates protons) as well as a base (i.e., accepts protons).

Examples of amphoteric molecules include amino acids (i.e., an amine and carboxylic acid group) and self-ionizable compounds such as water.

25. B is correct.

Strong acids (i.e., reactants) proceed towards products.

$$K_a = \text{[products] / [reactants]}$$

The molecule with the largest K_a is the strongest acid.

$$pK_a = -\log K_a$$

The molecule with the smallest pK_a is the strongest acid.

Strong acids dissociate a proton to produce the weakest conjugate base (i.e., most stable anion).

Weak acids dissociate a proton to produce the strongest conjugate base (i.e., least stable anion).

26. B is correct.

Balanced reaction:

$$H_3PO_4 + 3\ LiOH = Li_3PO_4 + 3\ H_2O$$

In neutralization of acids and bases, the result is always salt and water.

Phosphoric acid and lithium hydroxide react, so the resulting compounds are lithium phosphate and water.

27. B is correct.

Base strength is determined by the stability of the compound. If the compound is unstable in its present state, it seeks a bonding partner (e.g., H+ or another atom) by donating its electrons for the new bond formation.

The 8 strong bases are: LiOH (lithium hydroxide), NaOH (sodium hydroxide), KOH (potassium hydroxide), $Ca(OH)_2$ (calcium hydroxide), RbOH (rubidium hydroxide), $Sr(OH)_2$, (strontium hydroxide), CsOH (cesium hydroxide) and $Ba(OH)_2$ (barium hydroxide).

28. D is correct.

The formula for pH:

$$pH = -\log[H^+]$$

Rearrange to solve for $[H^+]$:

$$[H^+] = 10^{-pH}$$

$$[H^+] = 10^{-2} \text{ M} = 0.01 \text{ M}$$

29. C is correct. An electrolyte is a substance that dissociates into cations (i.e., positive ions) and anions (i.e., negative ions) when placed in solution.

30. C is correct.

A base is a chemical substance with a pH greater than 7 and feels slippery because it dissolves the fatty acids and oils from skin and therefore reduces the friction between the skin cells.

Under acidic conditions, litmus paper is red, and under basic conditions, it is blue.

Many bitter tasting foods are alkaline, because bitter compounds often contain amine groups, which are weak bases.

Acids are known to have a sour taste (e.g., lemon juice) because the sour taste receptors on the tongue detect the dissolved hydrogen (H^+) ions.

31. E is correct.

The 7 strong acids are: HCl (hydrochloric acid), HNO_3 (nitric acid), H_2SO_4 (sulfuric acid), HBr (hydrobromic acid), HI (hydroiodic acid), $HClO_3$ (chloric acid) and $HClO_4$ (perchloric acid).

The 8 strong bases are: LiOH (lithium hydroxide), NaOH (sodium hydroxide), KOH (potassium hydroxide), $Ca(OH)_2$ (calcium hydroxide), RbOH (rubidium hydroxide), $Sr(OH)_2$, (strontium hydroxide), CsOH (cesium hydroxide) and $Ba(OH)_2$ (barium hydroxide).

32. C is correct. The Arrhenius acid–base theory states that acids produce H^+ ions in H_2O solution and bases produce ^-OH ions in H_2O solution.

The Brønsted-Lowry acid–base theory focuses on the ability to accept and donate protons (H^+).

A Brønsted-Lowry acid is the term for a substance that donates a proton in an acid–base reaction, while a Brønsted-Lowry base is the term for a substance that accepts a proton.

Lewis acids are defined as electron pair acceptors, whereas Lewis bases are electron pair donors.

33. A is correct.

By the Brønsted-Lowry acid–base theory:

An acid (reactant) dissociates a proton to become the conjugate base (product).

A base (reactant) gains a proton to become the conjugate acid (product).

The definition is expressed in terms of an equilibrium expression:

acid + base ↔ conjugate base + conjugate acid.

34. D is correct. With polyprotic acids (i.e., more than one H^+ present), the pK_a indicates the pH at which the H^+ is deprotonated. If the pH goes above the first pK_a, one proton dissociates, and so on.

In this example, the pH is above both the first and second pK_a, so two acid groups are deprotonated while the third acidic proton is unaffected.

35. E is correct. It is important to identify the acid that is active in the reaction.

The parent acid is defined as the most protonated form of the buffer. The number of dissociating protons an acid can donate depends on the charge of its conjugate base.

$Ba_2P_2O_7$ is given as one of the products in the reaction. Because barium is a group 2B metal, it has a stable oxidation state of +2. Because two barium cations are present in the product, the charge of P_2O_7 ion (the conjugate base in the reaction) must be –4.

Therefore, the fully protonated form of this conjugate must be $H_4P_2O_7$, which is a tetraprotic acid because it has 4 protons that can dissociate.

36. C is correct.

The greater the concentration of H_3O^+, the more acidic is the solution.

37. B is correct.

A triprotic acid has three protons that can dissociate.

38. B is correct.

KCl and NaI are both salts.

Two salts only react if one of the products precipitates.

In this example, the products (KI and NaCl) are both soluble in water, so they do not react.

39. B is correct.

Sodium acetate is a basic compound, because acetate is the conjugate base of acetic acid, a weak acid ("the conjugate base of a weak acid acts as a base in water").

The addition of a base to any solution, even a buffered solution, increases the pH.

40. E is correct.

An acid anhydride is a compound that has two acyl groups bonded to the same oxygen atom.

Anhydride literally means *without water* and is formed via a dehydration (i.e., removal of H_2O) reaction.

Practice Set 3: Questions 41–60

41. A is correct.

The Brønsted-Lowry acid–base theory focuses on the ability to accept and donate protons (H^+).

A Brønsted-Lowry acid is the term for a substance that donates a proton (H^+) in an acid–base reaction, while a Brønsted-Lowry base is the term for a substance that accepts a proton.

42. A is correct.

Strong acids (i.e., reactants) proceed towards products.

$$K_a = [\text{products}] / [\text{reactants}]$$

The molecule with the largest K_a is the strongest acid.

$$pK_a = -\log K_a$$

The molecule with the smallest pK_a is the strongest acid.

Strong acids dissociate a proton to produce the weakest conjugate base (i.e., most stable anion).

Weak acids dissociate a proton to produce the strongest conjugate base (i.e., least stable anion).

43. D is correct.

Learn the ions involved in boiler scale formations: CO_3^{2-} and the metal ions.

44. E is correct.

A buffer is an aqueous solution that consists of a weak acid and its conjugate base, or vice versa.

Buffered solutions resist changes in pH, and are often used to keep the pH at a nearly constant value in many chemical applications. It does this by readily absorbing or releasing protons (H^+) and ^-OH.

When an acid is added to the solution, the buffer releases ^-OH and accepts H^+ ions from the acid.

To create a buffer solution, there needs to be a pair of a weak acid/base and its conjugate, or a salt that contains an ion from the weak acid/base.

Since the problem indicates that sulfuric acid/H_2SO_2 needs to be in the mixture, the other component would have a HSO_2^- ion.

45. C is correct.

Acidic salt is a salt that still contains H^+ in its anion. It is formed when a polyprotic acid is partially neutralized, leaving at least 1 H^+.

For example:

$H_3PO_4 + 2\ KOH \rightarrow K_2HPO_4 + 2\ H_2O$: (partial neutralization, K_2HPO_4 is acidic salt)

While:

$H_3PO_4 + 3\ KOH \rightarrow K_3PO_4 + 3\ H_2O$: (complete neutralization, K_3PO_4 is not acidic salt)

46. E is correct.

An acid anhydride is a compound that has two acyl groups bonded to the same oxygen atom.

Anhydride literally means *without water* and is formed via a dehydration (i.e., removal of H_2O) reaction.

47. A is correct.

By the Brønsted-Lowry definition, an acid donates protons, while a base accepts protons.

On the product side of the reaction, H_2O acts as a base (i.e., conjugate base of H_3O^+) and HCl acts as an acid (i.e., conjugate acid of Cl^-).

48. D is correct.

The ratio of the conjugate base to the acid must be determined from the pH of the solution and the pK_a of the acidic component in the reaction.

In the reaction, $H_2PO_4^-$ acts as the acid and HPO_4^{2-} acts as the base, so the pK_a of $H_2PO_4^-$ should be used in the equation.

Substitute the given values into the Henderson-Hasselbalch equation:

$pH = pK_a + \log[\text{salt} / \text{acid}]$

$7.35 = 6.87 + \log[\text{salt} / \text{acid}]$

Since $H_2PO_4^-$ is acting as the acid, subtract 6.87 from both sides:

$0.48 = \log[\text{salt} / \text{acid}]$

The log base is 10, so the inverse log will give:

$10^{0.48} = (\text{salt} / \text{acid})$

$(\text{salt} / \text{acid}) = 3.02$

The ratio between the conjugate base or salt and the acid is 3.02 / 1.

49. B is correct.

An electrolyte is a substance that dissociates into cations (i.e., positive ions) and anions (i.e., negative ions) when placed in solution. The fact that the light bulb is dimly lit indicates that the solution contains only a low concentration (i.e., partial ionization) of the ions.

An electrolyte produces an electrically conducting solution when dissolved in a polar solvent (e.g., water). The dissolved ions disperse uniformly through the solvent. If an electrical potential (i.e., voltage) is applied to such a solution, the cations of the solution migrate towards the electrode (i.e., abundance of electrons), while the anions migrate towards the electrode (i.e., deficit of electrons).

50. B is correct.

An acid is a chemical substance with a pH less than 7 which produces H^+ ions in water. An acid can be neutralized by a base (i.e., a substance with a pH above 7) to form salt.

Acids are known to have a sour taste (e.g., lemon juice) because the sour taste receptors on the tongue detect the dissolved hydrogen (H^+) ions.

However, acids are not known to have a slippery feel; this is characteristic of bases. Bases feel slippery because they dissolve the fatty acids and oils from skin and therefore reduce the friction between the skin cells.

51. C is correct.

The Arrhenius acid–base theory states that acids produce H^+ ions (protons) in H_2O solution and bases produce ^-OH ions (hydroxide) in H_2O solution.

The Brønsted-Lowry acid–base theory focuses on the ability to accept and donate protons (H^+).

A Brønsted-Lowry acid is the term for a substance that donates a proton in an acid–base reaction, while a Brønsted-Lowry base is the term for a substance that accepts a proton.

52. A is correct.

By the Brønsted-Lowry acid–base theory:

An acid (reactant) dissociates a proton to become the conjugate base (product).

A base (reactant) gains a proton to become the conjugate acid (product).

The definition is expressed in terms of an equilibrium expression:

acid + base ↔ conjugate base + conjugate acid.

53. A is correct.

By the Brønsted-Lowry acid–base theory:

An acid (reactant) dissociates a proton to become the conjugate base (product).

A base (reactant) gains a proton to become the conjugate acid (product).

The definition is expressed in terms of an equilibrium expression:

acid + base ↔ conjugate base + conjugate acid.

HCl dissociates completely and therefore is a strong acid.

Strong acids produce weak (i.e., stable) conjugate bases.

54. D is correct.

A diprotic acid has two protons that can dissociate.

55. A is correct.

Protons (H^+) migrate between amino acid and solvent, depending on the pH of solvent and pK_a of functional groups on the amino acid.

Carboxylic acid groups can donate protons, while amine groups can receive protons.

For the carboxylic acid group:

If pH of solution $< pK_a$: group is protonated and neutral

If pH of solution $> pK_a$: group is deprotonated and negative

For the amine group:

If pH of solution $< pK_a$: group is protonated and positive

If pH of solution $> pK_a$: group is deprotonated and neutral

56. E is correct. Acidic solutions contain hydronium ions (H_3O^+). These ions are in the aqueous form because they are dissolved in water. Although chemists often write H^+ (*aq*), referring to a single hydrogen nucleus (a proton), it actually exists as the hydrogen proton (H^+).

57. A is correct.

With a K_a of 10^{-5}, the pH of a 1 M solution of the carboxylic acid, $CH_3CH_2CH2CO_2H$, would be 5 and is a weak acid.

Only $CH_3CH_2CH_2CO_2H$ can be considered a weak acid, because it yields a (relatively) unstable anion.

58. C is correct.

Condition 1: pH = 4

$$[H_3O^+] = 10^{-pH} = 10^{-4}$$

Condition 2: pH = 7

$$[H_3O^+] = 10^{-pH} = 10^{-7}$$

Ratio of $[H_3O^+]$ in condition 1 and condition 2:

$$10^{-4} : 10^{-7} = 1,000 : 1$$

Solution with a pH of 4 has 1,000 times greater $[H^+]$ than solution with a pH of 7.

Note: $[H_3O^+]$ is equivalent to $[H^+]$

59. B is correct.

The pH of a buffer is calculated using the Henderson-Hasselbalch equation:

$$pH = pK_a + \log([\text{conjugate base}] / [\text{conjugate acid}])$$

When [acid] = [base], the fraction is 1.

Log 1 = 0,

$$pH = pK_a + 0$$

If the K_a of the acid is 4.6×10^{-4}, (between 10^{-4} and 10^{-3}), the pK_a (and therefore the pH) is between 3 and 4.

60. C is correct.

$K_w = [H^+] \cdot [^-OH]$ is the definition of ionization constant for water.

==

Practice Set 4: Questions 61–80

==

61. A is correct. Weak acids react with a strong base, which is converted to its conjugate weak base, creating an overall basic solution.

Strong acids do react with a strong base, creating a neutral solution.

Weak acids only partially dissociate when dissolved in water; unlike a strong acid, they do not readily form ions.

Strong acids are much more corrosive than weak acids.

62. C is correct.

K_w is the water ionization constant (also known as water autoprotolysis constant).

It can be determined experimentally and equals 1.011×10^{-14} at 25 °C (1.00×10^{-14} is used).

63. D is correct.

All options are correct descriptions of the reaction, but the correct choice is the most descriptive.

64. A is correct.

The Brønsted-Lowry acid–base theory focuses on the ability to accept and donate protons (H^+).

A Brønsted-Lowry acid is the term for a substance that donates a proton in an acid–base reaction, while a Brønsted-Lowry base is the term for a substance that accepts a proton.

65. A is correct.

Buffered solutions resist changes in pH, and are often used to keep the pH at a nearly constant value in many chemical applications. It does this by readily absorbing or releasing protons (H^+) and ^-OH.

H_2SO_4 is a strong acid. Weak acids and their salts are good buffers.

A buffer is an aqueous solution that consists of a weak acid and its conjugate base, or vice versa.

When an acid is added to the solution, the buffer releases ^-OH and accepts H^+ ions from the acid.

When a base is added, the buffer accepts ^-OH ions from the base and releases protons (H^+).

66. E is correct.

The main use of litmus paper is to test whether a solution is acidic or basic.

Litmus paper can also be used to test for water-soluble gases that affect acidity or alkalinity; the gas dissolves in the water and the resulting solution colors the litmus paper. For example, alkaline ammonia gas causes the litmus paper to change from red to blue.

Blue litmus paper turns red under acidic conditions and red litmus paper turns blue under basic or alkaline conditions, with the color change occurring over the pH range 4.5-8.3 at 25 °C (77 °F).

Neutral litmus paper is purple.

Litmus can also be prepared as an aqueous solution that functions similarly. Under acidic conditions, the solution is red, and under basic conditions, the solution is blue.

The properties listed above (turning litmus paper blue, bitter taste, slippery feel and neutralizing acids) are all true of bases.

An acidic solution has opposite qualities.

It has a pH lower than 7 and therefore turns litmus paper red.

It neutralizes bases, tastes sour and does not feel slippery.

67. A is correct.

An electrolyte is a substance that dissociates into cations (i.e., positive ions) and anions (i.e., negative ions) when placed in solution. An electrolyte produces an electrically conducting solution when dissolved in a polar solvent (e.g., water). The dissolved ions disperse uniformly through the solvent. If an electrical potential (i.e., voltage) is applied to such a solution, the cations of the solution migrate towards the electrode (i.e., abundance of electrons), while the anions migrate towards the electrode (i.e., deficit of electrons).

An acid is a substance that ionizes when dissolved in suitable ionizing solvents such as water.

If a high proportion of the solute dissociates to form free ions, it is a strong electrolyte.

If most of the solute does not dissociate, it is a weak electrolyte.

The more free ions present, the better the solution conducts electricity.

68. A is correct.

The 7 strong acids are: HCl (hydrochloric acid), HNO_3 (nitric acid), H_2SO_4 (sulfuric acid), HBr (hydrobromic acid), HI (hydroiodic acid), $HClO_3$ (chloric acid) and $HClO_4$ (perchloric acid).

69. B is correct.

The activity series determines if a metal displaces another metal in the solution.

The reaction can only occur if the added metal is above (i.e., activity series) the metal currently bonded with the anion.

An activity series ranks substances in their order of relative reactivity.

For example, magnesium metal can displace hydrogen ions from solution, so it is more reactive than elemental hydrogen:

$$Mg\ (s) + 2\ H^+\ (aq) \rightarrow H_2\ (g) + Mg^{2+}\ (aq)$$

Zinc can also displace hydrogen ions from solution, so zinc is more reactive than elemental hydrogen:

$$Zn\ (s) + 2\ H^+\ (aq) \rightarrow H_2\ (g) + Zn^{2+}\ (aq)$$

Magnesium metal can displace zinc ions from solution:

$$Mg\ (s) + Zn^{2+}\ (aq) \rightarrow Zn\ (s) + Mg^{2+}\ (aq)$$

The metal activity series with the most active (i.e., most strongly reducing) metals appear at the top, and the least active metals near the bottom.

Li: $2\ Li\ (s) + 2\ H_2O\ (l) \rightarrow LiOH\ (aq) + H_2\ (g)$

K: $2\ K\ (s) + 2\ H_2O\ (l) \rightarrow 2\ KOH\ (aq) + H_2\ (g)$

Ca: $Ca\ (s) + 2\ H_2O\ (l) \rightarrow Ca(OH)_2\ (s) + H_2\ (g)$

Na: $2\ Na\ (s) + 2\ H_2O\ (l) \rightarrow 2\ NaOH\ (aq) + H_2\ (g)$

The above can displace H_2 from water, steam, or acids

Mg: $Mg\ (s) + 2\ H_2O\ (g) \rightarrow Mg(OH)_2\ (s) + H_2\ (g)$

Al: $2\ Al\ (s) + 6\ H_2O\ (g) \rightarrow 2\ Al(OH)_3\ (s) + 3\ H_2\ (g)$

Mn: $Mn\ (s) + 2\ H_2O\ (g) \rightarrow Mn(OH)_2\ (s) + H_2\ (g)$

Zn: $Zn\ (s) + 2\ H_2O\ (g) \rightarrow Zn(OH)_2\ (s) + H_2\ (g)$

Fe: $Fe\ (s) + 2\ H_2O\ (g) \rightarrow Fe(OH)_2\ (s) + H_2\ (g)$

The above can displace H_2 from steam or acids

Ni: $Ni\ (s) + 2\ H^+\ (aq) \rightarrow Ni^{2+}\ (aq) + H_2\ (g)$

Sn: $Sn\ (s) + 2\ H^+\ (aq) \rightarrow Sn^{2+}\ (aq) + H_2\ (g)$

Pb: $Pb\ (s) + 2\ H^+\ (aq) \rightarrow Pb^{2+}\ (aq) + H_2\ (g)$

The above can displace H_2 from acids only

$$H_2 > Cu > Ag > Pt > Au$$

The above cannot displace H_2

70. E is correct.

The Arrhenius acid–base theory states that acids produce H^+ ions (protons) in H_2O solution, and bases produce ^-OH ions (hydroxide) in H_2O solution.

71. A is correct.

By the Brønsted-Lowry acid–base theory:

An acid (reactant) dissociates a proton to become the conjugate base (product).

A base (reactant) gains a proton to become the conjugate acid (product).

The definition is expressed in terms of an equilibrium expression:

acid + base ↔ conjugate base + conjugate acid.

72. D is correct.

Henderson-Hasselbach equation:

$$pH = pK_a + \log(A^- / HA)$$

A buffer is an aqueous solution that consists of a weak acid and its conjugate base, or vice versa.

Buffered solutions resist changes in pH, and are often used to keep the pH at a nearly constant value in many chemical applications. It does this by readily absorbing or releasing protons (H^+) and ^-OH.

When an acid is added to the solution, the buffer releases ^-OH and accepts H^+ ions from the acid.

73. C is correct.

The weakest acid has the smallest K_a (or largest pK_a).

The weakest acid has the strongest (i.e., least stable) conjugate base.

74. E is correct.

The balanced reaction:

$$2\ H_3PO_4 + 3\ Ba(OH)_2 \rightarrow Ba_3(PO_4)_2 + 6\ H_2O$$

There are 2 moles of H_3PO_4 in a balanced reaction.

However, acids are categorized by the number of H^+ per mole of acid.

For example:

HCl is monoprotic (has one H^+ to dissociate).

H_2SO_4 is diprotic (has two H^+ to dissociate).

H_3PO_4 is triprotic acid (has three H^+ to dissociate).

75. E is correct.

Because Na^+ forms a strong base (NaOH) and S forms a weak acid (H_2S), it undergoes a hydrolysis reaction in water:

$$Na_2S + H_2O \rightarrow 2\,Na^+ + 2\,HS^- + {}^-OH$$

Removing Na^+ ions from both sides of the reaction:

$$S^{2-} + H_2O \rightarrow 2\,HS^- + {}^-OH$$

76. A is correct.

HNO_3 is a strong acid, which means that $[HNO_3] = [H_3O^+] = 0.0765$.

$$pH = -\log[H_3O^+]$$

$$pH = -\log(0.0765)$$

$$pH = 1.1$$

77. C is correct.

Strong acids dissociate a proton to produce the weakest conjugate base (i.e., most stable anion).

Weak acids dissociate a proton to produce the strongest conjugate base (i.e., least stable anion).

Bicarbonate (H_2CO_3) has a pK_a of about 10.3 and is considered a weak acid because it does not dissociate completely.

Each of the listed strong acids form an anion stabilized by resonance.

HBr (hydrobromic acid) has a pK_a of –9.

HNO_3 (nitrous acid) has a pK_a of –1.4.

H_2SO_4 (sulfuric acid) is a diprotic acid and has a pK_a of –3 and 1.99.

HCl (hydrochloric acid) has a pK_a of –6.3.

78. A is correct.

It is important to recognize all the chromate ions:

Dichromate: $Cr_2O_7^{2-}$

Chromium (II): Cr^{2+}

Chromic/Chromate: CrO_4^-

Trichromic acid: does not exist.

79. B is correct.

The Brønsted-Lowry acid–base theory focuses on the ability to accept and donate protons (H^+).

A Brønsted-Lowry acid is the term for a substance that donates a proton in an acid–base reaction, while a Brønsted-Lowry base is the term for a substance that accepts a proton.

80. C is correct.

In the Arrhenius theory, acids are defined as substances that dissociate in aqueous solution to produce H^+ (hydrogen ions).

In the Arrhenius theory, bases are defined as substances that dissociate in aqueous solution to produce ^-OH (hydroxide ions).

This page is intentionally left blank

Explanations: Electrochemistry & Oxidation-Reduction Reactions

===

Practice Set 1: Questions 1–20

===

1. D is correct. In electrochemical (i.e., galvanic) cells, oxidation always occurs at the anode, and reduction occurs at the cathode.

Br^- is oxidized at the anode, not the cathode.

2. C is correct.

As ionization energy increases, it is more difficult for electrons to be released by a substance. Release of electrons would increase the charge of the substance, which is the definition of oxidation.

Substances with higher ionization energy are more likely to be reduced. If a substance is reduced in a redox reaction, it is considered an oxidizing agent because it facilitates oxidation of the other reactant.

Therefore, with the increase of ionization energy, a substance will be more likely to be reduced or be a stronger oxidizing agent.

3. E is correct.

Half reaction:

$$H_2S \rightarrow S_8$$

Balancing half-reaction in acidic conditions:

Step 1: Balance all atoms except for H and O

$$8 H_2S \rightarrow S_8$$

Step 2: To balance oxygen, add H_2O to the side with less oxygen atoms

There is no oxygen at all, so skip this step.

Step 3: To balance hydrogen, add H^+:

$$8 H_2S \rightarrow S_8 + 16 H^+$$

Balance charges by adding electrons to the side with higher/more positive total charge.

Total charge on left side: 0

Total charge on right side: $16(+1) = +16$

Add 16 electrons to right side:

$$8 H_2S \rightarrow S_8 + 16 H^+ + 16 e^-$$

4. B is correct.

An electrolytic cell is a nonspontaneous electrochemical cell that requires the supply of electrical energy (e.g., battery) to initiate the reaction.

The anode is positive and the cathode is the negative electrode.

For both electrolytic and galvanic cells, oxidation occurs at the anode, while reduction occurs at the cathode.

Therefore, Co metal is produced at the cathode, because it is a reduction product (from oxidation number of +3 on the left to 0 on the right). Co will not be produced at the anode.

5. C is correct.

The anode in galvanic cells attracts anions.

Anions in solution flow toward the anode, while cations flow toward the cathode.

Oxidation (i.e. loss of electrons) occurs at the anode.

Positive ions are formed while negative ions are consumed at the anode.

Therefore, negative ions flow toward the anode to equalize the charge.

6. E is correct.

By convention, the reference standard for potential is always hydrogen reduction.

7. C is correct.

Calculate the oxidation numbers of all species involved and look for the oxidized species (increase in oxidation number). Cd's oxidation number increases from 0 on the left side of the reaction to +2 on the right.

8. D is correct. The oxidation number of Fe increases from 0 on the left to +3 on the right.

9. D is correct.

Salt bridge contains both cations (positive ions) and anions (negative ions).

Anions flow towards the oxidation half-cell, because the oxidation product is positively charged and the anions are required to balance the charges within the cell.

The opposite is true for cations; ithey will flow towards the reduction half-cell.

10. E is correct.

A redox reaction, or oxidation-reduction reaction, involves the transfer of electrons between two reacting substances. An oxidation reaction specifically refers to a substance that is losing electrons and a reduction reaction specifically refers to a substance that is gaining reactions. The oxidation and reduction reactions alone are called half-reactions, because they always occur together to form a whole reaction.

The key to this question is that it is about the *transfer* of electrons between *two* species, so it is referring to the whole redox reaction in its entirety, not just one half reaction.

An electrochemical reaction takes place during the passage of electric current and does involve redox reactions. However, it is not the correct answer to the question posed.

11. A is correct.

The cell reaction is:

$$Co\ (s) + Cu^{2+}\ (aq) \rightarrow Co^{2+}\ (aq) + Cu\ (s)$$

Separate it into half reactions:

$$Cu^{2+}\ (aq) \rightarrow Cu\ (s)$$

$$Co\ (s) \rightarrow Co^{2+}\ (aq)$$

The potentials provided are written in this format:

$$Cu^{2+}\ (aq)\ |\ Cu\ (s)$$

$$+0.34\ V$$

It means that for the reduction reaction:

$Cu^{2+}\ (aq) \rightarrow Cu\ (s)$, the potential is +0.34 V.

The reverse reaction, or oxidation reaction is:

$Cu\ (s) \rightarrow Cu^{2+}\ (aq)$ has opposing potential value: –0.34 V.

Obtain the potential values for both half-reactions.

Reverse sign for potential values of oxidation reactions:

$$Cu^{2+}\ (aq) \rightarrow Cu\ (s) = +0.34\ V\ \ (reduction)$$

$$Co\ (s) \rightarrow Co^{2+}\ (aq) = +0.28\ V\ \ (oxidation)$$

Determine the standard cell potential:

Standard cell potential = sum of half-reaction potential

Standard cell potential = 0.34 V + 0.28 V

Standard cell potential = 0.62 V

12. E is correct.

The other methods listed involve two or more energy conversions between light and electricity.

It is an electrical device that converts the energy of light directly into electricity by the photovoltaic effect (i.e., chemical and physical processes).

The operation of a photovoltaic (PV) cell has the following requirements:

1) Light is absorbed, which excites electrons.

2) Separation of charge carries opposite types.

3) The separated charges are transferred to an external circuit.

In contrast, solar panels supply heat by absorbing sunlight. A photoelectrolytic / photoelectrochemical cell refers either to a type of photovoltaic cell or to a device that splits water directly into hydrogen and oxygen using only solar illumination.

13. A is correct.

Each half-cell contains an electrode; two half-cells are required to complete a reaction.

14. B is correct.

A: electrolysis can be performed on any metal, not only iron.

C: electrolysis will not boil water nor raise the ship.

D: it is probably unlikely that the gases would stay in the compartments.

E: electrolysis will not reduce the weight enough to float the ship.

15. C is correct.

Balanced reaction:

$$Zn \ (s) + CuSO_4 \ (aq) \rightarrow Cu \ (s) + ZnSO_4 \ (aq)$$

Zn is a stronger reducing agent (more likely to be oxidized) than Cu. This can be determined by each element's standard electrode potential ($E°$).

16. E is correct.

The positive cell potential indicates that the reaction is spontaneous, which means it favors the formation of products.

Cells that generate electricity spontaneously are considered galvanic cells.

17. B is correct.

The joule is a unit of energy.

18. C is correct.

Electrolysis of aqueous sodium chloride yields hydrogen and chlorine, with aqueous sodium hydroxide remaining in solution.

Sodium hydroxide is a strong base, which means the solution will be basic.

19. C is correct.

Balanced equation:

$$Ag^+ + e^- \rightarrow Ag\ (s)$$

Formula to calculate deposit mass:

mass of deposit = (atomic mass × current × time) / 96,500 C

mass of deposit = [107.86 g × 3.50 A × (12 min × 60 s/min)] / 96,500 C

mass of deposit = 2.82 g

20. E is correct.

The anode is the electrode where oxidation occurs.

A salt bridge provides electrical contact between the half-cells.

The cathode is the electrode where reduction occurs.

A spontaneous electrochemical cell is called a galvanic cell.

Practice Set 2: Questions 21–40

21. A is correct.

Ionization energy (IE) is the energy required to release one electron from an element.

Higher IE means the element is more stable.

Elements with high IE are usually elements that only need one or two more electrons to achieve stable configuration (e.g., complete valence shell – 8 electrons, such as the noble gases or 2 electrons, as in hydrogen). It is more likely for these elements to gain an electron and reach stability than lose electron. When an atom gains electrons, its oxidation number goes down and it is reduced. Therefore, elements with high IE are easily reduced.

In oxidation-reduction reactions, species that undergo reduction are oxidizing agents, because their presence allows the other reactant to be oxidized. Because elements with high IE are easily reduced, they are strong oxidizing agents.

Reducing agents are species that undergo oxidation (i.e., lose electrons).

Elements with high IE do not undergo oxidation readily, and therefore are weak reducing agents.

22. D is correct. Balancing a half-reaction in basic conditions:

The first few steps are identical to balancing reactions in acidic conditions.

Step 1: Balance all atoms except for H and O

$$C_8H_{10} \rightarrow C_8H_4O_4{}^{2-} \quad \text{C is already balanced}$$

Step 2: To balance oxygen, add H_2O to the side with less oxygen atoms

$$C_8H_{10} + 4\,H_2O \rightarrow C_8H_4O_4{}^{2-}$$

Step 3: To balance hydrogen, add H^+ to the opposing side of H_2O added in the previous step

$$C_8H_{10} + 4\,H_2O \rightarrow C_8H_4O_4{}^{2-} + 14\,H^+$$

This next step is the unique additional step for basic conditions.

Step 4: Add equal amounts of OH^- on both sides. The number of OH^- should match the number of H^+ ions. Combine H^+ and OH^- on the same side to form H_2O. If there are H_2O molecules on both sides, subtract accordingly to end up with H_2O on one side only.

There are 14 H^+ ions on the right, so add 14 OH^- ions on both sides:

$$C_8H_{10} + 4\,H_2O + 14\,OH^- \rightarrow C_8H_4O_4{}^{2-} + 14\,H^+ + 14\,OH^-$$

Combine H^+ and OH^- ions to form H_2O:

$$C_8H_{10} + 4\,H_2O + 10\,OH^- \rightarrow C_8H_4O_4{}^{2-} + 14\,H_2O$$

H$_2$O molecules are on both sides, which cancel and some H$_2$O remain on one side:

$$C_8H_{10} + 14\ OH^- \rightarrow C_8H_4O_4^{2-} + 10\ H_2O$$

Step 5: Balance charges by adding electrons to the side with higher/more positive total charge

Total charge on left side: $14(-1) = -14$

Total charge on right side: -2

Add 12 electrons to right side:

$$C_8H_{10} + 14\ OH^- \rightarrow C_8H_4O_4^{2-} + 10\ H_2O + 12\ e^-$$

23. A is correct.

In electrochemical (i.e., galvanic) cells, oxidation always occurs at the anode and reduction occurs at the cathode.

Therefore, CO$_2$ is produced at the anode because it is an oxidation product (carbon's oxidation number increases from 0 on the left to +2 on the right).

24. A is correct. Cu^{2+} is being reduced (i.e., gains electrons), while Sn^{2+} is being oxidized (i.e., loses electrons).

Salt bridge contains both cations (positive ions) and anions (negative ions).

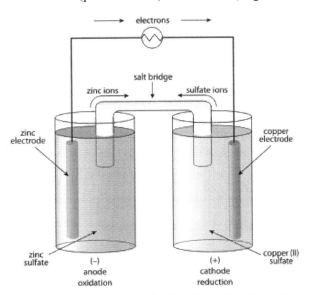

Schematic example of a Zn–Cu galvanic cell

Anions flow towards the oxidation half-cell, because the oxidation product is positively charged and the anions are required to balance the charges within the cell. The opposite is true for cations; they flow towards the reduction half-cell.

25. B is correct.

In all cells, reduction occurs at the cathode, while oxidation occurs at the anode.

26. C is correct.

ZnO is being reduced; the oxidation number of Zn decreases from +2 on the left to 0 on the right.

27. E is correct.

Consider the reactions:

$$Ni\ (s) + Ag^+\ (aq) \rightarrow Ag\ (s) + Ni^{2+}\ (aq)$$

Because it is spontaneous, Ni is more likely to be oxidized than Ag. Ni is oxidized, while Ag is reduced in this reaction.

Now, arrange the reactions in an order such that the metal that was oxidized in a reaction is reduced in the next reaction:

$$Ni\ (s) + Ag^+\ (aq) \rightarrow Ag\ (s) + Ni^{2+}\ (aq)$$

$$Cd\ (s) + Ni^{2+}\ (aq) \rightarrow Ni\ (s) + Cd^{2+}\ (aq)$$

$$Al\ (s) + Cd^{2+}\ (aq) \rightarrow Cd\ (s) + Al^{3+}\ (aq)$$

Lastly, this reaction $Ag\ (s) + H^+\ (aq) \rightarrow$ no reaction should be first in the order, because Ag was not oxidized in this reaction, so it should be before a reaction where Ag is reduced.

$$Ag\ (s) + H^+\ (aq) \rightarrow \text{no reaction}$$

$$Ni\ (s) + Ag^+\ (aq) \rightarrow Ag\ (s) + Ni^{2+}\ (aq)$$

$$Cd\ (s) + Ni^{2+}\ (aq) \rightarrow Ni\ (s) + Cd^{2+}\ (aq)$$

$$Al\ (s) + Cd^{2+}\ (aq) \rightarrow Cd\ (s) + Al^{3+}\ (aq)$$

The metal being oxidized in the last reaction has the highest tendency to be oxidized.

28. A is correct.

The purpose of the salt bridge is to balance the charges between the two chambers/half-cells.

Oxidation creates cations at the anode, while reduction reduces cations at the cathode. The ions in the bridge travel to those chambers to balance the charges.

29. B is correct.

Since $G° = -nFE$, when $E°$ is positive, G is negative.

30. C is correct.

The electrons travel through the wires that connect the cells, instead of the salt bridge. The function of the salt bridge is to provide ions to balance charges at both the cathode and anode.

31. A is correct.

Electrochemistry is the branch of physical chemistry that studies chemical reactions that take place at the interface of an ionic conductor (i.e. the electrolyte) and an electrode.

Electric charges move between the electrolyte and the electrode through a series of redox reactions, and chemical energy is converted to electrical energy.

32. B is correct.

Light energy from the sun causes the electron to move towards the silicon wafer. This starts the process of electric generation.

33. B is correct.

Oxidation number, also known as oxidation state, indicates the degree of oxidation (i.e. loss of electrons) in an atom.

If an atom is electron-poor, this means that it has lost electrons, and would therefore have a positive oxidation number.

If an atom is electron-rich, this means that it has gained electrons, and would therefore have a negative oxidation number.

34. B is correct.

Reduction potential is the measure of a substance's ability to acquire electrons (i.e. undergo reduction). The more positive the reduction potential, the more likely it is that the substance will be reduced. Reduction potential is generally measured in volts.

35. D is correct.

Batteries run down and need to be recharged, while fuel cells do not run down because they can be refueled.

36. A is correct.

Disproportionation reaction is a reaction where a species undergoes both oxidation and reduction in the same reaction.

The first step in balancing this reaction is to write the substance undergoing disproportionation twice on the reactant side.

37. A is correct.

The terms spontaneous electrochemical, galvanic and voltaic are synonymous.

An example of a voltaic cell is an alkaline battery – it generates electricity spontaneously.

Electrons always flow from the anode (oxidation half-cell) to the cathode (reduction half-cell).

In this reaction, Sn is oxidized, so electrons flow from the Sn electrode to the Cu electrode.

38. B is correct.

Reaction at anode:

$$2 H_2O \rightarrow O_2 + 4 H^+ + 4e^-$$

Oxygen gas is released and H^+ ions are added to the solution, which causes the solution to become acidic (i.e., lowers the pH).

39. D is correct.

Nonspontaneous electrochemical cells are electrolysis cells.

In electrolysis, the metal being reduced is always produced at the cathode.

40. B is correct.

Electrolysis is always nonspontaneous, because it needs an electric current from an external source to occur.

Practice Set 3: Questions 41–60

41. C is correct.

Electronegativity indicates the tendency of an atom to attract electrons.

An atom that attracts electrons strongly would be more likely to pull electrons from another atom. As a result, this atom would be a strong oxidizer, because it would cause other atoms to be oxidized when the electrons are pulled towards the atom with high electronegativity.

A strong oxidizing agent is also a weak reducing agent – they are opposing attributes.

42. E is correct.

MnO_2 is being reduced into Mn_2O_3.

The oxidation number increases from +4 on the left to +3 on the right.

43. C is correct.

Electrolytic cell: needs electrical energy input

Battery: spontaneously produces electrical energy. A dry cell is a type of battery.

Half-cell: does not generate energy by itself.

44. B is correct.

The anode in galvanic cells attracts anions.

Anions in solution flow toward the anode, while cations flow toward the cathode. Oxidation (i.e. loss of electrons) occurs at the anode.

Positive ions are formed, while negative ions are consumed at the anode.

Therefore, negative ions flow toward the anode to equalize the charge.

45. B is correct.

In electrochemical (i.e., galvanic) cells, oxidation always occurs at the anode and reduction occurs at the cathode.

Therefore, Al metal is produced at the cathode, because it is a reduction product (from oxidation number of +3 on the left to 0 on the right).

---

46. B is correct.

Anions in solution flow toward the anode, while cations flow toward the cathode.

Oxidation is the loss of electrons. Sodium is a group I element and therefore has a single valence electron. During oxidation, the Na becomes Na^+ with a complete octet.

47. A is correct.

A salt bridge contains both cations (positive ions) and anions (negative ions).

Anions flow towards the oxidation half-cell, because the oxidation product is positively charged and the anions are required to balance the charges within the cell.

The opposite is true for cations; they will flow towards the reduction half-cell.

Anions in the salt bridge should flow from Cd to Zn half-cell.

48. B is correct.

This can be determined using the electrochemical series:

Equilibrium	E°
$Li^+ (aq) + e^- \leftrightarrow Li (s)$	–3.03 volts
$K^+ (aq) + e^- \leftrightarrow K (s)$	–2.92
$*Ca^{2+} (aq) + 2\,e^- \leftrightarrow Ca (s)$	–2.87
$*Na^+ (aq) + e^- \leftrightarrow Na (s)$	–2.71
$Mg^{2+} (aq) + 2\,e^- \leftrightarrow Mg (s)$	–2.37
$Al^{3+} (aq) + 3\,e^- \leftrightarrow Al (s)$	–1.66
$Zn^{2+} (aq) + 2\,e^- \leftrightarrow Zn (s)$	–0.76
$Fe^{2+} (aq) + 2\,e^- \leftrightarrow Fe (s)$	–0.44
$Pb^{2+} (aq) + 2\,e^- \leftrightarrow Pb (s)$	–0.13
$2\,H^+ (aq) + 2\,e^- \leftrightarrow H_2 (g)$	0.0
$Cu^{2+} (aq) + 2\,e^- \leftrightarrow Cu (s)$	+0.34
$Ag^+ (aq) + e^- \leftrightarrow Ag (s)$	+0.80
$Au^{3+} (aq) + 3\,e^- \leftrightarrow Au (s)$	+1.50

In order for a substance to act as an oxidizing agent for another substance, the oxidizing agent has to be located below the substance being oxidized in the series.

Cu is being oxidized, which means only Ag or Au are capable of oxidizing Cu.

49. E is correct.

Anions in solution flow toward the anode, while cations flow toward the cathode.

Oxidation (i.e., loss of electrons) occurs at the anode.

Positive ions are formed while negative ions are consumed at the anode.

Therefore, negative ions flow toward the anode to equalize the charge.

50. B is correct.

Electrochemistry is the branch of physical chemistry that studies chemical reactions that take place at the interface of an ionic conductor (i.e. the electrolyte) and an electrode.

Electric charges move between the electrolyte and the electrode through a series of redox reactions, and chemical energy is converted to electrical energy.

51. E is correct.

E° tends to be negative and G positive, because electrolytic cells are nonspontaneous.

Electrons must be forced into the system for the reaction to proceed.

52. C is correct.

In order to create chlorine gas (Cl_2) from chloride ion (Cl^-), the ion needs to be oxidized.

In electrolysis, the oxidation occurs at the anode, which is the positive electrode.

The positively-charged electrode would absorb electrons from the ion and transfer it to the cathode for reduction.

53. B is correct.

In electrolytic cells:

Anode is a positively charged electrode where oxidation occurs.

Cathode is a negatively charged electrode where reduction occurs.

54. C is correct.

Nonspontaneous electrochemical cells are electrolysis cells.

In electrolysis, the metal that is being oxidized always dissolves at the anode.

55. D is correct.

Dry-cell batteries are the common disposable household batteries. They are based on zinc and manganese dioxide cells.

56. C is correct.

A disproportionation is a type of redox reaction in which a species is simultaneously reduced and oxidized to form two different products.

$2 H_2O \rightarrow 2 H_2 + O_2$: decomposition

$H_2SO_3 \rightarrow H_2O + SO_2$: decomposition

$Mg + H_2SO_4 \rightarrow MgSO_4 + H_2$: single replacement

57. D is correct.

Electrolysis is the same process in reverse for the chemical process inside a battery.

Electrolysis is often used to separate elements.

58. A is correct.

Fuel cell automobiles are fueled by hydrogen and the only emission is water (the statement above is reverse of the true statement).

59. A is correct.

Impure copper is oxidized, so it would happen at the anode. Then, pure copper would plate out (i.e., be reduced) on the cathode.

60. B is correct.

Electrolysis is a chemical reaction which results when electrical energy is passed through a liquid electrolyte.

Electrolysis utilizes direct electric current (DC) to drive an otherwise non-spontaneous chemical reaction. The voltage needed for electrolysis is called the decomposition potential

===

Practice Set 4: Questions 61–80

===

61. D is correct.

Calculate the oxidation numbers of all species involved and identify the oxidized species (increase in oxidation number).

Zn's oxidation number increases from 0 on the left side of reaction I to +2 on the right.

62. C is correct.

The lack of an aqueous solution makes it a dry cell. An example of a dry cell is an alkaline battery.

63. B is correct.

Half reaction: $C_2H_6O \rightarrow HC_2H_3O_2$

Balancing half-reaction in acidic conditions:

Step 1: Balance all atoms except for H and O

$\qquad C_2H_6O \rightarrow HC_2H_3O_2$ (C is already balanced)

Step 2: To balance oxygen, add H_2O to the side with less oxygen atoms

$\qquad C_2H_6O + H_2O \rightarrow HC_2H_3O_2$

Step 3: To balance hydrogen, add H^+ to the opposing side of H_2O added in the previous step

$\qquad C_2H_6O + H_2O \rightarrow HC_2H_3O_2 + 4\ H^+$

Step 4: Balance charges by adding electrons to the side with higher/more positive total charge

Total charge on left side: 0

Total charge on right side: $4(+1) = +4$

Add 4 electrons to right side:

$\qquad C_2H_6O + H_2O \rightarrow HC_2H_3O_2 + 4\ H^+ + 4\ e^-$

64. B is correct.

In electrochemical (i.e., galvanic) cells, oxidation always occurs at the anode, and reduction occurs at the cathode.

Therefore, CCl_4 will be produced at the anode because it is an oxidation product (carbon's oxidation number increases from 0 on the left to +4 on the right).

65. C is correct.

Battery: spontaneously produces electrical energy. A dry cell is a type of battery.

Half-cell: does not generate energy by itself

Electrolytic cell: needs electrical energy input

66. D is correct. Anions in solution flow toward the anode, while cations flow toward the cathode. Oxidation (i.e., loss of electrons) occurs at the anode.

Positive ions are formed, while negative ions are consumed at the anode.

Therefore, negative ions flow toward the anode to equalize the charge.

67. A is correct. A reducing agent is the reactant that is oxidized (i.e., loses electrons).

Therefore, the best reducing agent is most easily oxidized.

Reversing each of the half-reactions shows that the oxidation of Cr (*s*) has a potential of +0.75 V, which is greater than the potential (+0.13 V) for the oxidation of Sn^{2+} (*aq*).

Thus, Cr (*s*) is stronger reducing agent.

68. B is correct. A salt bridge contains both cations (positive ions) and anions (negative ions).

Anions flow towards the oxidation half-cell, because the oxidation product is positively charged and the anions are required to balance the charges within the cell.

The opposite is true for cations; they will flow toward the reduction half-cell.

Anions in the salt bridge should flow from Cd to Zn half-cell.

69. B is correct.

When zinc is added to HCl, the reaction is:

$Zn + HCl \rightarrow ZnCl_2 + H_2O$,

which means that Zn is oxidized into Zn^{2+}.

The number provided in the problem is reduction potential, so to obtain the oxidation potential, flip the reaction:

$Zn (s) \rightarrow Zn^{2+} + 2 e^-$

The $E°$ is inverted and becomes +0.76 V.

Because the $E°$ is higher than hydrogen's value (which is set to 0), the reaction occurs.

70. E is correct.

Calculate the mass of metal deposited in cathode:

Step 1: Calculate total charge using current and time

$$Q = \text{current} \times \text{time}$$

$$Q = 1 \text{ A} \times (10 \text{ minutes} \times 60 \text{ s/minute})$$

$$Q = 600 \text{ A·s} = 600 \text{ C}$$

Step 2: Calculate moles of electron that has the same amount of charge

$$\text{moles e}^- = Q \,/\, 96,500 \text{ C/mol}$$

$$\text{moles e}^- = 600 \text{ C} \,/\, 96,500 \text{ C/mol}$$

$$\text{moles e}^- = 6.22 \times 10^{-3} \text{ mol}$$

Step 3: Calculate moles of metal deposit

Half-reaction of zinc ion reduction:

$$Zn^{2+} (aq) + 2 \text{ e}^- \rightarrow Zn (s)$$

$$\text{moles of Zn} = (\text{coefficient Zn} \,/\, \text{coefficient e}^-) \times \text{moles e}^-$$

$$\text{moles of Zn} = (\tfrac{1}{2}) \times 6.22 \times 10^{-3} \text{ mol}$$

$$\text{moles of Zn} = 3.11 \times 10^{-3} \text{ mol}$$

Step 4: Calculate mass of metal deposit

$$\text{mass Zn} = \text{moles Zn} \times \text{molecular mass of Zn}$$

$$\text{mass Zn} = 3.11 \times 10^{-3} \text{ mol} \times (65 \text{ g/mol})$$

$$\text{mass Zn} = 0.20 \text{ g}$$

71. A is correct. Oxidation number of Mg increases from 0 to +2, which means that Mg loses electrons (i.e., is oxidized).

Conversely, the oxidation number of Cu decreases, which means that it gains electrons (i.e., is reduced).

72. D is correct.

Electrolysis is a method of using a direct electric current to provide electricity to a nonspontaneous redox process to drive the reaction. The direct electric current must be passed through an ionic substance or solution that contains electrolytes.

Electrolysis is often used to separate elements.

73. D is correct.

Oxidation is the loss of electrons, while reduction is the gain of electrons.

74. D is correct.

E° for the cell is always positive.

75. B is correct.

Galvanic cells are spontaneous and generate electrical energy.

76. D is correct.

In electrolytic cells:

Anode is a positively charged electrode where oxidation occurs.

Cathode is a negatively charged electrode where reduction occurs.

77. B is correct.

Balanced equation:

$$Cu^{2+} + 2\ e^- \rightarrow Cu\ (s)$$

Formula to calculate deposit mass:

mass of deposit = atomic mass × moles of electron

Since Cu has 2 electrons per atom, multiply the moles by 2:

mass of deposit = atomic mass × (2 × moles of electron)

mass of deposit = atomic mass × (2 × current × time) / 96,500 C

4.00 g = 63.55 g × (2 × 2.50 A × time) / 96,500 C

time = 4,880 s

time = (4,880 s × 1 min/60s × 1 hr/60 min) = 1.36 hr

78. C is correct.

Alkaline and dry-cell are common disposable batteries and are non-rechargeable.

Fuel cells require fuel that is going to be consumed and are non-rechargeable.

79. E is correct.

Electrolytic cells do not occur spontaneously; the reaction only occurs with the addition of an external electrical energy.

80. D is correct.

A redox reaction, or oxidation-reduction reaction, involves the transfer of electrons between two reacting substances. An oxidation reaction specifically refers to the substance that is losing electrons, and a reduction reaction specifically refers to the substance that is gaining reactions.

The oxidation and reduction reactions alone are called half-reactions, because they always occur together to form a whole reaction.

Therefore, half-reaction can represent either a separate oxidation process or a separate reduction process.

We want to hear from you

Your feedback is important to us because we strive to provide the highest quality prep materials. If you have any questions, comments or suggestions, email us, so we can incorporate your feedback into future editions.

Customer Satisfaction Guarantee

If you have any concerns about this book, including printing issues, contact us and we will resolve any issues to your satisfaction.

info@sterling-prep.com

To access the online SAT tests at a special pricing visit:
http://SAT.Sterling-Prep.com/bookowner.htm
